Prose Comprehension Beyond the Word

Arthur C. Graesser

Prose Comprehension Beyond the Word

With 27 Figures

Springer-Verlag
New York Heidelberg Berlin

ARTHUR C. GRAESSER
Department of Psychology
California State University, Fullerton
Fullerton, California 92634
U.S.A.

To my parents, Roy and Esther

Library of Congress Cataloging in Publication Data

Graesser, Arthur C
Prose comprehension beyond the word.

Bibliography: p. 275
Includes index.
1. Comprehension. 2. Listening. 3. Reading, Psychology of. I. Title.
BF325.G7 153.7 80-29582

Softcover reprint of the hardcover 1st edition 1981

9 8 7 6 5 4 3 2 1

ISBN-13: 978-1-4612-5882-7 e-ISBN-13: 978-1-4612-5880-3
DOI: 10.1007/978-1-4612-5880-3

Preface

When individuals read or listen to prose they try to understand what it means. This is quite obvious. However, the cognitive mechanisms that participate in prose comprehension are far from obvious. Even simple stories involve complexities that have stymied many cognitive scientists. Why is prose comprehension so difficult to study? Perhaps because comprehension is guided by so many domains of knowledge. Perhaps because some critical mysteries of prose comprehension reside between the lines—in the mind of the comprehender.

Ten years ago very few psychologists were willing to dig beyond the surface of explicit code in their studies of discourse processing. Tacit knowledge, world knowledge, inferences, and expectations were slippery notions that experimental psychologists managed to circumvent rather than understand. In many scientific circles it was taboo to investigate mechanisms and phenomena that are not directly governed by the physical stimulus. Fortunately, times have changed. Cognitive scientists are now vigorously exploring the puzzles of comprehension that lie beyond the word.

The study of discourse processing is currently growing at a frenetic pace. Linguists are analyzing the formal composition of connected discourse. Researchers in artificial intelligence are programing computers to interpret sentences in text. Cognitive psychologists are conducting experiments that examine how prose is comprehended, remembered, and cognitively represented. As a consequence of this collective enthusiasm, there has been a staggering increase in the number of books, new journals, and conferences that focus on some aspect of discourse processing. As a cognitive psychologist who has nourished an active research program in this area, I find that keeping abreast of scientific and scholarly developments has become a challenge (and also a financial liability).

I had four major objectives in mind when writing this book. One goal was to report some research conducted in my laboratory during the past four years. Some of the contributions of the Cognitive Research Group at California State University at Fullerton were large-scale projects that could not easily be partitioned and condensed in the form of journal articles. It was important to develop a theoretical and empirical context for this research and also to present a coherent picture of the research program. Consequently, this book is not an exhaustive survey of all there is to know about psychological research in discourse processing.

A second goal was to pursue a schema-based framework for exploring prose comprehension and knowledge representation. The schema construct has penetrated nearly all of the disciplines in the cognitive sciences. The framework also provides a satisfactory theoretical foundation for the research that will be reported. Unfortunately, it is beyond the scope of this book to evaluate how well a schema-based framework explains the reported research compared to alternative frameworks. There are no detailed comparisons of alternative models. At this rather underdeveloped stage in the discourse processing enterprise, there is something to be said for pursuing a widely accepted framework and discovering what can be learned. Critical tests between models will come later.

A third objective was to integrate the reported research with developments in different areas of the cognitive sciences. I tried to relate the findings to issues and relevant contributions in artificial intelligence, linguistics, and philosophy. Some contact with other disciplines is important for developing a psychological theory of discourse processing.

A fourth objective was to introduce some new methods for exploring discourse processing. Most of the studies in this book incorporated methods that are not in the standard repertoire of experimental psychologists. In particular, verbal protocols were collected in the studies in the second half of the book. Subjects were probed with questions either during or after the comprehension of passages. A content analysis of these question-answering protocols uncovered some new findings about symbolic mechanisms and representational structures that are constructed during prose comprehension. This is perhaps the most important contribution of this book. Cognitive scientists have long acknowledged the potential of collecting think-aloud protocols or question-answering protocols. However, there has always been the troublesome problem of how to analyze complex verbal protocols.

There is a long list of people who helped me prepare this book. I deeply appreciate their interest and kindness. The following individuals reviewed one or more of my chapters: John Black, Gordon Bower, Bruce Britton, Leslie Clark, Nancy Johnson, Wendy Lehnert, Allen Lesgold, George Mandler, Gary Olson, Scott Robertson, James Voss, and Patricia Worden.

I am endlessly indebted to Jim Riha for preparing the figures in this book, and to Lea Adams, Patricia Anderson, and Leslie Clark for spending hour after hour typing and revising this book on the text-editing system.

The research reported in this book would not have been conducted without the resources provided by certain institutions and individuals. The research was supported, to various extents and at various times, by National Institute of Mental Health Grants MH-31083 and MH-33491. I would also like to thank Chris Cozby, Dave Perkins, Mike Scavio, Hiro Yasuda, and the California State

University at Fullerton for providing the computer facilities, space, and environment that are needed for maintaining a research program.

There is a special group of individuals to whom I am profoundly indebted. Without the enthusiasm and dedication of the members of the Cognitive Research Group at Cal State Fullerton, my life at Fullerton would surely be uneventful and unproductive. The following individuals have at some time or another conducted research and actively participated in the cognitive research meetings during the past four years: Lea Adams, Patricia Anderson, Leslie Clark, Andy Cohen, Marcy Doyle, Liz Francis, Sharon Goodman, Sallie Gordon, Rosemarie Harold, Kathy Hauft-Smith, Mike Higginbotham, Nick Hoffman, Dan Kowalski, Ed Lovelace, Glenn Nakamura, Jim Riha, Scott Robertson, Brian Ronk, John Sawyer, Don Smith, Pam Stevenson, and Professor Stanley Woll.

Finally, I owe an enormous debt to Leslie Clark and Al Kreinheder for their emotional support while writing this book.

Fullerton, California ARTHUR C. GRAESSER

Contents

1. A Schema-Based Framework for Representing Knowledge **1**
Cognitive Psychology and Cognitive Science 2
Domains of Knowledge and Levels of Structure 4
Linguistic Knowledge 5
Rhetorical Knowledge 13
Causal Conceptualizations 19
Intentional Conceptualizations 23
Spatial Knowledge 26
Knowledge about Roles, Personalities, and Objects 28
Schemas 29
The Functioning of Schemas 32

2. Allocation of Cognitive Resources During Prose Comprehension **36**
Allocating Cognitive Resources to Different Components of Reading 39
The Relationship Between Resource Allocation During Comprehension and Performance on Comprehension and Retention Tests 55
Models of Reading 59
Extracting Information from Newspapers 63

3. A Schema Pointer Plus Tag Model of Prose Memory **68**
Representational Assumptions of the SP+T Model 73
Memory for Scripted Action Sequences 75
Memory for Stereotype-Based Personality Descriptions 81
Generating Guesses in Recall and Recognition 84
Retrieval Mechanisms During Recall and Recognition 88
Effects of Retention Interval on Memory for Typical and Atypical Items 95
Mathematical Formulation of the SP+T Model 100
Alternative Explanations and Models 105
Extensions of the Model 107

4. The Conceptual Representation of Prose in Memory **109**
Goals of the Proposed Theory of Prose Representation 111
A System for Representing Prose 116
A Question-Answering Method of Exposing Prose Inferences 130
Conceptual Graph Structures for Narrative Passages 134
Conceptual Graph Structures for Expository Passages 149
Differences Between Narrative and Expository Prose 151
Conceptual Graph Structures for Schemas 157
Additional Issues Concerning the Conceptual Graph Structures 165

5. The Utilization of Prose Representations **172**
Question Answering 179
Verification of Nodes 192
Recall of Prose 202
Conceptual Graph Structures Revisited 214

6. The Construction of Prose Representations **215**
A Question-Answering Method of Exploring the Construction of Prose Representations 220
Effects of Prior Context on the Interpretation of Statements 227
Generation and Disconfirmation of Inferences and Expectations 233
A Structural–Conceptual Analysis of On-line Comprehension 249
Some Considerations for a Model of On-line Prose Comprehension 262
Final Comments 272

References **275**

Author Index **302**

Subject Index **308**

1

A Schema-Based Framework for Representing Knowledge

Life is normally easy to comprehend. We are rarely challenged when we comprehend the social and physical world. In fact, most of our everyday experiences are familiar and predictable. Imagine the stereotypical working male. During weekdays he gets up, eats breakfast, goes to work, talks with friends and enemies, works, drinks coffee, tells jokes, eats lunch, works some more, goes home, eats supper, putters around with the family, drinks beer, watches television, and maybe reads the newspaper. Almost everything that happens makes sense. Events that do not make sense are probably ignored.

Adults do manage to learn about new things as they live in their repetitious, familiar worlds. Experiences are never exactly the same. However, the experience of learning a new skill or a new domain of knowledge requires effort and is usually avoided. Intentional learning is reserved for students, certain professionals, and bookworms. Comprehension is easy as long as the comprehender is not very inquisitive.

From the perspective of many theories in psychology, it is a miracle that adults are able to comprehend so easily. Cognitive psychologists have emphasized the fact that humans have a limited span of attention, consciousness, and immediate memory. During a given time span, humans are able to complete a limited number of cognitive operations, to encode a limited number of information units, and to utilize a limited supply of processing resources. Despite these severe limitations of processing capacity, the comprehender is automatically able to interpret input that appears to be very complex and rich.

Consider reading. The reader performs analyses at different levels of prose structure. Patterns of lines, angles, and curves are translated into letters; letters are grouped into syllables; syllables are grouped into words; words are grouped into phrases, phrases are grouped into sentences; and sentences are grouped into paragraphs. The reader analyzes the syntax of sentences. The reader interprets the meaning of explicitly stated information and draws inferences. Sometimes readers generate mental images. The reader relates the information in the reading material to his previous knowledge base. The motives of the author are often analyzed. The fact that all of these analyses are performed simultaneously and quickly seems inconsistent with the notion that there are severe limitations in the amount of information that can be processed during a short time span. Does this imply that the theories in cognitive psychology are wrong? Not necessarily. Reading and comprehension are highly organized activities that somehow fit within the constraints of certain bottlenecks in the human information processing system. One of the goals in this book is to examine this organization in some detail.

Although the emphasis in this book is on the comprehension of prose, in principle the analyses apply to other forms of stimulus input. When individuals comprehend pictorial stimuli, physical event sequences, and social interactions, they perform rather sophisticated interpretive analyses. These analyses are executed when we witness events in the world, as well as when we read or listen to verbal renditions of events in the world. The claim here is not that the observation of some activity is strictly equivalent to comprehending a passage about the activity; rather, some common conceptual analyses are performed when comprehenders receive input in different forms and modalities.

Cognitive Psychology and Cognitive Science

The study of discourse processing is a relatively new area in psychology. Ten years ago researchers in experimental psychology would not have tried to understand how discourse is comprehended. Such a goal would have been much too general and ambitious. Research in verbal learning and memory revealed how lists of words, paired-associates, and nonsense syllables are acquired and remembered. Research in reading was confined primarily to the processing of isolated words, letters, and speech sounds. A few scattered studies used prose as stimulus materials, but these studies were designed to answer relatively simple questions. For example, one popular research area was the exploration of the phenomenon that individuals remember the meaning of prose passages very well, but tend to forget the exact wording and syntax. Very few studies examined how inferences are generated and how meaning is cognitively represented and structured.

In contrast to 10 years ago, today's cognitive psychologists are focusing more on the processing of *ecologically valid* stimulus material (Neisser, 1976). Ecologically valid material is representative of the stimulus input that is normally encountered in the everyday world. For example, adults normally comprehend discourse rather than memorize nonsense material or lists of unrelated items. The investigation of prose comprehension is therefore more ecologically valid than the investigation of how word lists are acquired. It is fair to say that most psychologists welcome the shift to examining ecologically valid processing conditions. The resulting theories will certainly be easier to generalize to the real world. Practical applications of the theories will at least be more obvious.

Cognitive psychology is also becoming more interdisciplinary. In fact, many cognitive psychologists now call themselves cognitive scientists. A cognitive psychologist would find it important to examine methods of studying cognition in such areas as computer simulation and linguistics. Cognitive scientists would add other disciplines to the list, such as education, sociology, anthropology, philosophy, mathematics, artificial intelligence, and man-machine studies. An important difference between cognitive psychology and cognitive science lies in the methodology that is used to examine cognitive mechanisms and to defend theories. Cognitive psychology has strong roots in traditional experimental psychology. A cognitive psychologist would try to convince colleagues that a theory is plausible by reporting a series of well-controlled experiments on humans. The experiments would demonstrate how specific psychological events are caused by other psychological events, or how certain processing components are distinct from other processing components. A cognitive scientist might also conduct experiments on humans. In addition, a cognitive scientist might try to convince colleagues that a model or theory is plausible by writing a computer program that behaves like humans in some general activity. Cognitive scientists are not committed to or constrained by a specific methodology. A diversity of methods is a virtue.

Cognitive scientists have developed several computer programs that simulate the way in which humans comprehend sentences and prose. These programs embody a vast panorama of knowledge in the form of facts, rules, knowledge structures, and symbolic procedures. As the knowledge base increases, and the scope of the computer system expands, the modeler gains a better understanding of the relative importance of different components in the system. The modeler recognizes problems and discovers what is missing. The computer programmer and the program grow together symbiotically as more knowledge domains are assimilated. As the programmer implements more ideas into the computer system, the program comprehends more sentences and passages. As the program accounts for more sentences and passages, the programmer discovers what impact certain implemented ideas have on the system. An implemented idea often has repercussions that the programmer never anticipated since the operation of the system as a whole is too sophisticated to keep track of all at once.

We might not live to see a computer program that can explain how individuals comprehend *any* prose passage. Nevertheless, cognitive scientists will continue to develop computer systems that capture theories and models of prose comprehension. Comprehension is a complex mechanism that involves many different knowledge domains. As more knowledge domains are identified and understood, comprehension will seem less mysterious.

Cognitive psychologists have traditionally investigated comprehension mechanisms differently than the computer programmer. A cognitive psychologist would examine in detail one or a few components of the comprehension system. For example, a cognitive psychologist might spend 10 years investigating how humans analyze sentence syntax. The researcher would achieve an impressively detailed understanding of how syntax is processed according to some pet theory. There are advantages and disadvantages to this "divide and conquer" approach. A negative consequence is that the researcher tends to overlook how the component under examination interacts with other components that are not investigated. Moreover, after the researcher devotes 10 years to understanding how syntax is processed, the researcher might inflate the importance of syntax in the comprehension mechanism as a whole. On the other hand, an advantage to the cognitive psychologists' approach is that their conclusions and theories have a close correspondence to the way in which humans behave. Most scientists appreciate a close correspondence between theory and data.

It is obvious that many domains of knowledge participate in guiding the comprehension of prose. Some domains of knowledge can be identified by virtually everyone, whereas other domains are not very obvious and can be identified only when there is a theoretical understanding of comprehension mechanisms. It would certainly be difficult and tedious to identify all of the knowledge domains that are relevant to the comprehension of all types of prose passages. However, an extensive inventory of the knowledge required for comprehension might prove to be an important prerequisite for a sophisticated understanding of comprehension. There are many simple, parsimonious models of comprehension that focus on a small number of knowledge domains and processes. However, these models may be inadequate, or even misleading.

The reader may wonder whether this book falls under the rubric of cognitive psychology or cognitive science. The answer is both. The recent advances in the cognitive sciences are refreshing, sometimes impressive, and cannot safely be ignored. Yet it is also important to conduct appropriately designed experiments on humans in order to test theories, models, and hypotheses about human cognition. An important goal in this book is to help bridge an existing gap between (a) advances in some of the cognitive sciences whose foundations and methodologies are not rooted in experimental psychology and (b) supporting empirical data that would be palatable to experimental psychologists.

A few comments should be made about "gap bridging." An attempt to interface the contributions of two or more fields is a slippery enterprise because the goals of separate disciplines are usually different. Occasionally, the more temperamental members of a field become upset when their pet theories are not translated perfectly during the course of interfacing and they poke holes in the work of the interfacers. The goal of experimental psychologists (as interfacers or gap bridgers), however, is not to test directly the theories and ideas proposed in other disciplines. Instead, the experimental psychologists formulate their own theories, models, and hypotheses after considering the knowledge base that has accumulated in other disciplines.

Domains of Knowledge and Levels of Structure

The Czar and His Daughters

Once there was a Czar who had three lovely daughters. One day the three daughters went walking in the woods. They were enjoying themselves so much that they forgot the time and stayed too long. A dragon kidnapped the three daughters. As they were being dragged off they cried for help. Three heroes heard the cries and set off to rescue the daughters. The heroes came and fought the dragon and rescued the daughters. Then the heroes returned the daughters to their palace. When the Czar heard of the rescue, he rewarded the heroes.

The comprehender must have access to many knowledge domains in order to understand a simple story such as *The Czar and His Daughters.* A cognitive scientist would enjoy listing one or two dozen. For the purpose of providing a background for the issues and studies discussed in this book, we will refer to six basic knowledge domains that are involved in prose comprehension:

(1) Linguistic
(2) Rhetorical
(3) Causal
(4) Intentional
(5) Spatial
(6) Roles, personalities, and objects.

This list does not exhaust the total set of domains that are needed in a complete model of comprehension. There also may be a more natural categorization scheme. However, this categorization scheme does provide a framework for the issues and research that will be discussed in this book.

Linguistic Knowledge

In order to comprehend prose, the comprehender must obviously have knowledge of language. Linguists have segregated this knowledge into different levels. First, there is the *phonemic* level. Visual or acoustic input is recoded into basic speech sounds called phonemes. In English the word *Czar* contains three phonemes: /z/, /a/, and /r/. Second, there is a *lexical* level, which roughly corresponds to words. Comprehenders have access to a large mental dictionary. For each word there is a description of its phonemic composition, its definition and meaning, what it generally refers to in the world, and how the word is used. Third, there is a *syntactic* level, which includes a set of rules that specify how categories of words are to be grouped and ordered. Fourth, there is a *semantic* level, which specifies how the meanings of sentences are constructed. The meaning of a sentence is not simply the summation of the lexical meanings of the words in the sentence. Fifth, there is a *pragmatic* level, which corresponds to the use of language in dialogues and social interactions. When does a speech utterance constitute a question, a statement of fact, a request, a command, a threat, or a promise?

In this book the semantic and pragmatic aspects of the comprehension mechanism will be examined in some detail. Obviously, linguistic knowledge is an essential prerequisite for prose comprehension. However, an extensive discussion of linguistic knowledge can be circumvented here because the above description of most of these levels is sufficient for understanding the topics discussed in this book. Of the five levels, only the semantic and pragmatic levels need to be discussed further. Sources are available for those readers who are curious about linguistic knowledge and processing. In the past 20 years linguists and psycholinguists have written dozens of books that examine in detail one or more of the five levels of linguistic knowledge (Bates, 1976; Chomsky, 1965; Chomsky and Halle, 1968; Clark and Clark, 1977; Fillmore, 1968; Fodor, Bever, and Garrett, 1974; Massaro, 1975; Miller and Johnson-Laird, 1976; Stockwell, Schachter, and Partee, 1973).

During comprehension individuals normally focus on the meaning of the message rather than the exact wording and syntax (the surface structure). As a consequence, individuals normally remember the semantic and pragmatic aspects of passages rather than the surface structure code (Anderson and Paulson, 1977; Graesser and Mandler, 1975; Sachs, 1967, 1974). Of course, there are unusual circumstances when it is important or of interest to focus on the surface structure. Not surprisingly, individuals retain surface structure code in these conditions (Graesser and Mandler, 1975). Surface structure code is also impressively retained for conversations that individuals have with one another (Bates, Masling, and Kintsch, 1978; Keenan, MacWhinney, and Mayhew, 1977). The style, wording and syntax of spoken utterances are apparently important (pragmatically meaningful) when individuals interact in natural conversations. Nevertheless, individuals normally forget the wording and syntax of prose.

A propositional system will be adopted for capturing the semantic content of sentences in prose. Propositional representations are very popular in psychological theories of comprehension (Anderson and Bower, 1973; Clark and Clark, 1977; Frederiksen, 1977; Kintsch, 1974; Norman and Rumelhart, 1975; Wanner, 1974). A number of experiments have been reported that appear to support the hypothesis that propositions are natural psychological units in comprehension and memory (Buschke and Schaier, 1979; Carpenter and Just, 1975; Dosher, 1976; Graesser, 1977, 1978b; Kintsch and Keenan, 1973; Ratcliff and McKoon, 1978). According to these propositional systems, sentences are segmented into sets of propositions that are structurally related. It is important to mention that propositions have also been adopted as meaning constituents in several theories in linguistics and philosophy.

The propositional representation of a passage is known as its *microstructure* (Kintsch, 1974). Prose microstructure does not capture the complete representation of a passage. Sentences are also interrelated by *macrostructure* levels of analysis which will be discussed later. Moreover, the propositional content of sentences does not include inferences that the comprehender generates by virtue of prior knowledge and the information in the extended passage context. The propositional representation depicts the semantic content of what is directly stated.

What is a proposition? There is no ironclad agreement among and within disciplines as to what information is incorporated into propositions. However, most theories would include the following four claims (Clark and Clark, 1977; Kintsch, 1974; Norman and Rumelhart, 1975; Vendler, 1967).

(1) A proposition is a semantic unit that contains one or more arguments.
(2) Propositions denote states or events.
(3) Some propositions denote facts about other propositions.
(4) Some propositions qualify aspects of other propositions.

Some discussion is needed to clarify these four claims.

In the proposed propositional system, the ***arguments*** correspond to the specific referential entities and indices that are relevant to a particular passage. These contextually specific arguments correspond to specific persons, objects, parts of people, parts of objects, locations, points in time, ideas, other propositions, and a variety of other indices that will be discussed shortly. ***Predicates*** operate as functions that ascribe properties to arguments. Predicates are captured by virtually any class of lexical items. Predicates correspond to verbs, adverbs, adjectives, prepositions, connectives, and nouns.

One way to convey the nature of the proposed propositional system is to provide examples. Table 1.1 shows a propositional representation of *The Czar and His Daughters.* The nine sentences in the story contain a total of 41 propositions. Each proposition is assigned a number (e.g., P1, P2, etc.). The arguments of each proposition are in parentheses. The arguments are specific entities or indices in the passage. For example, proposition P1 expresses the fact that a specific Czar (C1) had some specific daughters (C2). Whenever a proposition refers to this Czar, the proposition would include the C1 argument. The properties of "Czarness" are ascribed to C1 by virtue of proposition P2. The properties of "daughterness" are ascribed to the argument C2 by virtue of proposition P5. Throughout

Table 1.1. List of Propositions for *The Czar and His Daughters*

P1:	have (C1, C2)	P22:	cry (C2, T6)
P2:	Czar (C1)	P23:	DURING (T6, T5)
P3:	EXIST (C1, T1)	P24:	GET (C2, X2)
P4:	once (T1)	P25:	help (X2)
P5:	daughter (C2)	P26:	in order to (P22, P24)
P6:	lovely (C2)	P27:	hear (C4, P22)
P7:	three (C2)	P28:	hero (C4)
P8:	walk (C2, L1, T2)	P29:	three (C4)
P9:	in (L1, O1)	P30:	set off (C4)
P10:	woods (O1)	P31:	rescued (C4, C2)
P11:	DURING (T2, T3)	P32:	in order to (P30, P31)
P12:	one day (T3)	P33:	come (C4)
P13:	enjoy (C2, C2, M1)	P34:	fight (C4, C3)
P14:	so much (M1)	P35:	rescue (C4, C2, T7)
P15:	forget (C2, X1)	P36:	return to (C4, C2, L2)
P16:	time (X1)	P37:	IN (L2, O2)
P17:	stay (C2, L1, T4)	P38:	palace (O2)
P18:	too long (T4)	P39:	hear of (C1, P35, T8)
P19:	kidnap (C3, C2)	P40:	reward (C1, C4, T9)
P20:	dragon (C3)	P41:	AFTER (T9, T8)
P21:	drag off (C3, C2, T5)		

the story there are four distinct characters, C1, C2, C3, and C4, which refer to the specific Czar, daughters, dragon, and heroes, respectively. A reference to a specific character is to be distinguished from the generic concept that predicates the character. For example, the specific daughters in the story are different from the generic concept of *daughter*, i.e., daughterness in general. In addition to those arguments that refer to specific story characters, there are references to the following: specific objects, e.g., the woods (O1) and the palace (O2); specific abstract entities, e.g., some help (X2); specific location indices (L1 and L2); specific time indices (T1 through T9); the specific manner in which a given proposition occurred (M1); and other propositions in the passage.

The predicates in Table 1.1 are usually captured by lexical items that are stated in the passage. The predicates corresponded to verbs (*have, walk, enjoy, forget, stay, kidnap, cry, hear, rescue, come, fight, reward*), adjectives (*lovely, three*), prepositions (*in*), connectives (*in order to*), nouns (*Czar, daughter, woods, time, dragon, help, hero, palace*), verb-preposition combinations (*drag off, set off, return to, hear of*), adverb-adjective combinations (*so much, too long*), and other word combinations that seem to operate in a unitary fashion (*one day*). Some of the predicates in Table 1.1 are in small capital letters. These predicates correspond to underlying predicates that were elliptically deleted from the passage (GET, DURING, IN) or to predicates that are more consistent with the meaning of the proposition than would be captured by words that were explicitly stated (DURING instead of *as*, AFTER instead of *when*).

As was mentioned earlier, some propositions denote states or events, some propositions denote facts about other states or events, and some propositions qualify other propositions. For example, the following propositions from *The Czar and His Daughters* conveyed an ongoing state in the physical world, social world, or mental world of a character.

P1: *The Czar had daughters;*
P6: *The daughters were lovely.*

The following propositions convey events, that is, state changes in the physical, social, or mental worlds.

P15: *The daughters forgot the time.*
P22: *The daughters cried.*

The following example illustrates a proposition that denotes a fact about another proposition.

P27: *The heroes heard the daughters cry.*

The heroes' hearing the daughters cry denotes a fact about the daughters crying (P22). In this example, P22 is an argument of P27. In the example below, one proposition modifies some argument or index of another proposition.

The daughters walked at some locations at some point in time (P8); the locations were in the woods (P9) and the time was one day (P12).

Proposition P9 qualifies the location index of P8. Proposition P12 qualifies the temporal index of P8.

It is important to mention what the propositional analysis does not capture about the information in the passage. The predicates of the various propositions included most, but not all of the words that were stated in the passage. Determiners (*a, the*) and pronouns (*their, they, who, he*) are not predicates and therefore are not included among the list of predicates in Table 1.1. The function of determiners and pronouns lies in the process of referring to arguments. Pronouns refer to arguments that have already been introduced in the passage. When the determiner ***the*** accompanies a noun or phrase, it means that the noun or phrase (or some aspect of the noun or phrase) has already been introduced. The determiner ***a*** usually signals the introduction of a new distinct argument (Chafe, 1972). For example, ***a Czar*** was stated when this character was first introduced in the story; later references to this character included the following descriptions: ***the Czar*** and ***he***. There are other words and aspects of the words that the propositional analysis does not directly incorporate. The analysis does not incorporate the tense of verbs (past, present, or future) and also certain auxiliary verbs are ignored. The fact that the propositional analysis does not incorporate these words should not be construed as a problem. The goal of a propositional analysis is to specify the semantic base structure of the explicitly stated information. In theory, the explicit phrasing and surface structure of a passage can be generated from the propositional representation by virtue of syntactic and pragmatic rules (Kintsch, 1974).

A propositional analysis of prose does not always specify how sentences and certain propositions are related conceptually. This deficit could be solved in a trivial way by linking propositions with certain connectives, such as ***and, and then,*** and ***in addition***. However, these connectives are not very informative. Propositions are often linked by elaborate conceptual chains of causes and reasons that are inferred by the comprehender. The rich conceptualizations that interrelate actions and events in stories are hardly captured by semantically depleted connectives such as ***and***. Again, this does not mean that there is a problem with propositional analyses. The processes involved in generating inferences and conceptually linking certain propositions will be performed by macrostructure analyses (van Dijk, 1977; Kintsch, 1974; Kintsch and van Dijk, 1978).

As mentioned earlier, predicates ascribe properties to arguments and interrelate arguments. Predicates serve as functions that operate on argument variables. The number and types of arguments in a given proposition depend on what the predicate is. The case structure grammars in linguistics (Fillmore, 1968; Stockwell et al., 1973) categorize verbs according to their case roles. One dimension for classification is simply the number of ***obligatory*** arguments. Obligatory arguments are explicitly mentioned in the sentence, whereas ***optional*** arguments need not be specified explicitly. In English there are verbs with one obligatory argument (*X* ***cry***), two obligatory arguments (*X* ***kill*** *Y*), and three obligatory arguments (*X* ***give*** *Y to Z*). Interestingly, there are few (if any) verbs that require four or more obligatory arguments in English or any other language (Weinreich, 1963). Other types of lexical items may also be classified according to the number of obligatory arguments. Prepositions have two arguments (*X in Y*), or three arguments (*X between Y and Z*), but again there are no prepositions that require four or more arguments. There is only one obligatory argument when the lexical item is an adjective (*X is red*), an adverb (*X occurs quickly*), or a noun (*X is a Czar*). Connectives usually have two arguments (*X in order to Y*).

A second dimension for classifying predicates is the type of obligatory arguments. Again, linguists who have developed case structure grammars have examined what case roles are required by different classes of verbs. Consider the present system of segmenting sentences into propositions. Some verbs, such as *cry, sleep,* and *die,* are accompanied by character arguments, but not object or abstract idea arguments. Dogs, children, and elves can sleep, but not rocks, grass, or brooms. Of course, there are exceptions to these types of constraints, particularly in metaphorical expressions, e.g., *The rocks cried when the earthquake hit Los Angeles* (Verbrugge and McCarrell, 1977). The fact that these constraints are violated partly explains why metaphors enrapture some readers and irritate others. Some types of predicates require propositions as arguments. For example, connectives ordinarily link propositions together, e.g., P26 and P32 in Table 1.1. Verbs such as *say* require propositional arguments, e.g., *The man said that the earthquake was dangerous.*

In addition to the specific configuration of arguments that are obligatory for a predicate, there are a number of indices that are part of virtually any proposition. Some of these indices have been discussed in theories of semantics in philosophy (Lewis, 1972). There is a pragmatic index that captures the fact that a proposition is expressed by a specific speaker to a specific listener. Propositions are bounded by time and location indices. A proposition has a truth value. Arguments of propositions may or may not exist. The truth of propositions and the existence of arguments are evaluated on the basis of the specific "world" or knowledge structure that the speaker intends to convey to the listener. Absolute truth (truth with respect to all possible worlds) is irrelevant for propositions in many passages (fiction). The propositional analysis in Table 1.1 does not list these arguments and indices for each proposition. For the most part, the comprehender fills in or constructs this information. These arguments and indices are specified only when there is explicitly stated information that embellishes an index of a given proposition. A time, location, or manner argument is included in a proposition only when there is another proposition that serves as a modifier. For example, P9 modifies P8 in Table 1.1; *the daughters walked at a specific location* (P8) and *this location was in the woods* (P9).

Regarding the speaker/listener, truth, and existence aspects, there are some pragmatic rules that simplify the analysis. Unless there are elements in the prose that indicate otherwise, propositions are true, arguments exist, and the same speaker is writing or speaking. The pragmatic rules reflect the fact that there are conversational rules that must be obeyed in order for communication to take place (Austin, 1962; Grice, 1975; Searle, 1969). The honest speaker does not assert untrue propositions about the knowledge structure that is conveyed. The speaker should not introduce arguments that do not exist in the world under consideration. The speaker should be coherent; arguments and propositions should not be expressed unless they are relevant to the world or knowledge structure under consideration.

Propositions are often embedded within other propositions. A result of this embedding is that some propositions are interrelated in a hierarchical fashion. A proposition that modifies aspects of another proposition is more subordinate than the proposition it modifies. Studies by Kintsch (Kintsch, 1974; Kintsch and Keenan, 1973) and other researchers (Manelis, 1980; Meyer, 1975, 1977a, 1977b) support the hypothesis that the likelihood of recalling a proposition tends to decrease as a proposition is more subordinate in an underlying structural hierarchy. Thus, recall for P13 (*daughters enjoy themselves*) should be higher than for P14 (the manner of P13 was *so much*). Stated differently, there is poorer recall for those propositions that modify, qualify, or embellish some aspect of a given proposition than for the proposition that is modified. This prediction is intuitively plausible and has been supported by recall data.

The propositional analysis that is adopted here is similar to many of the available propositional theories in psychology. According to all propositional theories, propositions contain a predicate and a number of arguments. Propositions also may be embedded within other propositions. As mentioned earlier, however, the available propositional theories differ in a number of ways. It is informative to consider briefly how the present propositional analysis compares to other propositional theories.

The present propositional analysis treats nouns as predicates. This assumption is consistent with some theories in linguistics (Bach, 1968; McCawley, 1970), philosophy (Reichenbach, 1947), and psychology (Clark and Clark, 1977). This assumption differs from some case structure theories in linguistics (Fillmore, 1968; Simmons, 1973) and Kintsch's microstructure theory (Kintsch,1974). According to the latter theories, nouns serve as arguments of propositions rather than as predicates. The issue of whether nouns correspond to predicates or arguments can be examined from a number of perspectives and criteria. From the present perspective, it is important to distinguish between words and the underlying concepts to which the words refer in a specific context. Treating nouns as predicates seems to preserve this distinction more naturally than when nouns are treated as arguments. The rationale for the present position has been discussed elsewhere (Bach, 1968; Clark and Clark, 1977; McCawley, 1970).

In the present propositional analysis, each proposition contains some arguments that are obligatory, a number of optional arguments, and a number of semantic indices. Whereas the obligatory arguments must be captured by explicit linguistic expressions, the optional arguments and indices need not be. Additional propositions are created whenever an optional argument or index is embellished with prepositional phrases or other linguistic expressions. This analysis is somewhat different from case structure theories in which both the obligatory arguments and explicitly embellished optional arguments are part of the same proposition (Fillmore, 1968; Stockwell et al., 1973).

A central goal of propositional theories in philosophy is to specify a device that determines whether or not propositions are true or false. The device contains a set of inference rules that generates a set of true new expressions from a given set of true expressions. The present propositional analysis, as well as other propositional theories in linguistics and psychology, is not designed to generate true inferences. Pragmatic rules of conversation render the problem of evaluating the truth of propositions as trivial. Unless the passage states otherwise, the truth values of stated propositions are *true.* Furthermore, the propositional theories in psychology are not designed as analytical devices that generate inferences. Inferences are generated by virtue of macrostructure analyses.

A propositional analysis of sentences in prose is designed to capture the semantic code of explicit information. The propositional representation provides a natural interface between language code and nonlinguistic knowledge of the world. Propositional representations have therefore been a level of scrutiny in both linguistic theories and theories of knowledge representation. In fact, there has been some debate as to whether propositions should be construed as units for linguistic analysis, units for representing nonlinguistic knowledge, or both. In any case, the propositional representation is important to incorporate in theories of prose comprehension.

The pragmatic level of linguistic analysis has only been discussed in passing in this section. This does not imply that the pragmatic level is not important. The pragmatic level is indeed essential for an adequate theory of communication and comprehension. However, the pragmatic level is the least understood aspect of linguistic analysis. There is also some question as to whether pragmatics should be extensively investigated in linguistics. It may be more natural to reserve the pragmatic level for theories of communication, social psychology, or sociology. Nevertheless, there are linguistic regularities that map onto a pragmatic code and linguistics have contributed a great deal to our understanding of pragmatics (Bates, 1976; Gordon and Lakoff, 1971).

The pragmatic level deals with the interaction between the speaker and listener, or the author and reader. When sentences are spoken (or written), the speaker produces the utterances for certain purposes. For example, an utterance is a statement when the speaker wants the listener to know about some fact or event, and a question when the speaker wants the listener to tell him about something. An utterance is a request when the speaker wants the listener to do something and a promise if the speaker agrees to do something that the listener wants him to do. Thus, speech acts are executed with intentions, just as physical actions are. These intentions are examined at the pragmatic level. It is important to distinguish between the *performative* aspect of a speech act and the *literal* or explicit content of what is said (Austin, 1962). Another issue for pragmatic analysis resides in the common knowledge that is shared between the speaker and listener. Some knowledge and conventions about language must be shared by the speaker and listener for communication to take place (Grice, 1975; Norman and Rumelhart, 1975; Rommetveit, 1974; Searle, 1969). Some of these conventions were introduced earlier in the context of propositional analysis. For example, the speaker and listener both assume that spoken propositions are true unless specified otherwise. Although the pragmatic aspects of statements are sometimes not manifested in linguistic elements, they are essential for effective communication.

Sometimes the performative aspect of an utterance is captured directly by linguistic regularities. For example, it would not be difficult to identify by linguistic cues which of the following utterances constitute a statement of fact, a question, or a command.

What did Judy say on the telephone?
Tell Marcy to give Kathy her telephone number.
Andy is attracted to Sharon.

However, syntactic regularities do not perfectly determine the performative aspect of an utterance (Austin, 1962; Gordon and Lakoff, 1971). Indirect requests and commands may be delivered in the form of a question syntactically.

Could you give me your telephone number?
Would you pass me the salt?

Indirect requests may also be expressed in the form of a statement.

I need your telephone number.
There is the salt.

The performative aspect of an utterance is evaluated by virtue of the social world, the physical world, and the discourse context in addition to linguistic cues (Clark, 1979; Clark and Lucy, 1975; Gibbs, 1979; Schweller, Brewer, and Dahl, 1976).

Rhetorical Knowledge

In the present context, rhetorical knowledge will be construed in the broadest possible sense. Rhetorical knowledge is knowledge that the comprehender has about how statements should be introduced, ordered, and interrelated in different kinds of prose so that the message has an optimal impact on the listener or reader. The development of a prose passage follows a certain logical form and set of conventions. Points are delivered in a prescribed order, and some points are emphasized more than others. The set of rhetorical rules that is appropriate for a particular passage depends on the conceptual content of the message.

A large number of distinct types of prose can be easily identified. There are stories, jokes, encyclopedia articles, scientific journal articles, speeches, newspaper articles, newspaper editorials, ads in the classified section, and movie reviews, just to name a few. Each of these types of prose has its own special set of rhetorical conventions. Consider the rhetorical conventions for a newspaper article. There usually is a short, condensed title that refers to an important event or situation. The paragraphs are short; often a single sentence constitutes a paragraph. The reporter tries to incorporate the important aspects of the situation at the beginning of the article and elaborates on details at the middle and end. The reader should be able to answer *who, what, when, where, how,* and *why* questions after reading the first two or three paragraphs of the article. When conveying why the event or situation occurred, the reporter quotes experts or witnesses rather than interjecting the reporter's own opinion. Reporters state their opinions in editorials rather than news articles.

A good instructor for a course in English composition tries to teach students the conventions of different types of prose. Prose passages are categorized into different prose *genres.* In the traditional categorization scheme, there are four different prose genres: descriptive, expository, narrative, and persuasive (Brooks and Warren, 1972). Descriptive prose resembles a listing of static concepts, attributes, and relationships. The description of a spatial scenario or a character's personality in a novel is an example of descriptive prose. Expository prose describes something and explains why it is the way it is. An encyclopedia article about earthquakes is a good example of expository prose. Narrative prose conveys actions and events that unfold in time. Stories and folk tales are prototypical examples of narrative prose. The persuasive genre is pretty much self-explanatory. Examples of persuasive prose include debates, sermons, and advertisements.

Most of the psychological research in discourse processing has examined the rhetorical conventions of the narrative genre. Story grammars have been developed to capture these conventions (van Dijk, 1972, 1973; Johnson and Mandler, 1980; Rumelhart, 1975, 1977c; Stein and Glenn, 1979; Thorndyke, 1977). The grammars specify the important components of stories, i.e., the characters, the setting, the plot, etc. The grammars also specify the order in which concepts and parts of the story are introduced. For example, Rumelhart's grammar (1975) includes the following rewrite rule for a story.

Story → Setting + Episodes*

This is not a very complicated rewrite rule. It captures the convention that the writer should introduce aspects of the setting before presenting the series of episodes in the plot. (The asterisk denotes that there may be more than one episode.) The setting includes the introduction and description of certain characters, the location, and the time frame in which the episodes occurred. A typical beginning of a story would be a sentence such as *Once upon a time in a deep dark forest there lived an elf.* This sentence introduces one of the characters, a location or scenario, and a vague reference to the time in which the episodes occurred. Of course, the setting and episodes are often fictitious. It is a good policy to elaborate on the setting before conveying the plot. A rich setting establishes a firm conceptual grounding and adds color.

Story grammars usually incorporate a list of rewrite rules and each rewrite rule contains a set of elements. For example, listed below are the first five rewrite rules of Thorndyke's grammar (1977).

(1) Story → Setting + Theme + Plot + Resolution
(2) Setting → Characters + Location + Time

(3) Theme → (Event)* + Goal
(4) Plot → Episode*
(5) Resolution → {Event | State}

According to these rewrite rules, a story is more than a setting and a sequence of episodes. A story has an overall theme. The theme is some primary goal that the protagonist wants to accomplish. Sometimes the theme is precipitated by some event. For example, suppose that the elf story was continued as follows:

Once upon a time in a deep dark forest there lived an elf. The elf became very lonely and needed a companion.

The elf's becoming lonely is an event that precipitates the goal of getting a friend. This would probably serve as the theme of the story. The theme provides a frame for the story plot. The actions of the plot might involve the elf executing a plan of action designed to achieve the goal of the theme. However, the physical and social world might not be particularly cooperative with the elf and his goals. The plot should be more complicated if the story is to be interesting (Beaugrande and Colby, 1979; Brewer and Lichtenstein, 1980; Bruce, 1978; Bruce and Newman, 1978; Wilensky, 1978b, 1978c). The plot of a large number of stories is organized around a problem solving theme with a protagonist wanting to achieve some goal by performing actions and overcoming barriers in the social or physical world (Rumelhart, 1977c). The resolution occurs at the end of the story. If the theme goal is achieved in the elf story, then the elf would find a friend. Alternatively, the elf would live as a loner for the rest of his days—perhaps for the better.

The *episode* unit is an important part of virtually all of the story grammars. The plot consists of an organized series of episodes. According to the various story grammars and other theories of representing stories, the episode unit includes a number of components. Listed below are rules for episode units in different theories.

Episode → Subgoal + Attempt + Outcome (Thorndyke, 1977)
Episode → Event + Reaction (Rumelhart, 1975)
Episode → *Beginning* cause *Development* cause *Ending* (Johnson and Mandler, 1980)
Episode → Initiate (Initiating Event, Response) (Stein and Glenn, 1979)
Episode Schema → Episode about protagonist P
(1) Event E causes P to desire Goal G
(2) P tries to get G until outcome O occurs (Rumelhart, 1977c)

It is apparent that the various systems of organizing stories are not in complete agreement about what information is carried within an episode. The differences can be appreciated only when the entire sets of rules are known and the objectives of the theories are articulated. The last rewrite rule incorporates more of the semantic regularities of an episode than do the other four. This is because

Rumelhart's 1977 theory attempted to interface the syntactic (rhetorical) regularities of stories with a semantic theory. Taken together, however, the various rules systems indicate that episodes contain a number of subparts. Some event initiates a response by a character, including the adoption of a goal (not to be confused with the primary theme goal). The character attempts to achieve a goal by performing actions and the attempt leads to some outcome. Of course, characters interact in stories. The goal-driven action of one character would be an initiating event that produces a goal in another character. For example, in the Czar story, the episode of the daughters crying would be an initiating event for another episode in which the heroes set off to rescue the daughters.

A major objective of the text grammar approach is to specify sets of rules that discriminate between passages of different genres. For example, the rules for a general story grammar would successfully parse all stories and would not accommodate passages in the expository, descriptive, and persuasive genres. There is a controversy, however, over whether the available story grammars fulfill this objective (Black and Wilensky, 1979; Mandler and Johnson, 1980). According to Black and Wilensky (1979), the available story grammars accommodate some passages that are not stories and fail to accommodate some passages that are stories. On the other hand, Mandler and Johnson (1980) argue that the classification errors pointed out by Black and Wilensky are not really classification errors. Regardless of whether the story grammars perfectly discriminate between stories and nonstories, the story grammar approach has clearly uncovered and articulated some important regularities that stories possess.

Novels are generally not pure narrative. Paragraphs may involve description, such as when the author devotes a few pages to describing the spatial scenario or the characters. Sometimes portions of the novel involve exposition: the author explains why certain characters or situations are the way they are. There may also be an element of persuasion in a novel: the author tries to convince the reader that a social or ethical ideal is good. Some shorter forms of narrative also have a persuasive impact. For example, the following rewrite rule highlights an important aspect of fables.

Fable → Story + Moral

Fables are presumably written to persuade the reader that a certain truism is justified. The story constitutes the evidence.

In the final analysis, it might be untenable to claim that there is a rigid categorization scheme applicable to all passages. It may be more plausible to view passages as varying along four or more different genre dimensions, including description, narrative, exposition, and persuasion. Several schemes for categorizing prose have been proposed in linguistics, literary criticism, and other areas in cognitive science. However, it is well beyond the scope of this section to compare and contrast the various schemes.

Writers sometimes violate the conventions that are appropriate for a particular prose genre. For example, novels sometimes incorporate foreshadowing. A novel begins with some episode that is interesting or related to the climax. Thereafter, the novel proceeds with the setting and the natural chronology of episodes. Novels also occasionally incorporate flashbacks to episodes that occurred prior to the time span of the main story sequence. Readers may notice the deviations from the normative rules for a genre. The reading is more unusual and captivating when the violations are used effectively. Of course, too many violations produce prose that is either unreadable or reserved for those who want to be challenged cognitively.

Psychologists have conducted experiments to test whether the representations generated by the story grammars correspond to the representations that humans construct as a result of comprehension. Investigators have collected (a) recall or summarization protocols after stories are comprehended (Mandler, 1978; Mandler and Johnson, 1977; Rumelhart, 1977c; Thorndyke, 1977), (b) ratings of the comprehensibility or importance of the sentences (Mandler and Johnson, 1977), and (c) reading times for sentences during comprehension (Haberlandt, 1980). Recall has served as the most popular test of story grammars. From a psychological perspective, the best grammar would perhaps be the best predictor of recall. The story grammars have provided the theoretical context for examining some predictions regarding recall. However, the predictions of the story grammars have had mixed success.

One type of prediction that some story grammars have offered is that recall for statements in stories varies as a function of their *hierarchical level.* The rewrite rules of a story grammar serve as a generative device that (a) assigns statements to categories of nodes and (b) relates the nodes structurally in a hierarchical fashion. Early research reported that there is poorer recall for those statements that are relatively subordinate in the structural hierarchy (Thorndyke, 1977). However, later research found this strong prediction to be unsupported when a larger sample of stories was examined. Recall is sometimes, but not always predicted by hierarchical level. The conditions in which recall can be predicted by hierarchical level depend on what node categories are involved and the semantic composition of structural configurations (Black and Bower, 1980; Johnson and Mandler, 1980; Rumelhart, 1977c). Thus, the semantic content and the relationships between story statements are apparently more critical for predicting recall than are the syntactic constraints of the story grammars.

A second prediction provided by the story grammar approach is that recall varies among the different categories of nodes. Mandler (1978) has reported that recall is poorer for statements referring to the *internal reactions* of characters and the *endings* of episodes, than statements capturing the *setting,* the *beginnings* of episodes, the *attempts* at achieving goals, and the *outcomes* of attempts at achieving goals. Such differences in recall among the different node categories are robust and they emerge in different cultures (Mandler, Scribner, Cole, and DeForest, 1980) and different age groups (Mandler, 1978; Mandler and Johnson, 1977; Mandler et al., 1980). However, these persistent trends may be explained by semantic phenomena as well as the story grammars. There may be poorer recall for episodic endings and internal reactions of characters because such information can be inferred semantically from other information that is articulated

(Black and Bower, 1980; Johnson and Mandler, 1980). The differences in recall among node categories may perhaps be explained by intrinsic properties of the statements.

A third prediction of the story grammars involves transformations of the chronological order of the actions and events. When stories are transformed by permuting the order of events, individuals recall the stories in a manner that obeys the narrative conventions (Mandler and Johnson, 1977; McClure, Mason, and Lucas, 1979; Stein and Nezworski, 1978). When a passage contains two separate stories, with the events of each story mixed together by interleafing, individuals tend to segregate the events of the two stories in their recall protocols (Mandler, 1979; Mandler and DeForest, 1979). Once again, however, these trends may be accommodated by a semantic explanation. Semantic theories would certainly assume that the most natural way for telling a story would honor the chronology of the sequences. Similarly, information that is semantically related should cluster together at recall. Thus, there has not yet been an unequivocal demonstration that the story grammars can predict recall. Part of the problem of providing convincing support for the story grammars stems from the fact that the rhetorical conventions are inextricably bound to the meaning and content of the material.

Most of the discussion about genre has focused on narrative. This is because cognitive scientists have studied the representation of narrative prose in more detail than other genres. There are only a few scattered studies in psychology that have examined the rhetorical conventions of other prose genres and how recall or reading times can be explained by them (Kieras, 1978; Munro, Lutz, and Gordon, 1979; Olson, Duffy, and Mack, 1980; Thorndyke, 1979). Perhaps future research will unveil the conventions of genres other than narrative.

Memory research has shown that narrative prose is remembered particularly well compared to other discourse genres (Bower and Clark, 1969; Cohen and Graesser, 1980; Graesser, Hauft-Smith, Cohen, and Pyles, 1980; Kozminsky, 1977; Thorndyke, 1977). The Graesser et al. (1980) study demonstrated this fact very nicely. Graesser et al. selected 12 passages that ranged in the degree to which they were familiar to the reader and the degree to which they were narrative versus expository. Subjects rated the passages on two 7-point scales. The narrativity scale ranged from "passage conveys static information" (1) to "passage conveys active information with events unfolding in time" (7). The familiarity scale ranged from "not at all familiar with the information in this passage" (1) to "very familiar with the information in this passage" (7). These two dimensions were found to be uncorrelated, $r = -.03$. Another group of subjects listened to the passages and later recalled them. The proportion of propositions recalled from the passages was found to be highly correlated with the narrativity ratings, $r = .92$. Thus, narrativity accounted for 84% of the recall variance. A third group of subjects listened to the passages and later received a 3-alternative, forced choice comprehension test on the material. The comprehension scores were also found to be highly correlated with narrativity ratings, $r = .62$. An interesting outcome of the study was that the familiarity ratings did not significantly predict retention. In fact, there was a slightly negative correlation between familiarity ratings and (a) recall, $r = -.11$, and (b) comprehension scores, $r = -.29$. The negative correlation between passage familiarity and memory is counterintuitive and will be discussed further in Chapter 3.

Why is narrative prose acquired so easily and remembered so well? Some semantic properties will undoubtedly need to be examined before a satisfactory answer to this question is in reach. It is unlikely that the linguistic or rhetorical organization of a passage is responsible for the fact that recall for narrative prose is nearly twice as good as that for expository prose. Available research has shown that variations in linguistic and rhetorical aspects of a message have either no effect or a very modest effect on prose acquisition and understanding (Kintsch, 1974; Kintsch, Mandel, and Kozminsky, 1977; Rothkopf, 1972; Thorndyke, 1979). The systematic variations in the surface structure of passages that differ in prose genre are probably not responsible for the fact that narrative is easiest to understand and remember. The deeper levels of understanding will be discussed in subsequent sections.

Causal Conceptualizations

Statements in prose are often related by causal conceptualizations. Consider the following three events from *The Czar and His Daughters.*

(1) *The daughters were enjoying themselves.*
(2) *The daughters forgot the time.*
(3) *The daughters stayed too long.*

The three events form a causal chain. The daughters' enjoying themselves *caused* the daughters to forget the time, which in turn *caused* the daughters to stay too long. In the present context, causal conceptualizations refer to sequences of events and states that unfold in a mechanistic or nonintentional manner.

The links that causally relate statements in a causal chain are not always necessary and sufficient causes. Strictly speaking, enjoyment does not cause people to forget time. The three example events are really successive *outcomes* that are products of complex, causally driven sequences of events. Some event leads to another event as a consequence of some causally driven mechanism. The underlying causal conceptualization is usually more elaborate than is indicated by an event chain that is expressed explicitly. A number of implicit events and states intervene between explicitly mentioned events. For example, the first and second events in the above example probably involve the following two states that are inferred.

(4) *The daughters were preoccupied.*
(5) *The daughters were not paying attention to the time.*

On the basis of explicitly stated event chains, the comprehender constructs an underlying causal conceptualization.

Causal conceptualizations involve both events and states. States are properties of the physical world, social world, or mental world of a character. The states remain unchanged throughout the time course of a mechanism that causally unfolds. Events are state changes. Some examples of states and events are shown below.

The boy was tall. (State)
The boy became tall. (Event)
The sun was shining. (State)
The sun started to shine. (Event)
The boss was angry. (State)
The boss became angry. (Event)

In the above examples the states contain the static linking verb *was,* whereas the events contain incoative verbs denoting changes of state, *became* and *started to.* Although these examples convey the difference between states and events, it is important to mention that the difference between states and events is not perfectly captured by linguistic properties of the statements in passages. Consider the example below.

When the boss heard about the restrictions on pay increases, the boss was angry.

In this example *the boss was angry* is an event despite the fact that it contains the verb *was.* The boss changed from the state of not being angry to the state of being angry as a consequence of hearing the bad news about pay increases. It is important to evaluate the context of a statement when deciding whether or not it refers to a state or an event. The linguistic form is often uninformative.

Cognitive scientists have explored the representations of causal conceptualizations that are constructed when individuals comprehend a passage (Black and Bern, 1980; Norman and Rumelhart, 1975; Rumelhart, 1975, 1977c; Schank, 1972, 1973, 1975; Schank and Abelson, 1977; Warren, Nicholas, and Trabasso, 1979; Wilks, 1977) or acquire knowledge in a more extended educational setting (Brown, Collins, and Harris, 1978; Collins, 1977; Collins, Brown, and Larkin, 1980; Stevens and Collins, 1977, 1979; Stevens, Collins, and Goldin, 1979). Of course, the causal conceptualizations that are constructed during prose comprehension or the course of education do not perfectly correspond to the deterministic systems that are prominent in scientific theories. The average reader is not that knowledgeable. The cognitive representations of causally driven systems in technology and the physical world are incomplete, are often incorrect, and may be internally inconsistent (Stevens et al., 1979).

Smith, Kinney, and Graesser (1980) recently reported a study that dramatically demonstrates how poorly college students understand passages that describe scientific mechanisms. College students read 200-300-word passages that described such mechanisms as nuclear reactors, photosynthesis, the development of stars, and the operation of galvanometers. The passages were written in simple language, with very few complicated terms and no formulas. In other words, the passages were quite readable. Subjects were allowed 5 minutes to read and study each passage. Five minutes was a relatively long time since subjects normally require only 1.5 minutes for reading such a passage when they are asked to read for comprehension and reading times are collected. After the subjects read each passage, they were given a 3-alternative, forced choice comprehension test. Some of the questions on the test were inference items. In order to answer the inference items correctly, subjects had to draw valid inferences and reason on the basis of explicitly stated information. An interesting, but rather depressing outcome of the study was that college students were entirely unable to identify valid inferences about the scientific mechanisms. In fact, the proportion of correct answers on the inference items did not differ at all from a group of control subjects who never read the passages. Even college students have a great deal of difficulty understanding scientific mechanisms.

The fact that scientific mechanisms are very difficult to understand is quite apparent to educators. A solution to this problem is nowhere in sight. Collins and his associates have explored how students conceptually represent scientific mechanisms by analyzing the conceptual errors in their reasoning processes (Collins, 1977; Collins et al., 1980; Stevens and Collins, 1977; Stevens et al., 1979). These errors and their genesis were exposed in student-tutor dialogues in which tutors asked students questions and offered corrective feedback to students when certain errors were identified. The practical purpose of this research was to diagnose conceptual errors and explore methods of modifying the students' knowledge structures when they were faulty or inadequate. It is quite apparent that successfully detecting and rectifying errors are not simple, straightforward processes.

Even experts of a scientific phenomenon may not have a single coherent picture of how a mechanism operates. Instead, experts may understand the mechanism from multiple perspectives or "models" (Collins et al., 1980; Norman, 1980; Stevens and Collins, 1977; Stevens et al., 1979). Each model captures different aspects of the mechanism. Stevens et al. (1979) have illustrated the notion of multiple models in the context of rainfall. How can the ever-present phenomenon of rainfall be explained by a meteorologist? Stevens et al. have identified one model that captures certain aspects of the evaporation process. According to a rudimentary version of this model of evaporation, molecules are viewed as billiard balls that bounce around, collide, and occasionally move from the water to the air. Meteorologists call this Brownian motion. An increase in temperature causes an increase in the speed of the motion. Therefore, an increase in temperature increases the incidence of the particles moving from the water to the air (evaporation).

This simple model is helpful for explaining how evaporation is influenced by wind or the surface area on the water, as well as temperature. However, the model is inadequate when it comes to explaining the shape of the function that relates evaporation to the temperature of the air and the water. Evaporation rate increases with temperature according to some complex function. An explanation of the complex function would require a second model. The second model would provide several predictions about evaporation that would not be provided by the first model. When considering all aspects of rainfall, there may be several models that the expert calls upon. As more models are acquired by the expert, his ability to predict rainfall will be improved. In summary, an expert may not understand a complex phenomenon by a single complex mechanism, but rather by a collection of simpler models that capture parts of the mechanism.

Although a valid explanation of a causally driven phenomenon may be cumbersome and complex, the average comprehender manages to get by with a simpler representation. Event 1 somehow causally leads to event 2, and event 2 somehow causally leads to event 3, and so on. States and events may intervene between successive events. The degree to which the comprehender "fills in" these gaps depends on the comprehender's expertise and motivation. If all else fails, the comprehender may conclude that event *n* causally leads to event *n*+1 by magic.

At the most basic level, causal conceptualizations may be captured by a network of events and states. Three types of causal links relate events and states in causal conceptualizations. LEADS TO links relate two events in a causal chain. ENABLE links exist when a state enables an event to occur. RESULT links occur when an event results in a state. For example, consider the four statements below.

(1) *The daughters cried.* (Event)
(2) *The heroes were nearby.* (State)
(3) *The heroes heard the cries.* (Event)
(4) *The heroes knew someone was crying.* (State)

The event of the daughters crying *leads to* the event of the heroes hearing the cries. The state of the heroes being nearby *enables* the event of the heroes hearing the cries. The event of the heroes hearing the cries *results* in the state of the heroes knowing that someone was crying. Enabling states participate in a causal chain by virtue of other events that occur together with the enabling states. Event 1 and state 2 together lead to event 3.

Causal configurations will be discussed in more detail in Chapter 4. For our present purposes, it is important to keep three points in mind. First, causal conceptualizations consist of a network of states and events that are causally linked. Second, the causal conceptualizations that are constructed during prose comprehension are not as complete and logically rigorous as causal systems in science; there are lapses in causal connectivity and sometimes even distortions. Third, the causal chains that are explicitly mentioned in prose do not capture the richness of causal conceptualizations. The stated information merely highlights informative outcomes of the causal conceptualizations. The comprehender constructs a more detailed conceptualization that attempts to explain what is stated explicitly.

Intentional Conceptualizations

Goals, plans, and actions are organized by virtue of intentional conceptualizations. Consider the statements below.

(1) *The heroes went to the dragon.*
(2) *The heroes fought the dragon.*
(3) *The heroes rescued the daughters.*

The heroes intentionally executed each of these plans and actions. The heroes went to the dragon in order to fight the dragon in order to rescue the daughters. It has been postulated that intentional action sequences are organized by hierarchical structures of goals and plans (Abbott and Black, 1980; Becker, 1975; Bruce, 1978; Charniak, 1977; Graesser, 1978a; Miller, Galanter, and Pribram, 1960; Pew, 1974; Wilensky, 1978b, 1978c). For example, statement 1 captures the most subordinate goal and statement 3 the most superordinate goal. It is believed that goal-oriented conceptualizations are fundamentally different from causal conceptualizations (Graesser, Robertson, and Anderson, 1981; Graesser, Robertson, Lovelace, and Swinehart, 1980; Wilks, 1977; von Wright, 1971) and that theories should capture this natural distinction.

Statements that refer to actions have both a goal-oriented aspect and a behavioral aspect. The goal-oriented aspect is particularly important when actions are embedded in prose. The behavioral aspect is often inconsequential. For example, in the Czar story either of the following statements could easily be substituted for *The heroes went to the dragon* without substantially changing the meaning.

The heroes ran to the dragon.
The heroes rode to the dragon.

These two statements express two different methods of transportation but roughly the same goal and outcome. The goal and outcome is the heroes arriving at a location near the dragon. Moving by horse or by foot are two alternative forms of behavior. The goal and outcome are more important than the exact behavior in the context of this story. This example is typical for stories. The weak claim here is that the behavioral aspects of an action are not as important as the goal and outcome in many instances.

When a character has a goal, the character desires some future state or event. The character executes some behavior to achieve the goal. The goal may be achieved directly by the character, by the help of another character, or by a cooperative physical world. Sometimes goals are not achieved and the character becomes frustrated or emotional. Sometimes the behavior and physical world unfold in a manner that satisfies a character's goals and sometimes the goals remain unsatisfied. The actions of a character may also lead to events and states that were not intended by the character.

An important difference between goal-oriented conceptualizations and causal conceptualizations is that goals and actions are *future* directed, whereas events and states are driven by *past* occurrences in causal systems. The interface between the two systems is the behavioral aspect of intentional action. The character is satisfied when the causally driven outcomes match the character's goals. Again, the social and physical worlds are not always that cooperative.

Simple stories often center around a single character who has a primary goal. The goal may or may not be satisfied by the actions and events unfolding in the plot. Single-protagonist stories have been studied by researchers who have pursued story grammars (Johnson and Mandler, 1980; Rumelhart, 1975, 1977c; Stein and Glenn, 1979; Thorndyke, 1977) and other theories of story representation (Black and Bower, 1980; Lichtenstein and Brewer, 1980; Nicholas and Trabasso, 1980; Omanson, 1979; Warren et al., 1979). In a sense, the story plot traces the problem-solving process that the protagonist enacts or experiences as the protagonist tries to achieve his or her primary goal.

Black (Black and Bower, 1980) proposed a *hierarchical state transition* theory of story organization and memory that incorporates some principles of problem solving. A state transition network summarizes a problem-solving process as a series of (a) states and (b) actions that invoke state changes. What states need to be changed and what actions are performed to change the states? At the beginning of a story, the protagonist is faced with a beginning state and wants to achieve some primary goal state. The protagonist executes a plan of actions in order to change from the beginning state to the goal state of the primary goal. Consider the mundane story below.

> Josh had been playing on the beach for hours and wanted some food. Josh put on his clothes, picked up his toys, walked to his bicycle, and rode home. He opened the refrigerator door, took out some ice cream, and ate it.

Josh has the primary goal of eating food but he initially finds that he is miles from home. Josh then applies a plan that ultimately fulfills his goal—he ends up eating ice cream.

One strategy of closing the gap between the beginning state and a goal state is *means-end analysis* (Newell and Simon, 1972). The protagonist performs an action or a plan that reduces the distance between the current state and a goal state. Eventually the goal state may be attained as the actions and state transitions get closer to the goal. For example, Josh went home in order to get physically closer to the refrigerator. Josh opened the refrigerator in order to get physically closer to the food. A second strategy is called a *problem reduction analysis,* which imposes a hierarchical structure to the problem solving (Nilsson, 1971). The problem solver continuously segregates the problem into a set of manageable subproblems that have a high likelihood of being achieved. For example, Josh would perhaps divide his problem into three subproblems: *getting home, obtaining food,* and *eating the food.* Each subproblem can be segmented further into sub-subproblems. For example, Josh would subdivide the *getting home* subproblem into two sub-subproblems: *preparing to go* and *transporting himself home.*

As a result of problem reduction, the story would be hierarchically organized. At the most superordinate level there are the actions or plans that directly link the protagonist's beginning state with his primary goal state. This is what Black and Bower (1980) call *the critical path.* The more subordinate levels would include actions that embellish the state transitions at the higher levels.

Black's hierarchical state transition theory impressively predicts recall of information in single-protagonist stories. According to the theory, recall is predicted to decrease as actions deviate further from the critical path in the hierarchical structure. This predicted trend accounted for 65-81% of the variance for recall of the actions in the three stories that were analyzed. Moreover, the hierarchical state transition theory predicted recall far better than the theoretical hierarchies generated by alternative theories of story memory structure, including Kintsch's microstructure theory (1974), the available story grammars, and Schank's (1975) causal chain theory.

In the Josh story, Josh did not encounter any difficulties while he executed his plan of getting something to eat. In most stories, the social and physical world is not particularly cooperative. In fact, interesting stories include obstacles that challenge the protagonist as the primary goal is pursued (Beaugrande and Colby, 1979; Bruce, 1978; Bruce and Newman, 1978). Obstacles may involve physical events or actions of other characters in the story. Often the protagonist temporarily abandons pursuing the primary goal in order to deal with the obstacle. After the obstacle is dealt with, the protagonist continues pursuing the primary goal. An interesting ironic twist occurs when the protagonist ends up achieving his primary goal while dealing with the obstacle.

Many stories do not involve a single protagonist pursuing a primary goal. Instead, there are two or more characters and each of them pursues his or her own goal. An important part of narrative comprehension involves the recognition of the plans, goals, and motives of different characters (Owens, Bower, and Black, 1979; Schmidt, 1976; Schmidt, Sridharan and Goodson, 1978). The characters' plans may interact. Goals of different characters may conflict. The villain may set up an obstacle to the victim's goal, and then a hero may set up an obstacle to the villain's goal while facilitating the victim's goal. Consider the Czar story. The dragon (villain) has a goal of kidnapping the daughters (victim). The kidnapping serves as an obstacle to the daughters' goal of enjoying themselves. Then along comes the heroes. The heroes construct a goal of saving the daughters by setting up an obstacle to the dragon's kidnapping goal. As a consequence of the heroes' rescuing the daughters, the dragon's goal is blocked and the daughters' goal is facilitated. Stories may be analyzed by tracing the goal structures of each character as the plot progresses (Beaugrande and Colby, 1979; Bruce, 1978, 1980; Bruce and Newman, 1978; Graesser et al., 1981; Lehnert, 1980; Nicholas and Trabasso, 1980; Warren et al., 1979; Wilensky, 1978b, 1978c). The plan of two characters may *conflict* or compete (the daughters and the dragon, the dragon and the heroes). There may be *goal concord* between two characters, such as when an alliance is formed or when one character helps another character (the daughters and the heroes).

Characters may interact either physically or by conversation. The speech acts that characters perform reflect goal conflicts or goal concord between characters. As was mentioned earlier in this chapter, speech acts serve a pragmatic function in addition to carrying a literal meaning. The pragmatic functions of speech acts are intimately related to the plans and goals of the speaker and hearer. One way of solving problems and achieving goals is to get other individuals to do things. Speech acts are needed to implement these plans.

In many conversations there is a goal concord between the speaker and listener. Communication is a cooperative effort. The speaker and hearer agree on topics or themes to discuss as well as conversational goals. Sometimes one character wants another character to do something. Character 1 would make a *command* or *request* that the other character do it. If the requested action can be executed immediately, the second character does it immediately, assuming that goal concord is desired. Sometimes the requested action cannot be done immediately. In this case the second character would perform a speech act that signifies a *promise* that the second character will do the requested action in the future. Without speech acts, it would be much more difficult for individuals to get others to do things for them. Some speech acts are not designed to get others to do things. *Questions* serve the function of requesting information from another character. The requested information presumably involves something that the questioner needs or wants to know. When the speech act is a *statement*, one character gives another character information. Again, the information that the character volunteers is presumably information that the other character needs or wants to know. Fulfilling conversations nourish the needs and goals of the participants. When the goals are not met, the conversation becomes pallid. Of course, some conversations do end up being pallid and there are individuals who are not particularly sensitive to the goals of the listener.

All speech acts and conversations do not involve a goal concord. Goal conflicts between characters may occur in conversations. There are arguments. Character 1 wants character 2 to believe X, but character 2 refuses to believe X. The situation becomes more stirring when character 2 simultaneously wants character 1 to believe Y, but character 1 refuses to believe Y. Of course, X and Y are not congruent. Sometimes speech acts serve as threats. Character 1 wants to do some action A. Character 2 performs a threat that character 1 not do A because character 2 does not want character 1 to do A. There is a goal conflict in this situation, and character 2 tries to resolve it by displaying his power and issuing a threat. The pragmatic functions of speech acts are intimately tied to the goals of the speech participants.

Spatial Knowledge

The comprehender often constructs scenarios that provide spatial contexts for the actions, events, and states that are expressed in prose. Individuals virtually always experience life in a spatial context (even blind people), so it is not surprising that spatial scenarios are often constructed when people comprehend prose. One effective strategy of acquiring and remembering difficult verbal material is to generate vivid mental images of objects, characters, and events within a spatial framework (Bower, 1970; Levin and Pressley, 1978; Paivio, 1971). Of course, an important issue to examine is how spatial knowledge is represented in memory (Bregman, 1977; Clark, 1973; Kosslyn and Pomerantz, 1977; Kosslyn and Schwartz, 1977; Kuipers, 1978; Minsky, 1975; Palmer, 1977; Pylyshyn, 1973; Stevens and Coupe, 1978).

Some passages specify the spatial context in rich detail. Novels often begin with a colorful description of spatial regions, paths, landmarks, and loci, e.g., the neighborhood, the house, the street, the city, the tower, the door, etc. Other passages leave most of the burden on the comprehender to construct the spatial setting. A single word may be sufficient to foreground a rich scenario. In the Czar story the reference to the woods was sufficient to conjure a scenario that included many components and attributes, e.g., trees, green grass, flowers, meadows, birds, dangerous animals, people, etc.

Once a spatial scenario is constructed, the actions and events in prose lead the comprehender to focus on specific objects, people, and regions that are part of the scenario. In a sense, the comprehender has a "mind's eye" (Kosslyn, 1973) or mental camera that moves, looms, and zooms throughout the spatial context. Sometimes the mental camera is stationed in the form of a third-person narrator who overlooks the entire scenario and set of activities. At other times the mental camera is stationed from the point of view of one of the characters. Studies have shown that movements and transformations of the mental camera systematically increase processing time (Black, Turner, and Bower, 1979; Graesser, 1977; Kosslyn, 1973, 1975; Kosslyn and Pomerantz, 1977; Lea, 1975). For example, reading times for sentences increase when the mental camera shifts from the point of view of one character to that of another (Black et al., 1979).

Passages are written with cues that direct the mental camera during comprehension. Consider the following excerpt from the Czar story.

The daughters went walking in the woods.

Whereas the woods provide the spatial setting, the camera is focused on the daughters, who are at some location within the woods. The camera is usually focused on actions, events, or the characters executing the actions. There are at least two other cues that direct the mental camera. One of these cues are prepositional phrases with references to locations, as in the following statement in the Czar story:

The heroes returned the daughters to the palace.

This statement directs the camera from the woods to the palace. The other cue is the *deictic* features of verbs of motion (Black et al., 1979; Brewer and Harris, 1974). Consider the pair of statements below.

(1) *The heroes set off.*
(2) *The heroes came.*

Statement 1 presupposes that the mental camera is placed where the heroes had been before setting off; statement 2 presupposes that the mental camera is stationed where the heroes end up. Diectic aspects of verbs ascribe directionality to motion and reference points for the positioning of the mental camera.

Knowledge about Roles, Personalities, and Objects

Characters in stories fulfill roles. There is the mean villain that does mean things, the young and innocent victim who has only good intentions, and the strong hero who can overcome all obstacles. Roles and stereotypes enrich our impressions about characters in stories. Individuals have personalities and roles.

Novels often begin by describing characters in detail, whereas short narratives rely on role labels or stereotype labels to convey impressions of characters. In the Czar story we infer that the heroes are strong, benevolent, young, and chivalrous despite the fact that none of these traits are mentioned explicitly. The labels that are used to refer to characters express a great deal about the traits of characters in prose. The nouns convey roles, e.g., hero, king, secretary, cowboy, and father. If the comprehender knows that the character is a cowboy, then there are other traits that are known as well: the person wears a hat, the person has a gun, the person rides a horse, etc. The adjectives that are used to describe characters often convey stereotypes. For example, if we know that a character is a shy female, then we would suspect that the following traits are correct.

> The person is difficult to know, is unsociable, is a loner, never starts a conversation, does not speak up, is frustrated, has few friends, is uninvolved, is self-conscious, is insecure, gets embarrassed easily, is withdrawn, has a low self-esteem, is quiet, blushes, avoids attention, and is timid.

Researchers in the area of social cognition have explored the attributes of roles and stereotypes, as well as the processes of constructing personality impressions (Cantor, 1978; Cantor and Mischel, 1977; Taylor and Crocker, 1980; Taylor, Crocker, and D'Agostino, 1978; Wegner and Vallacher, 1977; Wyer and Carlston, 1979). The personality impressions are constructed on the basis of the nouns and adjectives that are used to describe individuals, as well as the actions the individuals perform and their reactions to events. When comprehenders recall stories, their recall protocols substantially differ when they take the perspective of different characters (Anderson and Pichert, 1978; Bower, 1978).

When characters are part of stories, the story structure may impose certain traits on the characters. For example, the Czar story has a victim-villain-hero format. The villain places the victim in jeopardy and the hero saves the victim by decapacitating the villain. In most stories these three types of characters have distinctive attributes. The villain is ugly, dark, vain, plotting, and bad. The victim is young, innocent, small, and helpless. Of course, the hero is strong, light, humble, intelligent, and good. These properties are sometimes ascribed to various characters by virtue of the overall story configuration.

The comprehender constructs information about inanimate objects as well as animate characters. Objects have physical properties. Psychologists have conducted hundreds of experiments using reaction time measures in order to examine how humans search their semantic memory and verify whether objects or animals possess specific physical properties (Collins and Loftus, 1975; Collins and Quillian, 1969; Noordman-Vonk, 1979; Smith, Shoben, and Rips, 1974). Objects also have functional properties in the sense that there is a relatively small set of actions that humans typically perform with any given object (Lehnert, 1978b; Lehnert and Burstein, 1979; Nelson, 1974, 1977; Nickerson and Adams, 1979). Objects are used instrumentally for humans to achieve their goals. The functional knowledge of objects is just as important as their physical characteristics.

The domains of knowledge that have been discussed thus far do not exhaust the arena. Moreover, some of the knowledge domains that have been discussed have received little more than a passing reference. More could be said about the conventions of dialogues (Cohen and Perrault, 1979; Fetler, 1979; Fine, 1978; Goffman, 1974; Goodenough and Weiner, 1978; Hobbs and Robinson, 1979; Levin and Moore, 1977; Miyake and Norman, 1979; Reichman, 1979; Sacks, Schegloff, and Jefferson, 1974; Schank, 1977; Schank and Lehnert, 1979), belief systems (Abelson, 1973, 1975, 1980a; Carbonell, 1978; K. M. Colby, 1973), attitudes (Schank, Wilensky, Carbonell, Kolodner, and Hendler, 1978; Tesser, 1978; Tesser and Leone, 1977), and emotions (Brewer and Lichtenstein, 1980; Faught, Colby, and Parkison, 1979; Lehnert, 1980; Mandler, 1976). Nevertheless, enough has been described to portray a rough sketch of what is involved in the comprehension process. Our knowledge is rich, complex, and multifaceted. Subsequent chapters will explore some knowledge domains in more detail. Before proceeding, however, there is one other notion that needs to be introduced and examined: *schemas* guide comprehension.

Schemas

Schemas are generic knowledge structures that guide the comprehender's interpretations, inferences, expectations, and attention when passages are comprehended. A schema is a structured summary of the components, attributes, and relationships that typically occur in specific exemplars (Rumelhart and Ortony, 1977). Without these schemas, the comprehender would have little or no basis for making sense out of the incoming information in a specific passage (Adams and Collins, 1979; Bransford and McCarrell, 1974).

A good demonstration of schemas in the comprehension process was reported by Bransford and Johnson. Bransford and Johnson (1972, 1973) conducted a series of experiments that demonstrated the importance of identifying critical schemas during comprehension (see also Dooling and Lachman, 1971). Consider the passage below.

> The procedure is actually quite simple. First you arrange items into different groups. Of course, one pile may be sufficient depending on how much there is to do. If you have to go somewhere else due to lack of facilities, that

is the next step; otherwise, you are pretty well set. It is important not to overdo things. That is, it is better to do a few things at once than too many. In the short run this may not seem important but complications can easily arise. A mistake can be expensive as well. At first the whole procedure will seem complicated. Soon, however, it will become just another facet of life. It is difficult to foresee any end for this task in the immediate future, but then, one never can tell. After the procedure is completed one arranges the materials into different groups again. Then they can be put into their appropriate places. Eventually they will be used once more and the whole cycle will then have to be repeated. However, that is a part of life.

The above passage is relatively difficult to comprehend and recall. Experiments by Bransford and Johnson have shown that subjects give the passage low comprehension ratings and their recall of the passage is relatively low. Why is this passage difficult? The reader does not identify the schema that interrelates the statements. The overriding schema of this passage is *washing clothes.* Once the comprehender knows this, the passage makes sense. When the passage is preceded by the title *Washing Clothes,* the comprehension ratings are substantially higher and recall performance is twice as good. Identifying critical schemas is important for comprehension.

A specific passage invokes schemas from a number of different knowledge domains and levels of structure. At the molecular level, there are schemas that correspond to the meaning of individual words, i.e., the predicates of the propositions. At the more global level, there are schemas that organize action sequences, stereotypes about personalities and roles, and spatial scenarios, just to name a few. These schemas provide the background knowledge that is needed for interpreting the statements in a specific passage.

It is important to emphasize the distinction between generic schemas and cognitive representations of specific passages. The distinction is similar to Tulving's (1972) distinction between semantic memory and episodic memory. When an individual comprehends some specific input at a specific time and place, the individual constructs a specific memory trace for the experience. These memory representations are dated. Schemas, on the other hand, are created after years of experience with specific exemplars. For example, individuals have a schema for eating at a restaurant. The content of the schema is a product of hundreds of experiences of eating at a restaurant. Consequently, it is very unlikely that an experimental psychologist will be able to study the creation and development of a schema in the course of an experiment that lasts 1 hour, 4 hours, or even 1 week. Experimental psychologists normally examine the representation and development of specific memory traces, or at best a collection of memory traces.

A distinction has been made between two stages of schema utilization (Norman and Bobrow, 1976, 1979; Schank and Abelson, 1977) that will be called schema *identification* and schema *application.* The comprehender initially completes a relatively data-driven process of pattern recognition which identifies a schema that provides a good fit to some aspects of the input. During comprehension schemas are identified at different levels of structure and different domains of knowledge. Once a given schema has been identified, the course of schema application guides interpretations, expectations, attention, and inference processes in a conceptually driven fashion. Thus, comprehension proceeds by identifying and applying schemas corresponding to various knowledge domains and levels of structure.

It is convenient to examine schemas from two perspectives. The first perspective is to specify the informational content of specific schemas or classes of schemas. It is worthwhile to categorize schemas according to schema content. The second perspective is to explore how schemas function and operate during comprehension. The content of schemas will be discussed first.

Researchers in the cognitive sciences have identified different categories of schemas. To some extent, the domains of knowledge discussed in previous sections might provide some guidelines for categorizing schemas. A given category of schema would have its own characteristic type of information. For example, goal-oriented schemas would include goals, plans, and actions, whereas person schemas would include typical traits, attitudes, and actions. On the other hand, it might be more accurate to categorize schemas differently and to incorporate many of the knowledge domains into each schema category. Consider a person schema for *fireman.* An understanding of *fireman* would include typical traits (firemen are brave and strong), but also goals and plans (firemen stop fires), some causal conceptualizations (how fires get started and maintained), some objects (hoses and fire extinguishers), and some spatial knowledge (firemen are usually at fire stations). Schemas are natural packets of knowledge that humans possess. An important goal for research and theory is to discover how schemas are categorized and differentiated in the human mind. In recent years cognitive scientists have identified many different types of schemas and a staggering number of terms have been introduced and reintroduced: *scripts, stereotypes, themes, roles, models, frames,* and *memory organization packages* (MOPs).

In addition to categorizing schemas according to content, it is informative to consider some general properties that apply to virtually any schema or class of schemas. For example, Rumelhart and Ortony (1977) have proposed four properties of schemas.

(1) Schemas have variables.
(2) Schemas can embed, one within the other.
(3) Schemas vary in abstractness.
(4) Schemas represent knowledge rather than definitions.

These four characteristics will be clarified by some brief comments and examples.

The first characteristic is that schemas have variables. The variables of a restaurant script include character variables (customer, waitress, hostess, cook), object variables (tables, chairs, food, menu), and action, plan, or goal variables (the customer is seated, orders food, eats, pays the bill). There is a conventional or logical order in which the action variables are executed. The variables of a schema are related in a complex way that is specified by the schema. A schema is said to be *instantiated* in a passage when the variables have been filled and interrelated. Variables may be filled by virtue of explicitly stated information or by inference. It is important to emphasize that the variables are interrelated by a very rich network of interrelationships. When one variable of an instantiated schema is filled, there may be drastic repercussions on the other variables. For example, if a restaurant has no hostess, then one would not expect to be impressed with the quality of the cuisine.

The second characteristic of schemas is that they may embed. Consider the restaurant schema. There are a number of subschemas that are embedded in the restaurant schema. An eating schema and a paying schema are two subschemas. The fact that schemas may embed within one another implies that schemas may be related in a hierarchical fashion. Although all schemas do not fit within the constraints of a strictly hierarchical structure, it is possible to identify hierarchical orderings that interrelate some sets of schemas.

The third characteristic is that schemas vary in abstractness. Some schemas are very concrete and specific, whereas others are vague and abstract. Consider the following list of animate beings.

Animal
Mammal
Dog
Collie

There is a schema for each of these concepts. *Animal* is more abstract than *mammal, mammal* is more abstract than *dog,* and *dog* is more abstract than *collie.* Moreover, it is easy to form a mental image of a collie, but it is difficult to form an image of the universal animal.

The fourth characteristic of schemas is that they represent knowledge rather than definitions. This is an important characteristic that dispells certain misunderstandings that occur when a researcher tries to convince colleagues that a given schema has such and such attributes, components, and relationships. A property of a schema is not a definition in the sense that the property does not need to apply to *all* instantiations of a schema (Gaines, 1976; Oden, 1977, 1979; Rosch, 1978; Rosch and Mervis, 1975; Zadeh, 1975). The components, attributes, and relationships of a schema are not always necessary, certain, and universal; they are possible, probable, likely, or whatever. In other words, attributes of a schema vary in typicality with respect to a schema (Rosch, 1978). Paying the bill in the restaurant is typical, but not strictly necessary.

The Functioning of Schemas

The utilization of a schema can be subdivided into two basic processes: schema identification and schema application. Schema identification is essentially a pattern recognition process. At some point in time the comprehender accrues enough information from the input or previous conceptual elaborations to identify a particular schema as being relevant. Schema identification is a data-driven process. In what sense is it data-driven? The schema is essentially activated by information that is available to the comprehender just before the schema is identified. Stated metaphorically, all the schemas in long-term memory are waiting around to be identified and called to duty by the information that has been accrued. Schemas are analogous to the *demons* that have been introduced in the theories of pattern recognition (Lindsay and Norman, 1977; Neisser, 1967).

There are at least two factors that influence the course of schema identification. The first factor is goodness-of-fit. The appropriate (relevant) schema has a high likelihood of being identified if there is a good match between the target schema and the information that has accrued. Goodness-of-fit can only be evaluated with respect to alternative schemas in long-term memory. In the best of worlds, the match between the target schema and the available information is better than the match between the available information and any other schema. Ambiguity occurs when more than one schema provides a good match to the information that has accrued. A second variable that influences schema identification is the amount of information that accrues. As the amount of information increases, there generally is a higher likelihood that the appropriate schema will be identified. As more information accumulates, (a) the informational array is more distinctive, (b) fewer alternative schemas will fit the data, and (c) the target schema is more uniquely determined. Of course, humans occasionally identify an incorrect schema.

Once a schema has been identified, the schema invokes a number of processes in a conceptually driven fashion. Conceptually driven processes are governed by the content and procedures provided by the schema. Metaphorically speaking, schemas are very active, temperamental, and finicky creatures. A schema makes sure it is on duty by scanning the information array for images of its elements. The schema is not comfortable until there is information that satisfies its important variables. Until the schema finds information that can be bound to its important elements or variables, the schema is unhappy and may not be instantiated. Thus, the schema actively seeks information that satisfies and embellishes its variables. When information is bound to the important variables, the variables are structured and interrelated according to the constraints of the schema.

Theorists have identified a number of processes that the schema executes during schema application (Adams and Collins, 1979; Bobrow and Norman, 1975; Bregman, 1977; Minsky, 1975; Norman and Bobrow, 1975, 1979; Norman, Gentner, and Stevens, 1976; Ortony, 1978; Rumelhart and Ortony, 1977; Schank and Abelson, 1977). First, a schema provides the background knowledge or context that is needed for guiding the *interpretation* of specific input that is relevant to the schema. It would be virtually impossible to make sense out of a specific event without this background knowledge. Any simple stimulus event can be interpreted in hundreds of ways.

A second function of a schema is to provide the background knowledge that is relevant for generating *inferences.* When statements are comprehended in prose, the comprehender constructs a cognitive representation that contains a rich configuration of inferences. These inferences come from somewhere and their source is not always supplied by linguistic knowledge. Consider the following sentence.

(1) *A policeman held up his hand and stopped the car.*

In the predominant reading of this sentence, the comprehender may draw a large number of inferences, including those that are listed below.

(2) *The driver of the car pushed his brake pedal.*
(3) *The policeman wanted the car to stop.*
(4) *The brake shoes rubbed up against the brake drum.*
(5) *The driver knows that the policeman wanted his car to stop.*

Specific schemas are needed in order to generate these inferences. Relevant schemas include knowledge of *traffic control* and *brake systems in automobiles.*

A third function of schemas is to generate *expectations.* Once a schema is identified, the content of the schema provides the knowledge needed for the comprehender to expect and predict future events and states (Schank and Abelson, 1977; Tannen, 1979). For example, while reading a story the comprehender might conclude that the story involves rescuing. Consider what is known in the Czar story up through the sentence *The heroes heard the daughters cries.* A rescue schema has probably been identified at this point, based on the following information.

(1) *The dragon* (villain) *kidnapped the daughters* (victims).
(2) *Three heroes were near the kidnapping.*

A villain-victim-hero configuration would lead the reader to expect that the heroes will rescue the daughters in the story. In fact, this expectation would turn out to be correct. Expectations are generated by schemas at different levels of structure and knowledge domains. A subset of the expectations is ultimately correct, whereas another subset is eventually disconfirmed.

A fourth function of a schema is to guide the comprehender's *attention* (Neisser, 1976; Neisser and Becklen, 1975; Norman and Bobrow, 1976, 1979). There are two different ways that schemas guide attention. First, schemas direct attention toward regions of the information array where parts of the schema are expected to occur. The schema verifies that its important parts are present in the information array by issuing commands to seek and examine areas in the information array where schema elements are expected to be. If the information array does not contain an important part of the schema, then attention will fixate on the area where the missing part should be. An embarrassing example of this is when someone is missing a part of the body. It is difficult to avoid paying attention to a missing finger or a missing ear. Second, attention is directed to areas of the information array that deviate from the content of the schema. It would be difficult to avoid paying attention to a hand that has six fingers or a string hanging from a person's mouth. In summary, attention is directed to parts of the information array that deviate from the schema (Loftus and Mackworth, 1978; Mackworth and Morandi, 1967). The deviation may involve the deletion of important schema-related information or the insertion of atypical information.

A fifth function of a schema is relevant when the schema corresponds to goal-oriented action sequences and skills. The schema *corrects and adjusts* schema-relevant actions while receiving *feedback* about previous actions and consequences of these actions (Schmidt, 1975). While performing goal-oriented behavior, individuals execute actions in order to achieve consequences that satisfy goals. Consequently, the individual must perceive the outcomes of the actions in order to verify that goals are satisfied. The outcomes may not satisfy goals and there are sometimes unintended consequences (Norman, 1979). The individual adjusts to these disturbances by executing actions that attempt to correct the malfunctions. Therefore, goal-oriented schemas have two important capacities. First, they perceive and monitor feedback. Second, they execute commands and actions. Some commands and actions are automatically enacted and are not sensitive to the feedback. The execution of other commands and actions is contingent on the context and feedback.

Several schemas are relevant to the comprehension of a specific passage. Somehow the schemas must communicate with one another. The products of one instantiated schema are passed to other schemas. The course of instantiating one schema requires inputs from other schemas that are (become) instantiated. The process of schema interaction cannot be summarized in a few short paragraphs. Chapter 2 includes a discussion of an interactive model of reading that addresses this problem in more detail. The important points to keep in mind are that schemas must "know" how to communicate with other schemas and that there has been a great deal of theorizing on how this is accomplished.

One issue that will not be examined in this book is how schemas develop. Schemas are assumed to exist and are believed to be needed for comprehension. Problems and issues involved in schema development are difficult ones that are beyond the scope of this book. Most schemas develop over the course of years and modifying them is not an easy task. There are several discussions and theories of schema development that the reader may pursue (Flavell, 1963; Nelson, 1974, 1977; Piaget, 1953; Rumelhart and Norman, 1978).

The previous discussion of schemas and schema functioning suggests that schemas are very intelligent knowledge structures. They direct interpretations of input, generate inferences, generate expectations, guide attention, and sensitively adjust to incoming feedback. The underlying belief here is that the information processing system possesses a large inventory of active, generic, semiautonomous knowledge structures called schemas. Each schema does its job according to its particular content, constraints, and rules. The course of comprehension proceeds by employing a subset of a very large inventory of specialists. These specialists are called schemas.

2

Allocation of Cognitive Resources During Prose Comprehension

When readers comprehend prose they identify and utilize schemas that correspond to various levels of structure and domains of knowledge. These processes take time to accomplish. Time is required for readers to process letters, syllables, words, propositions, syntax, and new concepts in sentences. Time is required to integrate the content of different sentences. Some components of reading are interpreted very quickly without difficulty, whereas others are time consuming and demand effort. How do readers distribute resources to different components of reading? This question and some related issues will be explored in this chapter. The focus here is on reading printed material rather than listening to prose.

Models of reading have incorporated a few basic assumptions that pertain to resource allocation. One assumption is that readers have a limited supply of processing resources during any given time span (Kintsch and van Dijk, 1978; Norman and Bobrow, 1975; Perfetti and Lesgold, 1977). This limitation is believed to be a general constraint on human information processing systems (Broadbent, 1958; Kahneman, 1973; Norman, 1976). Available theories of information processing have contributed a great deal of thought and research in isolating the loci of this bottleneck in capacity. It has been suggested, for example, that capacity limitations constrain consciousness (Mandler, 1976; Mandler and Graesser, 1976; Posner and Warren, 1972), short-term memory (Atkinson and Shiffrin, 1968; Norman, 1976; Waugh and Norman, 1965), attention (Broadbent, 1958; Kahneman, 1973; Treisman, 1964), response execution (Keele, 1973), and even the coding of visual features from visual input (Rumelhart, 1970). It is beyond the scope of this chapter to review the research that has attempted to pinpoint exactly where the bottlenecks occur during reading. The important point is that readers do not have a infinite cognitive capacity for interpreting input. There clearly are limitations. Processing resources must be distributed among components of reading in a manner that falls within such limitations.

A second assumption that has been adopted in most models of reading is that some components are interpreted automatically (LaBerge, 1975; LaBerge and Samuels, 1974; Neely, 1977; Perfetti, 1980; Posner and Snyder, 1975; Schneider and Shiffrin, 1977; Shaffer and LaBerge, 1979; Shiffrin and Schneider, 1977). What does it mean to say that a component is interpreted automatically? It has been proposed by some researchers (Perfetti and Roth, 1980; Posner and Warren, 1972) that there are four characteristics of units that are encoded automatically.

(1) The processing of automatized units does not require consciousness, focal attention, and effort.
(2) The reader is generally unable to consciously introspect on the course of processing automatized units.
(3) The interpretation of automatized units is relatively unaffected by the goals of the reader.
(4) The interpretation of automatized units does not suffer interference from other processing mechanisms.

It is important to mention that the automaticity assumption does not imply that automatized units require zero processing time. The speed of interpreting such units is indeed quick and several units may be interpreted simultaneously. However, the speed of interpreting such units is not zero. The automaticity assumption does imply that the processing of automatized components is not easily detected in experiments that are not particularly accurate or sensitive.

How does a reading component come to be processed automatically? Overlearning is an important contributor to automaticity (LaBerge and Samuels, 1974). A unit becomes overlearned when an individual interprets it in thousands, if not millions of exposures. Letters of the alphabet and common words are good examples of overlearned units. A unit is not overlearned in a 1-hour experimental session, as LaBerge and Samuel's research has shown. There is a difference between overlearning a unit and simply learning it. An individual can acquire a unit perfectly, as reflected by perfect retention in a memory task or a perceptual discrimination task. However, the item may not be overlearned and automatized. An important developmental condition for automaticity is that an item has been experienced in diverse encoding contexts. Such diversity ordinarily requires time that can be measured in weeks, months, or years. If an item is to be interpreted automatically, without conscious attention, and without the influence of the interpreter's goals, it must be resilient to fluctuations in reading contexts. Exposure to an item in diverse encoding contexts appears to be important precondition for developing an automatized unit.

Most processing resources are allocated to nonautomatic processes, such as those that conceptually relate words in sentences or sentences in passages. The units that are interpreted in a nonautomatic fashion are usually novel. A reader rarely experiences the same sentence twice. Moreover, the interpretation of the same sentence usually differs in different passage contexts. Novel aggregations of units are rarely automatically processed. The interpretation and integration of a unique code is time consuming, requires effort and attention, and is demanding on the reader's available supply of processing resources.

An economic metaphor is applicable to the present discussion of cognitive resources. Just as a person's bank account has a limited amount of cash during any given month, there is a limited supply of cognitive processing resources during a given time span. A worker can increase the amount of cash by applying more effort through work, but there is still some ill-defined upper bound in the amount of cash supply. Similarly, more cognitive resources are available when individuals apply more effort in a task (Kahneman, 1973). Nevertheless, there is an upper bound in available cognitive resources.

The economic metaphor can be extended further. What about costs? Living costs money and these costs are absorbed by tapping the bank account. Similarly, the processing of a reading component taps the available supply of cognitive resources. Automatized components are not very expensive, whereas the interpretation of novel configurations is very costly. There are inexpensive penny components (letters), nickel components (syllables), dime components (words), and quarter components (propositions). There are expensive components that require dollars, such as interpreting sentences, establishing causal chains, and forming mental images. Consciousness, attention, and thought are required when processing \$20 or \$50 components; there is a substantial investment. Pennies, nickels, and dimes are spent without conscious thought. If too many \$5 and \$20 items are purchased, the cash supply in the bank will become depleted and someone will get shortchanged, even at the level of the penny, nickel, and dime items.

The economic metaphor can be extended still further. How much is the buyer willing to pay for a given item? Context is clearly important. A worker usually pays about \$1 for a glass of wine and 25¢ for a coke. However, in a French restaurant an individual will pay \$3 for a glass of wine and \$1 for a coke. Similarly, the time to process a word may require 20 milliseconds in some context, 100 milliseconds in another context, and 1000 milliseconds in still another. Context clearly plays an important role in determining how much processing resources are allocated to a given unit of reading. Nevertheless, one can still assess the average cost when averaging across contexts, and compare the costs of different components of reading. The processing of an average syllable is probably less demanding than the processing of an average proposition. Similarly, a coke is generally less expensive than a glass of wine. Enough of this!

The question arises as to how the reader allocates the available cognitive resources to different reading components. Of course, the question can be posed differently. How much of the supply of cognitive resources is needed to process specific reading components? Most of the studies reported in this chapter examined these questions by collecting reading times for sentences in passages. The assumption here is that reading time is a reasonable index of how much cognitive resources are expended. Sentences are read more quickly when they are less demanding on available resources. One can observe how reading times differ among sentences that vary in complexity with respect to several different components of reading. The pattern of reading times among sentences should ultimately reveal how resources are distributed among different reading components.

Allocating Cognitive Resources to Different Components of Reading

Researchers have collected reading times in order to test hypotheses about the comprehension of isolated sentences and sentences in context. However, these studies have usually focused on only one or two components at a time. Such an approach is usually sufficient for testing specific hypotheses, but it does not address the question of how resources are allocated to a diverse set of components during reading. There is also a methodological problem with such an approach. When a researcher reports that a given component predicts reading times, there is a possibility that some third variable is correlated with the predictor variable and that the third variable is responsible for the pattern of reading times. Consider a trivial example involving word processing. Suppose that reading times can be robustly predicted by the number of words in a sentence. Does this mean that lexical encoding per se robustly predicts reading time? Not necessarily. There are other variables that are highly correlated with the number of words in a sentence. The number of letters and number of syllables are clearly correlated with the number of words. What is responsible for the fact that reading time can be predicted by the number of words? Is it lexical encoding, letter encoding, syllable encoding, or meaning encoding at higher levels?

The studies reported in this section used multiple regression techniques for isolating the specific contributions of various components to reading time. Reading times were collected for a large number of sentences that appeared in different passages. The sentences varied in complexity along many different dimensions. The multiple regression analyses provided a basis for estimating the independent contribution of a component after partialing out the contributions of other components. The amount of processing time that is required for a given component was estimated from the slope parameters in the multiple regression analyses. Since a large number of predictor variables were examined, the slope values were believed to be reasonably valid estimates of processing time.

Before discussing which reading components were examined, a few comments should be made about some limitations of multiple regression analyses and how the limitations constrain the interpretation of results. The first limitation lies in the assumption that a given component influences reading times in a linear fashion. The linearity assumption is the simplest approach to take at this stage of the enterprise because of the lack of research on the question. It is possible to assume that a particular reading component predicts reading time according to a more complex function (logarithmic or exponential). Unfortunately, there are an infinite number of functions to test. The linearity assumption is therefore frequently adopted in research that uses multiple regression analyses, unless there is a theoretical rationale for adopting more complex functions. At the same time, it is important to point out that the slope parameter for a given component will be affected if the true function deviates from linearity.

A second comment about multiple regression analyses pertains to the slope parameters. The slope for a specific component measures the amount of time to process a single unit of that component. For example, suppose the slope is 125 milliseconds (msec) when measuring how reading time varies as a function of the number of words in sentences. This slope would indicate that it takes roughly 125 msec to process an average word. In fact, the latter conclusion is not correct, strictly speaking. The values of the slope parameters are to some extent dependent on the set of other predictor variables that enter into the predictive equation. Suppose that there were n predictors of reading time. The predictive equation for reading time is shown below.

$$\text{Reading time} = s_1C_1 + s_2C_2 + s_3C_3 + \cdots + s_nC_n + K \tag{2.1}$$

S_i is the slope, C_i is a value on the predictor variable, and K is a constant. In addition to the set of measured variables, C_1-C_n, there are additional unmeasured variables C_{n+1}-C_m, that may predict reading time and may be intercorrelated with the measured variables. The slope parameter, s_i, for a measured variable, C_i, would be different in two multiple regression analyses, one with variables C_1-C_n, and the other with variables C_1-C_m.

How serious is the above problem in interpreting the slope parameters? Fortunately, the problem becomes progressively less serious as more variables are measured and entered into the equation. Generally speaking, as n increases, the slope for C_i will become progressively more stable. In short, the slope values should be more valid as more variables are included in the multiple regression analyses.

A final problem with multiple regression analyses is that they do not uncover ways in which components interact in predicting reading times. Multiple regression analyses will not assess interactions unless the investigator anticipates special interactions among components before performing the analysis and incorporates interaction terms in the predictive equation. It should be rather obvious by now that multiple regression analyses will not perfectly segregate the independent contributions of different reading components on reading times. However, this approach does provide an informative first step in examining how reading times are predicted by a large number of predictor variables.

It is time to turn to some studies. Most of the data reported in this section consist of a reanalysis of the data reported in a study by Graesser, Hoffman, and Clark (1980). This study included two experiments in which reading times were collected for 275 sentences. The sentences were part of 12 different passages that varied in familiarity and text genre. An example passage is listed in Table 2.1. The sentences varied from 9 to 15 words in length, with a mean of 11.92 words. The number of sentences per passage varied from 17 to 32, with a mean of 22.92 sentences. The titles of the passages are listed below.

The Princess and the Pea	Earthquakes
Bodisat	Emotions
The Serpent and the Judge	Armadillos

Snow White	Earth's Motions
Noah	Harvester Ants
Jonah	Coal Energy

The experimental procedure was very simple. Subjects read a number of sentences presented on a display scope, one at a time, and pressed a button when they were finished reading each sentence. Subjects were told that they would later be tested on the passages.

In the Graesser et al. study, the sentences were scaled on seven dimensions. However, the data reported in this section include nine dimensions. Each of these components will now be described.

Table 2.1. Sentences in an Example Passage Used in Reading Time Experiments

Earth's Motions
Motions of the Earth may be viewed from different points in space.
The most obvious motion is the Earth's daily rotation on its axis.
This is the motion responsible for the alteration of day and night.
A particular place on Earth may face away or toward the sun.
Less obviously, the Earth also revolves around the sun each year.
The Earth's revolution sweeps 600 million miles and takes 365.25 days.
The Earth's revolution around the sun is responsible for the succession of the seasons.
The orbit around the sun is not a perfect circle, but an ellipse.
The Earth averages a 92.9 million mile distance from the sun.
This average varies by about 3,100,000 miles during the course of the year.
However, seasonal variation has little to do with distance from the sun.
The Earth is closest to the sun during the northern hemisphere's winter.
The path round the sun is not centered precisely at the Earth's center.
The Earth and the moon are locked together thoughout the path around the sun.
The Earth-moon partnership is locked by gravitation and behaves like a dumbbell.
There is a large ball at one end and a small one at the other.
There also is a center of mass for this asymmetrical dumbbell.
The center of mass actually causes the Earth's ellipse around the sun.
The Earth is more than 80 times heavier than the moon.
The center of mass lies more than 3000 miles from the Earth's center.
As the moon circles the Earth, the Earth's center traces an "S" curve.
There is a range of almost 6000 miles along the path around the sun.
Other gravitational forces are also acting upon this wiggle in orbit.
There are some insignificant gravitational forces exerted by other planets.
These planets are much heavier than the moon, but further away.
The Earth's rotation about its axis is also not altogether steady.
The moon is the main source of irregularity in the Earth's rotation.
The moon's attraction for the oceans on the Earth causes the tides.
The weight of the tides causes an imbalance in the Earth's spin.
Also the moon has a gravitational effect on the Earth.
The moon passes first south and then north of the equator.
This causes the Earth's axis to wobble like an ill-spun top.

(1) **Letters**. The first component was the number of letters in a sentence. The obvious prediction is that more time is required to read sentences with more letters. The slope parameter in the multiple regression analysis is expected to be a reasonably valid estimate of how long it takes to interpret an average letter from a printed array. Of course, the processing time should be relatively fast.

(2) **Syllables.** The next component was simply the number of syllables in a sentence. Reading time should increase with the number of syllables.

(3) **Words.** The third variable was the number of words in a sentence. Reading time should increase with the number of words. According to previous studies, the average reading speed is 150-400 words per minute, or 150-400 msec per word (Carpenter and Just, 1977b; Gibson and Levin, 1975; Tinker, 1965). Of course, overall reading speed does not reveal how long it takes to process words, since the influence of other variables is not segregated from the overall estimate of reading speed. The slope of the word component in a multiple regression analysis corresponds to the time to access a word unit on the basis of the available letter code and syllable code, as well as higher levels of context.

(4) **Propositions**. The next variable was the number of propositions in a sentence. A proposition was defined according to Kintsch's (1974) system of representation. Kintsch's system of segmenting sentences into propositions is roughly equivalent to the system described in Chapter 1 except for one modification: in Kintsch's system nouns are not predicates. Therefore, any proposition with noun predicates (according to Chapter 1) is not counted. Kintsch's research (Kintsch, 1974; Kintsch and Keenan, 1973) has shown that reading times increase linearly with the number of propositions. The slope of the proposition-reading time function was between 1 and 4 seconds depending on the length of the passage.

(5) **Syntax**. The next variable was the syntactic complexity of the sentence. A more detailed discussion needs to be devoted to this variable because syntax has been studied extensively in psychology and linguistics (Chomsky, 1965; Fillmore, 1968; Fodor et al., 1974; Lakoff, 1972; Stevens and Rumelhart, 1975), and there are substantial differences among theories of syntax.

The goals of a linguistic theory of syntax are quite different than the goals of a psychological theory. Linguistic theories of syntax analyze sentences as a whole, without consideration of the fact that words in sentences are read from left to right. The primary goal of a linguistic theory does not necessarily involve explaining the cognitive processes that interpreters execute when performing syntactic analyses. An important goal of most linguistic theories is to formulate a syntactic device that generates all possible grammatical sentences, but not ungrammatical sentences. A psychological theory, on the other hand, needs to capture the cognitive strategies that are imposed as words are processed from left to right (Bever, 1970; Clark and Clark, 1977); the formulation of a syntactic device that generates all possible grammatical sentences is not a primary goal of a psychological theory. It is not surprising, therefore, that linguistic theories of syntax have not explained psychological data with much success (Fodor et al., 1974). The goals of the two enterprises are quite different.

Augmented Transition Network (ATN) parsers have recently been developed in order to capture syntactic processing when words are read from left to right (Anderson, 1977; Kaplan, 1975; Rumelhart, 1977a; Stevens and Rumelhart, 1975; Woods, 1970). An ATN parser formulates predictions about the syntactic class of word $n+1$ in a sentence, based on the knowledge available from words 1 through n. An important property of an ATN parser is its predictive nature. As Stevens and Rumelhart (1975) state it, "following each word in the sentence there is an explicitly ordered set of expectations with respect to the syntactic class and other characteristics of the next word" (p. 138). For example, if the first two words in a sentence are *the old,* the reader expects the next word to be a noun. If the first three words are *the old ship,* the reader expects the next word to be either a verb, a preposition, or a relative pronoun. Of course, expectations are not always confirmed. Consider the sentence *the old ship fruit.* By the time the interpreter inputs *the old ship,* the word *ship* is categorized as a noun. However, when *fruit* is received, the ATN mechanism must reanalyze *the old ship* by reassigning *old* to a noun class and *ship* to a verb class. Ambiguities and reanalyses of prior input require additional computations and should demand additional processing time for humans. The ATN parsers attempt to capture these facts.

Stevens and Rumelhart (1975) have developed an ATN parser that can account for the reader's expectations about the syntactic classes of words in sentences. Their parser has been tested in a number of experiments. In one experiment subjects read passages presented on a computer. The subjects were periodically stopped and asked to generate the next word that they believed would be stated in the passage. The ATN parser accounted for the syntactic classes of the generated words in 97% of the observations. An informative outcome of the experiment was that there usually was only one syntactic class that subjects generated at any point in a sentence. Although the ATN parser would accept a set of alternative syntactic classes at any given point in a sentence, only one of the alternatives was generated by subjects with a high likelihood (.90, as computed from Table 6.1 in Stevens and Rumelhart, 1975). Generally speaking, readers *predict* only one syntactic class at any point in a sentence, but they can *accommodate* several alternative classes when they receive an incoming word.

A plausible prediction of an ATN model is that an incoming word would demand less processing time if it conforms to the expected syntactic class than when it does not conform to the reader's expectation. Thus, a sentence should take more time to process as fewer incoming words match the expectations formulated by the ATN. The proposed measure of syntactic complexity was based on this assumption. The syntactic complexity of a sentence was measured by computing the proportion of words in the sentence that did not turn out to be in the syntactic class that was most likely to be expected by Stevens and Rumelhart's ATN parser. Reading time was expected to increase as the syntactic complexity of the sentence increased.

(6) **New argument nouns.** The next variable was the number of arguments in a sentence that were introduced in the passage for the first time. In this context,

an argument consists of a noun and refers to a character, object, location, or basic concept. Since new argument nouns are *foregrounded* (Chafe, 1972) in a passage when they first appear, additional processing time is needed for integrating their significance to the rest of the passage. This prediction has been supported by experiments that collected reading times (Kintsch, 1974; Kintsch, Kozminsky, Streby, McKoon, and Keenan, 1975; Manelis and Yekovich, 1976) and eye movements (Carpenter and Just, 1977b). Just as the arguments in a sentence may be categorized as new versus old, propositions may be segregated into those that convey new information with respect to the passage versus those propositions that refer to information that has already been either stated or inferred in the passage context. One would predict that those sentence propositions that convey new information require more resources than propositions that refer to old information (Lesgold, Roth, and Curtis, 1979). Nevertheless, the studies reported in this section did not scale sentences on the number of new propositions because propositions were rarely repeated in the passages.

(7) **Passage familiarity**. The next variable assessed the familiarity of the topic discussed in the passage. Some passages discussed topics that subjects were familiar with before reading the passage, whereas other passages conveyed information about unfamiliar topics. Obviously, it is predicted that the reader would spend more time reading sentences in unfamiliar passages. It is informative to note, however, that there is a lack of evidence for this prediction. The 12 stimulus passages were rated on familiarity in an earlier study by Graesser, Hauft-Smith, Cohen et al. (1980). In that study subjects rated each passage on a 7-point familiarity scale ranging from "very unfamiliar with the topic discussed in the passage" (1) to "very familiar with the topic discussed in the passage" (7). The mean familiarity ratings for the passages ranged from 2.25 to 5.00 with a mean of 3.57. Each sentence of a given passage received the same familiarity rating.

(8) **Passage narrativity**. The next variable assessed the genre of the passage. It is rather obvious that narrative passages (e.g., stories) are easier to read than expository passages. Consequently, narrative passages are predicted to be read faster. The 12 stimulus passages were rated on narrativity as well as familiarity in the Graesser, Hauft-Smith, Cohen et al. (1980) study. Each passage was rated on a 7-point narrativity scale ranging from "passage conveys static information" (1) to "passage conveys active information, with actions and events unfolding in time" (7). The mean narrativity ratings ranged from 1.58 to 6.75, with a mean of 4.31. Again, all sentences in a given passage received the same narrativity rating.

(9) **Serial position**. The final variable was the serial position of the sentence in a given passage. Graesser (1975) has reported that reading times decrease as a function of the serial position of the sentence in the passage. There are two basic explanations of this trend. According to the simplest explanation, the reader has a general strategy of spending more time reading sentences at the beginning of a passage in order to establish a solid framework to build on. The second explanation asserts that serial position has no direct influence on reading times. Instead, the obtained trend may be an indirect consequence of the fact that the beginning of a passage contains special time-consuming components. For example, there is a higher incidence of new argument nouns at the beginning of the

passage than at the middle and end. The new argument variable may be responsible for the fact that reading times decrease with serial position.

It is convenient to classify the variables into *microstructure components* and *macrostructure components.* Those variables that correspond to components within sentences are microstructure components, whereas macrostructure components integrate information between sentences. The letter, syllable, word, proposition, and syntax variables are microstructure components; the familiarity, narrativity, and new argument noun variables are macrostructure components. The serial position variable is in a separate category because it does not refer to a structural component.

In the study by Graesser, Hoffman, and Clark (1980), multiple regression analyses were performed in order to determine how the various components affected reading times. The Graesser et al. study examined all of the above variables except for letters and syllables. The analyses that will be reported here consist of a reanalysis of the data from the second experiment in the Graesser et al. study and included the letter and syllable components in the multiple regression analyses.

In the first set of analyses a correlation matrix was computed for the nine predictor variables. This correlation matrix is shown in Table 2.2. Table 2.2 includes the correlations between reading components. The last column in Table 2.2 lists the simple correlations between each component and mean reading times for sentences, averaging over subjects. All of the correleations are in the expected direction, although three of the nine correlations were not significant (serial position, syntax, and familiarity). There were positive correlations between reading time and the number of letters, syllables, words, propositions, new argument nouns, and syntactic complexity. There were negative correlations between reading time and familiarity, narrativity, and serial position.

Table 2.2. Correlation Matrix for Reading Times and the Nine Predictors of Reading Time

	L	S	W	P	Syn	NAN	F	N	Reading Time
Serial Position (SP)	-.08	-.05	.04	-.10	-.03	-.31	.18	.03	-.12
Letters (L)		.71	.38	.53	.04	.24	-.14	-.53	.57
Syllables (S)			.31	.40	.02	.20	-.10	-.48	.52
Words (W)				.40	.07	.05	-.01	-.11	.32
Propositions (P)					.13	.25	-.08	-.39	.50
Syntax (Syn)						.10	.15	-.10	.05
New argument nouns (NAN)							-.09	-.17	.30
Familiarity (F)								-.08	-.10
Narrativity (N)									-.59

Based on data collected in Experiment 2 of Graesser, Hoffman, and Clark (1980).
A correlation of .15 is significant at $p < .05$.

There is a problem in accepting simple correlations as tests of whether particular variables predict reading times. Many of the predictor variables are intercorrelated with one another, as Table 2.2 clearly shows. For example, there is a high correlation between the number of words in a sentence and the number of propositions. This correlation presents problems in interpreting the large correlation between reading time and number of propositions. Is the .50 correlation explained by propositions per se, or by some covariates, such as words? The fact that predictor variables are significantly intercorrelated calls for multiple regression analyses in which the independent effects of each variable can be assessed.

The outcome of the multiple regression analyses is shown in Table 2.3. A multiple regression analysis was performed on each of the 36 subjects' reading times. There was also one overall analysis on the *z*-score transformation of the subjects' times. For each subject, a *z* score was computed on the reading time of a sentence. A mean *z* score was subsequently computed for each sentence, averaging over subjects. Table 2.3 includes a slope value, an *F* score, and the proportion of reading time variance (r^2) that was predicted by each of the nine variables. The slope values are means that were derived from the analyses of individual subjects. The *F* scores and the proportions of predicted variance were based on the overall analysis on the *z* scores. In each multiple regression analysis, all nine variables were entered simultaneously.

The *F* scores shown in Table 2.3 reveal which reading components significantly predict reading times and which components do not. All but two of the components significantly predicted reading times at the $p < .10$ level. The reading times increased with syntactic complexity, but not significantly. Serial position also had no effect on reading times. Thus, the finding that reading times tend to decrease with serial position is apparently explained by the fact that certain

Table 2.3. Multiple Regression Analyses on Reading Time Data

Reading component	Slope (msec)	Standard deviation	F score	Proportion of variance predicted
Macrostructure variables				
Narrativity	-169	177	32.38**	.294
Familiarity	-65	177	2.87*	.012
New argument nouns	155	157	7.46**	.031
Microstructure variables				
Propositions	117	128	4.29**	.015
Syntax	363	988	.08	.003
Words	131	99	7.83**	.110
Syllables	45	35	9.22**	.057
Letters	24	25	8.90**	.018
Serial position	-8	14	.14	.014

Based on data collected in Experiment 2 of Graesser, Hoffman, and Clark (1980).

** $p < .05$

* $p < .10$

structural components are correlated with serial position. In particular, new argument nouns tend to occur at the beginning of passages. The additional time needed to foreground new argument nouns perhaps explains much of the obtained serial position effect.

The last column in Table 2.3 is a list of the proportion of reading time variance that is predicted by each of the reading components. These proportions reflect how robustly any given component predicts reading times. The nine variables together predicted .554 of the reading time variance. However, the components predicted reading times to different degrees. Narrativity predicted most of the variance. The proportion of *predicted* variance that was explained by narrativity was .531 (.294/.554). The second most robust predictor was the number of words, which explained .199 of the predicted variance (.110/.554). The third most robust predictor was the number of syllables (.103 of predicted variance), and the fourth was the number of new argument nouns (.056 of predicted variance). The other five variables accounted for a modest amount of the predicted variance.

The slope values in Table 2.3 appear to be valid estimates of how many milliseconds were needed to process a single unit along each of the predictor variables. More global units of analysis generally required more processing time, although this trend was not perfect. The interpretation of an average word demanded more processing time (131 msec) than that of a syllable (45 msec), and the interpretation of a syllable demanded more processing time than that of a letter (24 msec). However, more time was required to interpret a word than a proposition (117 msec), despite the fact that propositions are more global units than words. The foregrounding of a new argument noun (155 msec) also took longer than the interpretation of a proposition.

The slope for the propositions supports Kintsch's claim that reading time increases as a linear function of the number of propositions in prose (Kintsch, 1974; Kintsch and Keenan, 1973). However, the slopes in this study showed that only 117 msec is needed to interpret a proposition, which is substantially faster than the estimates from Kintsch's research (1000-4000 msec). What is the reason for this discrepancy? It is unlikely that the source of the difference lies in stimulus materials. The simple correlation between the number of propositions and reading time was .50 in this study, which is equal to the .50 correlation in Kintsch's research. The discrepancy appears to be a result of components that covary with the number of propositions. What are these components? Table 2.2 shows that six components significantly covaried with propositions: the number of letters, syllables, words, new argument nouns, syntactic complexity, and narrativity. Some of these covariates would not be responsible for the discrepancy between Kintsch's slope and the slope for propositions reported here. Since Kintsch's studies controlled for number of words, it is unlikely that the word, syllable, and letter variables account for the discrepancy. Moreover, syntactic complexity did not significantly affect reading time, so it is reasonable to eliminate syntax as the source of the discrepancy. The source of the discrepancy seems to lie in the narrativity and new argument noun variables.

Sentences with more propositions do tend to have more new argument nouns. When a new character, object, location, or concept is introduced for the first time in a passage, it is normally accompanied by a number of adjectives, prepositional phrases, and other descriptors that modify the concept. These elaborations increase the number of propositions in a sentence. For example, when the wolf is first introduced in the story of *Little Red Riding Hood,* the wolf is called *the big bad wolf.* Thereafter, the sentences simply refer to *the wolf.* It appears that a portion of Kintsch's slope estimate is confounded with the time needed to foreground a new argument.

Narrativity is another component that is confounded with the number of propositions. Sentences in narrative passages tend to have fewer propositions than sentences in expository passages. Since narrative passages are read faster, the sentences with fewer propositions would tend to come from narrative excerpts and be read faster by virtue of narrativity. The narrativity component could explain a large portion of Kintsch's proposition-reading time function and the fact that Kintsch's slope estimate is inflated.

The most substantial predictor of reading time was passage narrativity. The reading time for a sentence changed by 169 milliseconds for a 1-unit change on the 7-point narrativity scale. Therefore, a 12-word sentence in a perfectly expository passage (rating = 1) would take 1014 msec more time to read than a comparable sentence in a perfectly narrative passage (rating = 7). Narrativity is an interesting variable that will be discussed throughout this chapter.

The influence of passage familiarity on reading times was surprisingly small. The slope for 1-unit of change on the 7-point familiarity scale was only 65 msec. Familiarity only marginally predicted reading times ($.05 < p < .10$). A 12-word sentence in a completely unfamiliar passage (rating = 1) required approximately 390 msec more time to process than a sentence in a perfectly familiar passage (rating = 7). One would have expected familiar passages to have been read faster because there is a rich body of knowledge and repertoire of schemas to guide interpretations and to formulate expectations. However, the advantage of having prior knowledge about a topic had a rather small influence on reading times. Of course, it is possible that two processes influence reading times in an antagonistic manner. On the one hand, prior familiarity may decrease reading times because the richer knowledge base provides for easier interpretations and more expectations. On the other hand, prior familiarity may increase reading times because (a) more inferences are constructed when reading familiar passages and (b) reading times increase with the number of inferences that the reader generates (Miller and Kintsch, 1980; Olson, Mack, and Duffy, 1980).

It is rather disturbing that the syntactic component had a small and nonsignificant influence on reading times. The fact that this component was nonsignificant suggests that the measure of syntactic complexity may not have captured differences between sentences with complex syntax and those that had a simpler syntactic composition. However, if the 363 msec slope value is accepted as valid, then it took 363 more msec to process a 12-word sentence in which all of the words were in unexpected syntactic classes than a sentence in which all word classes were expected by an ATN parser. The slope suggests that it takes 30 more msec (363/12 = 30) to process a word in an unpredicted syntactic class than a word in a predicted syntactic class.

One reason that the syntax component did not significantly affect reading times is that an average eye fixation incorporates approximately two or three words instead of only one (Levin and Turner, 1968; Rayner and McConkie, 1977). Moreover, some information can be extracted from the reader's peripheral or parafoveal vision (Poulton, 1962; Rayner, 1978; Rayner, McConkie, and Ehrlich, 1978), especially when the sentences are embedded in prose (Rayner, 1975). The present measure of syntactic complexity was an inverse function of syntactic predictability. Syntactic predictability was measured as the likelihood of predicting the syntactic class of word *n*+1 given that there is knowledge of words 1 to *n*. However, since several words may undergo processing within a eye fixation, some previewing and preliminary analyses are performed on word *n*+1 while most cognitive resources are allocated to previous words. The fact that words are usually processed in chunks or phrases would undermine the correspondence between ATN mechanisms and the syntactic processing of readers.

It is conceivable that other measures of syntactic complexity would be more valid indices. One type of measure could assess the degree to which certain syntactic constructions impose demands on short-term memory load as sentences are read from left to right (Kaplan, 1975; Perfetti and Goldman, 1976; Rumelhart, 1977a; Wanner and Maratsos, 1974; Yngve, 1960). For example, consider the following sentence, which contains multiple embedded relative clauses.

(1) *The woman who loves the poem that I wrote is a phony.*

The reader must maintain *the woman* in memory while processing the embedded propositions *write(I, poem)* and *love(woman, poem)*. Maintaining an unfinished proposition in memory imposes demands on processing resources. This phenomenon occurs in sentences that have syntactic constructions with left embedding (Fodor et al., 1974). The processing is simplified when the sentence syntax provides right embedding, as in the following sentence.

(2) *I wrote a poem that is loved by a woman who is a phony.*

In sentence 2 there are no unfinished propositions that need to be maintained in memory while other propositions are being processed. Consequently, sentence 2 would impose less demands on short-term memory than would sentence 1. It is possible to measure the memory load at a particular point in a sentence in terms of the number of uncompleted constituents that are held in memory awaiting completion. A mean memory load across all words in a sentence would then serve as a measure of syntactic complexity.

There are still other ways of measuring the syntactic complexity of sentences. One could measure the number of decisions and operations that an ATN parser applies when parsing a sentence (Kaplan, 1975; Rumelhart, 1977a). Sentence complexity would increase with more decisions and operations. Another measure would assess the degree to which syntactic form isolates the underlying propositional segmentation (Fodor et al., 1974). For example, consider the following sentences.

(3) *I knew the man who died was a phony.*
(4) *I knew that the man who died was a phony.*

Sentence 4 is somewhat easier to read than sentence 3 because the *that* signals the reader that *the man* is part of an embedded proposition (*the man is a phony*) rather than being a direct object of *know* (*I know the man*). Sentence 4 clarifies what would otherwise be an ambiguous sentence construction (Foss, 1970). Sentence 4 would be read faster than sentence 3 despite the fact that sentence 4 has an additional word (*that*).

It should be obvious by now that there are many ways to assess syntactic complexity. Not only are there several theories of syntax to test, but there are also several alternative processing assumptions that specify different ways that a given syntactic theory is applied to psychological functioning. The fact that the specific measure of syntactic complexity in the Graesser, Hoffman, and Clark (1980) study did not predict reading times does not imply that syntax has no effect on reading times in general. It may suggest that there is a better way of measuring syntactic complexity. Let us elaborate on this point a bit. A decade of research in psycholinguistics led to the dismissal of a derivational theory of complexity (Fodor et al., 1974). This theory attempted to predict reading times by the number of syntactic transformations that was needed to arrive at the deep structure of a sentence from its surface structure (Chomsky, 1965). The fact that the derivational theory of complexity failed to predict reading times suggested that the theory did not satisfactorily apply to the cognitive processing of sentence syntax; it did not imply that syntactic complexity fails to predict processing time. Other cognitive theories of sentence syntax fared better (Bever, 1970).

The data presented in Table 2.3 reveal how readers allocate their cognitive resources to different reading components. From the slope values it is possible to arrive at a predictive equation for reading times. The seven variables that significantly predicted reading times will be assigned the following symbols:

L = number of letters in a sentence
S = number of syllables in a sentence
W = number of words in a sentence
P = number of propositions in a sentence
N = number of new argument nouns in a sentence
E = the degree to which a passage is expository (i.e., 7 - narrativity rating)
U = the degree to which a passage is unfamiliar (i.e., 7 - familiarity rating)

The values of these variables are assigned to a given sentence in order to determine its predicted reading time. For each variable, reading time increases as the value of the variable increases. The slopes of the variables correspond to the slopes reported in Table 2.3. As a result, the reading time for a sentence is predicted by the formula below.

$$\text{Reading time (in milliseconds)} = 1 + 24L + 45S + 131W + 117P + 155N + 65U + 169E \qquad (2.2)$$

The Graesser, Hoffman, and Clark (1980) study examined two additional questions regarding the allocation of cognitive resources during reading. First, how do relatively slow readers allocate their resources differently than fast readers? Second, how do readers allocate their resources differently when they read for different purposes? The data reported in this section were in fact obtained under two different conditions that were designed to vary the goals of the reader. Before reading the passages, the subjects in an *essay* condition were told they would later be given an essay recall test on the passages. Subjects in a *multiple choice* condition were told they would later be given a multiple choice test. Within these two conditions, a median split criterion was used to segregate fast and slow readers, based on the mean reading time per sentence.

Table 2.4 shows the mean slope parameters, the mean intercept values, and the mean reading times for the four groups of subjects. The times in Table 2.4 are means of the values derived from the regression analyses of individual subjects. In order to test for differences between groups of subjects, the slope values for each variable were submitted to an analysis of variance with a 2 (essay vs. multiple choice) × 2 (fast vs. slow reader) factorial design.

Differences between fast and slow readers will be considered first. Analyses on the slope values indicated that the microstructure variables predicted differences between fast and slow readers. The slope values of slow readers were significantly higher than those of fast readers for the four microstructure components, but not the three macrostructure components. The following reading time formulas reflect this pattern.

Reading time (fast reader) =

$$189 + 15L + 19S + 93W + 59P + 140N + 81U + 165E \quad (2.3)$$

Table 2.4. Reading Time Data for Four Groups of Subjects

	Condition			
	Easy		Multiple choice	
	Fast	Slow	Fast	Slow
Microstructure variables				
Letters	.015	.036	.015	.031
Syllables	.026	.068	.012	.074
Words	.092	.196	.094	.140
Propositions	.072	.157	.045	.192
Macrostructure variables				
New argument nouns	.204	.234	.076	.104
Unfamiliarity	.096	.128	.066	−.031
Expository	.243	.227	.086	.120
Intercept	.409	−.152	−.032	−.223
Mean reading time	3.590	5.990	3.176	5.356

Based on data collected in Experiment 2 of Graesser, Hoffman, and Clark (1980). The scores are the mean slope values in seconds.

Reading time (slow reader) =

$$-188 + 34L + 71S + 168W + 175P + 169N + 49U + 174E \quad (2.4)$$

Relative to the fast readers, the slower readers took 2.27 times as long to interpret a letter, 3.74 times as long to interpret a syllable, 1.81 times as long to process a word, and 2.97 times as long to process a proposition. However, there were no differences in the macrostructure variables.

The fact that differences in reading speed among subjects emerge in the microstructure components supports some earlier studies. Studies have shown that skilled readers incorporate more information within each reading fixation (Gibson and Levin, 1975; Gilbert, 1959; Huey, 1968; Jackson and McClelland, 1975; Patberg and Yonas, 1978; Taylor, 1965). Skilled readers also have a highly refined facility for encoding, generating, and manipulating representations at the microstructure level. Compared to unskilled readers, skilled readers require less time to establish letter codes (Hunt, Lunneborg, and Lewis, 1975; Jackson and McClelland, 1979), phonological codes (Perfetti and Lesgold, 1977, 1979; Shankweiler, Liberman, Mark, Fowler, and Fischer, 1979), and lexical codes (Lesgold and Perfetti, 1978; Perfetti and Hogaboam, 1975; Perfetti and Lesgold, 1977; Perfetti and Roth, 1980). Skilled readers are able to group words into phrases (such as propositions) at a faster rate than less skilled readers (Aaronson and Scarborough, 1977). In contrast, available research suggests that skilled and unskilled readers do not substantially differ in the time to execute macrostructure analyses (Aaronson and Scarborough, 1977; Perfetti and Lesgold, 1977). There is not as extensive evidence for the latter conclusion, but there are some findings that point in its direction.

To summarize, both the results reported here and the results from other studies support the generalization that differences between skilled and unskilled readers can be attributed to the time to execute linguistic analyses within clauses and to establish language codes. Most of these processes are accomplished automatically. In contrast, the time to integrate information from different sentences does not significantly differ between skilled and unskilled readers.

How do readers allocate their resources differently when they read for different purposes? The slopes reported in Table 2.4 indicate that variations in reading goals influence the time to perform macrostructure analyses but not microstructure analyses. There were significant differences between the essay and multiple choice conditions with respect to the macrostructure variables, but not the microstructure variables. The following predictive equations capture this trend.

Reading time (essay) =

$$129 + 26L + 47S + 144W + 115P + 219N + 112U + 235E \quad (2.5)$$

Reading time (multiple choice) =

$$-128 + 23L + 43S + 117W + 119P + 90N + 18U + 103E \quad (2.6)$$

Compared to the multiple choice condition, in the essay condition the slopes were 2.43 as steep for new argument nouns, 6.22 as steep for unfamiliarity, and 2.28 as steep for the expository components. Therefore, reading goals influence the time-consuming processes that interrelate information from different sentences, but the automatized units and linguistic processes are not effected. The fact that automatized processing components are not influenced by the comprehender's goals is consistent with many information processing models. (LaBerge and Samuels, 1974; Perfetti, 1979; Posner and Warren, 1972; Schneider and Shiffrin, 1977).

To summarize the findings, individual differences in reading speed depend on the time to complete microstructure analyses, whereas variations in reading goals influence the time to perform macrostructure analyses. Together, these results suggest that it is natural to view linguistic processing (microstructure) and extended conceptual analyses (macrostructure) as separate reading skills. Such a division has indeed been advocated either explicitly or implicitly by other researchers (Bever, Garrett, and Hurtig, 1973; Calfee, 1977; Clark and Lucy, 1975; Hurtig, 1978; Kintsch and van Dijk, 1978; Perfetti and Lesgold, 1977; Spilich, Vesonder, Chiesi, and Voss, 1979; Vipond, 1980).

Available research converges on the generalization that extended conceptual analyses are particularly prevalent at causal junctures (Aaronson and Scarborough, 1977; Bever et al., 1973; Caramazza, Grober, Garvey, and Yates, 1977; Clark and Sengul, 1979; Fodor et al., 1974; Hurtig, 1978; Jarvella, 1971; Jarvella and Herman, 1972; Just and Carpenter, 1980; Mitchell and Green, 1978; Perfetti and Lesgold, 1977; Townsend and Bever, 1978). Clauses appear to be natural units for linguistic analyses, and they have an interesting relationship with short-term memory. Words within a clause are maintained in short-term memory until the end of the clause is reached. The maintenance of words in a short-term buffer is of course demanding on cognitive resources; interpretive processes break down if the limited-capacity buffer memory is exceeded by a slow formation of lexical code (Lesgold and Perfetti, 1978; Perfetti and Goldman, 1976). Three events occur at the end of the clauses. First, syntactic analyses are completed. Second, the reader performs semantic and extended conceptual analyses on the clause. Third, the clause is compiled as a unit in working-memory or long-term memory. The latter process has the important consequence of freeing capacity and resources in the buffer. The buffer is cleared for the processing of the subsequent clauses. The proposed clause-by-clause processing mechanism serves as one solution for circumventing the capacity limitations of a human information processing system.

In the studies reported thus far reading times were used to assess how readers allocate their cognitive resources to different components of reading. It is assumed that those sentences that require more reading time also are more demanding on the limited supply of cognitive resources. This assumption is of course intuitively plausible.

Britton has pursued another method of examining the allocation of cognitive resources during reading. Britton investigated the general question of what type of passages are relatively demanding on the limited supply of cognitive resources. Britton used a secondary task technique to measure the amount of cognitive capacity that was utilized in a reading task. The primary task was reading passages. While the subject read the passages, a click was occasionally presented. Subjects were instructed to release a response key whenever they heard a click.

Responding to the click was the secondary task. The reaction time latency to respond to the click provided a measure of how much of the processing capacity was devoted to the reading material. As the latency to the secondary task increased, readers were presumably allocating more resources to the reading material (Britton and Price, 1980). This secondary task technique has been used in experiments that involve primary tasks other than reading (Kahneman, 1973; Kerr, 1973; Posner and Snyder, 1975).

Britton's research uncovered some interesting, and often counterintuitive findings regarding the types of passages that are relatively demanding on cognitive resources. Easy passages require more cognitive capacity than relatively difficult passages (Britton, Westbrook, and Holdredge, 1978; Britton, Zeigler, and Westbrook, 1980). Passages require more capacity when sentences are more cohesively related, or what Britton has called having more "discourse-level meaning" (Britton, Holdredge, Curry, and Westbrook, 1979). Less capacity is used when the passages contain more familiar words and a simpler syntax, and when there are certain words and phrases in the text that signal the reader about the structure of the text at the macrostructure level (Britton, Glynn, Meyer, and Penland, 1980). Passages use more capacity when they are being studied for a delayed test than for an immediate test (Britton, 1980). Narrative passages use more capacity than expository passages (Britton, Hamilton, Graesser, and Penland, 1980). The latter study included one experiment that used the same 12 passages as those used in the Graesser, Hoffman, and Clark (1980) study and other studies by Graesser (Cohen and Graesser, 1980; Graesser, Hauft-Smith, Cohen, and Pyles, 1980).

Britton's findings are particularly interesting when they are compared to experiments that measure the amount of time to read a passage. Passages that are easy, more cohesive, or more narrative apparently take up more capacity. However, such passages are also read faster. It appears that the time to read a passage is inversely related to the amount of cognitive capacity that is utilized. This relationship is puzzling to say the least. However, the relationship can perhaps be accommodated by a number of explanations. One explanation that Britton has proposed is that more capacity is associated with processes used in acquiring knowledge from text (Britton, Piha, Davis, and Wehausen, 1978). This explanation seems to be supported by the fact that easy, narrative, and cohesively organized passages are remembered better, and also that more capacity is used in conditions that promote better acquisition of a passage (Britton, Holdredge, Curry, and Westbrook, 1979; Britton, Piha, Davis, and Wehausen, 1978). A second explanation of the puzzling relationship is that more inferences are generated in easy, cohesive, and narrative passages compared to difficult, loosely organized, and expository passages (see Chapter 4). A third explanation is that the easier, more cohesive, and more narrative passages are particularly *absorbing* and easier to concentrate on. Absorbing passages are read faster and, at the same time, they utilize more cognitive resources. More research is clearly needed before this enigma can be unraveled any further.

The Relationship Between Resource Allocation During Comprehension and Performance on Comprehension and Retention Tests

Can prose acquisition be explained by the way in which readers allocate resources to different components during reading? The research reported in this section suggests that the relationship is rather complex. The obvious prediction is that the amount of information acquired and retained from a passage increases as more resources are allocated to the passage during comprehension. However, this prediction needs to be substantially qualified when certain data are considered.

There are data that seem to contradict the above prediction. In the study by Graesser, Hauft-Smith, Cohen, and Pyles (1980) recall protocols were collected for the 12 stimulus passages in the Graesser, Hoffman, and Clark (1980) study and the research reported in the previous sections. Subjects received a prompted recall test immediately after they listened to a passage. The amount of information remembered was measured as the proportion of presented propositions that were correctly recalled. The Graesser, Hauft-Smith, Cohen, and Pyles (1980) study revealed that there was a .92 correlation between the mean narrativity rating of a passage and the recall proportion for a passage. Recall increased robustly with the narrativity of a passage. However, reading time is known to decrease with the narrativity of these passages (Graesser, Hoffman, and Clark, 1980). When the reading times for the passages were correlated with recall proportions (controlling for number of words), there was a robust negative correlation, $r = -.87$, $p < .05$, between reading time and memory. Narrative passages are read faster but are also better remembered. This outcome is puzzling because it runs counter to the simple hypothesis that more is remembered about passages that are read for a longer duration. It should be noted that *passages* were used as the unit of analysis. When passages were used as the unit of analysis, recall was negatively correlated with reading time; this relationship accounted for 76% of the recall variance.

When *sentences* in passages are used as the unit of analysis, a different picture emerges. The amount of cognitive resources that a sentence receives does not substantially predict how well it is comprehended or the likelihood it will be recalled. Statements that are more superordinate in the passage structure have been shown to be recalled better than the more subordinate statements (Britton, Meyer, Simpson, Holdredge, and Curry, 1979; Kintsch, 1974; Kintsch and Keenan, 1973; Meyer, 1975, 1977a, 1977b). However, subordinate statements do not draw more cognitive resources during comprehension (Britton, Meyer, Hodge, and Glynn, 1980; Britton, Meyer, Simpson, Holdredge, and Curry, 1978). Graesser, Gordon, and Sawyer (1979) reported that recognition memory is substantially better for statements that are atypical than those that are typical of a generic script or schema that organizes statements in a passage. Recall is also better for atypical than typical statements when subjects are tested within 1 hour after acquisition (Graesser, Woll, Kowalski, and Smith, 1980). However, the differences in memory for atypical and typical statements are not explained by the amount of resources allocated to statements during comprehension (Graesser et al., 1979). The amount of resources that are allocated to sentences in prose also cannot explain the fact that sentences are recalled better when they are more concrete, more comprehensible, and more interesting (Johnson, 1970). Thus, available research indicates that statements that are recalled better were not allocated more cognitive resources during comprehension. The correlation between comprehension (acquisition) and reading time is essentially zero when sentences are used as the unit of analysis.

What is the relationship between comprehension and the amount of allocated resources when *subjects* serve as the unit of analysis? This question was examined in an experiment reported by Hoffman, Hoffman, and Graesser (1980). Reading times were collected for the 275 sentences in the 12 passages used by Graesser, Hoffman, and Clark (1980). The subjects were 48 college students who were told to read the passages for comprehension because they would later receive a comprehension test. A three-alternative, forced choice (3AFC) test was administered to the subjects after all 12 passages had been read. The questions in this 3AFC test had also been used in the Graesser, Hauft-Smith, Cohen, and Pyles (1980) study. There were 10 questions per passage and therefore 120 questions algether. A comprehension score was computed based on all 12 passages combined.

A mean reading time per sentence was computed for each subject, along with the subject's comprehension score. The mean comprehension score was 83.9 with a standard deviation of 9.4. When a correlation was computed between the mean reading time per sentence and the comprehension score for a subject, the correlation was significantly negative, $r = -.33, p < .05$. Thus, subjects who read faster also tended to achieve higher comprehension scores. This outcome agrees with other research (Curtis, 1980; Jackson and McClelland, 1975; Lesgold and Curtis, 1980).

There clearly is a complicated relationship between acquisition of information in a passage and the amount of resources that are allocated to the passage during comprehension. The correlation is dramatically negative when passages are used as a unit of analysis, zero when sentences are used as a unit of analysis, and modestly negative when subjects are used as a unit of analysis. However, if a given subject were to vary his or her reading speed, comprehension scores would presumably increase when more cognitive resources are allocated during comprehension. The increase would possibly be modest, but there certainly would not be a decrease.

Can the acquisition of information in a passage be explained by the way in which subjects distribute their resources to different reading components during comprehension? This question was examined in the study by Hoffman et al. (1980). For each subject a multiple regression analysis was performed on the reading times just as reported in the previous section. The slope parameters for each of the nine predictors of reading time were computed for each subject separately. The means and standard deviations of the slopes for the nine predictor variables are shown in Table 2.5, in addition to the *F* scores and the amount of predicted variance that each variable accounted for. The latter two values were based on an overall analysis in which mean *z* scores were obtained for each sentence.

The data in Table 2.5 are quite comparable to those in Table 2.3. The nine predictor variables predict .569 of the reading time variance, which compares favorably to the .554 value in the study reported in the previous section. As in the previous study, narrativity accounted for most of the predicted variance, followed by words, syllables, and finally new argument nouns. To summarize, the data in Table 2.5 essentially replicate those in Table 2.3. The only discrepancy is that the slope parameters for letters was significantly above zero in the earlier study, but not in the present study.

The correlation coefficients between the subjects' slope parameters for the nine predictor variables and the subjects' comprehension scores are shown in Table 2.6. The correlations were uniformly low, ranging from −.27 to .18. In fact, the only variable which approached significance was narrativity. There was a marginally significant ($p < .10$) negative correlation between comprehension scores and the slope parameters of narrativity. Thus, comprehension scores were higher for those subjects who spent more time reading expository passages compared to narrative passages. The comprehension scores were not robustly predicted by the amount of resources that were allocated to the other reading components.

The last column in Table 2.6 involved a slightly different correlational analysis. This analysis excluded subjects whose times were not substantially predicted by the set of reading components. It is plausible that these eliminated subjects were pacing themselves while reading the sentences in the passages. Instead of allocating their reading times according to the difficulty of the sentences, these

Table 2.5. Multiple Regression Analyses on Reading Time Data

Reading components	Slope (msec)	Standard deviation	*F* score	Proportion of variance predicted
Macrostructure variables				
Narrativity	−107	93	30.53*	.312
Familiarity	−77	92	5.45*	.027
New argument nouns	123	108	13.18*	.037
Microstructure variables				
Propositions	74	83	4.57*	.020
Syntax	72	1114	.33	.003
Words	82	91	5.57*	.107
Syllables	51	40	17.00*	.048
Letters	4	20	.01	.003
Serial position	5	13	.91	.005
Comprehension score	83.91	9.35		

Data from Hoffman, Hoffman, and Graesser (1980).
* $p < .05$.

Table 2.6. Correlations Between Comprehension Scores and the Slope Values of the Nine Predictors of Reading Time

Reading components	Correlation between slope value and comprehension score	Correlation between adjusted slope and comprehension score
Macrostructure variables		
Narrativity	-.27*	-.48**
Familiarity	-.19	-.24
New argument nouns	.08	.09
Microstructure variables		
Propositions	.00	.06
Syntax	.17	.11
Words	.18	.17
Syllables	.05	.24
Letters	-.13	-.26
Serial position	-.16	-.18

* $p < .10$.
** $p < .05$.

eliminated subjects may have allocated a more or less constant amount of time to each sentence. Ten of the 48 subjects were eliminated because the 9 predictor variables together accounted for less than 10% of their reading time variance (r^2). The correlations in the last column are also based on an adjusted slope value for each predictive component. The adjusted slope values are relative to the subject's mean reading time per sentence, as shown below.

$$\text{Adjusted slope} = \text{slope/mean reading time.} \qquad (2.7)$$

The adjusted slope values correlated with comprehension scores in essentially the same way that the regular slope values did.

In summary, the slope function of the narrativity variable was the only aspect of the reading time that predicted comprehension scores. Readers who adjusted their reading time according to the genre of the passages performed best on the comprehension test. In other words, they spent a lot of time reading sentences in expository prose and relatively little time on narrative prose. Subjects with poorer comprehension scores spent about the same amount of time reading expository and narrative passages. They did not speed up or slow down as a function of the difficulty of the passage, at least not to the same extent as did those subjects who had higher comprehension scores. In order to illustrate the phenomenon being discussed here, consider the course of reading a novel. A skilled comprehender reads quickly when comprehending the plot (narrative) and slows down in expository sections in which the author is describing a setting, a character, an object, or the nature of a situation. The unskilled comprehender does not adjust his or her reading rate according to prose genre.

Except for the narrativity variable, comprehension scores were not significantly predicted by the amount of resources that were allocated to various reading components. However, the reported correlations do not unequivocally establish a lack of relationship between comprehension scores and the allocation of resources during comprehension. A significant relationship may be found when individual subjects are assigned to different comprehension conditions that encourage subjects to allocate their cognitive resources differently. Experiments that impose within-subject manipulations may be needed before anything more can be said on the matter.

One implication of the above findings is that properties of prose representation and organization are probably more critical predictors of comprehension than is the sheer amount of resources that are allocated to text during comprehension. The data reported in this section agree with Perfetti's (1979) conclusion that "something other than processing time . . . is critical for achieving deeper levels [of understanding] and more durable memories" (p. 159). The amount of processing time probably does not account for the patterns of memory and comprehension data that have proliferated in the literature. Probably the only situation in which processing time is substantially correlated with comprehension is when the passage is particularly complex or technical. However, such a situation deals with extended study rather than a normal reading experience.

Models of Reading

The previous sections in this chapter provided some insights about (a) how cognitive resources are allocated during reading and (b) the degree to which characteristics of resource allocation can predict the comprehension and retention of prose. The reported findings leave some important questions unanswered. How do the various processing components interact during reading? Is there an order in which the components are interpreted during comprehension?

These questions have been heatedly debated in recent years. Models of reading incorporate different assumptions about the interaction among components and the temporal order of their execution. A brief review of some reading models should clarify the points of controversy.

One issue addresses the order in which reading components are interpreted. The strongest claim about processing order is that there is a fixed, sequential order in which components are interpreted (Gough, 1972; Mackworth, 1972). Letters are interpreted first, then syllables, then words, then syntax and propositions, and so on. The components are interpreted in a bottom-up, sequential order such that the encoding of units at level n does not begin until all of the units at level $n-1$ are interpreted. Such a model is bottom-up in the sense that a global unit, such as a proposition, is not interpreted until its component units (words, syllabes, and letters) have been interpeted.

Most models of reading have not adopted a purely bottom-up, sequentially ordered mechanism. However, there are some models that approximate such a viewpoint. Gough's (1972) model of reading is one such example. The course of reading begins when visual features are briefly registered in an icon while pattern recognition processes operate on the icon in order to identify letters. In the second stage, the letters are translated into a phonemic or phonological representation. The third stage involves the phonemic strings being matched against items in the lexicon, i.e., the mental dictionary for words. Beyond the word level, Gough does not make specific assertions about the ordering of processing components. In fact, Gough refers to a TPWSGWTAU, which stands for "the place where sentences go when they are understood." This "place" corresponds to a memory register. Gough clearly did not intend to commit himself on issues such as whether syntax is processed before semantics. Nevertheless, Gough's model has bottom-up characteristics, with input being sequentially transformed from the letter level to higher level encodings. Some experimental investigations offer weak support to a bottom-up mechanism. For example, they have reported that the time needed to identify a word is accomplished automatically and autonomously, i.e., it is not influenced by the semantic, sentential context in which the word is embedded (Cairns and Kamerman, 1975; Forster, 1976; Foss and Jenkins, 1973; Swinney, 1979; Tanehaus, Leiman, and Seidenberg, 1979). However other investigators have reached just the opposite conclusion (Danks and Glucksberg, 1980; Foss, Cirilo, and Blank, 1979; Marslen-Wilson and Welsh, 1978; Stanovich and West, 1979; Swinney and Hakes, 1976).

One property of Gough's model is that the letter code is transformed into a phonemic code. The implication of this assumption is that the visual array or the letter code does not provide direct access to the lexical code. The reader must first arrive at a phonemic code, which is an intermediate code that provides direct access to lexical items. The establishment of such an intermediate code may have some advantages (Lesgold and Perfetti, 1978). Since the phonemic code is a representation that is common to both reading and listening, the lexicon would only need to be identified by virtue of its phonemic code rather than there being both phonemic and visual codes. Alternatively, the phonemic code may facilitate processing speed because it serves as another criterial dimension for directing pattern match processes between specific input and generic concepts. There is some experimental work that has addressed the question of whether this phonemic translation stage must occur. Unfortunately, the issue is unsettled. Some investigators argue that phonemic translation must occur (Foss and Blank, 1980; Rubenstein, Lewis, and Rubenstein, 1971), as Gough's model suggests. However, most studies suggest that phonemic recoding is not executed in all reading environments or by all readers (Baron, 1973; Coltheart, Davelaar, Jonasson, and Besner, 1977; Davelaar, Coltheart, Besner, and Jonasson, 1978; Frederiksen and Kroll, 1976; Kolers, 1970; Mason, 1978; Schulman, Hornak, and Sanders, 1978). Readers may access the lexical code either directly from the visual array, or, alternatively, after phonemes have been identified. For example, skilled readers may execute the phonemic translation stage more consistently and quickly than unskilled readers (Lesgold and Perfetti, 1978).

Other models of reading have preserved the bottom-up property, but have relaxed other constraints. In these models it is assumed that lexical codes may be identified from visual features; intermediate stages of letter identification and phonemic translation are not strictly necessary (LaBerge and Samuels, 1974; McClelland, 1977, 1979). Nevertheless, the models described thus far have no provisions for top-down processing, in which higher level units (e.g., words) affect the identification of lower level units (e.g., letters). In strictly bottom-up models it is assumed that higher level units do not modify, facilitate, or preclude the identification of lower level units.

Rumelhart (1977b) has described an "interactive" model of reading that allows for both bottom-up analyses and top-down analyses to proceed simultaneously (see also Drewnowski and Healy, 1977; Goodman, 1966; Hochberg, 1970; Lesgold and Perfetti, 1978; Marslen-Wilson and Welsh, 1978; Morton, 1969; Rieger, 1978; Perfetti, 1980). In a book edited by Lesgold and Perfetti (1981) a number of studies are reported that examine the nature of the interactive processes in reading. The interactive property was in part proposed because certain empirical outcomes called some bottom-up models to task. For example, the amount of time to identify a letter often depends on the surrounding letters and whether or not the letters form a word (Johnson, 1975, 1977, 1979; Johnston, 1978; Reicher, 1969; Smith and Spoehr, 1974; Wheeler, 1970). The time to identify a word is influenced by its syntactic and semantic environment (Blank and Foss, 1978; Cole and Perfetti, 1980; Foss et al., 1979; Kleiman, 1975; Kolers, 1970; Marslen-Wilson and Welsh, 1978; Meyer and Schvaneveldt, 1971; Morton, 1969; Perfetti, Goldman, and Hogaboam, 1979; Tulving and Gold, 1963; Tulving, Mandler, and Baumal, 1964). Syntactic analyses are to some extent dependent on semantic content (Graesser and Mandler, 1975; Masson and Sala, 1978; Tyler and Marslen-Wilson, 1977) and the extend prose context (DeJong, 1979). The reading speed and interpretation of sentences depends on the meaning of the prose context (Bransford and McCarrell, 1974; Clark and Haviland, 1977; Gibbs, 1979; Graesser, Robertson, and Clark, 1980; Haberlandt and Bingham, 1978; Hobbs, 1979; Kieras, 1978). It appears that the interpretation of a unit at one level influences and is influenced by analyses of units at other levels—both higher and lower. Of course, there may be an asymmetry (Perfetti, 1980). At least a preliminary analysis of lower levels often needs to be accomplished before that of higher levels; yet lower levels can begin execution before the influence of higher levels is imposed. The interactive properties of processing components are important to capture in models of reading, but it is too early to draw detailed conclusions about the particular types of interactions.

In Rumelhart's (1977b) interactive model, there is a *message center* and a set of independent *knowledge sources*. The knowledge sources include many of the reading components that were described in the earlier sections. Knowledge sources possess specialized knowledge in the form of schemas about specific components of reading. Readers have knowledge about letters, syllables, words, syntax, and a variety of semantic-conceptual domains. The interactive aspects of Rumelhart's model are captured both by the operation of the message center and the specialized knowledge of the knowledge sources. The message center is a global, highly structured data-storage device that allows for communication between and among different interpretive components. The message center maintains a running list of hypotheses; each hypothesis is relevant to one or more knowledge sources. When a hypothesis is active in the message center, it is evaluated by the appropriate knowledge source(s). The evaluation process produces a number of outcomes. A hypothesis may be confirmed or disconfirmed. A hypothesis may be removed from the message center or the relevant knowledge source(s) may add new hypotheses to the message center. At some point, the knowledge sources converge on decisions as to which hypotheses are most likely to be correct. In addition, the message center is "highly structured so that knowledge sources know exactly where to find relevant hypotheses and so that dependencies among hypotheses are easily determined" (Rumelhart, 1977b, p. 590).

Rumelhart represents the message center as a 3-dimensional space containing the following three levels.

(1) The position along the line of the text.
(2) The level of the hypothesis (letter, word, proposition, etc.).
(3) The set of alternative hypotheses at a particular level.

When a decision is made for some unit at a given level of analysis, it will modify the set of alternatives at other levels and other positions. For example, suppose that the reader encounters the phrase *the cat.* At one point in time the message center might conclude that the second word has three letters, that the first letter is *c*, and the third is *t*; no decision has been made about the middle letter. This information eliminates some alternative hypotheses at the word level. The alternatives are narrowed to *cat, cut,* and *cot.* At another point in time the reader learns from semantic analyses that the passage involves a *zoo* schema. This decision at a semantic level narrows down the three alternatives at the word level even further; *cat* is the most likely guess. At this point the message center decides the word is *cat.* This lexical decision directs the interpretation of the middle letter as an *a* in top-down fashion. Eventually, decisions will be made at all levels and all positions in the sentence.

It is important to emphasize that this interactive model sometimes generates errors in identifying and interpreting components. The system generates errors because the interpretation of any given component is based on hypotheses and guesses. The guesses accumulate and narrow as knowledge is passed from level to level. If the knowledge sources and message center were designed in a certain way, then the errors would be expected to correspond to errors that humans make. Of course, a psychological model of reading would be expected to generate encodings with human-like errors.

What implications does Rumelhart's model have for the reading time studies reported earlier? There are certain implications about the slope parameters that were extracted from the multiple regression analyses. Consider the word component. The data in Tables 2.3 and 2.5 indicate that it took 107 msec to process an average word. This time presumably partialed out the time to encode the letters and syllables within each word. What processes occur during the 107 msec? According to a strictly bottom-up model, such as Gough's, the 107 msec is the time to scan the reader's lexicon in order to find a match between the phonemic input and a lexical item in the mental dictionary. The scanning and matching operations took 107 milliseconds for the average word of the average reader. The data in Table 2.4 indicate that faster readers scan and match more quickly. An interpretation of the 107 msec would be more complicated according to Rumelhart's interactive model. The 107 msec reflects the time it takes for the message center to arrive at a decision about an average unit at the word level. This decision time would not only depend on the available letter and syllable code, but also the *context* within which the word is embedded. The syntactic and semantic levels could facilitate or inhibit decision time at the word level in a top-down fashion. Thus, the 107 msec corresponds to the time to arrive at a guess or a decision about an average word for the average reader in *the average context* as knowledge accumulates and hypotheses are narrowed down about a word. In Rumelhart's model, the lexical decision time would vary from context to context, whereas lexical decision time would be relatively context free in a strictly bottom-up model.

The multiple regression approach seemed appropriate for obtaining "ball park" estimates of how cognitive resources are allocated to different reading components. However, in order to understand the complex ways that components influence one another in an interactive model of reading, researchers will need to adopt some assessment procedure other than multiple regression. The multiple regression analysis approach is limited when it comes to discovering (a) interactions between and among components and (b) the quantitative functions that relate reading time to specific predictive components. Computer simulation techniques are better suited for exploring these more challenging, esoteric issues.

Extracting Information from Newspapers

The issues in this section will differ from those in previous sections in two ways. First, the studies and models in the previous sections have addressed the problem of resource allocation and comprehension during relatively short time spans. One goal was to account for reading times of sentences, a time span that takes about 3-8 seconds. In this section the extraction of information over a longer time span of roughly 15 minutes will be examined. Specifically, how do readers allocate their resources when they read newspapers? Second, the previous studies examined resource allocation and acquisition in situations in which the reader was told to read the material and was expected to be tested on it. The passages were read in a *task-induced* situation because readers were extrinsically motivated to read. In this section we will also examine acquisition in *self-induced* reading environments, in which readers are intrinsically motivated to read. What do readers read when they want to read?

Psychologists have generally lost sight of the phenomenon of self-induced knowledge acquisition. We have some understanding of how knowledge is acquired in experimental settings. We know next to nothing about how adults acquire information that they genuinely want to acquire in everyday life. Are the two reading environments expected to differ fundamentally? Possibly. In task-induced settings, the resources would presumably be distributed somewhat more uniformly, especially when the goals are ill-defined. In contrast, readers should be more selective when they acquire information in self-induced comprehension settings. Readers normally read what interests them and they skirt the acquisition of uninteresting material. The average news reader reads about the illicit affairs of celebrities. Articles on political reform are not particularly captivating. National politics is more captivating than international politics. Cinema is in; oil painting is out. Reading in self-induced conditions is probably more selective than reading in task-induced conditions.

Graesser, Higginbotham, Robertson, and Smith (1978) compared how readers extract information when newspapers are read under task-induced versus self-induced conditions. In the self-induced condition college students voluntarily picked up and read a sheet from a sensationalist news weekly, the *National Enquirer.* The subjects believed they were waiting around to participate in an experiment while they were reading in this self-induced condition. It is interesting to note that 98% of the college population will spontaneously read a sheet from a sensationalist weekly while waiting for an experiment. *Time Magazine, The Wall Street Journal,* and *Playboy* don't fare as well.

An experimenter behind a one-way mirror timed the reading times of subjects in the self-induced condition. Immediately after subjects finished reading the sheet in the self-induced condition, the experimenter entered the waiting room, gave them another sheet from the *National Enquirer,* and told them to read it because they would be tested on their comprehension. This, of course, is the task-induced condition. The experimenter also told the subjects that they would be allotted a specific amount of time for reading. This critical time for reading in the task-induced condition was yoked to the reading time in the self-induced condition. If a subject read a sheet for 11 minutes in the self-induced condition, then they would be given 11 minutes for reading in the task-induced condition. Subjects were later tested on what they read and acquired.

The assessment of what the readers read and acquired was divided into two subproblems. What articles were selected to read? What type of information was acquired and retained from those articles that were read? Regarding article selection, we examined whether readers tend to choose articles on familiar topics or unfamiliar topics. Are readers attracted to familiar material or are they bored by it and attracted to novelties? Regarding the extraction of information within an article, we compared extraction of active, narrative information with that of static, expository information. Do readers focus on what happened, why it happened, and how it happened? Or do they focus on who did it, what was present, where it occurred, when it happened, how much, or how many? In other words, to what extent do readers have a *narrative basis* when extracting information from reading material?

During the test phase of the study, the subjects were tested on (a) the sheet from the self-induced condition, (b) the sheet from the task-induced condition, and (c) a control sheet that they never read. Of course, the three sheets were counterbalanced across subjects and conditions. The control sheet provided an assessment of base rate levels of responding. The testing procedure included five phases.

(1) **Title recognition.** The subjects indicated whether or not they had seen an article title. There were 12 articles from each of the three news sheets. The 36 titles were ordered randomly in the test form.
(2) **Article selection.** The subjects identified which articles they read.
(3) **Topic familiarity**. Subjects were again presented the list of 36 article titles and they rated each article (title) on how familiar they were with the topic before the experiment.
(4) **Topic interest.** The subjects were presented the list of 36 titles and rated how interesting the article was if they read it, or how interesting it would seem (based on title) if they did not read it.
(5) **Comprehension test.** A 3AFC test was used to assess acquisition of information from the articles. Two questions were included for each article. One question pertained to active information and the other to static information. Active questions probed knowledge about intentional actions, events, methods, plans, goals, and reasons. The static questions probed knowledge about actors, objects, locations, time, quantities, and attributes.

What differences were found in information extraction between the self-induced and task-induced reading conditions? In some ways, the two conditions did not differ. First, the subjects correctly recognized about 63% of the titles in both the self-induced and task-induced conditions. Only 5% of the titles on the control sheet were claimed to have been read. Second, subjects reported having read 57% of the articles in the two experimental conditions, while only 2% of the articles were said to have been read from the control sheet. Consequently, the same number of articles and titles were read in the self-induced and task-induced conditions.

Subjects were found to have read different types of articles in the self-induced condition than in the task-induced condition. The familiarity and interest ratings suggested that in both conditions the subjects tended to read those articles that were more familiar and more interesting. Unfortunately, there is a methodological problem in interpreting these ratings. Perhaps the subjects gave higher interest or familiarity ratings to articles they had read simply because they had read them.

Fortunately, there is a less problematic measure for assessing how familiarity influences article selection. Specifically, it is possible to assume that familiar articles would show higher base rate scores on the 3AFC test than would unfamiliar articles. Subjects would be expected to have more preexperimental knowledge about the more familiar articles. A critical comparison can be derived from the proportion of correct responses on the 3AFC questions in situations in which an article was *not* read. These proportions were .32, .45, and .41 in the self-induced, task-induced, and control conditions, respectively. These proportions were significantly lower in the self-induced condition than in the task-induced condition and the control condition. Thus, subjects tended to read articles on familiar topics in the self-induced condition because the scores on articles not read in this condition were lower than those not read in the control condition. Moreover, since the proportions were not different in the task-induced and control conditions, familiarity did not guide article selection in the task-induced conditions.

The above findings support the conclusion that subjects tend to select and read articles on familiar topics in conditions in which they genuinely want to read. Newspapers apparently enlighten their readers by modifying and adding new information to issues and events that they already know something about. Subjects tend to steer away from articles that introduce new issues and happenings. Adults apparently become exposed to new issues and happenings by other media and channels of communication if at all. For example, television, radio, and social interactions with peers probably expose adults to new news topics.

An informative outcome was that the familiarity bias in article selection disappears in the task-induced reading condition. When readers are forced to read newspapers in anticipation of being tested, they distribute their efforts more evenly or randomly. There is an equal likelihood of selecting articles on familiar topics and unfamiliar topics.

Those articles that were read were read differently in task-induced and self-induced reading conditions. Acquisition scores were computed for static versus active items in the two reading conditions. The acquisition scores controlled for guessing by subtracting out the base rate proportions, as shown below.

$$\text{Acquisition score} = p(\text{correct response/article read}) - p(\text{correct response/control sheet}) \quad (2.8)$$

The acquisition scores for active and static information in the self-induced versus task-induced reading conditions are shown in Table 2.7. Scores from both experiments in the Graesser et al. (1978) study are shown in order to demonstrate the reliability of the findings. Acquisition scores were roughly equal for active and static information in the task-induced conditions. However, acquisition scores in the self-induced condition were nearly four times as high for active information as for static information.

Table 2.7. Acquisition Scores for Active Versus Static Information in Self-Induced and Task-Induced Conditions

	Reading condition			
	Self-induced		Task-induced	
Experiment Number	Active	Static	Active	Static
1	.36	.11	.15	.08
2	.38	.09	.17	.16
Mean	.37	.10	.16	.12

Adapted from Graesser, Higginbotham, Robertson, and Smith (1978).

To summarize, for both article selection and extraction of information within articles, there were systematic differences between self-induced and task-induced conditions. In self-induced reading conditions subjects tended to read more familiar articles and tended to select more active information than static information from those articles that were read. Both of these effects disappeared when news sheets were read in task-induced conditions. When readers expected to be tested on the reading material, they tended to distribute their cognitive resources more evenly. After all, they are responsible for acquiring *everything.* The role of selectivity in information acquisition apparently is not a very prominent factor in studies that test subjects in task-induced conditions.

Readers have a narrative bias when they genuinely want to read a news article. They want to know what happened, why it happened, and how it happened. Readers are less concerned with static information, generally speaking. In the final analysis, narrativity has consistently emerged as a critical dimension that robustly predicts information acquisition and retention. Compared to static and expository code, narrative code tends to be selected for acquisition (Graesser et al., 1978), tends to be comprehended much faster (Graesser, Hoffman, and Clark, 1980), tends to be more absorbing (Britton, Hamilton, Graesser, and Penland, 1980), and tends to be better retained (Bower and Clark, 1969; Cohen and Graesser, 1980; Graesser, Hauft-Smith, Cohen, and Pyles, 1980; Kozminsky, 1977). Nelson (1977) has also proposed that action and event sequences are developed earlier than static and categorical codes. In order to understand why narrative has a special status in the information processing system, we need to know more about how narrative is represented in memory. How do the representations of passages in the narrative and expository genres compare? These representational issues will be examined in Chapters 4 and 5.

3

A Schema Pointer Plus Tag Model of Prose Memory

In Chapter 1 it was argued that comprehension consists of identifying and instantiating schemas that correspond to different knowledge domains and levels of structure. The schema is a critical theoretical construct in the proposed framework. What should a schema-based theory explain? A number of questions become important when a schema-based framework is seriously considered. How are various types of schemas cognitively represented? How do schemas guide comprehension? How does the comprehender construct prose representations by virtue of these schemas? These questions will be examined in later chapters. The goals in the present chapter are somewhat less ambitious. In this chapter we will examine how individuals represent and retrieve passages that are organized around some central, underlying schema. For example, consider a passage that describes a scripted activity, such as eating at a restaurant. How would such a passage be represented in memory? What retrieval processes are involved when the individual recalls or recognizes statements from such a passage?

Explaining memory performance has been the most popular approach to testing alternative theories of representation in psychology. Patterns of memory performance obviously reveal little about comprehension *processes* and how prose representations are constructed *during* comprehension. However, memory data can to some extent expose the representations that are available in memory *after* a passage is comprehended. Moreover, investigating the *result* of comprehension does sometimes indirectly suggest constraints on the comprehension process. Once there is some understanding of how a passage is ultimately represented, the researcher can examine how these representation are constructed during comprehension.

One question that a schema-based theory must address is how the comprehender deals with information that is typical of a schema versus information that is atypical. Specific experiences are rarely perfectly consistent with the schemas that organize them. There usually are aspects of the experience that deviate from established schemas. Information may be inconsistent with or unrelated to the underlying schemas. Consider the following three short passages.

(1) John was hungry so he went to a restaurant. He walked in, was seated by the hostess, and ordered food. After the waitress served the food, he sipped his coffee and took a pen out of his pocket. The waitress later brought John his check. He left a tip, paid the check, and left.

(2) Jane had always been very shy. She was unsociable, a loner, and had few friends. Jane was insecure, quiet, aggressive, self-conscious, and avoided attention.

(3) Daniel remembered the kitchen in the house he grew up in. He remembered the refrigerator, stove, sink, toaster, bookshelves, and cupboards.

Each of these passages foregrounds a schema that organizes most of the information. Most of the information is very typical of the schema. However, there is a statement in each passage that is clearly atypical. Taking a pen out of one's pocket is an atypical action when someone eats at a restaurant, although it certainly would not be outrageously unusual to do so. Similarly, being aggressive is an atypical trait of a shy female and bookshelves are not typically placed in kitchens. Atypical statements are often salient and capture the attention of the comprehender. How are the atypical items represented differently in memory than typical information? Do individuals have better memory for the typical or atypical information?

According to a *filtering hypothesis,* the typical information is preserved in memory whereas the atypical information tends to be filtered out. This relatively simple hypothesis assumes that the schema organizes the typical information in a cohesive manner. Cohesively organized material is retained in memory longer and is easier to retrieve from memory. The atypical information is loosely associated with the cohesively related typical information. Individuals should therefore find it difficult to retrieve the remotely associated atypical information from memory.

The filtering hypothesis has not been directly formulated by researchers in psychology. However, many researchers believe it is correct and incorporate it into their models and predictions about memory. For example, in the area of social cognition researchers claim that there is better memory for those traits and behaviors that are consistent with a stereotype than those items that are inconsistent, atypical, or unrelated (Cantor, 1978; Cantor and Mischel, 1977; Taylor and Crocker, 1980). Research in memory for discourse has demonstrated that individuals tend to recall statements that are consistent with the overall theme of a passage and tend to delete unrelated statements (Bransford, 1979; Kintsch and van Dijk, 1978; Spilich et al., 1979; Vipond, 1980). Chess players recall, reconstruct, and correctly recognize typical board configurations better than atypical configurations after a brief study period (Goldin, 1978). The research that appears to support the filtering hypothesis is based on one critical observation: there is a higher likelihood of recalling or recognizing acquisition items that are typical than those that are atypical of a central organizing schema.

Unfortunately, many of the findings that support the filtering hypothesis are misleading because of one crucial artifact: individuals often guess. When individuals recall passages such as those above, they often recall typical items that were not presented in the acquisition passages. For the first paragraph, subjects would probably recall that John ate, despite the fact that this action was not explicitly mentioned. These are called recall *intrusions*. Whereas the intrusion rate is relatively high for typical items, the intrusion rate is essentially zero for atypical items. The phenomenon of guessing therefore yields an unfair advantage for typical items compared to atypical items. The same problem exists in recognition tests in which subjects are presented a series of test items and asked to decide whether or not each test item had been presented in an acquisition passage. Individuals often guess that an unpresented typical item had been presented, whereas they rarely guess that an unpresented atypical item had been presented. A *false alarm* occurs when the individual decides that an item had been presented when in fact it had not.

Intrusion rates on recall tests and false alarm rates on recognition tests are higher for typical than for atypical items. This is a well-known and consistent finding in the memory literature (Bower, Black, and Turner, 1979; Brown, 1976; Cantor and Mischel, 1977; Graesser et al., 1979; Graesser, Woll, Kowalski, and Smith, 1980). These differences in guessing rates are important because they imply that the recall or recognition of presented items does not always provide an informative measure of memory. A good measure of what is remembered about a specific passage would assess the ability of subjects to discriminate between those items that were presented and those that were not presented in the acquisition passage.

The filtering hypothesis is not supported when appropriate measures of memory are used to assess memory for typical versus atypical actions. Experiments that assess recognition memory for actions in scripted activities (as in the first paragraph) have shown that memory discrimination is better for atypical than for typical actions (Bower et al., 1979; Graesser et al., 1979; Graesser, Woll, Kowalski, and Smith, 1980). This trend is also found for recall memory when individuals are tested within 1 hour after the acquisition passage is acquired (Graesser et. al., 1980). Memory performance after longer retention intervals (1 week or 1 month) shows a more complicated but interesting pattern that will be discussed later in this chapter. Similarly, studies have shown that there is better memory for traits and behaviors that are inconsistent with an overriding stereotype (Hastie and Kumar, 1979) or unrelated to a stereotype (Woll and Graesser, 1980) compared to traits and behaviors that are typical of a person stereotype. There is better recognition memory for faces that have unusual or atypical features than faces that are a close fit to an average, prototypical face (Going and Read, 1974; Light, Kayra-Stuart, and Hollander, 1979). Thus, available evidence clearly argues against the filtering hypothesis despite the fact that many theories presuppose or assert its validity.

The fact that memory is better for atypical than for typical information is consistent with a well-known phenomenon called the *von Restorff effect* (von Restorff, 1937). The von Restorff effect can be demonstrated by the following list of items:

Bear
Dog
Cat
Rabbit
Shoe
Cow
Horse

The word *shoe* stands out in this list because it saliently contrasts with the background of categorically related animal items. There is also better memory for the item that is unrelated to the set of categorically related items. This phenomenon has been replicated repeatedly in the verbal learning literature (Bruce and Gaines, 1976; Wallace, 1965).

Are there theories, models, or hypotheses that predict better memory for atypical than for typical information? Yes indeed! A *schema with correction hypothesis* was proposed decades ago in the context of memory (Bartlett, 1932), perception (Woodworth and Schlosberg, 1954), and action (Woodworth, 1958). This hypothesis offers interesting assertions about the cognitive representations that are constructed when individuals interpret input. The interpreter imposes a schema that fits the input along with specific "corrections" that correspond to aspects of the input that deviate from the schema. All of the schema-relevant information is structurally related as a whole, much like a single unit or chunk. However, each specific deviation from the schema is distinctively captured in the cognitive representation in the form of a correction. A correction specifies a discrepancy between schema and input. Since each correction is distinctively captured in the memory representation, such information should be relatively salient in memory.

A more recent adaptation of the schema with correction hypothesis has been introduced in the context of scripted activities. Scripts are a subclass of schemas that correspond to activities that are enacted frequently or in a conventional manner (Abelson, 1980b; Schank, 1979b; Schank and Abelson, 1977). Examples of scripts are *eating at a restaurant, washing a car,* and *getting married.* A *script pointer plus tag hypothesis* has been recently introduced in order to explain memory for actions that are typical versus atypical of a script (Graesser, Gordon, and Sawyer, 1979; Graesser, Woll, Kowalski, and Smith, 1980). The script pointer plus tag hypothesis makes interesting claims about the representations that are constructed when individuals comprehend scripted activities. The memory representation consists of (a) a *pointer* to the generic script which interrelates both the stated and inferred typical actions as a whole and (b) a set of tags that correspond to the various actions and events that are atypical of the script. A special tag is encoded for each of the atypical actions, but not for all of the typical actions. Thus, there should be better memory discrimination for the atypical information. As mentioned earlier, memory research supports this prediction (Bower et al., 1979; Graesser et al., 1979; Graesser, Woll, Kowalski, and Smith, 1980).

The script pointer plus tag hypothesis makes a strong prediction about memory for typical actions. The hypothesis states that typical actions in a passage are organized by virtue of a pointer to the generic script as a whole. Since the pointer addresses the content of the generic script as a whole, much of the implicit knowledge base for that script will be incorporated in the memory trace by default (Minsky, 1975). This implies that both the stated very typical actions and the inferred very typical actions will be constructed and be of similar status. Individuals will find it difficult to discriminate between which actions were stated and which actions were inferred when they later receive a memory test. This prediction has in fact been confirmed. Studies have reported zero memory discrimination between presented and unpresented actions that are very typical of a script (Graesser et al., 1979; Graesser, Woll, Kowalski, and Smith, 1980).

Scripts are only one subclass of generic knowledge structures or schemas. What about stereotypes and other types of schemas? The script pointer plus tag hypothesis may embody assumptions and predictions that can be extended to passages that instantiate other subclasses of schemas. For example, there is zero recognition memory for traits and behaviors that are very typical of a stereotype, and recognition memory is better for atypical than for typical traits and behaviors (Woll and Graesser, 1980). Perhaps we need to introduce a stereotype pointer plus tag hypothesis.

In this chapter a more general *schema pointer plus tag* (SP+T) model will be considered that should apply to many or all subclasses of schemas. The SP+T model has some similarities to other schema-based models of representation and memory (Bower et al., 1979; Bregman, 1977; Norman and Bobrow, 1979; Spiro, 1977; Thorndyke and Hayes-Roth, 1979). However, it is beyond the scope of this chapter to provide a detailed comparison of the SP+T model with other schema-based models. The SP+T model has been tested extensively on passages that are organized by generic scripts and to some extent on passages that are organized by generic stereotypes or roles. The question remains as to whether the SP+T model can generalize to passages that are organized by other subclasses of schemas.

The SP+T model was developed to explain memory performance from many angles and perspectives. Specifically, the model should account for the following data.

(1) Differences in memory for typical and atypical actions when tested after different retention intervals.
(2) Differences between recall and recognition memory.
(3) Patterns of hit rates, false alarm rates, and discrimination scores on recognition tests.
(4) Patterns of correct recalls, intrusions, and memory discrimination in recall tests.
(5) The generation of guesses in both recall and recognition tests.

The rest of this chapter is devoted to developing the SP+T model in more detail. After the basic assumptions and predictions of the model are described, some experiments will be reported that assess memory for statements in scripted activities and stereotype-based descriptions of personalities. A mathematical model will then be formulated in order to simulate recall and recognition memory data when memory for passages is tested after varying retention intervals. Finally, the model will be extended to studies in a different memory paradigm and some alternative explanations of the data will be discussed.

Representational Assumptions of the SP+T Model

The SP+T model assumes that the comprehender has a large inventory of generic schemas in memory. The schemas correspond to different knowledge domains and levels of structure. When a specific passage is comprehended, the comprehender identifies a number of schemas. However, for the present purposes, the focus will be on a central, global schema that interrelates most of the statements in an acquisition passage. For example, in passage 1 above, a restaurant script accommodates the typical actions. *Taking a pen out of one's pocket* is an atypical (irrelevant) action.

The SP+T model has three representational assumptions that specify the memory representation that is constructed when a passage is comprehended. Figure 3.1 captures these assumptions pictorially.

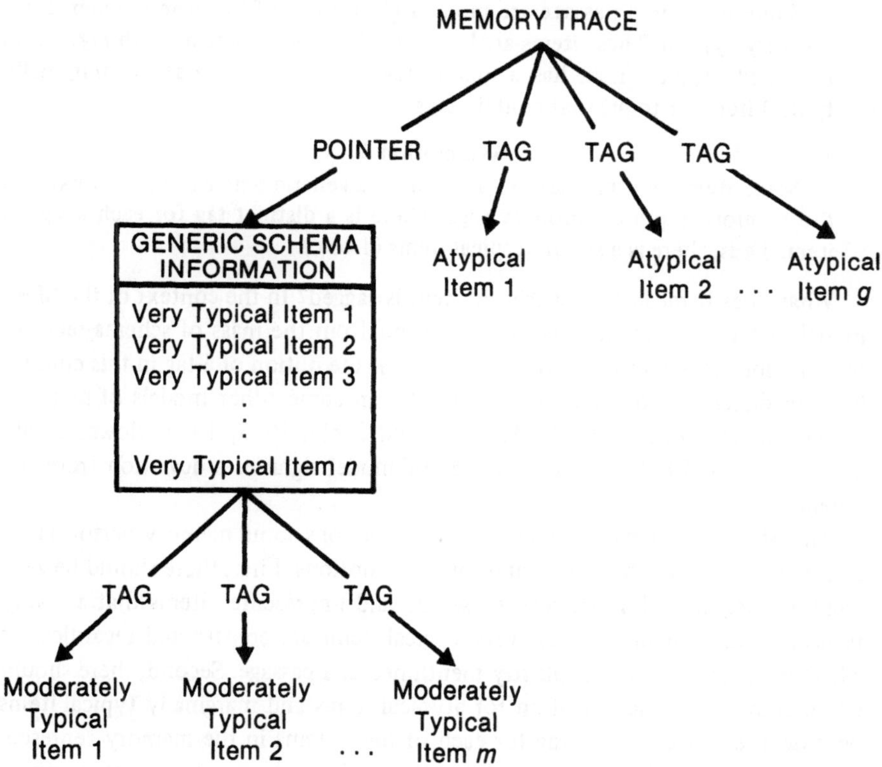

Figure 3.1. Representation of a schema-based passage according to the schema pointer plus tag model.

Assumption 1

The memory representation for a passage includes a *pointer* to the generic schema that best fits the input statements compared to the set of alternative schemas in memory. Since the schema is addressed by the pointer, both the stated and inferred very typical items are incorporated into the representation. Thus, the representation includes a set of very typical items (1 to n).

What does it mean to say that the specific memory trace has a pointer to a generic schema? It means that the elements, attributes, and relationships of the generic schema are copied into the specific memory trace that is constructed for the specific passage. How much generic information is passed to the memory trace? Perhaps all of the very typical information in the generic schema is passed to the memory trace. Alternatively, only a subset of the typical, generic information may be passed to the specific memory trace. Experiments conducted by Bower et al. (1979) suggest that the latter alternative is more plausible. Comprehension proceeds by selecting that generic information which is relevant to the comprehension of the passage statements. Of course, the very typical generic information would tend to be selected frequently and consistently when averaging over different stimulus passages. Moderately typical generic information would be passed to the memory traces of some passages, but not others.

Assumption 2

Some items in a passage are moderately typical of the generic schema but not very typical. These items are linked to the generic schema with *tags*. Each marginally typical item has a unique tag. Thus, there is a set of marginally typical items (1 to m) that contain tags.

Assumption 3

Some items in a passage are atypical of a generic schema and are linked to the memory representation by tags. There is a distinct tag for each atypical item. Thus, there is a set of atypical items (1 to g).

What does it mean to say that an item is tagged? In the context of the SP+T model, a tagged item designates a deviation from the mass of schema-relevant information. It is important to point out that the notion of a tag in this context is quite different from the notion of a tag in some other models of memory (Anderson and Bower, 1972; Atkinson and Juola, 1973, 1974; Bower et al., 1979; Kintsch, 1977a). A tag in the SP+T model signifies a deviation from the schema.

The SP+T model makes some obvious predictions about memory performance as a consequence of the representational assumptions. First, there should be zero memory discrimination between presented and unpresented items that are very typical of the schema because very typical items are constructed regardless of whether or not they are explicitly mentioned in a passage. Second, there should be an above zero discrimination for atypical items and marginally typical items because there is a distinct tag for each of these items in the memory representation. There is probably not a discrete division between items that are marginally typical and those that are atypical. Instead, there is a continuum, perhaps due to variations among individuals. Nevertheless, the model clearly predicts better memory for atypical than typical items.

The SP+T model also predicts a higher likelihood of guessing typical items than guessing atypical items. This prediction is a consequence of the fact that some unpresented typical items are inferred by virtue of Assumption 1. This prediction has direct consequences on recall and recognition performance. Compared to atypical items, the typical items should have higher false alarm rates on recognition tests and higher intrusion rates on recall tests. Regarding the hit rates on recognition tests and recall proportions on recall tests, it is uncertain how typical and atypical items will compare. This uncertainty is due to the trade-off between (a) the likelihood of retrieving a tagged item from the memory representation and (b) the likelihood of guessing an item. There is a higher likelihood that an atypical item will be tagged and retrieved from memory than will a typical item. However, there is a lower likelihood of guessing (or inferring) an atypical item than a typical item. Consequently, the patterns of hits and recall proportions may be relatively unsystematic compared to the patterns of false alarms, intrusions, and memory discrimination scores.

Memory for Scripted Action Sequences

In previous studies memory has been examined for actions in passages describing scripted activities (Bower et al., 1979; Graesser et al., 1979; Graesser, Woll, Kowalski, and Smith, 1980). The results of these studies have uniformly supported the SP+T model. In this section the primary focus will be on recognition memory because researchers have traditionally believed that recognition tests provide a more sensitive assessment of what is stored than other memory tasks, such as recall. Moreover, memory will be examined after relatively short retention intervals (within 1 hour) because the immediate question is how memory traces are represented after a passage has been comprehended. Memory performance after long retention intervals (days or weeks) will be examined in a later section.

The scripted activities in these studies were generated systematically. The typical actions consisted of actions that subjects had generated in a *free generation* condition. These subjects wrote down all actions and events that typically occur in a number of scripted activities. Some examples of the scripted activities are ***eating at a restaurant, cleaning an apartment,*** and ***visiting someone at a hospital.*** The pool of typical actions in a script included all actions that were listed by at least two subjects. This criterion eliminated the unusual actions that subjects listed in the free generation task. Thus, a typical action is defined as an action that is produced by at least two subjects in a free generation task.

An informative measure to compute is the likelihood of generating any given item in the free generation task. This measure will be called the ***generation likelihood.*** The generation likelihood is an index of how readily subjects can retrieve and express an element in the generic schema. It is unknown whether this measure reflects retrieval processes or articulation processes. A subject may retrieve an element from a schema but be unable or choose not to express it in language. Nevertheless, the generation likelihood of an item does provide an assessment of how readily the item can be produced overtly. Previous studies revealed that typical actions vary a great deal in generation likelihood. The frequency distribution for typical actions is an exponential function (Graesser et al., 1979). There is an exponential decrease in the frequency of typical actions as generation likelihood increases.

The atypical actions in the scripted activities were generated by the experimenters. It is important to emphasize that the typical actions were not unusually bizarre or ridiculously salient. The atypical actions could conceivably occur in a given script. For example, *taking one's pen out of one's pocket* is not an unusual action in a restaurant. It is best to construe the atypical actions as unrelated to the script rather than being inconsistent with the script or outrageously weird. The ratio of atypical to typical actions in a scripted activity varied from study to study. However, these variations are inconsequential because recognition memory for typical and atypical actions is not affected by the number of atypical actions that are inserted into a scripted activity (Graesser et al., 1979; Jebousek, 1978).

The actions in the scripted activities were also scaled on typicality. Subjects in a *normative rating group* rated all of the actions in each scripted activity on the following 6-point typicality scale.

1 = very atypical
2 = moderately atypical
3 = uncertain, but probably atypical
4 = uncertain, but probably typical
5 = moderately typical
6 = very typical.

In addition to the typicality ratings, subjects rated each item on a necessity scale which assessed how necessary it was for the action to occur in order for the script to be executed.

1 = very unnecessary
2 = moderately unnecessary
3 = uncertain, but probably unnecessary
4 = uncertain, but probably necessary
5 = moderately necessary
6 = very necessary.

The typicality ratings were found to be highly correlated with necessity ratings, $r = .92$ (Graesser et al., 1979), so subsequent analyses were performed on the typicality ratings. The typicality ratings were of course much higher for the typical items (4.5-6.0) than for the atypical items (1.2-4.3).

After the actions in each scripted activity were generated and scaled, a Jack story was prepared that included a number of scripted activities. There were two versions (A and B) of the Jack story in the Graesser, Woll, Kowalski, and Smith

(1980) study. The different versions contained different samples of actions. There were three sets of actions for each scripted activity.

(1) **Common typical.** A set of typical actions that were presented in both versions A and B of the Jack story.
(2) **A actions.** A set of typical and atypical actions that were presented in version A but not in version B.
(3) **B actions.** A set of typical and atypical actions that were presented in version B but not in version A.

Memory for typical and atypical actions was assessed by observing performance on the A actions and B actions. The common typical actions were not analyzed.

Subjects were presented the Jack stories, which were played from a tape recorder at a medium presentation rate (175 words per minute). Subjects were asked to listen to the passages carefully because they would later be asked to answer questions about the passage, including questions about Jack's personality. Half of the subjects received version A and half version B of the Jack story.

Within 1 hour after the subjects listened to the Jack story, the subjects completed a recognition test. The recognition test booklets included the title of each script, followed by a list of A and B actions (not the common typical actions). The subjects rated each test action on the following 6-point scale.

1 = positive that the item was not presented in the Jack story
2 = fairly sure that the item was not presented in the Jack story
3 = uncertain, but guess that the item was not presented in the Jack story
4 = uncertain, but guess that the item was presented in the Jack story
5 = fairly sure that the item was presented in the Jack story
6 = positive that the item was presented in the Jack story.

It was essential to design the experiments so that there were two versions (A and B) of each scripted activity. With this design feature, it was possible to measure both hit and false alarm rates as follows.

$$\text{Hit rate} = p(4, 5, \text{ or } 6 \text{ rating/action was presented})$$

$$\text{False alarm rate} = p(4, 5, \text{ or } 6 \text{ rating/action was not presented})$$

The relationship between hit rates and false alarm rates provides a measure of memory discrimination. The greater the difference between the hit rate and false alarm rate, the better the memory discrimination.

A number of experiments have incorporated the above procedures for generating stimulus materials, presenting the scripted activities, and testing the subjects' memories (Graesser et al., 1979; Graesser, Woll, Kowalski, and Smith, 1980). The differences among these experiments lie in the variations in (a) the scripts and (b) the actions that serve as test items. Despite these variations in script materials, the results were quite consistent from experiment to experiment. The mean hit rates and mean false alarm rates as a function of typicality are shown in Figure 3.2. The actions were segregated into the following typicality rating intervals: 1-1.99, 2-2.99, 3-3.99, 4-4.99, 5-5.99, and 6.0. The actions with 6.0 ratings had been rated as very typical by all subjects in the normative rating group.

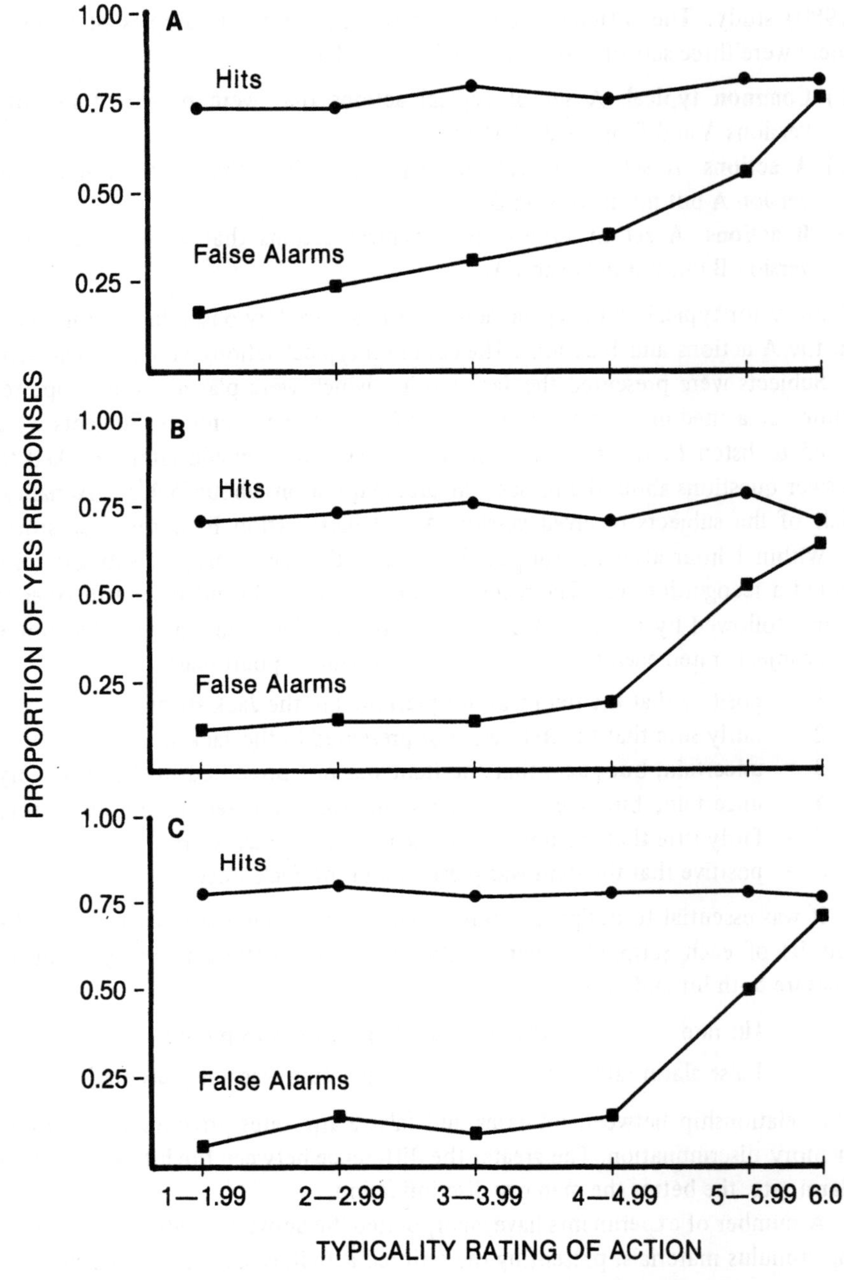

Figure 3.2. Hit and false alarm rates for actions in scripted activities as a function of typicality. (Data in part A from Graesser, Gordon, and Sawyer, 1979; data in parts B and C from Graesser, Woll, Kowalski, and Smith, 1980.)

The hit rates were not found to vary significantly as a function of typicality. When the data from the three experiments were combined, the mean hit rates were .72, .74, .74, .71, .76, and .74 in the 1-1.99, 2-2.99, 3-3.99, 4-4.99, 5-5.99, and 6.0 intervals, respectively. In contrast, the false alarm rates dramatically increased with increasing typicality, .14, .18, .20, .30, .52, and .71, respectively. The false alarm rates appear to increase in an exponential fashion as a function of typicality. In fact, an exponential function fits these means far better than does a linear function. To summarize, hit rates did not vary as a function of typicality, whereas there was an exponential increase in false alarm rates.

It is well known that the pattern of hit rates alone reveals nothing about how much is retained. Similarly, no conclusions about retention can be made from the pattern of false alarm rates alone. The amount of information retained can only be inferred from the relationship between hit rates and false alarm rates: the larger the difference between hits and false alarms, the better the retention. A popular measure for the discrimination between presented and unpresented items is a d' score. Therefore, d' scores were computed in order to assess retention as a function of typicality. These data are plotted in Figure 3.3. Figure 3.3 clearly shows that d' scores decreased as typicality increased. When the data from the three experiments were combined, the mean d' scores were 1.96, 1.87, 1.83, 1.43, .66, and .09 in the 1-1.99, 2-2.99, 3-3.99, 4-4.99, 5-5.99, and 6.0 typicality rating intervals, respectively.

The recognition memory data in Figures 3.2 and 3.3 consistently support the predictions of the SP+T model. First, memory was better for atypical than typical actions. Retention was found to decrease as typicality increased. Second, there was virtually no memory discrimination for very typical actions. The d' score was essentially zero ($d' = .09$) for very typical actions (6.0 typicality rating).

The question arises as to whether the above findings are found in recall tests as well as recognition tests. If the SP+T model is directly extended to recall, then the model would predict better memory for atypical than for typical actions, and no memory for very typical actions. On the other hand, it may be unjustified to assume that recall and recognition performance are comparable. In particular, there is some evidence that recall of text material involves abstraction and summarization processes (Cofer, Chmielewski, and Brockway, 1976; Gomulicki, 1956; Graesser, Robertson, Lovelace, and Swinehart, 1980; Rumelhart, 1977c; Spilich et al., 1979; Zangwill, 1972). When individuals are asked to recall text, they tend to include the highlights and main points and delete minor points that may nevertheless be available in memory. It is conceivable that the summary editor may tend to preserve the typical actions, which are part of the primary script, and to delete the atypical actions. If there is extensive summarization during recall, recall for typical actions would be better than that for atypical actions; just the opposite trend would occur for recognition performance.

The study of Graesser, Woll, Kowalski, and Smith (1980) included an experiment in which recall protocols were collected for the scripted activities. The procedure in this experiment was identical to that for the recognition studies except that subjects recalled the Jack story instead of receiving the recognition test.

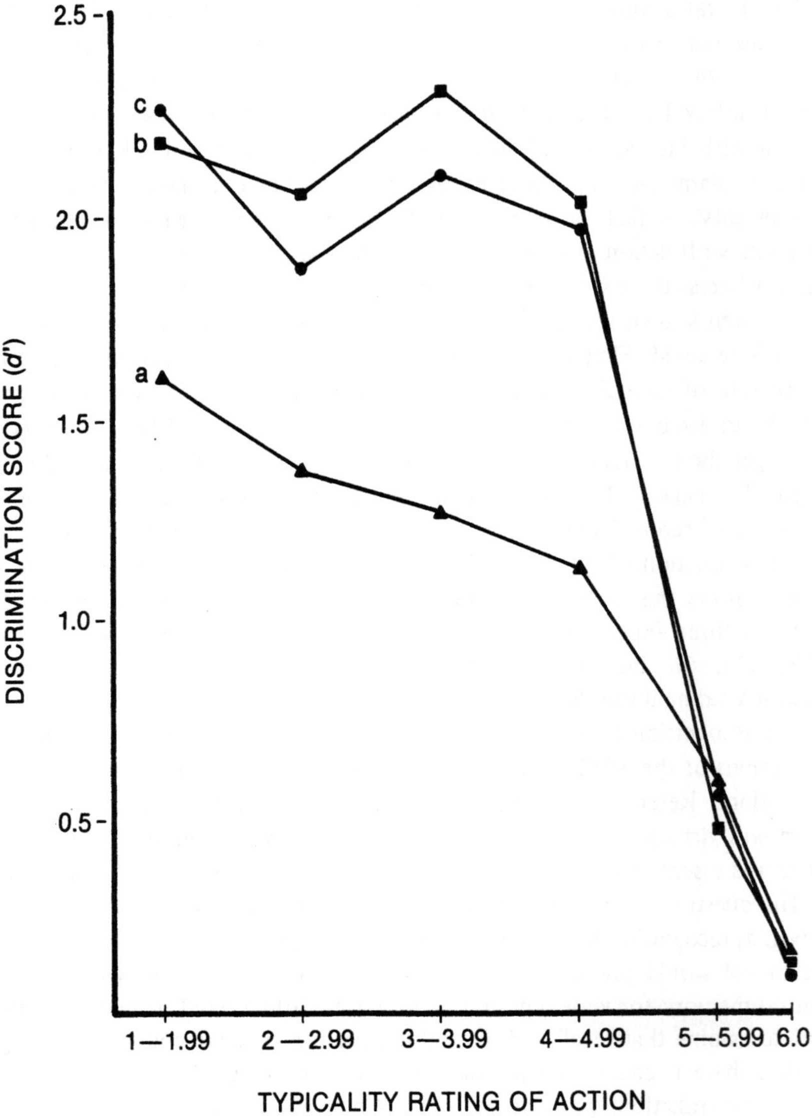

Figure 3.3. Memory discrimination (d' scores) for actions in scripted activities as a function of typicality. (Data for line *a* from Graesser, Gordon, and Sawyer, 1979; data for lines *b* and *c* from Graesser, Woll, Kowalski, and Smith, 1980.)

Within 1 hour after subjects listened to the Jack story, they were presented the script titles and asked to recall as many of the actions that occurred in the script as they could remember. Before recall, the experimenter pointed out that some actions were typical of the script whereas others were atypical. The subjects were encouraged to write down as many typical and atypical actions as they could remember.

The likelihood of recalling a presented action as a function of typicality is shown in Figure 3.4; the intrusion likelihoods for the test actions (i.e., A and B actions) are also shown. The pattern of recall proportions and intrusion proportions directly parallel the hit rates and false alarm rates in the recognition tests. Recall proportions did not vary systematically as a function of typicality. However, the intrusion proportions increased exponentially with increasing typicality.

Just as in recognition tests, an appropriate measure of retention cannot be estimated by the recall proportions alone. Subjects often guess that the typical actions had occurred. However, subjects never guess atypical actions. A retention score must be derived from the relationship (difference) between recall proportions and intrusion proportions. *Memory scores* were computed in order to provide an unbiased estimate of how well an action was acquired and retained.

$$\text{Memory score} = \frac{p(\text{recall}) - p(\text{intrusion})}{1 - p(\text{intrusion})} \tag{3.1}$$

It is important to mention that the intrusion proportions were based only on the A and B items, i.e., actions presented in one version of the Jack story but not the other. Subjects also incorrectly recalled other actions in their protocols, but these intrusions were not scored.

Memory scores are plotted in Figure 3.5. The memory scores for recall directly match the d' scores for recognition. Memory performance decreased as the typicality of an action increased, and there was no memory discrimination for very typical actions. Thus, the basic predictions of the SP+T model were supported both for recall and recognition memory.

The above data suggest that recall and recognition memory do not differ qualitatively. Nevertheless, there are some differences between recall and recognition after long retention intervals. Differences also emerge when mechanisms that generate guesses are examined. These differences will be discussed in more detail later. In the next section, the SP+T model will be tested further by using personality descriptions as stimulus material. If the SP+T model is a general model, it should account for passages that are organized around person schemas (roles and stereotypes) as well as action schemas (scripts).

Memory for Stereotype-Based Personality Descriptions

Previous studies in social cognition have assessed memory for personality descriptions that are organized around person schemas (Cantor, 1978; Cantor and Mischel, 1977; Cohen, 1977; Hastie and Kumar, 1979; Taylor and Crocker, 1980). Examples of person schemas are roles (*cowboy, secretary, professor, policeman*) and stereotypes (*macho male, nagging female*). Memory was examined in order to test some schema-based theories in social cognition. However, virtually none of these studies have collected the necessary data for determining whether there

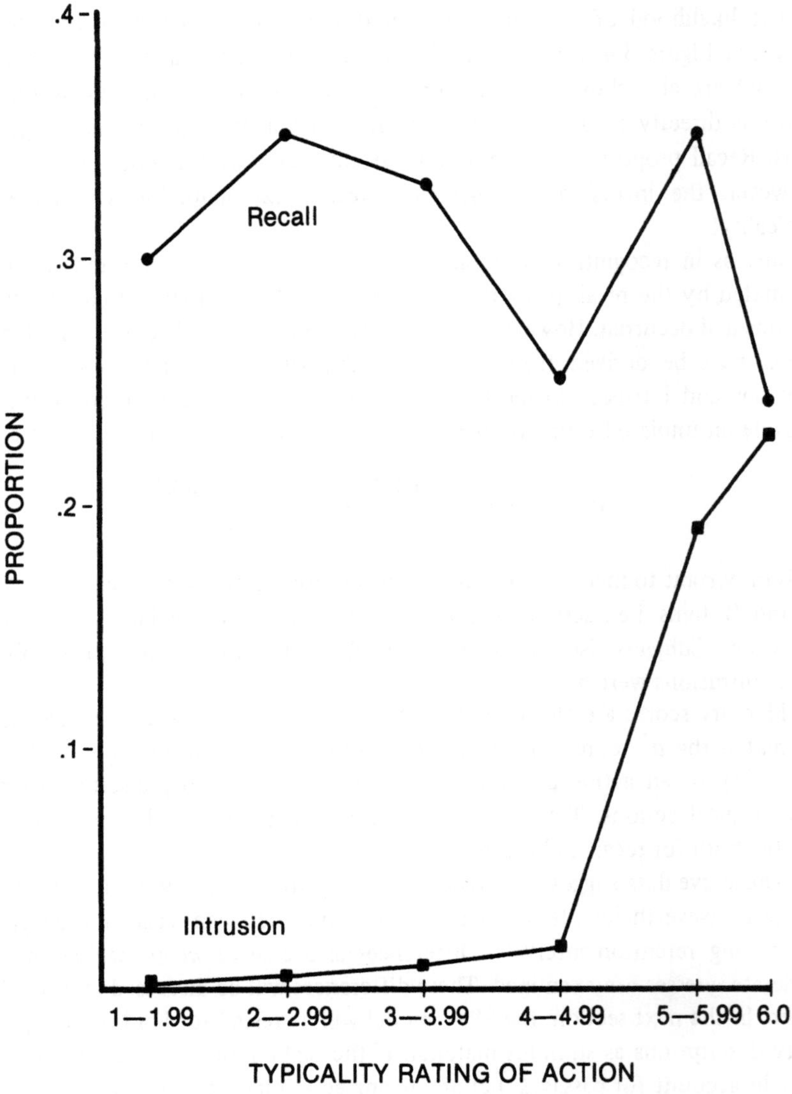

Figure 3.4. Recall and intrusion proportions for actions in scripted activities as a function of typicality. (Adapted from Graesser, Woll, Kowalski, and Smith, 1980.)

is better memory for typical information or for atypical information. In some studies recall protocols or recognition ratings were collected for behaviors and traits that are typical versus atypical of the person schema. Researchers have usually concluded that there is better memory for typical than for atypical information because hit rates and recall proportions are higher for items that are typical of the schema. Of course, these measures are uninformative because there are no provisions for guessing. On the other side of the coin, a number of studies have confirmed the prediction that false alarm rates are higher for distractor

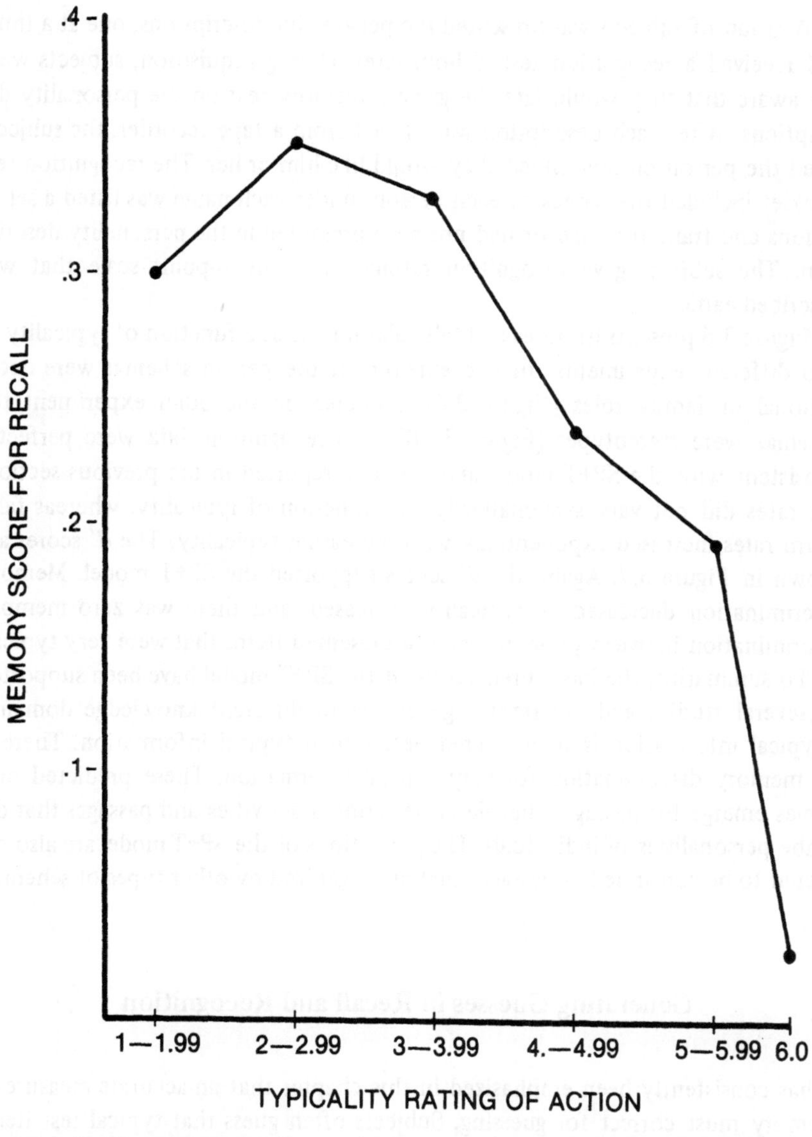

Figure 3.5. Memory scores for recall of actions in scripted activities as a function of typicality. (Adapted from Graesser, Woll, Kowalski, and Smith, 1980.)

items that are typical of the schema than those that are atypical. Unfortunately, the memory discrimination between presented and unpresented items was usually not examined in these studies.

Woll and Graesser (1980) examined recognition memory for actions and traits that vary in typicality with respect to person schemas. The methods of generating the acquisition passages were identical to those used in the previously reported studies involving scripted activities. Several personality descriptions were prepared with two different versions (A and B). A common male or female name (Robert, Sue) was assigned to each personality description.

A group of subjects was presented the personality descriptions, one at a time, and received a recognition test .5 hour later. During acquisition, subjects were not aware that they would later be given a memory test on the personality descriptions. After each description was played from a tape recorder, the subjects rated the person on how much they would like him or her. The recognition test booklet included the names of each person; under each name was listed a set of actions and traits that had or had not been presented in the personality description. The subjects gave recognition ratings using the 6-point scale that was described earlier.

Figure 3.6 presents hit rates and false alarm rates as a function of typicality in two different experiments. In one experiment the person schemas were occupational or family roles (Figure 3.6A), whereas in the other experiment the schemas were stereotypes (Figure 3.6B). The recognition data were perfectly consistent with the SP+T model and the data reported in the previous section. Hit rates did not vary systematically as a function of typicality, whereas false alarm rates increased exponentially with increasing typicality. The d' scores are shown in Figure 3.7. Again, the d' scores supported the SP+T model. Memory discrimination decreased as typicality increased, and there was zero memory discrimination between presented and unpresented items that were very typical.

To summarize, the basic predictions of the SP+T model have been supported in several studies and apparently generalize to different knowledge domains. Atypical information is remembered better than typical information. There is no memory discrimination for very typical information. These predicted outcomes emerge for passages that describe scripted activities and passages that describe personalities of individuals. The predictions of the SP+T model are also expected to be confirmed in passages that are organized by other types of schemas.

Generating Guesses in Recall and Recognition

It has consistently been emphasized in this chapter that an accurate measure of memory must correct for guessing. Subjects often guess that typical test items had been presented in a passage. Guesses rarely occur for atypical items. What mechanism generates guesses? Is the guessing mechanism different for recall and recognition tests? These questions will be examined in this section.

In one sense, it is misleading to refer to "guessing" processes in the present context. The notion of guessing has unfortunate connotations that are analogous to tossing coins or randomly generating responses. These analogies do not really capture what is going on in the minds of the subjects. When an individual incorrectly responds **YES** to a nontarget action on a recognition test, the individual probably did not mentally toss a two-sided coin that turned out to be **YES** rather than **NO**. Instead, the individual's decision was based on information that was retrieved from memory. This retrieved information may correspond to the specific memory trace (Figure 3.1) or the generic schema. When an individual formu-

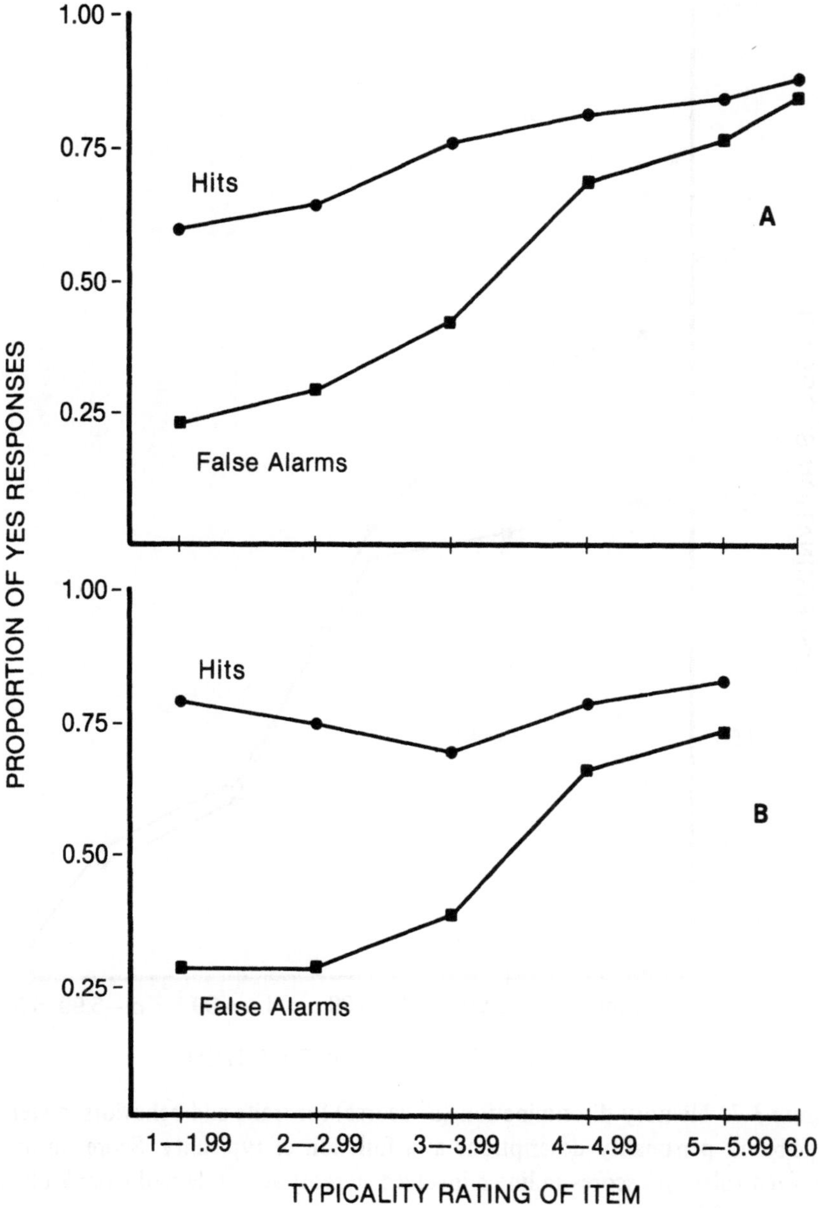

Figure 3.6. Hit and false alarm rates for traits and behaviors in stereotype-based personality descriptions. A. Descriptions involved roles. B. Descriptions involved stereotypes. (Adapted from Woll and Graesser, 1980.)

lates the judgment on the basis of the generic schema, then the context of the acquisition passage has no impact on the individual's response. In subsequent discussions, the notion of guessing refers to responses that are produced by information sources other than the presented information that is incorporated into the specific memory trace.

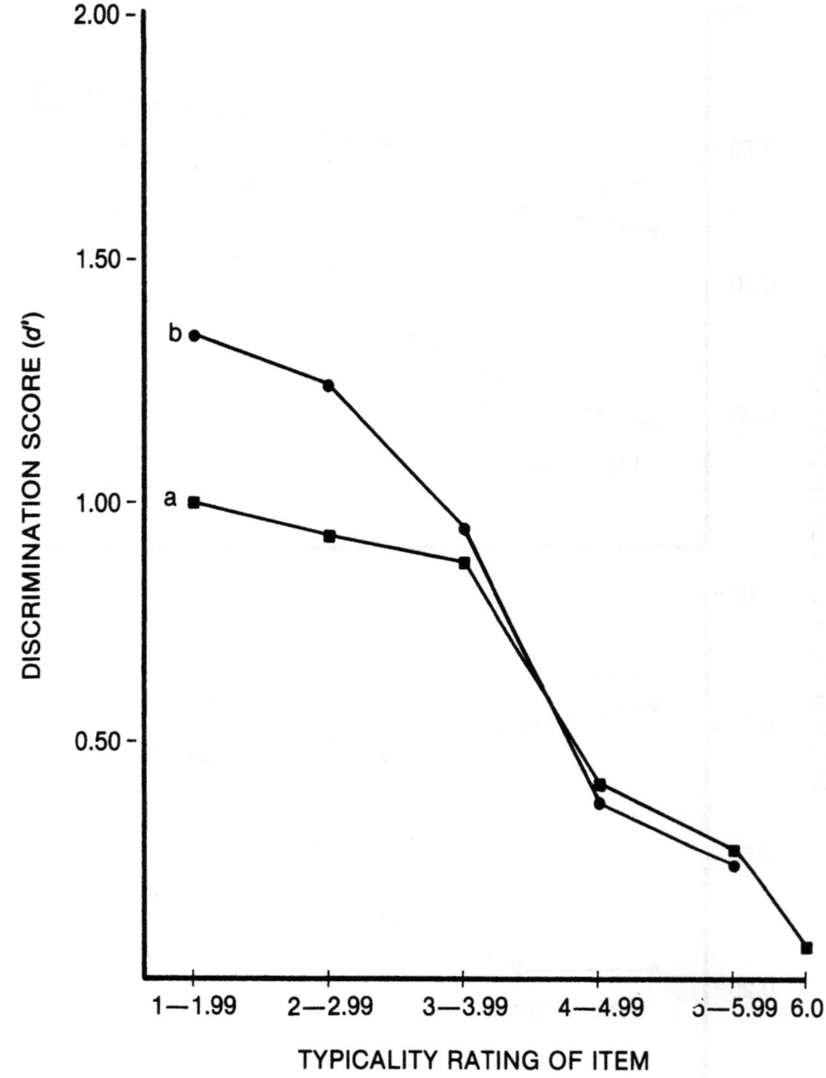

Figure 3.7. Memory discrimination (d' scores) for traits and behaviors in stereotype-based personality descriptions as a function of typicality. Scores in line *a* involved roles and scores in line *b* involved stereotypes. (Adapted from Woll and Graesser, 1980.)

Guessing mechanisms were examined separately for recall and recognition tests. An intrusion proportion corresponds to the likelihood of guessing a given item in a recall test whereas the false alarm rates reflect guessing on recognition tests. The initial question to consider is to what extent the false alarm rates and intrusion rates for the items can be predicted by (a) the typicality ratings and (b) the free generation proportions, i.e., the likelihood of generating a given item in the free generation task. Since subjects rarely guess atypical items in memory tests, the subsequent analyses will be restricted to the typical items.

Table 3.1. Correlation Matrix for Typical Actions in Scripted Activities

	False alarm rate	Intrusion rate	Typicality rating
Intrusion rate	.33**		
Typicality rating	.42**	.03	
Free generation proportion	.19*	.67**	.10

Adapted from Graesser, Woll, Kowalski, and Smith (1980).
* $p < .10$.
** $p < .05$.

The correlation matrix for the following four variables is presented in Table 3.1:

False alarm rates
Intrusion rates
Free generation proportions
Typicality ratings.

These data were extracted from the Graesser, Woll, Kowalski, and Smith (1980) study, in which recall and recognition memory for scripted activities were tested. The analyses are based on 64 typical actions.

The pattern of correlations revealed some interesting differences in guessing on recall versus recognition tests. The overall correlation between intrusion rates and false alarm rates was significant, but modest. This suggests that guessing processes might be somewhat different for recall and recognition. With regard to recall, the intrusion rates were significantly correlated with free generation proportions, but not with typicality ratings. Guessing on recognition tests showed the opposite trend. The false alarm rates were significantly correlated with the typicality ratings but not quite significantly ($.05 < p < .10$) with the free generation proportions. Furthermore, the typicality ratings were not significantly correlated with the free generation proportions.

Some conclusions about guessing mechanisms can be drawn from the obtained pattern of correlations. First, there is one type of guessing process that involves active generation, retrieval, and articulation of an element from a generic schema. An item's free generation proportion serves as an estimate of its *generic recallability*. Second, there is a different process that produces a judgment on how typical an item is for a generic schema. An item's typicality rating serves as an estimate of its *generic typicality*. These two processes are surprisingly uncorrelated for schema-relevant items. Items that have relatively high generic typicality do not systematically show high generic recallability. The fact that an item is very typical of a schema does not ensure that subjects will articulate it in a recall task; such an item may be inferred from other items that are mentioned. For example, *sitting down at a table* may be a very typical action in a restaurant script. However, this action may not be frequently produced in a free generation protocol because it can be inferred from other typical actions that are mentioned, e.g., *eating food*. Individuals usually sit down before they eat.

Two more assumptions can be made on the basis of the correlations in Table 3.1. These assumptions will be added to the earlier assumptions of the SP+T model.

Assumption 4

The likelihood of guessing an item at recall increases as a function of its generic recallability.

Assumption 5

The likelihood of guessing **YES** to an item at recognition increases as a function of its generic typicality. There is a residual effect of generic recallability on guessing at recognition.

Assumptions 4 and 5 are an attempt to capture systematic guessing processes that occur in recall and recognition tests. Subjects also occasionally guess randomly on recognition tests. Random guessing is not predicted by typicality or free generation and therefore would not be considered systematic. The false alarm rates for very atypical items (1-1.9) in Figure 3.2 are uniformly above zero (mean .14). These items reflect random guesses that subjects generate when (a) they do not retrieve an item from memory and (b) they do not judge the item as being presented by virtue of Assumption 5. Therefore, another assumption can be made for the SP+T model.

Assumption 6

There is some likelihood that subjects randomly guess **YES** on a recognition test when an item is not retrieved from memory and not judged as having occurred on the basis of its generic typicality and its generic recallability.

Retrieval Mechanisms During Recall and Recognition

It was mentioned earlier that memory theorists believe that retrieval processes are different in recall and recognition tests. The exact sources of these differences are currently under debate. This section includes the retrieval mechanisms for recall and recognition that will be adopted by the SP+T model. The retrieval mechanisms proposed here are quite similar to the models developed by Atkinson and Juola (1973) and Mandler (1972, 1980).

Other than guessing, there are two distinct components that determine a subject's correct retrieval of information that had been presented in the acquisition material. The first component will be called *conceptually driven retrieval.* In conceptually driven retrieval, organized retrieval strategies access a specific item that is part of a contextually specific memory trace. The recall of information is guided by this conceptually driven retrieval. There are two key notions that must be considered when examining conceptually driven retrieval. The first notion is *organization.* Retrieval strategies are structured and implemented in an organized manner. With regard to schema-based passages, the relevant generic schema plays a central role in guiding the organized retrieval strategies. The second notion is *context.* The context in which an item is embedded is just as important as the conceptual code corresponding to the item itself. In fact, an item would not be retrieved without its context being reinstated by virtue of the organized retrieval strategies. The contextually specific memory trace for schema-based passages is depicted in Figure 3.1.

The second component of the proposed retrieval mechanism will be called *data-driven retrieval.* Data-driven retrieval occurs in recognition tests but not in recall tests. The test item on the recognition test contains a number of informational cues that provide a relatively direct access to the item in memory. Data-driven retrieval is directed by the item itself as a "copy cue." Data-driven retrieval is analogous, although perhaps not strictly identical, to what has been called "detection of familiarity" (Atkinson and Juola, 1973; Mandler, 1980), in some models of recognition memory. There are some subtle differences between the notion of data-driven retrieval and the detection of familiarity, but the similarities are important from the present perspective. Specifically, data-driven retrieval is not always guided by organized retrieval strategies and does not always critically depend on reinstating the acquisition context in which a particular item was embedded. For example, an atypical action may be correctly recognized without the subject's remembering which scripted activity the action occurred in. A subject might quickly recognize that *Jack put his pen in his pocket,* but might not remember whether Jack did this in the *restaurant* script or the *washing clothes* script.

In the proposed model, the correct recognition of an item may be accomplished by data-driven retrieval or by conceptually driven retrieval. According to this dual-process model of recognition memory, data-driven retrieval and conceptually driven retrieval are additive and separate components. A tagged item may be accessed by data-driven retrieval, but not by conceptually driven retrieval, and vice versa. The application and mathematical formulation of this model is quite similar to other dual-process models of recognition memory (Atkinson and Juola, 1973; Mandler, 1972, 1980).

An example should clarify the different retrieval processes that occur during recall and recognition.

> One night I went to a fancy Hungarian restaurant with three friends. During the meal an arrogant violinist came to the table and played a romantic tune. During the schmaltzy melody, one of the strings snapped and there were snickers at our table and the surrounding tables. Three months later I was again having dinner with the same three friends at an inexpensive American restaurant. I questioned each of my friends separately about the violin episode. I asked Leslie to recall if anything unusual happened at the Hungarian restaurant. At first, she couldn't recall anything very unusual, but after 5 minutes she finally remembered the violin episode. This first person had to perform some active, effortful, and time-consuming retrieval processes that followed some organized strategy. Leslie's retrieval was conceptually driven. Liz was also asked whether anything unusual happened at the Hungarian

restaurant. This second person actively tried to recall an unusual episode for 10 minutes but did not recall the violin episode. I then gave Liz a recognition test. I asked Liz if she remembered the violinist's string breaking and she immediately answered **YES** with confidence in her decision. Liz retrieved the violin episode in a data-driven fashion by the copy cue, i.e., my asking her directly about the violinist's string breaking. Liz was unable to retrieve the episode by conceptually driven retrieval. The third person, Don, was questioned directly about the violinist breaking the string. At first Don did not recognize that the violin episode occurred in the Hungarian restaurant. However, after thinking about the matter for 5 minutes, he changed his mind and decided, with confidence, that the violinist did break the string. This third individual was unable to retrieve the violin episode by data-driven retrieval, but ultimately was able to retrieve it by invoking an organized retrieval strategy.

Listed below are summaries of how the three individuals successfully retrieved the violin episode.

Leslie. Retrieval by a conceptually driven organized retrieval strategy; status of data-driven retrieval is uncertain.

Liz. Retrieval by data-driven retrieval, but not by conceptually driven retrieval.

Don. Retrieval by conceptually driven retrieval, but not by data-driven retrieval.

Hopefully, the reader now has some intuitive understanding of the difference between (a) conceptually driven retrieval, which is active, time-consuming, and follows some organized strategy, and (b) data-driven retrieval, which is a more automatic process that is accomplished quickly and is driven by information in the test item. Only the organized retrieval strategies are available in a recall test. On recognition tests, however, access to an item may be conceptually driven or data driven. These retrieval processes are captured by the two assumptions below.

Assumption 7

Recall of an item is directed by an organized retrieval strategy that is conceptually driven.

Assumption 8

Recognition of an item is either data-driven through the copy cue, accessed by a conceptually driven retrieval strategy, or both.

One additional comment should be made about data-driven retrieval. There is a question as to how much context is reinstated when an item is retrieved by data-driven retrieval. It is plausible that some items are accessed without reviving the original context in which the item was embedded (Mandler, 1980). For example, a subject might correctly recognize that *Jack bought some mints* was presented in the Jack story without remembering which scripted activity the action occurred in. For other items, however, the context is reinstated during the course of data-driven retrieval. On the basis of the information in the test item, the subject might diagnostically predict the relevant schema and thereby accumulate more retrieval cues (Norman and Bobrow, 1979); the specific context may even be reinstated. For example, a subject might correctly recognize that *Jack left a tip* by (a) inferring that this action must have occurred in the restaurant script, (b) examining the memory trace of the restaurant activity, and (c) identifying the tipping episode as being part of the memory trace. In other words, an item might be retrieved by informational cues that are provided by the test item together with the schema that is associated with (predicted by) the test item.

According to the SP+T model, recall performance is explained by Assumptions 4 and 7 in addition to the representional Assumptions 1, 2, and 3. The likelihood of recalling a particular item depends on whether a tagged item is retrieved through an organized retrieval strategy (Assumption 7) and whether an item is guessed on the basis of the generic schema (Assumption 4). The intrusion proportion for an unpresented item can be predicted by the generic recallability of the item, as measured by its free generation likelihood. The fact that recall proportions do not vary systematically with typicality is a consequence of two antagonistic trends: (a) the likelihood of tagging an item at acquisition and of retrieving a tagged item at recall *decreases* with typicality (Assumptions 2, 3, and 7) and (b) the likelihood of guessing an item *increases* with typicality (Assumption 4). Assumptions 1, 2, and 3 explain the fact that there is no memory discrimination between presented and unpresented items that are very typical, and also the fact that memory discrimination is better for atypical than for typical items.

An explanation of recognition performance is somewhat more complicated. Figure 3.8 is a diagram of the mechanism involved in deciding whether or not a test item had been presented. The diagram incorporates the guessing Assumptions 5 and 6, the retrieval Assumption 8, and the representational Assumptions 1, 2, and 3. The mechanism includes three stages:

Stage 1. Memory trace examination.
Stage 2. Schema evaluation.
Stage 3. Random guessing.

The three stages will be discussed separately.

Stage 1 consists of a memory examination process that searches for a tagged item that corresponds to a test action. If there is a match between a test item and a tagged item, the subject answers **YES**. The likelihood of acquiring a tag (Assumptions 2 and 3) and later retrieving a tagged item (Assumption 8) decreases as an item's typicality increases; the likelihood approaches zero for very typical actions (Assumption 1). Memory discrimination, as measured by d' scores, is a direct function of the likelihood that an item is tagged. A tagged item may be retrieved either by data-driven access (the left vertical line below INPUT TEST ITEM in Figure 3.8) or by an organized, conceptually driven retrieval strategy (the right vertical line below INPUT TEST ITEM). If a tagged item is not retrieved during Stage 1, then the test item is evaluated by Stage 2.

Stage 2 is a schema evaluation stage. The test item is compared to the content of the appropriate generic schema. The subject evaluates the likelihood that an item could have been presented based on the content of the generic schema. The likelihood of a **YES** decision from Stage 2 *increases* with the typicality of an

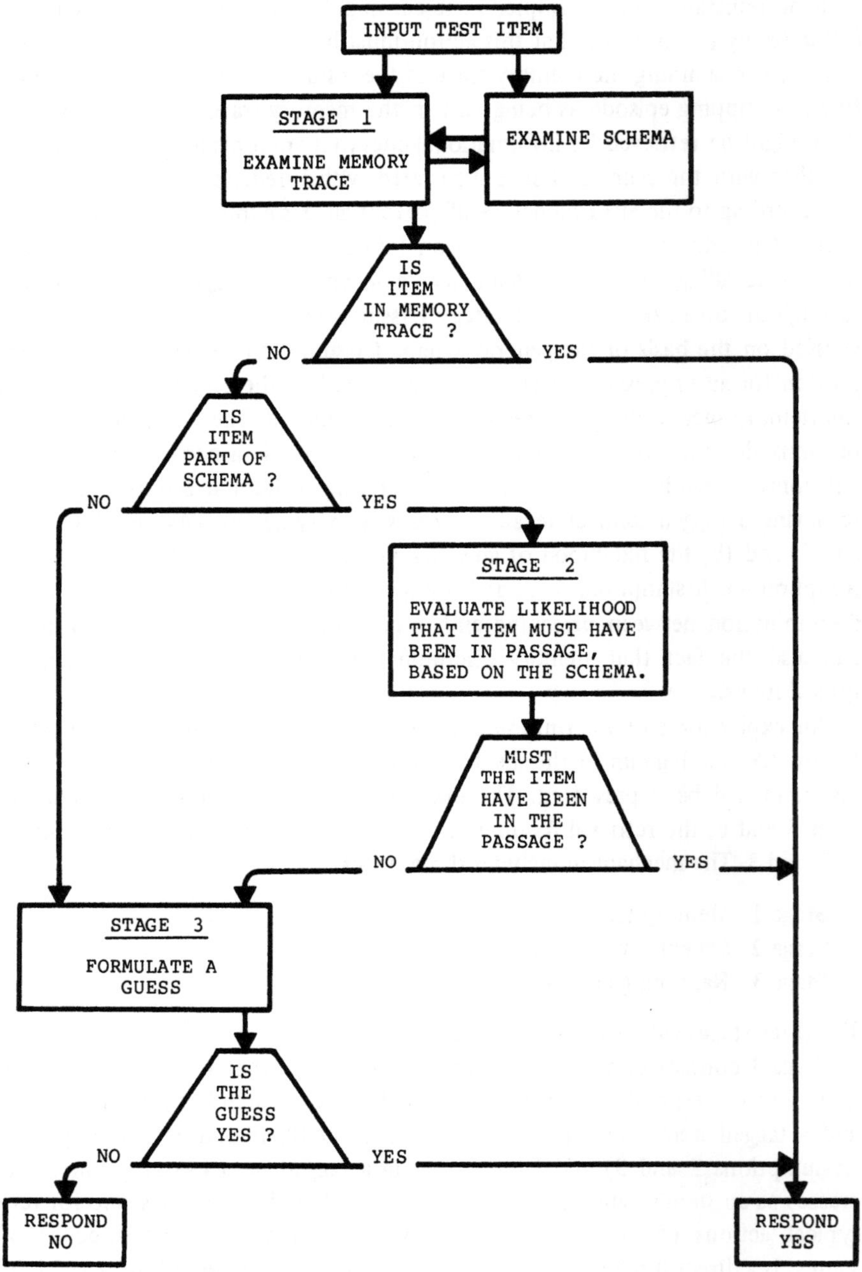

Figure 3.8. Mechanism for generating recognition responses.

item and is reflected in the false alarm rates. The likelihood of guessing that an item was presented depends on both its generic typicality and generic reliability (Assumption 5). When Stages 1 and 2 are considered together, there is no predicted pattern of hit rates as a function of typicality. The likelihood of generating a **YES** decision from Stage 1 *decreases* with typicality, whereas the likelihood of generating a **YES** decision from Stage 2 *increases* with typicality.

Whenever a **YES** decision is not generated from Stages 1 and 2, then a test action is passed to Stage 3. Stage 3 simply generates a random guess (Assumption 6).

There is an interesting question as to whether the output from Stage 2 is based on inference processes at acquisition or guessing processes at retrieval (or both). The likelihood of a **YES** decision from Stage 2 is clearly higher for typical items than for atypical items. Is this because individuals infer and encode typical items during comprehension, or because individuals judge at test time that typical items must have been presented? The plausible answer to this question is that both processes occur to some extent. The pattern of false alarm rates in Figure 3.2 suggests that individuals do sometimes judge at test time that an item must have been presented. The mean false alarm rates are .14, .18, .20, and .30 in the typicality intervals of 1-1.99, 2-2.99, 3-3.99, and 4-4.99, respectively. There clearly is an increase in false alarm rates within this range of typicality. However, it is very unlikely that subjects ever inferred these items at comprehension. The free generation proportions and intrustion proportions are virtually zero for all of the items within this range of typicality. Therefore, there is some evidence that the output from Stage 2 of the recognition mechanism is to some extent based on judgments occurring at test time rather than inference processing during comprehension.

There is also evidence that the high false alarm rates for typical actions are to some extent based on inference processing during comprehension. The question arises as to whether individuals sometimes circumvent memory trace examination when an item is typical of the schema. Individuals could conceivably apply schema evaluation (Stage 2) first and avoid any time-consuming retrieval processes that are involved at Stage 1. For example, suppose that an individual were given a recognition test on the first example passage about John. When asked whether *John ate* had been presented, the subject might prematurely conclude that the action must have been stated (based on Stage 2) and ultimately avoid executing a retrieval strategy that examines the specific memory trace (Stage 1). If Stage 1 is often circumvented when typical items are tested, then it is possible that there is good memory for typical items despite the poor recognition scores. The alternative possibility is that subjects do not circumvent Stage 1 when typical test items are judged.

An experiment in the Graesser, Woll, Kowalski, and Smith (1980) study was designed to test the above two possibilities. Subjects received either a standard **YES/NO** recognition test on the Jack story or a two alternative, forced-choice test (2AFC). Pairs of alternative actions on the 2AFC test were matched on generic typicality. If one item had a mean typicality rating of t, then the alternative item had a mean typicality of $t \pm .2$. This matching constraint on the 2AFC test was designed to eliminate schema evaluation (Stage 2) as a criterion for deciding whether an item had been presented. Since both alternatives of a pair would receive equal evalutations from Stage 2, the subjects would be forced to rely on memory trace examination (Stage 1) when formulating their decisions.

In Figure 3.9 the d' scores are shown as a function of typicality. Separate d' scores are shown for those subjects who received the 2AFC recognition test and

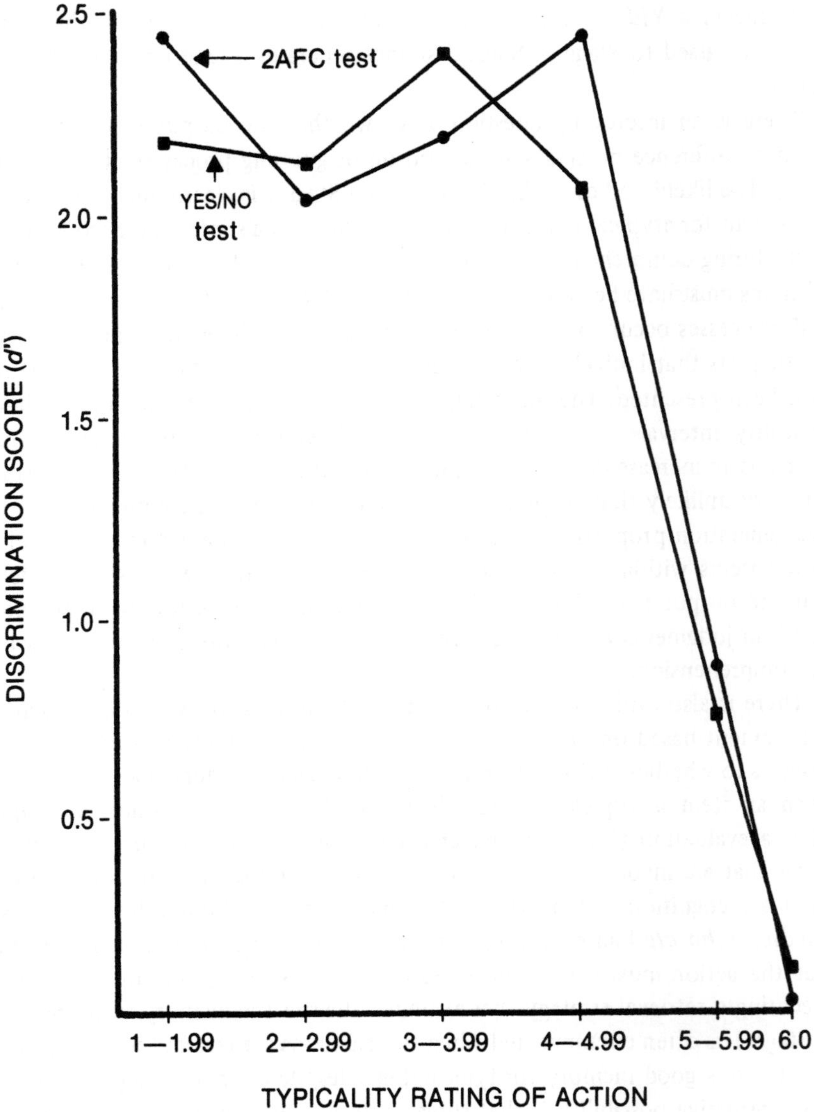

Figure 3.9. Memory discrimination (d' scores) for actions in scripted activities as a function of typicality and recognition test format. (Adapted from Graesser, Woll, Kowalski, and Smith, 1980.)

those who received the **YES/NO** recognition test. The patterns and magnitudes of the d' scores are virtually equivalent for the 2AFC and **YES/NO** recognition tests, just as would be predicted by signal detection theory (Green and Swets, 1966). The recognition test format had no significant influence on memory discrimination. These data support the conclusion that subjects do *not* avoid memory trace examination (Stage 1) when they judge typical test items. If they did, then the 2AFC test would have produced higher d' scores than the **YES/NO** test for typical actions. These results also support the claim that most of the typical actions were inferred during comprehension, rather than being guessed at test time.

The similarities and differences between recall and recognition mechanisms have been identified in this section. The differences will become more salient in the next section.

Effects of Retention Interval on Memory for Typical and Atypical Items

What is the fate of typical and atypical information when passages are tested after longer retention intervals? How do forgetting rates compare for typical versus atypical information? Does recall differ from recognition? Does access to tagged items differ for conceptually driven retrieval and data-driven retrieval? It has already been established that memory discrimination is better for atypical than typical information when subjects are tested within 1 hour after comprehension. Does this outcome persist over time?

Relatively few studies have been conducted on memory for text after very long retention intervals, such as a week, a month, or even a year. When Bartlett (1932) examined memory for stories after long and short retention intervals, he made a few informal observations. Memory for text initially tends to be "reproductive" in the sense of being close to what was explicitly stated. However, memory is more "reconstructive" as the retention interval increases (see also Cofer et al., 1976; D'Andrade, 1974; Dooling and Christiaansen, 1977; Kintsch, 1977a; Kintsch and van Dijk, 1978; Spiro, 1977).

What are the implications of memory being reconstructive? One implication is that individuals tend to preserve information that is consistent with the overriding schema. They delete unrelated or inconsistent details. If this generalization is correct, then there is some basis for expecting typical information to be forgotten at a slower rate than atypical information. In fact, there are a few studies on memory for pictures and stereotypes that appear to support this prediction (Cohen, 1977; Mandler and Ritchey, 1977; Wulff, 1922). The obvious explanation for the differential forgetting rate is that the schema plays a more important role in guiding retrieval as the retention interval increases.

Smith and Graesser (1980) examined both recall and recognition memory for actions in scripted activities. Subjects listened to the same Jack story that was used in the studies reported earlier in this chapter. The subjects were given a recall test or a recognition test after four different retention intervals: .5 hour, 2 days, 1 week, and 3 weeks. There were eight experimental scripts in the Jack story. Therefore, a within-subject design could be used to assess memory after the four different retention intervals and two testing formats (recall versus recognition). For any given subject, a particular script was tested only once by either testing format (not both formats) at only one of the retention intervals. Of course, appropriate counterbalancing procedures were imposed across subjects so that each script was tested by both recall and recognition at all four retention intervals. The 48 subjects who participated in this experiment received the Jack story that was used in the Graesser, Woll, Kowalski, and Smith (1980) study.

The memory data from the Smith and Graesser (1980) study are presented in Table 3.2. Hit rates and false alarm rates are reported for the recognition test; recall proportions and intrusion proportions are reported for the recall test. Of course, typical actions are segregated from atypical actions. Statistical tests on the data in Table 3.2 indicated that a number of main effects and interactions were significant. However, the fact that trends were significant was expected and not particularly informative. The important questions address how well the means quantitatively fit the SP+T model. The nature of the forgetting functions for typical versus atypical actions is also important.

According to the model, the recall data should provide a pure assessment of the likelihood of accessing a tagged item by means of conceptually driven retrieval. Conceptually driven retrieval utilizes the generic schema for guiding the course of memory trace examination. It is important to partial out guessing when estimating the likelihood of accessing a tagged item. Thus, the memory score in Formula 3.1 served as an estimate of the probability of accessing a tagged item by conceptually driven retrieval.

In Figure 3.10 the memory scores for typical and atypical items are plotted as a function of retention interval. The curves in Figure 3.10 show four informative trends. First, the memory functions appear to decay exponentially as a function of retention interval. Second, at a short (.5-hour) retention interval, memory is better for atypical than for typical actions. Third, memory approaches zero for both typical and atypical actions after a 3-week retention interval. Fourth, memory decays at a faster rate for atypical than for typical actions. Support for this fourth trend lies in an interesting crossover. Although memory is better for atypical than for typical actions after a short retention interval of .5 hour, just the opposite is the case after 1-week and 3-week retention intervals. Statistical

Table 3.2. Memory Data for Actions in Scripted Activities

Test format and item typicality	Memory measure	Retention interval			
		.5 hour	2 days	1 week	3 weeks
Recognition					
Typical	*p*(hit)	.781	.766	.728	.660
	p(false alarm)	.564	.553	.627	.628
Atypical	*p*(hit)	.728	.638	.564	.463
	p(false alarm)	.154	.250	.186	.261
Recall					
Typical	*p*(recall)	.288	.250	.245	.165
	p(intrusion)	.117	.159	.191	.144
Atypical	*p*(recall)	.288	.096	.032	.011
	p(intrusion)	.000	.000	.000	.000

analyses revealed that this crossover is significant (see also Graesser, Woll, Kowalski, and Smith, 1980).

The data shown in Figure 3.10 are consistent with the notion that schemas become progressively more important in guiding conceptually driven retrieval as the retention interval increases. Memory is relatively reproductive after short retention intervals. Atypical information is retrieved relatively well after short delays. However, after longer retention intervals, the atypical information drops out. Subjects are only able to reconstruct the tagged typical items that are accessed through the schemas.

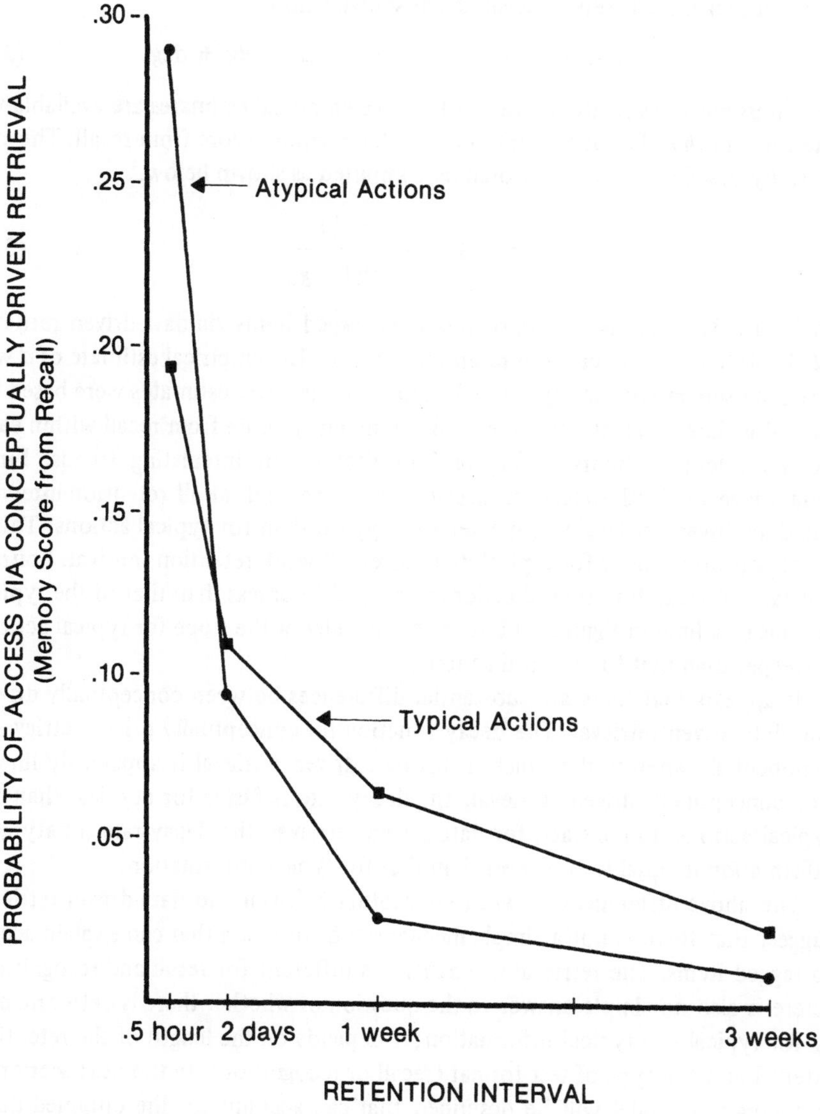

Figure 3.10. Probability of accessing actions in scripted activities via conceptually driven retrieval. (Adapted from Smith and Graesser, 1980.)

What about data-driven access to the tagged items on recognition tests? According to the model, recognition memory is determined both by conceptually driven and by data-driven retrieval. In order to estimate the likelihood of accessing a tagged item via data-driven retrieval, it is important to partial out two components: (a) access to a tagged item via conceptually driven retrieval and (b) guessing. The false alarm rates served as an estimate of guessing, g, whereas the memory scores in Figure 3.10 served as an estimate of the likelihood of recognizing an item via conceptually driven retrieval, c. The hit rate for items on the recognition test would be based on the guessing likelihood (g), the probability of accessing items via conceptually driven retrieval (c), and the likelihood of accessing items via data-driven retrieval (d), as shown below.

$$\text{Hit rate} = d + c + g - cg - dc - dg + dcg \tag{3.2}$$

It is possible to estimate the value of d since empirical estimates are available for the hit rate (h), the false alarm rate, and the memory score from recall. The empirically based estimate of d would be computed as shown below.

$$d = 1 + \frac{(h - 1)}{(1 - c)(1 - g)} \tag{3.3}$$

In Figure 3.11 the likelihood of accessing tagged items via data-driven retrieval (d) is plotted as a function of retention interval. The empirical estimate of d was obtained separately for typical and atypical items. The estimates were based on the false alarm rate, the hit rate, and the memory score from recall within each of the retention intervals. Figure 3.11 shows four interesting trends. First, data-driven retrieval appears to decay linearly. Second, at all retention intervals the data-driven retrieval was greater for atypical than for typical actions. Third, there was no memory for typical items after a 3-week retention interval. Fourth, the rate of decay for atypical actions was equal to or less than that of the typical actions (the lines in Figure 3.11 are either parallel or the slope for typical actions is steeper than that for atypical actions).

It appears that there are substantial differences between conceptually driven and data-driven retrieval. The decay function for conceptually driven retrieval is exponential, whereas the function for data-driven retrieval is apparently linear. For conceptually driven retrieval, the decay rate is faster for atypical than for typical actions. In contrast, for data-driven retrieval, the decay rate for atypical information is equal to or slower than that for typical information.

The above differences between conceptually driven and data-driven retrieval suggest that there is not a simple mechanism or function that can explain access to tagged items. The retrieval mechanism is different for recall and recognition. There is also no simple answer to the question of whether there is better memory for typical or atypical information; it depends on the length of the retention interval and the type of test format (recall or recognition). In the next section, a mathematical model will be described that can account for the obtained data. However, before turning to the mathematical model, the last two assumptions of the SP+T model will be articulated.

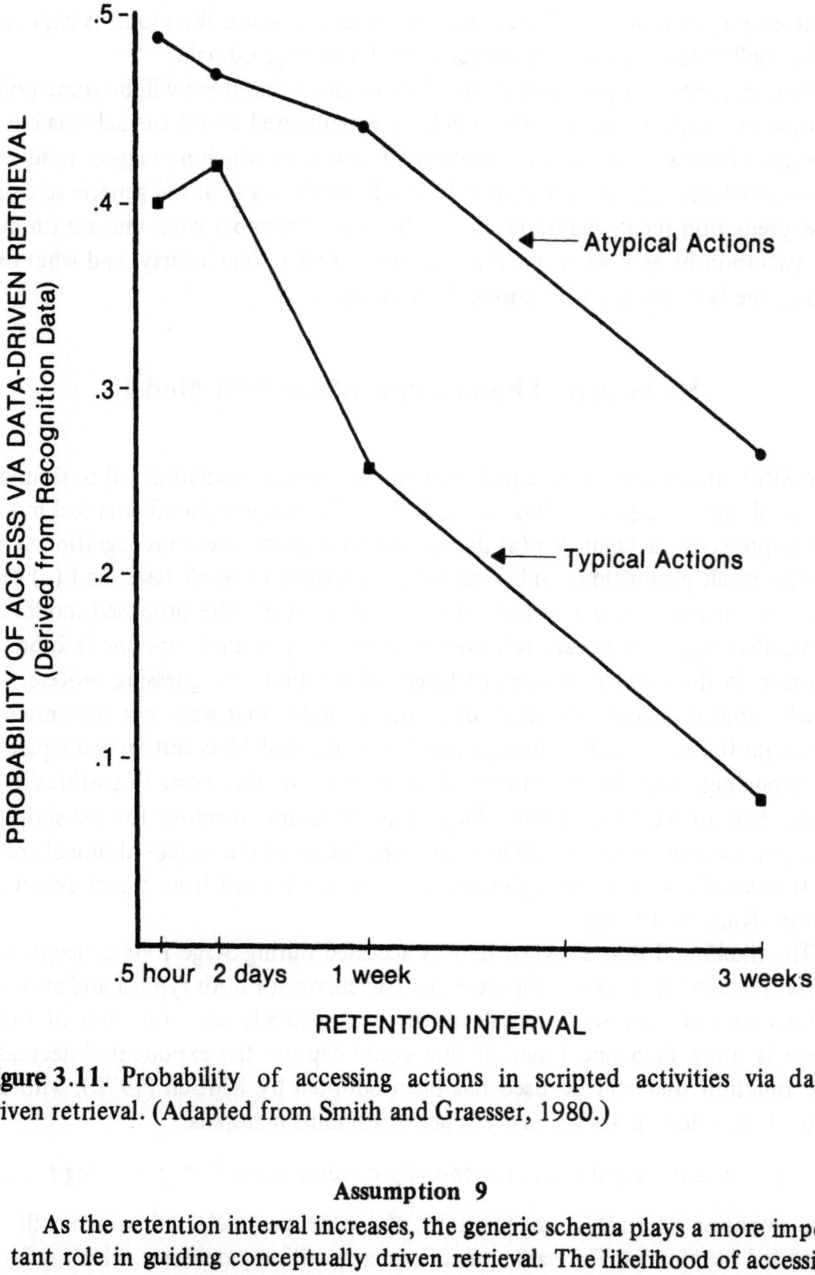

Figure 3.11. Probability of accessing actions in scripted activities via data-driven retrieval. (Adapted from Smith and Graesser, 1980.)

Assumption 9

As the retention interval increases, the generic schema plays a more important role in guiding conceptually driven retrieval. The likelihood of accessing an item via conceptually driven retrieval decreases exponentially over time and the atypical items have a faster decay rate than the typical items.

Assumption 10

The likelihood of accessing an item via data-driven retrieval decreases linearly as the retention interval increases. The decay rate for atypical information is equal to or slower than that for typical items.

At this point all of the assumptions of the SP+T model have been specified. Although the model has been applied in detail to scripted activities, and also to some extent to stereotype-based personality descriptions, the model is expected to be applicable to schemas in virtually any knowledge domain.

One interesting implication of the SP+T model is that there will be some point in time at which virtually nothing will be remembered about the schema-based passage. There is some critical retention interval after which no tagged items will be accessed and subjects will respond entirely on the basis of the generic schema. This prediction seems plausible. It is difficult to remember what one ate for dinner two months ago, what one drank at the last New Year's party, and what one said to the last solicitor who knocked on the door.

Mathematical Formulation of the SP+T Model

The SP+T model can be specified mathematically in sufficient detail to simulate the recall and recognition data in Table 3.2. The proposed mathematical model can impressively account for (a) the hit and false alarm rates in recognition tests, (b) the recall proportions and intrusion proportions in recall tests, and (c) variations in memory as a function of retention interval. The proposed model assumes that tagged items are retrieved from memory in an all-or-none fashion. In addition to the correct retrieval of tagged items, there are guessing processes in which subjects incorrectly recall or recognize items that were not presented in the acquisition material. Although an all-or-none model has certain inadequacies for modeling recognition memory of word lists, an all-or-none (high-threshold) model has proved to be quite adequate for modeling memory for the scripted passages. Of course, the mathematical formulation of the proposed model could be translated into more complex models that are derived from signal detection theory (Kintsch, 1977a).

The likelihood that a tagged item is accessed during Stage 1 via conceptually driven retrieval is shown in Figure 3.10. The curves for both typical and atypical actions suggest that retention decreases exponentially as a function of time. There is more than one function that could capture the exponential decrease. The function that will be used has been adopted by Kintsch (1970), who examined retention curves for many types of stimulus materials.

$$p(\text{access to tagged item/conceptually driven retrieval}) = a - b \log t \quad (3.4)$$

The retention interval is captured by the time parameter, t, which will be measured in minutes. The parameter a is an acquisition parameter, which reflects how well an item is initially learned. As a increases, the level of original acquisition becomes higher. The parameter b reflects the rate of forgetting, the decay rate. As b increases, the rate of forgetting increases.

The two free parameters, a and b, were computed for the curves in Figure 3.10 using a least squares criterion for goodness-of-fit. The acquisition parameter a was .277 for typical information and .427 for atypical information. This outcome, of course, agrees with earlier claims that memory is initially better for atypical than typical information. The forgetting rate parameter b was .023 for typical information and .041 for atypical information. Again, these parameter values support earlier claims that atypical information has a faster forgetting rate than typical information when access via conceptually driven retrieval is considered.

Before the recall data can be completely simulated, a guessing parameter must be estimated for typical information. The likelihood of guessing atypical information is, of course, zero. The intrusion proportions of typical information do not significantly vary as a function of retention interval. Therefore, the estimate for guessing typical information, g, will be assigned the mean intrusion proportion across the four different retention intervals. The estimate of g is .153. The predicted intrusion proportion would therefore be .153 for all retention intervals. The predicted recall proportion would be computed as shown below.

$$p(\text{recall}) = (a - b \log t) + g(1 - a + b \log t) \qquad (3.5)$$

The predicted and obtained values are shown in Figure 3.12.

According to the model, on a recognition test subjects may access a tagged item in Stage 1 either by data-driven retrieval or by conceptually driven retrieval. The exponential functions that were extracted from recall (Figure 3.10 and Formula 3.4) provide an empirical estimate of the conceptually driven retrieval during recognition. The data-driven retrieval functions are shown in Figure 3.11 for typical and atypical actions. The later functions appear to be linear rather than exponential and can be captured by the linear function shown below.

$$p(\text{access to tagged item/data-driven retrieval}) = c - dt \qquad (3.6)$$

The parameter c is the acquisition parameter, and d is the slope parameter that reflects the decay rate for forgetting. As c increases, the initial level of acquisition for an item increases; as d increases, the rate of forgetting increases. The parameter t is again the retention interval.

The two curves in Figure 3.11 were fit to linear functions with days used as the unit of time. Days were used instead of minutes in order to show a reasonably large value for the slope parameter. The acquisition parameter c was higher for atypical information than for typical information, .524 and .380, respectively. The rate of forgetting parameter d was steeper for typical than for atypical actions, .016 and .012, respectively. These parameter values agree with the earlier claims about data-driven retrieval.

If it is assumed that conceptually driven retrieval and data-driven retrieval are stochastically independent processes, then the likelihood of accessing a tagged item during Stage 1 can be computed for recognition as shown below.

$$p(\text{accessing a tagged item during recognition}) = (a - b \log t) - (1 - a + b \log t)(c - dt) \qquad (3.7)$$

Of course, the parameters would be estimated for typical and atypical items separately.

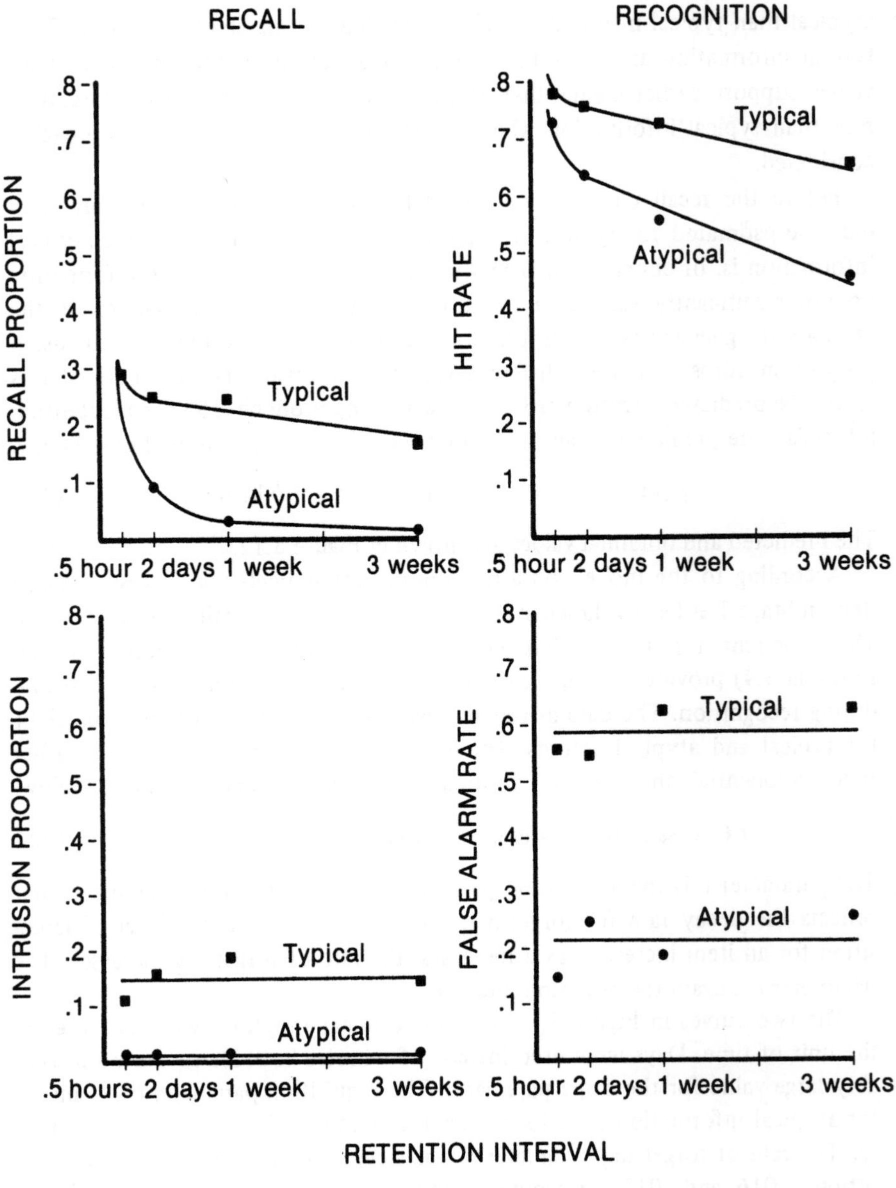

Figure 3.12. Expected (*lines*) and obtained (*points*) memory data for actions in scripted activities. (Adapted from Smith and Graesser, 1980.)

In order to specify mathematically the hit and false alarm rates at recognition, the phenomena of guessing must be dealt with. The false alarm rates serve as an index of guessing at recognition. The likelihood of guessing **YES** for an item is a product of three processes:

(1) **Generic recallability.** The estimate of guessing on the basis of generic recallability is g for typical items and zero for atypical items. These estimates are the same as those for recall.

(2) **Generic typicality.** The estimate of guessing on the basis of the generic typicality is s for typical items and zero for atypical items.
(3) **Random guessing.** Random guesses are products of Stage 3. Stage 3 decisions occur when no decision can be made on the basis of Stages 1 and 2. The likelihood of randomly guessing **YES**, r, is the same for typical and atypical items.

The mathematical model assumes that the three types of guesses are generated by stochastically independent processes. The fact that the g parameter is included as a parameter for recognition captures the fact that there is a modest correlation between false alarm rate and generic recallability. The positive correlation between generic typicality and false alarm rate is captured by the s parameter. Finally, the r parameter accounts for the fact that the subjects sometimes randomly guess **YES** on very atypical nontarget items. The false alarm rates for typical items can now be simulated by a simple stochastic process.

$$p(\text{false alarm/typical}) = g + s + r - gs - gr - sr + gsr \qquad (3.8)$$

The false alarm rate for atypical items would simply be r. It follows that the hit rate for a typical action would be computed as shown below:

$$p(\text{hit/typical}) = (a - b \log t) + (1 - a + b \log t)(c - dt) + [1 - (a - b \log t) - (1 - a + b \log t)(c - dt)](g + s + r - gs - gr - sr + gsr) \qquad (3.9)$$

The hit rate for atypical items would be computed the same way except that (a) there would be different parameter values for a, b, c, and d, and (b) the parameter values for g and s would be zero.

The expected and obtained memory data for recall and recognition are shown in Figure 3.12. The best fit values are shown below (with days used as the unit of time):

Guessing parameters: $r = .213$
$g = .153$
$s = .394$
Typical information: $a = .109$
$b = .023$
$c = .380$
$d = .016$
Atypical information: $a = .126$
$b = .041$
$c = .524$
$d = .012$.

The expected curves had an impressively good fit to the data. In fact, a chi-square statistic indicated that the expected values did not significantly deviate from the obtained values, $\chi^2(20) = 19.7, p > .50$.

It is important to consider how the proposed model compares with alternative models. There is an endless list of memory models that could be compared to the data, and it would be cumbersome to elucidate how dozens of alternative models would fail to accommodate the rich pattern of data. Some alternative models were tested, but these did not fit the data as well as the proposed model. Specifically, the following models did not fare as well.

(1) A model that assumes that the forgetting rate for conceptually driven retrieval follows a linear decay function rather than an exponential function.
(2) A model that assumes that the retrieval of tagged items (Stage 1) during recognition follows a single forgetting function (either linear or exponential). Indeed, there does seem to be both conceptually driven retrieval and data-driven retrieval during recognition!

There is at least one way in which the model could be improved in order to provide a better fit. The mathematical model assumes that the retention interval does not affect the guessing processes. However, the patterns of false alarm rates and intrusion rates indicate that the guessing increased slightly as the retention interval increased (see also Kintsch and van Dijk, 1978). Since there was a relatively large variability in the false alarms and intrusions, it is difficult to speculate on the shape of the functions that relate guessing and retention interval.

If the proposed model is correct, there are some additional implications concerning the fate of typical and atypical information in memory. For example, there is no simple generalization that can be made regarding memory for typical and atypical information. The question of whether memory is better for typical or atypical information depends on the testing format (recall or recognition) and the retention interval. If we use the parameter values obtained in the Smith and Graesser (1980) study, two trends emerge. First, recognition memory will always be better for atypical than for typical information. Second, recall performance will be equal for atypical and typical information after a retention interval of 3.3 days. Before 3.3 days, recall will be better for atypical than typical information; after 3.3 days recall memory will be better for typical than atypical items.

A second interesting implication of the model is that there will be some point in time at which there is absolutely no memory for typical and atypical information. Again, these critical times can be estimated from the reported parameter values. For conceptually driven retrieval (recall), there should be absolutely no memory for typical information after about 96 days and no memory for atypical information after about 21 days. For data-driven retrieval, which accounts for most of the recognition data, there should be no memory for typical information after about 23 days and no memory for atypical information after about 44 days. Thus, nothing specific should be remembered about the scripted activities after 3 months. At that point, it may even be difficult to remember what scripts were presented. There would be no way to discriminate the acquisition experience from the generic script. It should be emphasized that these predictions are entirely plausible.

Alternative Explanations and Models

The SP+T model has provided a reasonable explanation of memory for typical and atypical information. In order to place the model in perspective, it is worthwhile to discuss some possible alternative explanations. Some colleagues have entertained the possibility that the data can be explained by simpler hypotheses or that the data are artifacts of some well-known variables that have been studied in verbal learning. However, these alternative explanations fall short of the mark when examined closely.

Some researchers have questioned whether the differences in memory for typical versus atypical actions can be more easily explained by a *resource allocation hypothesis*. According to this hypothesis, the comprehender allocates more cognitive resources to atypical than to typical items during comprehension (Bobrow and Norman, 1975; Hastie, 1980; Hastie and Kumar, 1979). Studies have in fact shown that observers fixate more often and for a longer duration on objects that are atypical of a pictorial scene (an octopus in a farm scene) than on typical objects (a tractor in a farm scene) (Loftus and Mackworth, 1978; Mackworth and Morandi, 1967). Consequently, it would not be very surprising that atypical items are remembered better. As an individual allocates more cognitive resources to an item, there is an increase in one or more of the following cognitive processes or operations: (a) amount of attention, (b) amount of rehearsal, (c) depth of conceptual elaboration within an item, (d) number of associations with other items, and (e) number of processing operations.

The SP+T model, on the other hand, asserts that memory discrimination reflects primarily the properties of the representational code. The amount of resources allocated to an item at best indirectly predicts memory discrimination. Similarly, the number of elaborations or associations with other items is not expected to explain the obtained data.

Available evidence appears to support the representational position rather than the resource allocation position. For example, it is difficult for the resource allocation explanation to account for the zero memory discrimination for very typical items; subjects must have allocated some resources to such items at input and yet there is no memory. A resource allocation hypothesis could perhaps patch up this deficit by asserting that some minimal amount of resources must be allocated at input in order for there to be later memory discrimination. When less than the minimal amount of resources are allocated at input, there would later be no memory discrimination.

There is other evidence that seems to be inconsistent with the resource allocation hypothesis. First, results from several experiments (Graesser et al., 1979; Jebousek, 1978; Kowalski and Graesser, 1979) have indicated that memory for actions is unaffected by various types and amounts of script distortions.

(1) When scripts were distorted by saturating them with more and more atypical items, recognition memory for the actions did not decrease.

(2) When scripts were distorted by the interruption of one script with another script, recognition memory for the actions did not decrease, compared to a condition in which there was no interruption.
(3) When actions from different scripts were interleafed, recognition memory for the actions did not decrease, compared to a condition in which actions from scripts were blocked and segregated.

These findings seem to be inconsistent with the resource allocation hypothesis. Fewer resources would presumably be allocated to a given action as a scripted activity became more distorted from its prototype. Again, the resource allocation hypothesis could perhaps take care of these problematic outcomes by assuming that more resources are allocated to a scripted activity as there are more and more deviations from the script prototype. However, the resource allocation hypothesis would have to add another rather strong assumption: as the comprehender allocates more cognitive resources when faced with script distortions, the comprehender allocates just enough additional resources to ensure that later memory for typical and atypical actions remains unaffected by the script distortions. This strong assumption is possibly correct, but does seem implausible.

Probably the most devastating problem with the resource allocation hypothesis is the third bit of evidence. Recall for typical actions is better than for atypical actions after longer retention intervals. A resource allocation hypothesis would clearly not predict this reversal.

Taken together, the evidence seems to argue against the resource allocation hypothesis. This conclusion agrees with the research in verbal learning on the von Restorff effect in which word lists were used as stimuli. The von Restorff effect is better explained by organizational properties than by the amount of rehearsal, attention, and effort that is applied to the items during acquisition (Bruce and Gaines, 1976).

Researchers have also questioned whether the typical and atypical items differ on extraneous dimensions. Perhaps other dimensions account for the patterns of memory instead of typicality. For example, atypical items might be more concrete or evoke more vivid mental images than the typical items. Do the differences in memory reflect extraneous biases? More detailed analyses of the data have consistently failed to support this possibility (Graesser et al., 1979). A very abstract, imageless word can be very salient when there is a background of concrete words that evoke vivid mental images. The list below is an example of this possibility.

Rock
Sidewalk
Brick
Idea
Stone

Again, the finding that most seriously challenges the "third-variable artifact" hypothesis is that recall is better for typical than atypical actions after long retention intervals. If concrete items are remembered better after short retention intervals, then the same trend should hold after long retention intervals. However, there is a crossover in recall memory for typical and atypical actions as a function of retention interval.

Extensions of the Model

One test of the generality of a model is to assess whether it can account for phenomena that lie within its scope of prediction but are unrelated to the specific conditions and materials that were used to test its adequacy. In this section we will examine whether the SP+T model can account for data in different paradigms.

Most of the studies reported in the previous section have focused on scripted activities as stimulus material. Can the SP+T model explain memory for stimulus materials in other knowledge domains? The answer appears to be "yes." In the third section of this chapter it was shown that the predictions hold for personality descriptions. Within a .5-hour retention interval, there is better memory for traits and actions that are atypical of a role or stereotype than those items that are typical. There are also several studies that have examined recognition memory for faces. Faces that are very unique, distinctive, and deviant from a prototype are more accurately recognized in a later recognition test than those that approach a facial prototype (Cohen and Carr, 1975; Going and Read, 1974; Light et al., 1979). Studies on memory for categorized word lists have shown that recognition memory is lower for those exemplars of a category that are more prototypical (Rabinowitz, Mandler, and Patterson, 1977; Schnur, 1977). For example, if the subject studied a list of bird items, there would be poorer recognition memory for a very typical bird (*robin*) than a bird that is less prototypical (*chicken*). The fact that the predictions of the SP+T model are supported for materials involving radically different knowledge domains, i.e., action schemas, person schemas, pictorial schemas, and exemplars of conceptual categories, suggests that the model should generalize to any knowledge domain.

A second area to which the SP+T model can be extended is prose retention after different retention intervals. In a recent literature review Gagne (1978) examined the roles of familiarity and retention interval in memory for prose. Gagne reported that memory is better for unfamiliar than for familiar material at all retention intervals when memory is assessed by a recognition test format (see also Graesser, Hauft-Smith, Cohen, and Pyles, 1980). However, recall for prose shows a more complex pattern of results. Unfamiliar passages are recalled better after short retention intervals, whereas familiar passages are recalled better after long retention intervals. These results are consistent with the SP+T model (see the sixth section of this chapter) if it is assumed that the statements in unfamiliar passages have a higher likelihood of being tagged as atypical. As was reported in Table 3.2, recognition memory is consistently better for atypical than typical information; however, recall shows better memory for atypical information at short retention intervals and better memory for typical information at long retention intervals. This complex pattern of memory performance has been reported to occur for picture memory (Goodman, 1978; Mandler, 1979) as well as connected discourse.

The SP+T model should also explain performance in cognitive tasks that indirectly involve memory retrieval. For example, consider judgment and decision processes. Atypical information is predicted to be weighted higher than typical information when individuals formulate decisions , make judgments, or predict future events (Levin, Ims, Simpson, and Kim, 1977). For example, in recommendations for individuals applying for jobs or graduate schools, the unusual comments that deviate from the normal person (or the normal outstanding person) tend to capture the attention of the evaluator and are salient in memory. The atypical characteristics may be weighted to the point of radically affecting important decisions despite the fact that the more typical attributes are more validly diagnostic in predicting later performance (Dawes, 1976; Kahneman and Tversky, 1973). Of course, more research is needed in order to determine whether the SP+T model can be extended to judgment and decision processes.

Another extension of the SP+T model is in the area of aesthetics. There is a curvilinear function that relates aesthetic preference and stimulus complexity (Rapoport, 1977; Smets, 1971). Individuals tend to appreciate simuli that deviate somewhat from the prototype. Individuals do not prefer stimuli that are perfectly consistent with one's expectations, or stimuli that drastically deviate from some prototype to the point that they can't be recognized. There seems to be an optimal incidence of tagging for keeping the cognitive system attentive. A completely predictable world is so dull that the comprehender ends up pursuing his or her daydreams and fantasies; a completely unpredictable world is so congested that the comprehender suffers an uncomfortable information overload.

4

The Conceptual Representation of Prose in Memory

During the past decade cognitive psychologists have explored how prose is represented in memory. Many of the representational theories have been influenced by theoretical advances in other areas in cognitive science. Linguistics and artificial intelligence have been particularly influential. Of course, psychological theories have specific goals that set them apart from the sister sciences.

One goal of any theory of prose representation is to provide a symbolic system that assigns conceptual representations to specific passages. A general theory would accommodate any passage. However, most of the available representational theories do not have such an ambitious goal as being able to assign a representation to any passage. Instead theories have focused on some subset of passages, such as stories or scripted passages. The scope of some representational theories is even more restricted. There are theories that attempt to capture the representation of only well-formed stories. Some theories focus only on those well-formed stories that are organized around a single protagonist; stories that have multiple protagonists with shifting character perspectives are outside their scope. The fact that a representational theory handles only a small subset of passages does not necessarily undermine its usefulness. Some of these theories have provided informative insights that would have been missed if the researcher had pursued a more general theory. Moreover, it is conceivable that comprehenders in fact categorize prose into different subclasses or genres, with distinct organizational processes associated with any given subclass.

Representational theories may be analyzed, categorized, and evaluated on dimensions other than scope. Can the theory successfully assign representations to those passages for which it is designed? What aspect of prose organization does the theory capture? Is the symbolic system that generates the representations of passages formally well defined or articulated sufficiently? Is the theory decisive in the sense that passages can be analyzed with little difficulty or ambiguity? Is the theory parsimonious? Is the theory explanatory? An answer to the latter question obviously depends on what phenomena and data the investigator intends to explain.

A psychological theory of prose representation attempts to explain behavioral data. This goal gives such a theory a unique status. The representation that is assigned to a passage should provide the basis for predicting or accounting for patterns of data that are collected from experiments on humans. Can the theory predict what information in a passage tends to be recalled? Can the theory explain reading times? Can the theory account for the answers given to questions about the passage? The necessity to explain behavioral data imposes constraints on a psychological theory of prose representation. These constraints are not necessarily imposed on theories in other disciplines in cognitive science.

What does it mean to have a good psychological theory of prose representation? One property of a good theory is that the theoretical representations correspond to the conceptual representations that humans in fact construct. However, psychologists do not know what the true conceptual representations look like. The problem is further complicated by the fact that representations are somewhat different for different comprehenders. We can say, in principle, that any given theory does not perfectly match the true conceptual representations. The best that can be hoped for is a good approximation to the true conceptual representations. Although we cannot make an absolute judgment about the goodness of approximation for any given theory, we can make a comparative judgment between theories. We can say that theory A is better than theory B in approximating the true conceptual representations that humans construct. One theory is better than another theory to the extent that it accounts for behavioral data with greater accuracy and completeness.

Some psychologists have been skeptical about the goals of a psychological theory of representation. The skeptics have worried about the indeterminacy of testing such theories. The argument goes as follows. First, there is no direct way of observing what these representations look like. Second, behavioral data do not allow the investigator to infer distinctly how input is cognitively represented because there are several different representational theories that could explain any given set of data. Therefore, the assertions of a psychological theory of representation are impossible to test (Anderson, 1978). The arguments of the skeptics, along with the counterarguments, have led to a controversy about the role of representational theories in psychology.

Many researchers do not worry about the indeterminacy problems of representational theories. Indeterminacy is an issue that confronts all scientific endeavors. It is reasonable to examine representational theories that naturally or easily map onto behavioral data. Assertions about representations may be based on goodness-of-fit or ease-of-fit to the empirical data. Theories of representations may be tested by observing how well they predict behavioral data or how easy it is to accommodate data already collected. The ability to predict outcomes before data collection is a convincing test of a theory, particularly when other theories offer no predictions or offer opposing predictions. Another test of a theory is its ability to account for data after the data are collected. A good theory would accommodate existing data more easily or more naturally than would alternative theories.

It can be argued that those who are skeptical of developing a representational theory have a rigid representation of how science progresses (pun intended). The skeptics' view of scientific progress seems to follow a metaphysical metaphor: scientific questions are worthwhile to pursue only when the answers can be objectively and uniquely established by direct observation of underlying mechanistic components. This seems to be an unnecessarily constraining requirement that ultimately may be impossible to fulfill. There is a problem in determining which observations are direct because all observations are interpreted from the perspective of some underlying conceptual system. Direct observation also does not solve the indeterminacy problem. Many theories can explain any given set of behavioral data, set of neurophysiological data, or set of "direct" observations.

From the present perspective, a preferable metaphor for scientific development is a knowledge and perception metaphor. The goal of scientists is to perceive mechanisms and to accumulate knowledge about these mechanism. Human perception and knowledge acquisition are not always based on certainty and direct observables; neither is scientific knowledge.

The virtue of scientific knowledge is that there are special tools of measurement and experimentation that assist in perceiving these mechanisms and defending theories of the mechanisms. As more knowledge accumulates from the data, and as a phenomenon is perceived from more diverse perspectives, there are fewer alternative theories that fit the data. Eventually, more scientists become convinced that a given theory is plausible.

Goals of the Proposed Theory of Prose Representation

As was mentioned earlier, a theory of representation can only be evaluated with respect to the goals that such a theory intends to achieve. It is therefore important to state these goals. In this chapter a representational system will be presented that appears to meet the goals described below, to a large extent. At the risk of being prematurely pretentious, this representational system will be called a theory. In Chapter 5, the theory will be evaluated by examining the extent to which it explains behavioral data.

The first goal is to arrive at a representational theory that can be applied to a diversity of passages. A theory that applies to only a single prose genre or a small set of passages is inadequate. Consequently, some psychological theories will be rejected because they do not meet this goal. Story grammars (Johnson and Mandler, 1980; Mandler and Johnson, 1977; Rumelhart, 1975; Stein and Glenn, 1979; Thorndyke, 1977) are too narrow in scope because they can only be applied to well-formed narratives and, even then, only to a subset of passages in the narrative genre. Another class of theories that will be rejected are schema-based theories that focus on a restricted class of schemas. A script-based theory (Cullingford, 1979; Schank and Abelson, 1977), for example, is too narrow in scope.

A second goal of the representational theory is to account for behavioral data that are collected in experiments on humans. The theory should provide the framework for predicting performance in a variety of tasks. In addition, the theory should provide some basis for accommodating trends that are not predicted in a strict sense. There are data in a variety of experimental tasks that call for an explanation. The theory should explain which passage statements tend to be retrieved during recall, and what statements are produced when humans summarize passages. Verification (truth) ratings of inferences call for explanation, as well as reading times for explicitly stated information. The theory should explain why certain answers are given to questions about information in the passage. There are theories of representation in artificial intelligence (Schank and Abelson, 1977) and linguistics (Grimes, 1975; Halliday and Hasan, 1976) that have not attempted to explain behavioral data. These theories are not necessarily wrong or to be rejected as candidates for the proposed theory; they simply have not been tested with respect to this goal.

A third goal of the proposed theory is to incorporate inferences that are made during comprehension. The theory should include a broad range of inferences that are generated by virtue of schematic knowledge. Thus, the inferences should not be restricted to those that are analytically necessary or those that are derived linguistically. This goal eliminates several psychological theories that have focused exclusively or primarily on explicitly stated information. The latter theories include Kintsch's theory of prose microstructure (Kintsch, 1974), most of the story grammars, and other psychological theories of prose structure (Crothers, 1972, 1979; Meyer, 1975). It is believed that inference processes are fundamental to the comprehension process and cannot safely be ignored.

It is important to specify the range of inferences that will be incorporated in the proposed representational system. Among the available psychological theories, there are substantial variations in the number and types of inferences that have been incorporated into prose representations. Psychologists have preserved a distinction between *propositional* (necessary) inferences and *pragmatic* inferences (Chaffin, 1979; Crothers, 1978, 1979; Harris and Monaco, 1978; Hildyard, 1979; Hildyard and Olson, 1978; Kintsch, 1974). Most psychological theories of prose representation have attempted to incorporate propositional inferences, but few theories have seriously attempted to incorporate pragmatic inferences. What is the difference between these two classes of inferences?

Propositional inferences are regarded as necessarily true because they can be directly derived from the semantic content of the explicitly stated propositions. Propositional inferences are based on linguistic features of predicates. For example, certain necessary inferences are derived from implicative verbs (*know, forget, pretend, dream*) that have propositional compliments (Hildyard and Olson, 1980; Macnamara, Baker, and Olson, 1976).

Explicit information: *Kathy forgot to take her pill.*
Inference: *Kathy did not take her pill.*

There are verbs of transfer and possession (*give, take, buy, sell, borrow, keep*) that specify who owns or possesses an object (Norman and Rumelhart, 1975; Stillings, 1975).

Explicit information: *Chris bought Jeanie a new car.*
Inference: *Jeanie has the car.*

Another type of linguistically based inference involves comparative terms (*bigger, smaller, taller, shorter, younger, older*):

Explicit information: *Sue is older than Tarie.*
Inference: *Tarie is younger than Sue.*

Some predicates possess transitive properties that permit the application of syllogistic reasoning for deriving inferences (Revlin and Mayer, 1978). For example, transitive inferences can be derived from linear orderings (Potts, 1974, 1977; Potts and Scholz, 1975).

Explicit information: *Sue is older than Tarie and Tarie is older than Karen.*
Inference: *Sue is older than Karen.*

Syllogistic reasoning can be applied when there are relationships that convey class inclusion (Frase, 1978; Griggs, 1978).

Explicit information: *Lea is a cognitive psychologist and a cognitive psychologist is a scientist.*
Inference: *Lea is a scientist.*

Some types of propositional inferences do not involve the construction of unstated expressions. Instead, they ascribe a truth value or an existential specification to expressions or elements that are more or less stated explicitly. For example, there are presuppositions (Clark, 1977; Crothers, 1978, 1979; van Dijk, 1973; Haviland and Clark, 1974; Loftus, 1975; MacWhinney and Bates, 1978).

Explicit information: *Lisa was delighted that UCLA accepted her into graduate school.*
Inference: *UCLA accepted Lisa into graduate school.*

Existential presuppositions specify that some person, object, or entity exists.

Explicit information: *John fell asleep.*
Presupposition: *John exists.*

All of these types of propositional inferences are regarded as necessarily true. It is perhaps for this reason that they have received the most attention in psychological research.

Pragmatic inferences are regarded as plausible inferences that are not necessarily true. Pragmatic inferences are generated by virtue of at least two sources of knowledge. One is a set of global schemas that the comprehender identifies when comprehending sentences and groups of sentences. The other is a set of conversational rules that are shared by speakers and listeners of a message or writers and readers of text (Bates, 1976; Clark, 1977; Grice, 1975; Norman and

Rumelhart, 1975; Searle, 1969). For example, there are conventional rules that specify that the speaker is conveying information that he believes to be true and that the speaker is attempting to be coherent. The pragmatic inferences are derived from knowledge sources beyond the explicit, linguistic input. Without the schematic knowledge and the conversational knowledge, the pragmatic inferences would never be made. Despite this fact and the fact that such inferences are not necessarily true, pragmatic inferences are critical for understanding the meaning of prose (Adams and Collins, 1979; Bransford and McCarrell, 1974).

It would be a weary task to enumerate the different types of pragmatic inferences. Pragmatic inferences are constructed from world knowledge and social knowledge. Consequently, a taxonomy of pragmatic inferences would perhaps be as rich as a taxonomy of social and world knowledge—very rich indeed. Nevertheless, there are some types of pragmatic inferences that have attracted the attention of experimental psychologists. There are pragmatic inferences that can be derived from isolated sentences. For example, the instruments with which actions are performed are often inferred rather than explicitly stated (Corbett and Dosher, 1978; Singer, 1979).

Explicit information:	*The hunter stabbed the wolf.*
Inference:	*The hunter used a knife.*

Some types of pragmatic inferences are invoked by virtue of the conversational rules and speech context of an utterance. For example, the perlocutionary force of an utterance (the impact on the listener) may be inferred from the illocutionary force of an utterance (the speech act that the speaker performed) (Austin, 1962; Schweller, Brewer, and Dahl, 1976).

Explicit information:	*Lea told her boss she was not paid enough.*
Inference:	*Lea asked her boss for a raise.*

There are pragmatic inferences that are constructed by virtue of global schemas, such as scripts (Bower et al., 1979; Cullingford, 1979; Graesser et al., 1979; Schank and Abelson, 1977).

Explicit information:	*Dave walked into the restaurant, sat down, ordered food, read a newspaper, paid the bill, and then left.*
Inference:	*Dave ate food.*

Although these pragmatic inference are not necessarily true, they are probably true and the comprehender often draws such inferences in order to understand the meaning of the explicit information.

There is an issue of controversy that has been investigated and debated by researchers in psychology and artificial intelligence. Which inferences are in fact constructed during prose comprehension? Presumably one subset of inferences is constructed during the comprehension process, whereas another subset is merely derived when the comprehender is later asked questions or tested on the prose passage. Researchers in artificial intelligence have pointed out that it would be unfeasible to assume that prose comprehension proceeds by generating all possible propositional and pragmatic inferences that are relevant to the passage. There would be a horrendous computational explosion problem (Rieger, 1975, 1977). Hundreds, if not thousands of inferences would be generated from a very short passage. Consequently, researchers in artificial intelligence have proposed algorithms and heuristics that attempt to reduce the number of inferences to a manageable and more realistic set (Schank, 1979a).

Psychologists have conducted experiments to assess whether or not certain types of inferences are actually drawn at comprehension and what conditions facilitate inference generation (Brewer, 1977; Chaffin, 1979; Corbett and Dosher, 1978; Frederiksen, 1975; Goetz, 1979; Harris and Monaco, 1978; Hayes-Roth and Walker, 1979; Hildyard, 1979; Hildyard and Olson, 1978; Keenan, 1978; Kintsch, 1974; Reder, 1979; Schweller et al., 1976; Singer, 1979; Stillings, 1975; Walker and Meyer, 1980). However, it is too early to offer detailed generalizations about which inferences are drawn at comprehension versus at test time. The issue is complicated by the fact that there may be substantial differences among comprehenders. There is one rather basic generalization that is accepted by many researchers in psychology. Many psychological models of prose representation assume that the comprehender draws just enough inferences to provide coherence or conceptual connectivity among propositions that are explicitly stated in prose (Clark, 1977; Crothers, 1978, 1979; van Dijk, 1977; Kintsch, 1974, 1979; Kintsch and van Dijk, 1978; Spilich et al., 1979; Vipond, 1980). Thus, if an inference is not needed for bridging a conceptual gap between any of the stated propositions, then it would probably not be generated during comprehension. This principle of coherence or bridging serves as one criterion for restricting the number of inferences drawn at comprehension and thereby minimizing a computational explosion problem. However, experimental evidence for this solution is not particularly strong. Psychologists and researchers in artificial intelligence do not really know how many inferences comprehenders generate during comprehension.

There presently is no psychological theory of prose representation that has met all of the goals stated above. This fact has two implications. First, there is a great deal of latitude in developing a satisfactory representational theory since there is no psychological theory available. Second, it would be worthwhile to consider some of the representational theories in the cognitive sciences that have not been tested by collecting data from human subjects. It would be especially important to explore those theories that incorporate pragmatic inferences. For the most part, pragmatic inferences have not been adequately dealt with in the available theories in psychology.

There are some theories available that have attempted to incorporate pragmatic inferences and have been designed to capture psychological processes. None of these theories has been substantially tested by experimental data. Some studies have focused on inferences in narrative prose (Beaugrande and Colby, 1979; Bower et al., 1979; Nicholas and Trabasso, 1980; Rumelhart, 1977c; Warren et al., 1979). The LNR group has explored inference generation when the comprehender interprets isolated sentences (Norman and Rumelhart, 1975), story passages (Rumelhart, 1977c), and other diverse forms of input (Rumelhart and Ortony, 1977). Inference processes have been incorporated in Schank's Conceptual Dependency Theory (Lehnert, 1978a; Schank, 1972, 1973, 1975; Schank and Abelson, 1977; Wilensky, 1978b, 1978c). These studies had a major impact on the formulation of the proposed system of representing prose.

System for Representing Prose

The proposed system for representing prose is designed for a broad range of prose passages. In principle, passages in all prose genres should be accommodated by the system. In this system it is assumed that schemas guide the interpretation of verbatim information and guide the generation of inferences. The proposed system is therefore designed to incorporate inferences as well as explicitly stated information. The purpose of this section is to describe a representational system that segments information into basic units and relates these units conceptually.

The basic unit of information is roughly equivalent to a proposition or statement. The basic unit will be called a ***statement node.*** The statement node consists of the proposition unit described in Chapter 1 except for two differences. First, the referential propositions, which are captured by nouns as predicates, will not be counted as separate propositions. For example, the sentence *The dragon kidnapped the daughters* contains three propositions according to Chapter 1.

P1: kidnap (C1,C2)
P2: dragon (C1)
P3: daughters (C2).

However, only one statement node would be assigned to this sentence; the referential propositions (P2 and P3) would not be counted.

The second deviation from the earlier propositional analysis involves verb predicates that have propositional complements. For example, consider the sentences and propositional analyses below.

(1) *The dragon knew that the daughters were in the woods.*
    P1: know (dragon, P2)
    P2: in (daughters, woods)
(2) *The dragon wanted to keep the daughters.*
    P1: want (dragon, P2)
    P2: keep (dragon, daughters)
(3) *The daughters told the dragon to go home.*
    P1: tell (daughters, dragon, P2)
    P2: go to (dragon, home)

In sentences 1, 2, and 3 there is a predicate (*know, want, tell*) that has an embedded proposition as one of the arguments. Although there are two propositions in each of these example sentences, there is only one statement node. (Of course, the embedded proposition may be counted as a separate statement node.) In order to clarify what constitutes a statement node, the reader might want to review the third section in Chapter 1 and to refer to the list of statement nodes in Table 4.1.

The proposed system of representing inferences and stated information involves three steps. For the moment, the issue of how inferences are identified will be ignored.

Step 1

Segment inferences and stated information into statement nodes.

Step 2

Assign each statement node to a node category.

Step 3

Interrelate the nodes by a network of labeled, directed arcs.

Step 1 has already been discussed. Information is segmented into basic statements that roughly corrrespond to propositions. Step 2 and Step 3 need to be clarified. What are the categories of nodes and arcs? What are the criteria for assigning specific nodes to node categories? What are the criteria for relating nodes by the labeled, directed arcs?

Categories of Nodes

There are six categories of nodes in the proposed system of representation.

Physical Event (PE)
Physical State (PS)
Internal Event (IE)
Internal State (IS)
Goal (G)
Style (S)

A brief description of each node category is provided in Table 4.1, along with some examples. Each statement node is assigned to one and only one of the six node categories. Although Table 4.1 provides a general impression of the node categories, the categories need to be elaborated further because they will be incorporated in the analyses presented in the remaining chapters. The reader will need to understand these categories well in order to understand subsequent chapters in this book.

Physical State Nodes. These statements convey ongoing states in the physical or social world. The physical world includes objects, properties of objects, characters, properties of characters, and spatial information. The physical world has ongoing attributes such as those captured in the statements below.

The book was on the table.
The briefcase was brown.
The hand was sweaty.
The forest was cold.

Table 4.1. Six Node Categories in the Proposed Representational System

Node category	Identification criterion	Examples
Physical State (PS)	Statement refers to an ongoing state in the physical or social world	*The dragon was large.* *The ant was unable to swim.* *The heroes were not married.*
Physical Event (PE)	Statement refers to a state change in the physical or social world	*The boy fell.* *The stream carried away the ant.* *The man became an uncle.*
Internal State (IS)	Statement refers to an ongoing state of knowledge, attitude, sentiment, belief, or emotion in a character	*The heroes knew about the dragon.* *The mother loved roses.* *The boy did not believe in God.*
Internal Event (IE)	Statement refers to a state change in knowledge, attitude, sentiment, belief, or emotion in a character	*The heroes became angry.* *The heroes heard the cries.* *The man recognized the ring.*
Goal (G)	Statement refers to an achieved or unachieved state that a character wants, needs, or desires. An *action* involves a character executing behavior and achieving a goal; there may be goals that are not achieved and plans that are not applied by executing behavior	*The dragon kidnapped the daughters.* *The lady told the man to stop.* *The ant stung the birdcatcher.* *The baby wanted to eat.* *The father watched television.*
Style (S)	Statement or phrase that refers to details about the style in which an action or event occurred	*X occurred quickly.* *C did something with a knife.* *C moved one foot at a time.*

These are ongoing states in the physical world. They remain constant as events unfold in a narrative. Physical states may be captured by negative statements as well as positive assertions.

The book was not in the room.
The briefcase was not red.
The hand was not dry.
The forest was not cold.

These are descriptions of static properties of the physical world.

The social world includes kinship relationships, political institutions in a society, and normative obligations in a society. Separate categories could perhaps be included that distinguish the social from the physical world in the representational system. However, the two worlds will be combined in the proposed system for the sake of parsimony. Properties of the social world usually have consequences on the physical world, but this fact is not the primary reason for combining physical states and social states. In fact, it would probably be desirable to distinguish between the two worlds when certain passages are analyzed. Since social states were relatively rare in the narrative and expository passages that were analyzed, the social states were combined with physical states. Listed below are some example statements about the social world that would be categorized as Physical States.

The Czar had three daughters.
The psychologists were married.
The raise was not constitutional.
Heroes are supposed to help people.

There are some other types of statements that are categorized as Physical States. Characters or objects may have certain potentials or lack of potentials to perform certain activities; such potentials are categorized as Physical States.

The ant was unable to swim.
The table could not be moved.

Points in time are categorized as Physical States.

X occurred on September 4, 1968.
Once upon a time . . .

Biological states of characters are categorized as Physical States.

The dog was hungry.
The ant was thirsty.
The disease was chronic.
The prince was horny.

Physical Event Nodes. These statements convey state changes in the physical and social worlds. As a result of some activity, a state may change from not existing to existing, or from existing to not existing. States get destroyed or created as activities unfold in the physical or social world. Objects or characters may change location.

The boy fell down.
The ball rolled from the kitchen to the living room.

The attributes of objects or characters may change.

The toast burned.
The soldier died.
The baby was born.

Both the location and the attributes of objects or characters may change as a result of some activity.

The plane crashed.
The train blew up.

In the social world, objects or people may change possession.

The house became sold.
The child became adopted.

All of these statements are examples of Physical Events.

For some statements it is impossible to determine whether a Physical State or a Physical Event is the appropriate category. Knowledge of the passage is often needed to distinguish states from events. For example, consider the statement *The radio was broken.* In the following context this statement is a Physical State.

*The student's apartment was always in shambles. The walls were dirty, the clothes were unwashed, and **the radio was broken.***

However, in the following context the same statement would be a Physical Event.

*Last night the students had a wild party. The rug was stained, the windows were smashed, and **the radio was broken.***

In the latter context the events of the wild party caused the radio to change from being in working order to being broken. It is important to reemphasize that the assignment of statements to categories often requires a background context. A statement in isolation is usually ambiguous; a statement embedded in context is rarely ambiguous (Lehnert, 1978a).

Internal State Nodes. These statements describe the ongoing mental and emotional states of animate beings. An Internal State may refer to an ongoing state of knowledge.

The daughters knew where the forest was.
The boy was aware of his temper.

Internal States include sentiments.

The child loves parades.
The guests hate liver.

Ongoing attitudes and beliefs are Internal States.

The mother believes in corporal punishment.
The students were against racism.

Emotions that span a long period of time are Internal States.

The patient was depressed.
The professor was frustrated.

Sometimes there is a fine and fuzzy line between Physical States and Internal States. In the proposed system, certain biological states (thirst and hunger) are Physical States, whereas cognitive and emotional states are Internal States. The skin does not separate the internal from the external; rather, the mind does. It would be pointless to defend a more specific dividing line between mind and body, or between internal and external. The division perhaps lies somewhere in the autonomic nervous system. The issue of how to categorize pain is an open question that has no important consequences on the proposed representational system.

Internal Event Nodes. These statements convey changes in knowledge, sentiment, attitude, belief, or emotion in animate beings.

The child became angry.
The soldier found out about the spies.
The scientist discovered the formula.

Changes in knowledge state are often accomplished by sensory organs.

The policeman saw the killer.
The camper heard the bear.
The dog smelled the food.
The citizens felt the earthquake.

The sensory organs provide the vehicle for the creation of knowledge in the minds of the characters. Sometimes knowledge may flow in or out of a character's consciousness or memory, which results in an Internal Event.

The daughters forgot about the promise.
The heroes remembered the password.

Again, it is important to emphasize that the passage context is often needed in order to decide whether a specific statement is an Internal State or an Internal Event. For example, *The mother was angry* is a state in the following context.

The clinical psychologist read the mother's case history. The mother had low self-esteem and was usually ill. The mother was angry.

The same statement refers to an event in the following context.

The father was drunk and penniless when he came home from work. The mother was angry.

In the latter context the mother changed from being not angry to being angry as a result of the father's irresponsibility.

Goal Nodes. The above categories of nodes describe aspects of either causally driven or static knowledge domains. Causally driven event sequences are continuously driven by *prior* events and states. For any given event, there was a set of events that causally led up to it. A given event is never determined by events and states that follow it. Consider the following sequence of events.

(1) *The stream was rushing hard.*
(2) *The boy was pulled under water.*
(3) *The boy drowned.*

The event of the boy being pulled under water (statement 2) was to some extent caused by the rushing of the stream (statement 1), but not by the boy's drowning (statement 3). Causally driven conceptualizations are believed to differ fundamentally from goal-driven conceptualizations. Goal-oriented conceptualizations involve animate beings trying to attain *future* events and states. Goal-driven conceptualizations involve intentional actions, desires, and planned behavior.

Goals are statements that convey achieved or unachieved desired states. Statements are marked as a Goal+ when the goal is eventually achieved, as a Goal– when the goal is not achieved, and a Goal? when it is unknown whether or not a goal is achieved. Intentional actions are categorized as a Goal+.

The dragon kidnapped the daughters.
The boy ran to the store.
The father watched the baseball game.

In each of these statements an animate agent executes an organized plan of behavior that ultimately achieves some goal. The dragon executed some unspecified sequence of behavior that ultimately led to the state of the daughters being kidnapped. The dragon desired this end state. The kidnapping certainly did not occur by accident and was unlikely to have been directed by a causally driven sequence of events, i.e., a tornado moving the dragon. Similarly, the boy's running to the store is intended rather than being accidental or causally driven. Watching a game involves an organized strategy of moving one's eyes and focusing one's attention. Intentional actions always involve goals. Whereas Physical Events are causally driven, intentional actions are goal-driven. Of course, actions do involve physical behavior and therefore operate as events in some sense. The behavioral aspect of actions may causally drive subsequent events that may either be intended or not intended. Thus, actions (Goal+) have both an intentional aspect and a behavioral aspect that operates as an event (Searle, 1980). Physical Events, on the other hand, do not have an intentional aspect.

Again, it is sometimes difficult to decide whether a statement is a Physical Event or a Goal+ without knowing about the passage context. Consider *The man tripped the thief* in the following passages.

A thief stole a man's wallet in a parking lot. The man started running after the thief and finally caught up to him. The man tripped the thief and took back his wallet.

A thief robbed a store, started running down the street, and turned the corner. A man was carrying a ladder in the side street. The thief ran so quickly that he didn't see the man and the man tripped the thief. The startled man helped the thief up and apologized.

Sometimes goals are not achieved by characters in a passage but are nevertheless desired. The character may have executed some behavior in order to obtain the goal but ultimately failed.

The father tried to paint the ceiling.
The father never finished painting the ceiling.

Characters sometimes have a goal but never initiate a plan to achieve the goal. Unachieved goals can often be identified by such verbs as *want, desire, need, hope for,* and *wish.*

The politician wanted to be president.
The child wished he was an astronaut.

Style Nodes. These statements modify an action (Goal+) or an event. Style statements may convey information about the speed or intensity of an action or event.

X occurred quickly.
C did something quickly.
X occurred forcefully.
C did something forcefully.

A Style node may convey information about the instrument with which some action is accomplished.

C did something with a knife.
C did something with his fist.
C did something with his wit.

Actions and events occur with a specific quality of manner.

C moved one foot at a time.
X occurred in circles.

When actions or events occur, there may be movements in some direction.

The ball moved toward a tree.
The dragon carried the daughters toward the cave.

These statements that modify and qualitatively embellish an action or event are Style nodes.

Categories of Arcs

The specific nodes of a passage are structurally related by labeled, directed arcs. There are five categories of arcs in the proposed representational system.

Reason (R)
Initiate (I)
Consequence (C)
Manner (M)
Property (P)

Each arc category relates nodes of a specific category. Moreover, the nodes are related in a specific direction. The arc categories are defined in Table 4.2.

Reason Arcs. These arcs structurally relate Goal nodes. The Goal nodes and Reason arcs form the heart of goal-oriented conceptualizations. Organized action sequences are mediated by a structure of Goal nodes that are usually related in an hierarchical fashion. A character forms Goal 1 in order to achieve Goal 2. Goal 2 is constructed in order to achieve Goal 3, and so on. The goal hierarchy captures what some people call instrumental activity or means-end analyses.

The execution of organized action sequences involves problem solving. A person has a goal of ingesting a ham sandwhich. In order to eat the sandwich, the person must make the sandwich. In order to make the sandwich, the person must get the ingredients and prepare the sandwich. In order to get the ingredients, the person walks to the cupboard. Goal hierarchies are believed to underlie intentional activity and problem solving (Becker, 1975; Charniak, 1977; McDermott, 1978; Miller et al., 1960; Newell and Simon, 1972). These Goal structures are prevalent in narrative prose, as well as other genres of prose (Abbott and Black, 1980; Black and Bower, 1980; Bruce and Newman, 1978; Graesser, 1978a; Lichtenstein and Brewer, 1980; Rumelhart, 1977c; Schank and Abelson, 1977; Schmidt, 1976; Schmidt et al., 1978; Wilensky, 1978b). The Goal nodes are linked by Reason arcs. If Goal *n* is a subgoal of Goal *n*+1, then the two Goal nodes are related by the Reason arc in a forward direction.

$$\langle \text{Goal } n \rangle \quad \overset{R}{\rightarrow} \quad \langle \text{Goal } n{+}1 \rangle$$

It is believed that Goals are related in a hierarchical fashion. This means that any given Goal node is directly subordinate to at most one Goal node. A Goal hierarchy for getting a plant is presented in Figure 4.1.

A person goes to a plant store (G3) *and pays the clerk $4* (G4) *in order to buy a plant* (G2).

The person buys the plant (G2) *in order to have the plant* (G1).

Each Goal node has at most one Reason arc directly emanating from it in a forward direction ($\overrightarrow{R}$). However, a Goal node may dominate more than one subgoal. Goal 2 directly dominates Goal 3 and Goal 4. Goal 3 and Goal 4 emanate from Goal 2 by Reason arcs in the backward direction ($\overleftarrow{R}$). The claim here is that

Table 4.2. Arc Categories That Interrelate Nodes

Arc Category	Definition	Example
Reason (R)	One Goal node is a reason for another Goal node	*The dragon's kidnapping the daughters* (G1) is a reason for *the dragon's carrying off the daughters* (G2) $\langle G2 \rangle \xrightarrow{R} \langle G1 \rangle$
Initiate (I)	A State or Event node initiates a Goal node	The state of *being hungry* (PS) initiates the goal of *ingesting food* (G) $\langle PS \rangle \xrightarrow{I} \langle G \rangle$
Consequence (C)	A State, Event, or action (Goal+) node has the consequence of another State or Event node	*The ant being pulled under water* (PE1) has the consequence of *the ant drowning* (PE2) $\langle PE1 \rangle \xrightarrow{C} \langle PE2 \rangle$
Manner (M)	An Event or action (Goal+) node occurs with some style (Style or Goal node)	*The man walked* (G+) *in a manner that was quick* (S) $\langle G+ \rangle \xrightarrow{M} \langle S \rangle$
Property (P)	A character, object, or entity has some property that is a State node	*The man owned a jacket* (PS1) *that was red* (PS2) $\langle \text{Argument of } PS1 \rangle \xrightarrow{P} \langle PS2 \rangle$

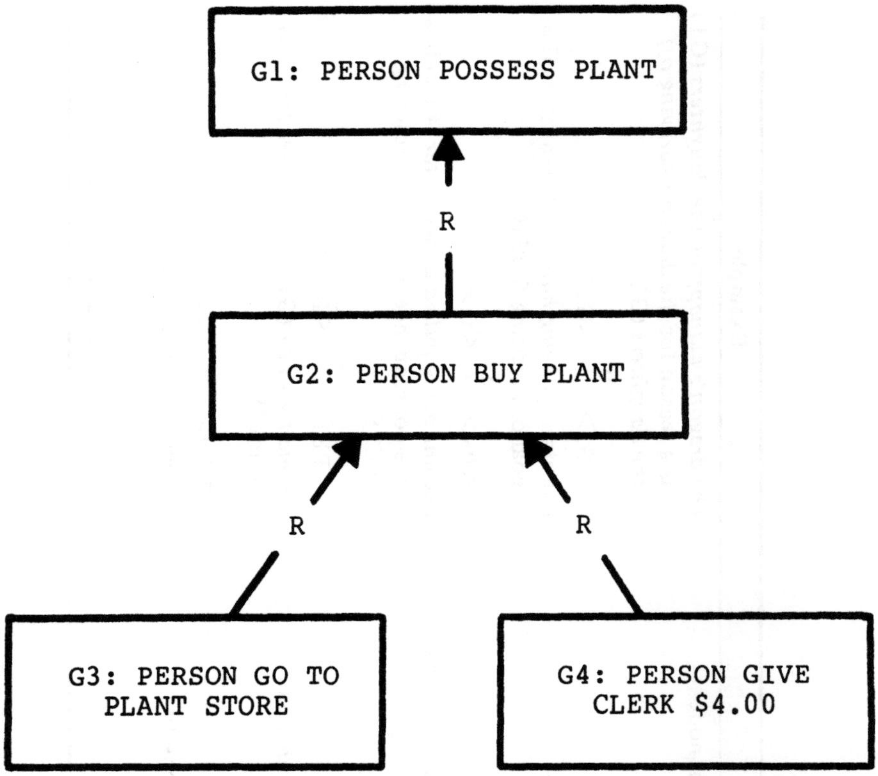

Figure 4.1. Goal-oriented hierarchical structure for buying a plant with Goal nodes.

Goal nodes are structurally related in a hierarchical fashion. However, the extent to which Goal structures are strictly hierarchical is an empirical question. The alternative would be a network structure in which a given Goal node can be dominated by more than one superordinate node. In either case, the first rule for generating Goal nodes is shown below. Note: An asterisk signifies that there may be more than one Goal node.

$$\textbf{Rule 1.}\quad \langle(\text{Goal*})\rangle \overset{R}{\rightarrow} \langle\text{Goal}\rangle$$

Initiate Arcs. Goals are created from somewhere. The goals of a character are initiated by states, events, and also actions of other characters. Initiate arcs link states, actions, and events to Goal nodes. Figure 4.2 includes a graph structure which illustrates how certain states and events initiate the goals in the plan for getting a plant. The four Goal nodes are initiated by specific states of the world.

The fact that *the person likes plants* (IS5) initiates the Goal of *possessing a plant* (G1).

The fact that *plants cost money* (PS6) initiates the Goal of *the person buying a plant* (G2).

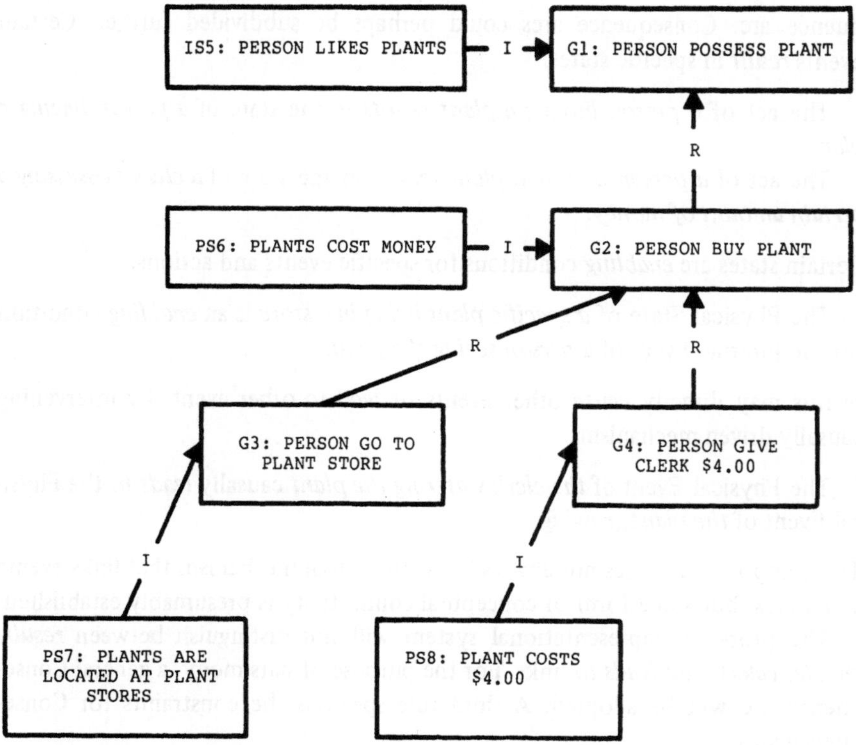

Figure 4.2. Goal-oriented hierarchical structure for buying a plant with Goal nodes and Goal initiators.

The fact that *plants are located at plant stores* (PS7) initiates the Goal of *going to a plant store* (G3).

The fact that *the plant of the person's choice costs $4* (PS8) initiates the Goal of *the person giving the clerk $4* (G4).

Thus, for every Goal node in a hierarchy, there are certain initiating states or events. In other words, the specific Goal hierarchy that a character establishes is sensitive to the context of existing states and events.

The states and events that initiate goals are ultimately internal events or states. Such information must be in the minds of the characters in order to create goals. This implies the rule below.

$$\textbf{Rule 2.}\quad < \begin{Bmatrix} \text{Internal State*} \\ \text{Internal Event*} \end{Bmatrix} > \quad \overset{I}{\rightarrow} \quad < \text{Goal} >$$

Physical events and states lead to internal events and states by perceptual activities.

Consequence Arcs. States, events, and actions may lead to other states and events by causally driven mechanisms. Similarly, states may be needed to enable or disenable events. Causal links and enabling links are captured by the Consequence arc. Consequence arcs could perhaps be subdivided further. Certain events *result* in specific states.

The act of *a person buying a plant* ***results*** in the state of *a person having a plant.*

The act of *a person buying a plant* ***results*** in the state of *a clerk possessing a certain amount of money.*

Certain states are *enabling* conditions for specific events and actions.

The Physical State of *a specific plant being in a store* is an ***enabling*** condition for the Internal Event of *a person seeing the plant.*

Events may directly *cause* other events or *lead to* other events by intervening causally driven mechanisms.

The Physical Event of *the clerk watering the plant* causally ***leads to*** the Physical Event of *the plant growing.*

The comprehender does not always know the causal mechanism that links events and states, but some form of conceptual connectivity is presumably established.

The proposed representational system will not distinguish between *result, enable, cause,* and *leads to* links. For the purpose of parsimony, a general Consequence arc will be adopted. A third rule specifies the constraints for Consequence arcs.

$$\textbf{Rule 3.}\quad < \begin{Bmatrix} \text{State} \\ \text{Event} \\ \text{Goal+} \end{Bmatrix} > \;\overset{C}{\rightarrow}\; < \begin{matrix}\text{State}\\ \text{Event}\end{matrix} >$$

Rule 3 is a very general rule that perhaps does not capture certain restrictions on causality. First, internal states and events cannot directly cause physical states and events, since telekinesis violates the average comprehender's view of causality. Second, a set of states alone cannot directly cause an event. An event is caused by a prior event together with a set of enabling states. Thus, there must be some prior event that starts the process going and ultimately leads to the event in question. These additional constraints have interesting implications but will nevertheless not be captured in the proposed representational system.

Causally driven conceptualizations are captured by a configuration of State and Event nodes. It is believed that causal conceptualizations are normally organized in a network fashion, in contrast to the hierarchically structured, goal-oriented conceptualizations (Graesser, Robertson, Lovelace, and Swinehart, 1980).

Figure 4.3 presents an example network for a causal conceptualization involving a plant falling from a shelf onto the toe of a clerk. The clerk becomes aroused by two chains of events. First, there is the arousal from the painful toes. Second, there is the arousal from the noise. Two separate event chains cause the arousal. Notice that a structure loop is formed from nodes 13, 16, 17, 18, and 19. These loops often occur in network structures, but rarely in hierarchical structures.

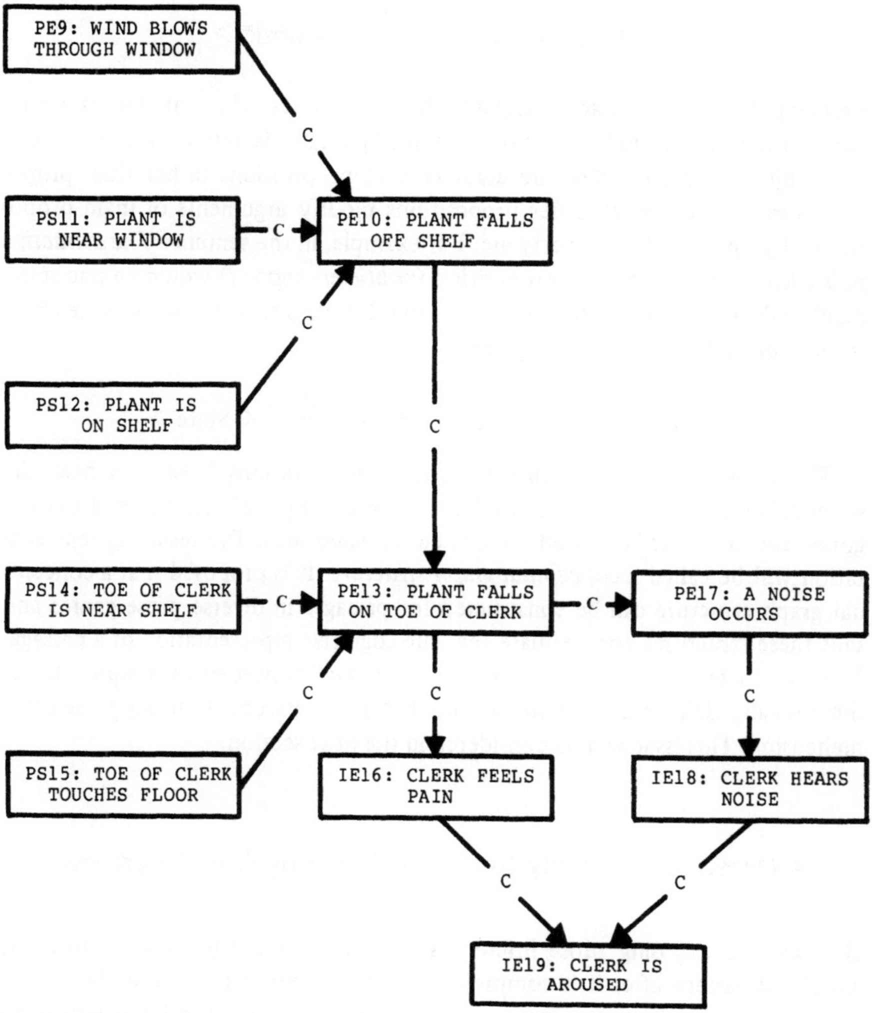

Figure 4.3. Causally oriented network structure for a plant falling off a shelf.

Manner Arcs. Actions (Goal+) and events may occur with some style. The Style nodes are connected to the Goal+ and Event nodes by Manner arcs. Therefore, there is a fourth rule.

$$\textbf{Rule 4.} \quad < \begin{Bmatrix} \text{Event} \\ \text{Goal+} \end{Bmatrix} > \quad \overset{M}{\rightarrow} \quad <\text{Style}>$$

Sometimes Goal nodes are connected to other Goal nodes by Manner arcs rather than Reason arcs. This occurs when subgoals embellish the style of some action but are not necessary for accomplishing the primary goal. For example, the person who buys the plant may unfold the four dollar bills when giving the clerk the four dollars. Such an action (Goal+) satisfies a separate "courtesy" goal (the person wants to be courteous), but does not *necessarily* function as a necessary subgoal for transferring the four dollars. Consequently, there is another rule that relates Goal nodes by Manner arcs:

Rule 5. $\langle \text{Goal+} \rangle \overset{\text{M}}{\rightarrow} \langle \text{Goal*} \rangle$

Property Arcs. Objects and characters have attributes. These attributes are related to the objects and characters by Property arcs. It is important to point out that objects and characters are arguments of propositions rather than propositions in themselves. Modifier propositions modify arguments of main propositions by virtue of the Property arc. For example, in the sentence *The attractive politician tripped*, the main proposition (*politician tripped*) would be one statement node with an argument (*politician*) that is linked to a statement node (*politician is attractive*) via a Property arc.

Rule 6. $\langle \text{Argument of node} \rangle \overset{\text{P}}{\rightarrow} \langle \text{State} \rangle$

The three steps of constructing prose representations have now been described. Statements that are inferred or mentioned explicitly are assigned to categories and structurally related by labeled, directed arcs. The resulting representation will be called a *conceptual graph structure.* It is proposed that a conceptual graph structure can be constructed for passages in diverse prose genres and that these structures approximate the true cognitive representation of a passage. In order to test these claims, however, a method is needed for empirically or theoretically delineating the inferences that are constructed during prose comprehension. This issue will be considered in the next section.

A Question-Answering Method of Exposing Prose Inferences

One way of exposing prose inferences is to ask the comprehender questions about the passage after it is comprehended. The experimenter resembles a news reporter who questions an expert, a victim, or a witness about an important event or situation. There are several questions that could be asked.

Why?
How?
Who?
What?
Where?
When?
How much (many)?
What kind?

The list goes on. Answers to such questions include inferences that the comprehender made during comprehension and also inferences that can be derived from the stored representation during question answering. For the moment, the issue will not be discussed as to which inferences were constructed during comprehension versus those derived at question answering.

Graesser (Graesser, 1978a; Graesser, Robertson, and Anderson, 1981; Graesser, Robertson, Lovelace, and Swinehart, 1980) has used a question-answering (Q/A) method for examining the inferences that are drawn when scripted passages and stories are comprehended. Answers to *why* questions exposed the reasons, causes, and initiating states of actions and events in narrative. The Q/A procedure is straightforward.

Step 1

The subject reads or listens to a passage.

Step 2

The subject answers a *why* question (and possibly other questions) about each statement in the passage.

Consider the following short passage.

A person went to a plant store and paid $4 for a plant. A plant fell off the shelf and landed on the clerk's toe.

After listening to this passage the comprehender would answer the following questions.

Why did the person go to the plant store?
Why did the person pay for the plant?
Why did the person pay $4?
Why did a plant fall off the shelf?
Why did the plant land on the clerk's toe?

The answers to these questions expose a large number and variety of inferences. The following is a sample Q/A protocol (see Figures 4.2 and 4.3).

Why did the person go to a plant store?
In order to get a plant (G1).
Because the person likes plants (IS5).
In order to buy a plant (G2).
Because plants are located at plant stores (PS7).
Why did a plant land on the clerk's toe?
Because the plant fell off the shelf (PE10).
Because the clerk's toe was near the shelf (PS14).

The answers include many of the nodes shown in Figures 4.2 and 4.3. Many of the nodes were never explicitly stated in the passage but were nonetheless involved in the interpretation of the passage. The Q/A method exposes these inferences.

The Q/A method does not expose all of the inferences that are generated during comprehension, but it does expose a large number of them. There are two ways to expose an increasing number of inferences. First, a statement may be probed with more categories of questions.

Why did the person go to the plant store?
How did the person go to the plant store?

When did the person go to the plant store?
What is the person like?
What is the plant store like?
Where is the plant store?

Previous research has shown that *why* questions and *how* questions generate the bulk of the information that is needed to construct conceptual graph structures for the narrative passages. Such questions expose the reasons, causes, enabling states, goal initiators, and so on. This information forms the heart of narrative representations (see Nicholas and Trabasso, 1980; Warren et al., 1979).

Answers to *where, what,* and *who* questions include a set of properties that are normally less critical, i.e., the fringe of the narrative representations. The representations examined in this chapter are based on answers to *why* questions and *how* questions.

A second way of exposing more prose inferences is simply to instruct the subject to answer questions more completely, with more detail. In the *standard* Q/A method, subjects give whatever answers seem informative and relevant to the question. In the *extended* Q/A method, the subjects are encouraged to give many answers, including information that would seem rather obvious. For example, subjects were instructed to give a minimum of four lines of information per question in the studies reported in this chapter.

The answers generated by the Q/A method include inference nodes in addition to statements that were explicitly mentioned in the passage. As a result, there are two sets of nodes to be included in the conceptual graph structures: (a) statements that were explicitly stated in the passage, and (b) inferences that were generated by the Q/A method.

Subjects occasionally became sarcastic, humorous, or off the wall when answering questions. Fortunately, there is a way to eliminate these bizarre answers. An answer was included in the analyses only when it was generated by at least two subjects. Although subjects are occasionally humorous, they are rarely off the wall in exactly the same way. Generally speaking, only a small proportion of the inference nodes (5%) are bizarre, and these inferences were eliminated by the criterion of having to be generated by at least two people.

Judgments need to be made as to which basic answers among the Q/A protocols have the same gist or meaning. In previous applications of the Q/A method this was accomplished by two steps.

Step 1

Decide which answer nodes have the same meaning when analyzing the various subjects' protocols for a specific question. It is possible to compute the proportion of subjects that generate a specific answer node for a specific question.

Step 2

Decide which answer nodes generated from different questions have the same meaning. It is possible to compute how many questioned statements generate a specific answer node.

Estimates have been made of interjudge reliability for these decisions. These estimates are substantially high, but do vary from passage to passage. Decisions on narrative passages normally have a somewhat higher interjudge reliability than those on expository passages. Interjudge reliability scores are slightly higher for Step 1 decisions than Step 2 decisions. Training judges on the representational system obviously improves reliability scores.

How may interjudge reliability scores be computed? The scoring procedure that has been used is fairly straightforward. Suppose that the subjects generate N basic answers to a given question. The objective is to determine which answers capture the same meaning. A judge is then presented all possible pairs of answers and gives a **YES/NO** decision as to whether the two answers of each pair have the same or a very similar meaning. There would be $N \times (N-1)/2$ possible pairs. An interjudge reliability score between *two* judges is computed as the proportion of decisions that the two judges agree on.

When judges are trained on the representational system, reliability scores are rather impressive. Reliability scores are approximately .90 for Step 1 decisions and .85 for Step 2 decisions. The scores are substantially lower when judges are not trained. The analyses reported in this chapter are based on decisions by trained judges.

Once Steps 1 and 2 are completed, a Q/A matrix is prepared that summarizes which answer nodes are generated from specific questions. Suppose that n statements in a passage are probed with why questions, yielding a set of explicitly stated nodes: $S_1, S_2, \cdots, S_n$. The answers to the questions sometimes refer to other statements in the passage that were explicitly stated, in addition to a set of unique inference nodes: $I_1, I_2, \cdots, I_m$. Thus, there is a total of $(m+n)$ nodes. For every probed statement, S_i, and specific node, N_j, there is a corresponding likelihood, p_{ij}, that the specific node is generated from the question:

$$p_{ij} = p(N_j/S_i).$$

This proportion is estimated by the proportion of subjects that give answer N_j to the probed statement S_i.

After the total set of nodes $(N_1, N_2, \cdots, N_{m+n})$ has been prepared, each node is assigned to a node category. The assignment of nodes to categories can be accomplished with high interjudge reliability provided that two conditions are met. First, the judges need to be sufficiently trained on the representational system. Second, the judges need to know about the passage content and context when making the decisions. Without knowledge of how a node fits in with the passage context, many decisions are completely ambiguous, as was discussed earlier. When these two conditions are met, the assignment of nodes to categories has substantial interjudge reliability scores (.70 or higher). Certain inconsistencies among judges frequently occur. Judges occasionally disagree whether a node is an Event versus a State, or Internal versus Physical. Whenever inconsistencies between judges arise, the node is assigned to the category that most judges assign it to.

The final step in constructing conceptual graph structures is to interrelate the labeled nodes by labeled, directed arcs. This is clearly the most challenging step in the analysis. It is analogous to solving a difficult puzzle. Judges clearly need to be highly trained when facing the task of structurally relating the nodes. It is difficult to evaluate the interjudge reliability in this final step, but a few remarks can be made. First, judges seem to agree more and more as there is more feedback among judges as to why they made their decisions when disagreements arise. Second, as structures are analyzed and reanalyzed a point is reached when judges become reasonably happy with the most recent version of a conceptual graph structure. At some point the debates cease, and a toast is made to the artistic creation.

It is important to mention that the judges do impose certain decisions on the shape and wiring of the representations when interrelating the nodes with arcs. These decisions lack a methodological purity that is appreciated in experimental psychology. The subsequent analyses will relax a certain degree of methodological purity in order to arrive at some solution for the objectives. At the same time, it is important to mention that the construction of the conceptual graph structures is not a completely subjective creation that is invented by the investigators. Subjects, not investigators, generated the nodes. Moreover, the puzzle must fit within the constraints of a representational system; the Reason, Initiate, Consequence, Manner, and Property arcs have specific constraints that must be reckoned with. The graph structures are neither completely objective nor completely subjective concoctions; they are somewhere between the two extremes. The question of whether the conceptual graph structures approximate true cognitive representation will be answered by observing whether they account for behavioral data in experiments that impose cleaner methods. Having made these hedges and humble remarks, it is time to embark on more substantial issues. What do the empirically derived conceptual graph structures look like? This question will be examined in the next section.

Conceptual Graph Structures for Narrative Passages

In a study by Graesser et al. (1981), conceptual graph structures were constructed for the four short narrative passages in Table 4.3. The graph structures were empirically derived from Q/A protocols using the analytical procedures described in the previous section.

A few details about the data collection should be mentioned. Q/A protocols were collected from eight college students who were paid $25 for participation. A computer monitored the entire course of the study. The computer presented each passage on a display scope, presented the questions, and collected the answer protocols which the subjects typed into a terminal. The study involved the following five phases:

Table 4.3. Narrative Passages

The Czar and His Daughters

Once there was a Czar who had three lovely daughters. One day the three daughters went walking in the woods. They were enjoying themselves so much that they forgot the time and stayed too long. A dragon kidnapped the three daughters. As they were being dragged off they cried for help. Three heroes heard the cries and set off to rescue the daughters. The heroes came and fought the dragon and rescued the maidens. Then the heroes returned the daughters to their palace. When the Czar heard of the rescue, he rewarded the heroes.

The Boy and His Dog

A boy was holding a dog by a leash when the leash broke. The dog ran away and the boy fell. A rabbit looked at the dog as the dog ran past him. When a fox saw the dog, the fox and the dog started fighting and the rabbit started running. The fox chased the dog and the dog chased the rabbit. The rabbit jumped into a hole. Then the dog jumped into the hole to safety. Soon the rabbit met the dog. Some rabbits gave the dog carrots and rode on him. When the dog left, the rabbits cried. The dog returned to the sad boy. The boy hugged the dog and they were happy to be together again.

John at Leone's

John went to New York by bus. On the bus he talked to an old lady. When he left the bus, he thanked the driver. He took the subway to Leone's. On the subway his pocket was picked. He got off the train and entered Leone's. He had some lasagna. When the check came, he discovered he couldn't pay. The management told him he would have to wash dishes. When he left, he caught a bus to New Haven.

The Ant and the Dove

A thirsty ant went to a river. He became carried away by the rush of the stream and was about to drown. A dove was sitting in a tree overhanging the water. The dove plucked a leaf and let it fall. The leaf fell into the stream close to the ant and the ant climbed onto it. The ant floated safely to the bank. Shortly afterwards, a birdcatcher came and laid a trap in the tree. The ant saw his plan and stung him on the foot. In pain the birdcatcher threw down his trap. The noise made the bird fly away.

(1) **Reading the passages.** Subjects read each of the four passages (Table 4.3) on three separate occasions.
(2) **Standard Q/A with *why* questions.** For each statement in a passage there was a corresponding *why* question. Subjects typed their answers into a computer. Statements were questioned in the same order as they appeared in the passage.
(3) **Standard Q/A with *how* questions.** For each statement in a passage there was a corresponding *how* question that subjects answered.

(4) **Extended Q/A with *why* questions.** *Why* questions were again asked for each statement. Subjects were told to type in answers that filled up at least four lines of text per question.
(5) **Extended Q/A with *how* questions.** *How* questions were again asked for each statement and subjects typed in a minimum of four lines per question.

Subjects were told to type in as much relevant information as they could think of in the extended Q/A phase. Subjects were told to include information that is true no matter how obvious it seemed to be.

The four passages sample a diversity of narrative forms. The passages have also been analyzed by other researchers. *The Czar and His Daughters* has been parsed by more than one story grammar (Johnson and Mandler, 1980; Rumelhart, 1975) and follows a conventional format for a simple story. *John at Leone's* is a script-based passage that has been analyzed by Schank and Abelson's (1977) computer program called the Script Applier Mechanism (**SAM**). *John at Leone's* is difficult or impossible to parse by available story grammars. *The Ant and the Dove* is a passage analyzed by Meehan (1977), who developed a computer program called **TAILSPIN** that generates simple stories. *The Ant and the Dove* is not script based, but can be parsed by some story grammars. *The Boy and His Dog* is not script based and cannot be parsed by available story grammars. This passage was selected from a chapter by Kintsch (1977b). *The Boy and His Dog* and the three other passages can be organized by Kintsch's microstructure theory. The selected passages therefore covered a large range of narrative forms.

A conceptual graph structure was constructed for each passage, thanks to the help of several members of the Cognitive Research Group at California State University at Fullerton who served as judges. A complete analysis of *The Czar and His Daughters* is provided in Table 4.4. Table 4.4 includes a listing of the node descriptions, along with the node categories that were assigned to each node. The nodes are listed in the left-hand column, and the arcs that relate the nodes are listed in the right-hand. The arcs are specified in a list format because it is cumbersome to draw a figure with over a hundred labeled nodes that are structurally related by labeled, directed arcs. However, sections of the structure will be captured by figures when specific points are to be made.

The analysis in Table 4.4 shows that a large number of inferences are generated from the Q/A method. In the Czar story there were 157 inference nodes and 19 stated nodes. Thus, there was a ratio of 8.26 inference nodes to 1 stated node. This ratio was roughly constant among stories. The ratio was 8.60, 8.0, and 8.0 in *The Ant and the Dove, The Boy and His Dog,* and *John at Leone's,* respectively. It appears that the stated information only skims the surface of the conceptualizations that are constructed when a passage is comprehended.

Most of the inference nodes were generated in the extended Q/A task. Among the four stories, .72 of the inference nodes were generated only in the extended Q/A task, whereas .28 were generated in the standard Q/A task (and usually also in the extended Q/A task). The number of generated nodes per questions did not differ significantly between *why* and *how* questions. An interesting outcome was that the extended Q/A procedure probed more knowledge than the standard Q/A procedure, but the quality of the answers did not decline. The mean proportion of subjects that generated a specific node in the extended Q/A method was equal to that in the standard Q/A method, .42 and .41, respectively. Thus, as subjects are requested to give more and more detailed answers, they do not give less plausible answers that have lower intersubject reliability; the subjects merely give more answers.

Table 4.4 shows that most of the nodes were categorized as Goals. Among the four stories, the nodes were distributed as shown below.

Goal	.52
Style	.09
Physical State	.12
Physical Event	.14
Internal State	.06
Internal Event	.07

Most of the Style nodes embellished Goal nodes rather than Physical Event nodes. Therefore, most of the nodes captured information about intentional, goal-oriented conceptualizations (.61). Physical States and Events are part of causally oriented conceptualizations and constituted .26 of the nodes. Information about the Internal States and Events of characters comprised .13 of the nodes.

Table 4.4 provides an impression of how the arcs were distributed among the five arc categories. Most of the arcs were Reason and Consequence arcs. Among the four stories, the arcs were distributed as shown below.

Reason	.48
Manner	.07
Initiate	.15
Consequence	.29
Property	.01

When the arc distributions and node distributions are considered together, it appears that roughly two-thirds of the graph structures consist of goal-oriented conceptualizations and one-third consists of causally oriented conceptualizations. Goal-oriented conceptualizations include Reason, Initiate, and Manner arcs that interrelate Goal and Style nodes. Causally oriented conceptualizations involve Consequence arcs that interrelate Event and State nodes. The interface between goal-oriented and causally oriented domains includes (a) the events and states that initiate goals and (b) goal-driven actions that causally lead to state changes in the physical, social, and internal domains. In order to obtain a clearer understanding of the graph structures, some figures will be presented that capture sections of the empirically generated graph structures.

Table 4.4. List of Labeled Nodes and Labeled, Directed Arcs in *The Czar and His Daughters*

	Nodes	Arcs
(0)[a]	PS: There were three daughters	$\langle \text{PS12} \rangle \overset{\text{P}}{\rightarrow} \langle \text{PS0} \rangle$
(1)	G−: Czar have sons	$\langle \text{IS2} \rangle \overset{\text{I}}{\rightarrow} \langle \text{G−1} \rangle$
(2)	IS: Czar liked boys more than girls	$\langle \text{G+3} \rangle \overset{\text{R}}{\rightarrow} \langle \text{G−1} \rangle$
(3)	G+: Czar had children	$\langle \text{G+4} \rangle \overset{\text{R}}{\rightarrow} \langle \text{G+3} \rangle$
(4)	G+: Wife had children	$\langle \text{G+5} \rangle \overset{\text{R}}{\rightarrow} \langle \text{G+4} \rangle$
(5)	G+: Czar married wife	$\langle \text{G+6} \rangle \overset{\text{R}}{\rightarrow} \langle \text{G+4} \rangle$
(6)	G+: Czar got wife pregnant	$\langle \text{G+7} \rangle \overset{\text{R}}{\rightarrow} \langle \text{G+6} \rangle$
(7)	G+: Czar had sex with wife	$\langle \text{G+6} \rangle \overset{\text{C}}{\rightarrow} \langle \text{PE8} \rangle$
(8)	PE: Wife had children	$\langle \text{PE8} \rangle \overset{\text{C}}{\rightarrow} \langle \text{PS9} \rangle$
(9)	PS: Children were born female	$\langle \text{PS9} \rangle \overset{\text{C}}{\rightarrow} \langle \text{PS11} \rangle$
(10)	PS: Genes were female	$\langle \text{PS10} \rangle \overset{\text{C}}{\rightarrow} \langle \text{PS9} \rangle$
(11)	PS: Czar had no sons	$\langle \text{PS9} \rangle \overset{\text{C}}{\rightarrow} \langle \text{PS12} \rangle$
(12)[a]	PS: Czar had daughters	$\langle \text{PS12} \rangle \overset{\text{P}}{\rightarrow} \langle \text{PS13} \rangle$
(13)	PS: Daughters looked attractive	$\langle \text{PE8} \rangle \overset{\text{P}}{\rightarrow} \langle \text{PS15} \rangle$
(14)	PS: Daughters looked like wife	$\langle \text{PE8} \rangle \overset{\text{C}}{\rightarrow} \langle \text{PS14} \rangle$
(15)	PS: Wife was attractive	$\langle \text{PS12} \rangle \overset{\text{P}}{\rightarrow} \langle \text{PS16} \rangle$
(16)	PS: Czar was attractive	$\langle \text{PS14} \rangle \overset{\text{C}}{\rightarrow} \langle \text{PS13} \rangle$
(17)	PE: Daughters were brought up rich	$\langle \text{PS15} \rangle \overset{\text{C}}{\rightarrow} \langle \text{PS13} \rangle$
(18)	PS: Daughters were well preserved	$\langle \text{PS16} \rangle \overset{\text{C}}{\rightarrow} \langle \text{PS13} \rangle$
(19)	PS: Daughters were well dressed	$\langle \text{PS13} \rangle \overset{\text{P}}{\rightarrow} \langle \text{PS20} \rangle$
(20)[a]	PS: Daughters were lovely	$\langle \text{PE17} \rangle \overset{\text{C}}{\rightarrow} \langle \text{PS18} \rangle$
(21)[a]	G+: Daughters enjoyed themselves	$\langle \text{PS18} \rangle \overset{\text{C}}{\rightarrow} \langle \text{PS13} \rangle$
		$\langle \text{PE17} \rangle \overset{\text{C}}{\rightarrow} \langle \text{PS19} \rangle$
		$\langle \text{PS19} \rangle \overset{\text{C}}{\rightarrow} \langle \text{PS20} \rangle$
		$\langle \text{G+21} \rangle \overset{\text{P}}{\rightarrow} \langle \text{PS20} \rangle$
(22)	IS: Daughters were bored	$\langle \text{IS22} \rangle \overset{\text{I}}{\rightarrow} \langle \text{G+21} \rangle$
		$\langle \text{G+26} \rangle \overset{\text{R}}{\rightarrow} \langle \text{G+21} \rangle$

Table 4.4 (continued)

Nodes			Arcs		
(23)	G+:	Daughters picked flowers	<PS29>	$\xrightarrow{I}$	<G+26>
			<G+28>	$\xrightarrow{R}$	<G+26>
(24)[a]	G+:	Daughters walked in woods	<G+24>	$\xrightarrow{R}$	<G+28>
(25)	IS:	Daughters liked flowers	<G+24>	$\xrightarrow{R}$	<G+27>
			<G+23>	$\xrightarrow{R}$	<G+21>
(26)	G+:	Daughters had picnic	<IS25>	$\xrightarrow{I}$	<G+23>
			<G+24>	$\xrightarrow{R}$	<G+23>
(27)	G+:	Daughters got fresh air	<IS32>	$\xrightarrow{I}$	<G+23>
(28)	G+:	Daughters got away from palace	<IS32>	$\xrightarrow{I}$	<G+33>
(29)	PS:	It was a nice day	<G+33>	$\xrightarrow{R}$	<G+21>
(30)	IS:	Daughters liked to walk in woods	<G+24>	$\xrightarrow{R}$	<G+33>
(31)	PS:	Palace was surrounded by woods	<G+34>	$\xrightarrow{R}$	<G+21>
(32)	IS:	Daughters liked nature	<IS35>	$\xrightarrow{I}$	<G+34>
(33)	G+:	Daughters watched baby animals	<G+36>	$\xrightarrow{R}$	<G+21>
(34)	G+:	Daughters talked	<G+37>	$\xrightarrow{R}$	<G+21>
(35)	IS:	Talking is fun	<IS30>	$\xrightarrow{I}$	<G+24>
(36)	G+:	Daughters laughed	<PS31>	$\xrightarrow{I}$	<G+24>
(37)	G+:	Daughters played	<G+24>	$\xrightarrow{M}$	<G+41>
(38)	S:	Daughters walked together	<G+41>	$\xrightarrow{M}$	<S42>
(39)	IS:	Daughters liked being together	<G+41>	$\xrightarrow{M}$	<S43>
(40)	S:	Daughters walked happily	<G+24>	$\xrightarrow{M}$	<S38>
(41)	G+:	Daughters moved feet	<IS39>	$\xrightarrow{I}$	<S38>
(42)	S:	Daughters moved one foot in front of other foot	<G+24>	$\xrightarrow{M}$	<S40>
(43)	S:	Daughters moved slowly	<G+21>	$\xrightarrow{C}$	<PE44>
(44)	PE:	Daughters were busy	<PE44>	$\xrightarrow{C}$	<IE53>
(45)	IS:	Daughters didn't pay attention to to time	<IE53>	$\xrightarrow{C}$	<IS45>
(46)	PS:	Daughters didn't have a watch	<IE53>	$\xrightarrow{C}$	<IS48>
(47)[a]	IE:	Daughters forgot the time	<PE44>	$\xrightarrow{C}$	<IS48>

Table 4.4 (continued)

	Nodes	Arcs
(48)	IS: Daughters didn't pay attention to the sun	<PE44> $\xrightarrow{C}$ <IS48>
(49)	IS: Daughters did not see the sun	<IS45> $\xrightarrow{C}$ <IE47>
(50)	IS: Daughters did not notice it was getting dark	<PS46> $\xrightarrow{C}$ <IE47>
(51)	PE: It was getting late	<IS48> $\xrightarrow{C}$ <IS49>
(52)	PE: It was getting dark	<IS49> $\xrightarrow{C}$ <IS50>
(53)	IE: Daughters were careless	<IS50> $\xrightarrow{C}$ <IE47>
(54)[a]	PE: Daughters stayed too long	<IE47> $\xrightarrow{C}$ <PS56>
(55)	PS: Daughters were supposed to be home before dark	<PS56> $\xrightarrow{C}$ <PS57>
(56)	PS: Daughters did not leave woods	<PS57> $\xrightarrow{C}$ <PE54>
(57)	PS: Daughters did not go home	<PE51> $\xrightarrow{C}$ <PE52>
(58)	IE: The dragon saw the daughters	<PE52> $\xrightarrow{C}$ <IS50>
(59)	G–: Dragon eat the daughters	<PE52> $\xrightarrow{C}$ <PE54>
		<PE55> $\xrightarrow{C}$ <PE54>
		<PE54> $\xrightarrow{C}$ <IE58>
		<IE58> $\xrightarrow{I}$ <G–59>
(60)	PS: Dragon was hungry	<PS60> $\xrightarrow{I}$ <G–59>
(61)[a]	G–: Dragon kidnapped daughters	<IS64> $\xrightarrow{I}$ <G–61>
		<G–61> $\xrightarrow{R}$ <G–59>
		<G–61> $\xrightarrow{R}$ <G–62>
(62)	G–: Dragon get ransom	<G–62> $\xrightarrow{R}$ <G–63>
(63)	G–: Dragon hurt Czar	<G–61> $\xrightarrow{R}$ <G–65>
(64)	IS: Dragon liked kidnapping	<IS66> $\xrightarrow{I}$ <G–65>
(65)	G–: Dragon keep daughters	<G–67> $\xrightarrow{R}$ <G–61>
(66)	IS: Dragon was lonely	<G–68> $\xrightarrow{R}$ <G–67>
(67)	G–: Dragon didn't want anyone to find daughters	<G+69> $\xrightarrow{R}$ <G–68>
(68)	G+: Dragon wanted daughters to be hidden	<PS70> $\xrightarrow{I}$ <G+69>

Table 4.4 (continued)

	Nodes	Arcs		
(69)	G+: Dragon wanted daughters to be in the cave	<G+71>	$\overset{R}{\rightarrow}$	<G+69>
(70)	PS: The cave was in the woods	<G+72>	$\overset{R}{\rightarrow}$	<G+71>
(71)	G+: Dragon carried daughters away	<G+72>	$\overset{C}{\rightarrow}$	<PE73>
(72)	G+: Dragon snuck up on daughters	<PE73>	$\overset{C}{\rightarrow}$	<IE74>
(73)	PE: Daughters were caught off guard	<G+75>	$\overset{R}{\rightarrow}$	<G+71>
(74)	IE: Daughters were surprised	<PS76>	$\overset{I}{\rightarrow}$	<G+75>
(75)[a]	G+: Dragon dragged off daughters	<G+77>	$\overset{R}{\rightarrow}$	<G+75>
(76)	PS: Carrying daughters is not easy	<G+77>	$\overset{M}{\rightarrow}$	<S78>
(77)	G+: Dragon grabbed daughters	<G+79>	$\overset{R}{\rightarrow}$	<G+75>
(78)	S: Grab was forceful	<G+79>	$\overset{M}{\rightarrow}$	<S80>
(79)	G+: Dragon picked up daughters	<G+79>	$\overset{M}{\rightarrow}$	<S81>
(80)	S: Dragon used claws	<G+82>	$\overset{R}{\rightarrow}$	<G+75>
(81)	S: Dragon used teeth	<G+82>	$\overset{M}{\rightarrow}$	<S83>
(82)	G+: Dragon pulled daughters	<G+82>	$\overset{M}{\rightarrow}$	<S84>
(83)	S: Daughters were pulled on the ground	<G+82>	$\overset{M}{\rightarrow}$	<S85>
(84)	S: Daughters were pulled by hair	<G+75>	$\overset{C}{\rightarrow}$	<IE86>
(85)	S: Daughters were pulled with feet in dragon's mouth			
(86)	IE: Daughters thought that dragon might do something bad	<IS86>	$\overset{I}{\rightarrow}$	<G+87>
(87)	G+: Daughters not be with dragon	<G+87>	$\overset{R}{\rightarrow}$	<G+88>
(88)	G+: Daughters not be kidnapped	<G+88>	$\overset{R}{\rightarrow}$	<G+89>
(89)	G+: Daughters not be eaten	<G+91>	$\overset{R}{\rightarrow}$	<G+87>
(90)	IE: Daughters were frightened	<G+92>	$\overset{R}{\rightarrow}$	<G+91>
(91)	G+: Daughters get rescued (saved)	<G+93>	$\overset{R}{\rightarrow}$	<G+92>
(92)[a]	G+: Daughters get help	<G+94>	$\overset{R}{\rightarrow}$	<G+93>
(93)	G+: Daughters wanted someone to come	<G+95>	$\overset{R}{\rightarrow}$	<G+94>
(94)	G+: Daughters wanted someone to hear them	<G+95>	$\overset{M}{\rightarrow}$	<S97>
(95)[a]	G+: Daughters cried	<IS86>	$\overset{C}{\rightarrow}$	<IE90>

Table 4.4 (continued)

		Nodes	Arcs
(96)	IS:	Daughters were desparate	<IE90> $\xrightarrow{C}$ <IE96>
(97)	S:	Cries were loud	<IE96> $\xrightarrow{C}$ <G+95>
(98)[a]	IE:	Heroes heard cries	<G+95> $\xrightarrow{C}$ <IE98>
(99)	PS:	Heroes were close by	<PS99> $\xrightarrow{C}$ <IE98>
(100)	G+:	Heroes were listening	<G+100> $\xrightarrow{C}$ <IE98>
(101)	S:	Heroes used ears	<G+100> $\xrightarrow{M}$ <S101>
(102)[a]	G+:	Heroes rescued daughters	<IE98> $\xrightarrow{I}$ <G+102>
			<G+102> $\xrightarrow{R}$ <G+103>
			<G+103> $\xrightarrow{I}$ <G+105>
(103)	G+:	Heroes wanted daughters to be free of dragon	<G+103> $\xrightarrow{R}$ <G+104>
(104)	G+:	Heroes wanted daughters to be safe	<G+87> $\xrightarrow{I}$ <G+105>
(105)	G+:	Daughters wanted to return to palace	<G+106> $\xrightarrow{R}$ <G+102>
(106)	G+:	Heroes killed dragon	<G+106> $\xrightarrow{C}$ <PE107>
(107)[a]	PE:	Dragon was defeated	<PS108> $\xrightarrow{C}$ <PS110>
(108)	PS:	Heroes outnumbered dragon	<PS110> $\xrightarrow{C}$ <PE107>
(109)	PS:	Heroes were skillful	<PS109> $\xrightarrow{C}$ <PE107>
(110)	PS:	Heroes were stronger than dragon	<PS111> $\xrightarrow{C}$ <PE107>
(111)	PS:	Good conquers evil	<PS112> $\xrightarrow{C}$ <PE107>
(112)	PS:	Dragon is bad	<PS113> $\xrightarrow{C}$ <PE107>
(113)	PS:	Heroes are good	<G+123> $\xrightarrow{R}$ <G+106>
(114)[a]	G+:	Heroes fought dragon	<G+114> $\xrightarrow{R}$ <G+123>
(115)	IS:	Heroes knew they could win	<IS115> $\xrightarrow{I}$ <G+114>
(116)	G+:	Heroes attacked dragon	<G+116> $\xrightarrow{R}$ <G+114>
(117)	G+:	Heroes surrounded dragon	<G+116> $\xrightarrow{C}$ <PE120>
(118)	S:	Attack was hard	<PE120> $\xrightarrow{C}$ <PE107>
(119)	S:	Heroes used weapons	<G+117> $\xrightarrow{R}$ <G+116>
(120)	PE:	Dragon became tired	<G+116> $\xrightarrow{M}$ <S118>

Table 4.4 (continued)

	Nodes		Arcs
(121)	G+:	Heroes stabbed dragon	<G+116> $\overset{M}{\rightarrow}$ <S119>
(122)	S:	Heroes used swords	<G+121> $\overset{R}{\rightarrow}$ <G+116>
(123)	G+:	Heroes wounded dragon	<G+121> $\overset{M}{\rightarrow}$ <S122>
(124)	G+:	Heroes crept up on dragon	<G+124> $\overset{R}{\rightarrow}$ <G+117>
(125)[a]	G+:	Heroes went to dragon	<G+125> $\overset{R}{\rightarrow}$ <G+117>
(126)	G+:	Heroes rode horses	<G+126> $\overset{R}{\rightarrow}$ <G+125>
(127)	G+:	Heroes got on horses	<G+127> $\overset{R}{\rightarrow}$ <G+126>
(128)	S:	Heroes rode quickly	<G+126> $\overset{M}{\rightarrow}$ <S128>
(129)	S:	Heroes rode cautiously	<G+126> $\overset{M}{\rightarrow}$ <S129>
(130)	G+:	Heroes followed sounds	<G+125> $\overset{M}{\rightarrow}$ <S132>
(131)	G+:	Heroes followed tracks	<G+131> $\overset{R}{\rightarrow}$ <G+125>
(132)	S:	Heroes went through woods	<G+130> $\overset{R}{\rightarrow}$ <G+125>
			<PS133> $\overset{I}{\rightarrow}$ <G+105>
(133)	PS:	Daughters lived in palace	<PS134> $\overset{I}{\rightarrow}$ <G+105>
(134)	PS:	Daughters are safe in palace	<G+105> $\overset{I}{\rightarrow}$ <G+142>
(135)	G+:	Daughters told heroes to return them to the palace	<G+142> $\overset{I}{\rightarrow}$ <G+143>
(136)[a]	G+:	Heroes returned daughters to palace	<G+143> $\overset{I}{\rightarrow}$ <G+144>
(137)	G+:	Heroes escorted daughters	<G+144> $\overset{C}{\rightarrow}$ <IE141>
(138)	G+:	Heroes carried daughters	<G+105> $\overset{I}{\rightarrow}$ <G+139>
(139)	G+:	Daughters returned to the Czar	<G+139> $\overset{I}{\rightarrow}$ <G+140>
(140)	G+:	Daughters told Czar about the rescue	<G+140> $\overset{C}{\rightarrow}$ <IE141>
(141)[a]	IE:	Czar heard about the rescue	<G+135> $\overset{R}{\rightarrow}$ <G+105>
(142)	G+:	Daughters told people about the rescue	<G+135> $\overset{I}{\rightarrow}$ <G+136>
(143)	G+:	People talked about the rescue	<G+136> $\overset{I}{\rightarrow}$ <G+145>
			<G+145> $\overset{C}{\rightarrow}$ <IE141>
(144)	G+:	Servant told Czar about the rescue	<G+136> $\overset{M}{\rightarrow}$ <G+137>
(145)	G+:	Heroes told Czar about the rescue	<G+136> $\overset{M}{\rightarrow}$ <G+138>
(146)	IE:	Czar became happy	<IE141> $\overset{C}{\rightarrow}$ <IE146>

Table 4.4 (continued)

Nodes		Arcs
		<IE146> $\xrightarrow{I}$ <G+148>
(147)	IE: Czar became grateful	<IE141> $\xrightarrow{I}$ <G+148>
(148)	G+: Czar repaid the heroes	<IE141> $\xrightarrow{C}$ <IE147>
(149)[a]	G+: Czar rewarded the heroes	<IE147> $\xrightarrow{I}$ <G+148>
		<G+149> $\xrightarrow{R}$ <G+148>
(150)	G+: Czar gave heroes money	<G+150> $\xrightarrow{R}$ <G+149>
(151)	G+: Czar gave heroes jewels	<G+151> $\xrightarrow{R}$ <G+149>
(152)	G+: Czar gave heroes land	<G+152> $\xrightarrow{R}$ <G+149>
(153)	G+: Czar knighted heroes	<G+153> $\xrightarrow{R}$ <G+149>
(154)	G+: Czar let heroes marry daughters	<G+154> $\xrightarrow{R}$ <G+149>
(155)	G+: Czar let heroes live in palace	<G+155> $\xrightarrow{R}$ <G+149>

[a] Stated node.

Goal-Oriented Conceptualizations

Figure 4.4 is a graph structure of a Goal hierarchy in the Czar story. The node descriptions are included in Table 4.4. Three characteristics of goal-oriented conceptualizations are captured in Figure 4.4.

(1) There is a hierarchically ordered stack of Goal nodes that are linked by Reason arcs. For example, there is a path from G+127 to G+104 that relates 10 Goal nodes. The 10 nodes are all linked by Reason arcs, which can be verbally articulated by two connectives: *in order to* and *so that.* The heroes got on the horses (G+127) in order to ride the horses (G+126) in order to go to the dragon (G+125) in order to surround the dragon (G+117) in order to attack the dragon (G+116) in order to fight the dragon (G+114) in order to wound the dragon (G+123) in order to kill the dragon (G+106) in order to rescue the daughters (G+102) so that the daughters would be free of the dragon (G+103) so that the daughters would be safe (G+104). The direction of Reason arcs is important. If G1 and G2 are linked by a forward arc ($\overrightarrow{R}$), then it makes sense to say *G1 in order to G2,* but not *G2 in order to G1.* For example, it makes sense to say *The heroes got on the horses in order to ride the horses,* but it does not make sense to say *The heroes rode the horses in order to get on the horses.* There is also a temporal constraint on the hierarchy. If all the goals in a hierarchy are successfully completed, then a superordinate goal is never achieved before a more subordinate goal. The heroes get on the horses before riding the horses;

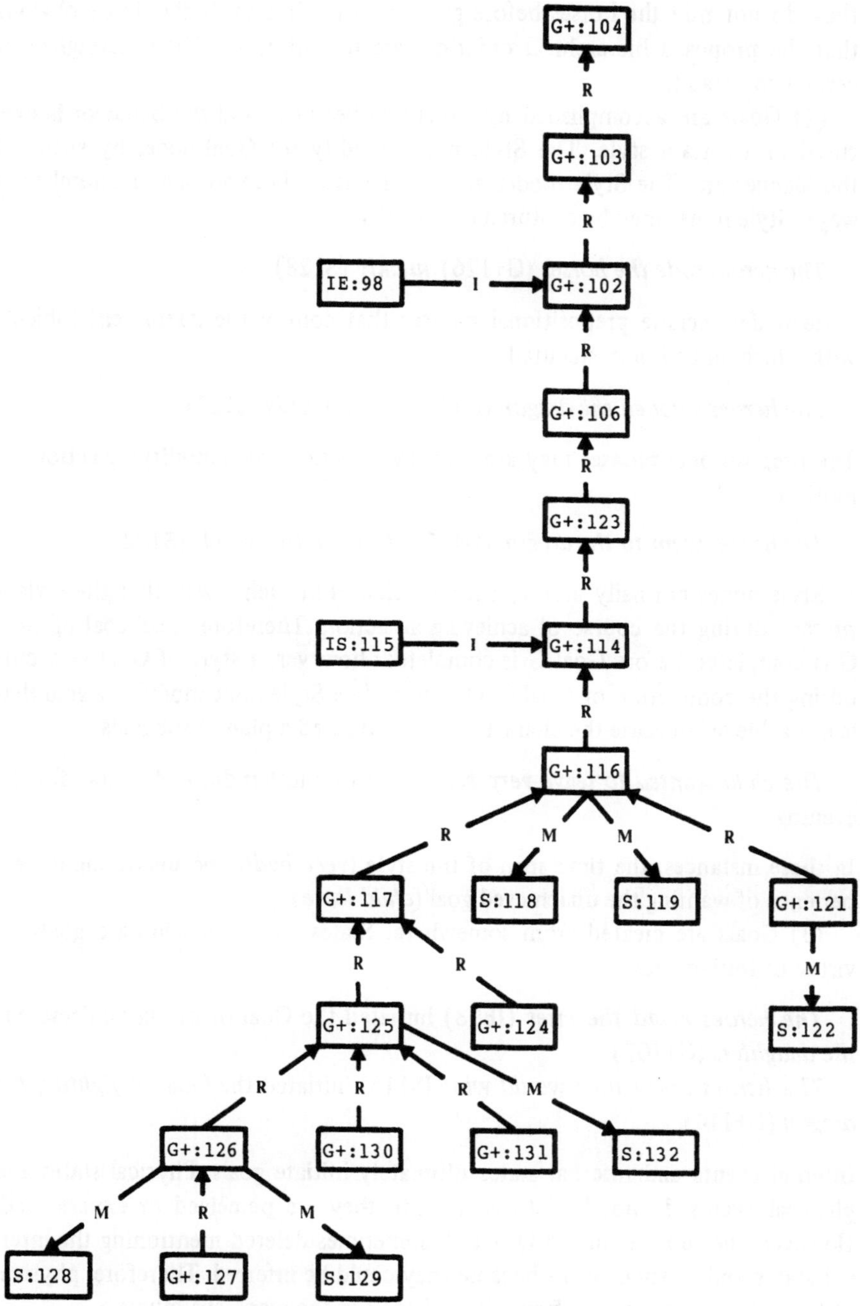

Figure 4.4. Goal-oriented conceptual structure from *The Czar and His Daughters*. (See Table 4.4 for identification of nodes.)

they do not ride the horses before getting on the horses. It should be obvious that the proposed hierarchical orderings are not arbitrary. The orderings meet certain constraints.

(2) Goals are accomplished by executing behavior and the behavior is executed in a certain style. The Style nodes modify the Goal nodes by virtue of the Manner arc. The Style modes may be linguistically expressed in a number of ways. Style nodes may be captured by adverbs.

The heroes rode the horses (G+126) *quickly* (S128).

Style nodes include prepositional phrases that convey the instrument (object) with which an action is executed.

The heroes stabbed the dragon (G+121) *with swords* (S122).

The prepositional phrases may also convey direction when modifying actions of motion.

The heroes went to the dragon (G+125) *through the woods* (S132).

Style nodes normally modify actions (Goal+) in such a way that the style is present during the course of achieving an action. Therefore, a subgoal of Goal G is completed before Goal G is completed; however, a style of Goal G occurs during the completion of Goal G. Occasionally a Style node modifies a goal that is not achieved because the character never executed a plan of subgoals:

The child wanted to leave very badly, but his mother decided to stay for the evening.

In these instances, the time span of the style (*very badly*) occurs during the experience of wanting the unachieved goal (*child leave*).

(3) Goals are created from somewhere. States and events initiate goals by virtue of Initiate arcs.

The heroes heard the cries (IE98) initiated the Goal of *the heroes rescuing the daughters* (G+102).

The heroes knew they would win (IS115) initiated the Goal of *fighting the dragon* (G+114).

Internal events and internal states ultimately initiate goals. Physical states and physical events do not lead to goals until they are perceived or experienced. However, the subjects in the Q/A task sometimes deleted mentioning the internal states and internal events because they could be inferred. Therefore, physical states and physical events often initiated goals in the graph structures.

An interesting structural characteristic of the goal-oriented graph structures was the hierarchical property. There rarely were structural loops. This property may be responsible for the fact that goal-driven action sequences are recalled well compared to expository text, in which structural loops prevail. Hierarchically organized Goal structures are perhaps easy to keep track of within the cognitive system compared to network structures that contain loops.

The question arises as to why goal-oriented conceptualizations seems to preserve the hierarchical structure. There is one plausible reason: The character completing the actions normally executes only one action or plan at a time and there is a logical order in which the actions must be executed for the plan to be accomplished successfully. A hierarchically organized Goal stack captures this ideal ordering of actions. Unless the physical and social worlds are uncooperative, the actions will be completed and the goals will be achieved according to the ideal Goal hierarchy.

Causally Oriented Conceptualizations

Figure 4.5 is a causally oriented structure from the Czar story. The structure is a network rather than a hierarchical structure because there are structural loops. Structural loops are quite common in causally oriented conceptualizations. There are other properties as well.

(1) Causally oriented conceptualizations contain Events and States that are interrelated by Consequence arcs. The Consequence arcs may be articulated linguistically by the connectives *lead to, caused,* or *had the consequence of.*

The daughters' being busy (PE44) led to *the daughters' not paying attention to the time* (IS45) which led to *the daughters' forgetting the time* (IE47) which led to *the daughters' not leaving the woods* (PS56) which led to *the daughters' not going home* (PS57) which led to *the daughters' staying too long* (PE54).

The connective *because* captures the Consequence chain in the backwards direction.

The daughters stayed too long (PE54) because *they did not go home* (PS57) because *they did not leave the woods* (PS56) because *they forgot the time* (IE47) because *they did not pay attention to the time* (IS45) because *they were busy* (PE44).

The Consequence chains are constrained by time. If Event E1 has the consequence of Event E2, then Event E1 occurred or existed before E2.

(2) Causally oriented structures often have enabling states that are important for a causally driven sequence to unfold.

The state of *the daughters' not paying attention to the time* (IS45) enabled *the daughters' forgetting the time* (IE47).

In a strictly causal system an event cannot be driven by a set of states alone. There must be events that start and maintain the causally driven flow of events. For example, *the daughters' forgetting the time* (IE47) should not occcur because the event was preceded only by static nodes: *The daughters did not notice it was getting dark* (IS50), *the daughters did not pay attention to the time* (IS45), and *the daughters did not have a watch* (PS46). However, events were often consequences of state configurations in the empirically derived graph structures. Why? Because subjects sometimes do not express all of the intervening events and

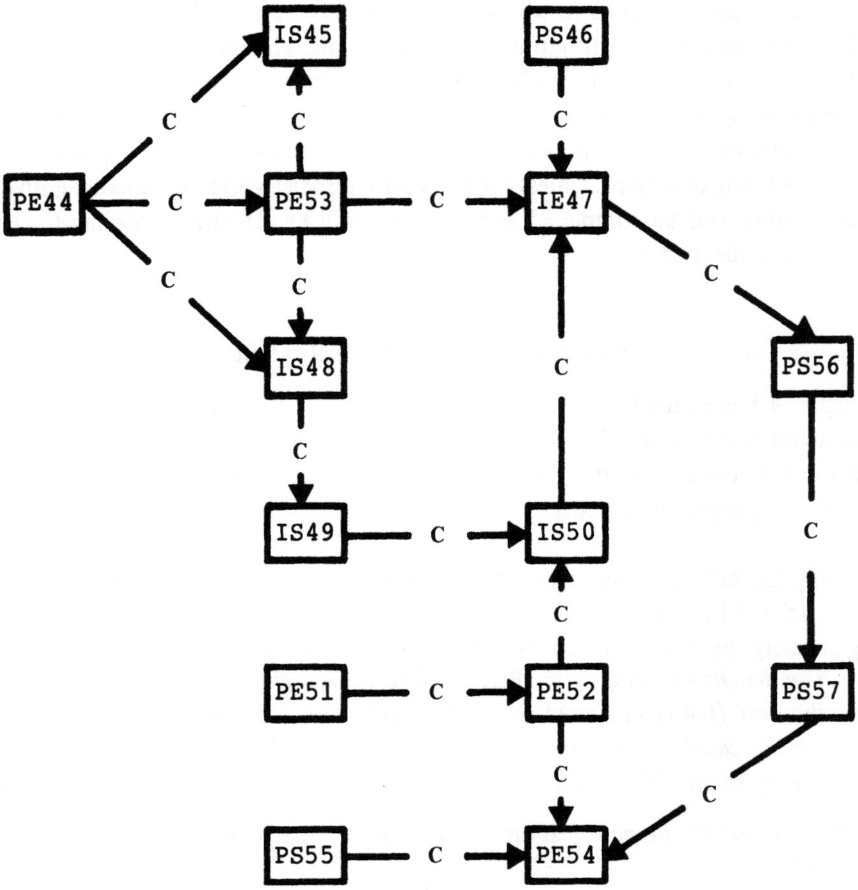

Figure 4.5. Causally oriented conceptual structure from *The Czar and His Daughters.* (See Table 4.4 for identification of nodes.)

states that participate in a causal conceptualization. In the case of *the daughters forgetting the time,* there presumably were intervening internal processes in which forgetting occurs with the passage of time; however, subjects did not express these intervening phenomena.

It is important to emphasize that the Consequence arcs are not *causes* in an absolute sense. A given event or state may only *participate* in the causal mechanism that causes another event or state without being the direct cause. For this reason, the Consequence arcs represent consequences rather than causes. The Consequence arcs are formulated on the basis of knowledge from generic schemas rather than a scientifically sound causal system. The goal here is to capture causal conceptualizations generated by the comprehender rather than to formulate a scientifically cohesive and valid causal system.

Property Arcs

A small proportion of the arcs in the graph structures were Property arcs.

A property of the daughters is that *they were attractive* (PS13).
A property of the Czar is that *he was attractive* (PS16).

The characters, objects, or concepts embedded in a statement may have certain static properties. When this is the case the modifying State node is linked to the modified statement by a Property arc. The modifying node is usually an Internal State or Physical State. Property arcs are quite prevalent at the beginning of stories when the setting is established.

Conceptual Graph Structures for Expository Passages

The Q/A method was applied to the four short passages shown in Table 4.5. These passages were of comparable length to the narrative passages in Table 4.3. The procedure was the same as that for the narrative passages with only two exceptions. First, the extended Q/A protocols were collected but not the standard Q/A protocols. Second, a different set of 10 subjects was questioned for each passage; 8 subjects were questioned on all passages when data was collected for the narrative passages. Of course, the same analytical methods were imposed on the expository passages as were imposed on the narrative passages. This study was conducted by Sharon Goodman, a member of the Cognitive Research Group at California State University at Fullerton.

There were a number of differences between narrative and expository passages when the graph structures of the two prose genres were compared. One or more of these differences may be responsible for the fact that narrative passages are recalled better and read faster than expository passages.

(1) Expository passages invoked fewer inferences than narrative passages. Among the four expository passages, the ratio of inference nodes to stated nodes was 2.43:1. In contrast, there was a 8.22:1 ratio among the four narrative passages. Thus, compared to narrative prose, the conceptual organization of expository prose tends to be transmitted by explicitly stated information.

(2) The distribution of nodes among the six node categories was clearly different for expository and narrative prose. These distributions are presented in Table 4.6. The narrative passages had a higher proportion of Goal, Style, Internal State, and Internal Event nodes than did the expository passages. The expository passages had a substantially higher proportion of Physical State nodes. It appears that narrative prose incorporates more goal-oriented conceptualizations than does expository prose; expository prose embodies more causally oriented and static conceptualizations.

Table 4.5. Expository Passages

Development of the Wagon

The wheel and the wagon developed at the same time, approximately 5000 years ago. At that time, human beings found that they could pull their sledges more easily if they fitted them with wheels of solid wood. The Egyptians were among the earliest people to use wagons. The Scythians wandered over the plains of southeastern Europe as early as 700 B.C., carrying their possessions on two-wheeled carts covered with reeds. However, until the middle ages, the wagons were no more than boxes set upon axles between wheels. Then the four-wheeled coach was developed in Germany.

Social Origins

Socially, the hunting ape had to increase his urge to communicate and to co-operate with his fellows. Facial expressions and vocalizations had to become more complicated. With all the new weapons available, he had to develop powerful signals that would inhibit attacks within the social group. On the other hand, with a fixed home base to defend, he had to develop stronger aggressive responses to members of rival groups.

The Placenta

The placenta is the organ through which the growing embryo obtains food and eliminates wastes. Blood vessels in the embryo go through the umbilical cord to the placenta and back again to the embryo. Nutrients from the mother animal are absorbed into the placenta. From it they flow into the blood vessels of the cord, and are taken to the growing embryo. Embryonic wastes flow from the embryo, through the umbilical cord, to the placenta, through the mother's blood stream, and are then eliminated by the mother's kidneys.

The Zeeman Effect

The Zeeman Effect is the splitting up of spectrum lines into two or more components. It is caused by placing a light source in a strong magnetic field. The components from any one line have a set of frequencies that are different for every known chemical element. These components make a symmetrical pattern around the original source of light. The patterns vary from line to line, and are plane, elliptical, or circularly polarized. By using the Zeeman Effect, astronomers can measure the strength of the magnetic field on the surface of the stars.

(3) The distribution of arcs among the five arc categories was different for narrative and expository prose. These distributions are presented in Table 4.6. There was a higher proportion of Reason arcs in narrative than in expository prose. Expository passages included more Consequence and Property arcs. Again, these distributions support the conclusion that narrative passages contain more goal-oriented conceptualizations and fewer causally oriented conceptualizations than does expository prose. There were also more static descriptions in expository prose.

Table 4.6. Distribution of Nodes and Arcs in Expository and Narrative Passages

Categories	Prose genre	
	Narrative	Expository
Nodes		
Goal	.52	.34
Style	.09	.04
Physical State	.12	.43
Physical Event	.14	.14
Internal State	.06	.02
Internal Event	.07	.03
Arcs		
Reason	.48	.21
Manner	.07	.08
Initiate	.15	.14
Consequence	.29	.41
Property	.01	.16

The differences between narrative and expository passages are perhaps quantitative rather than qualitative. Although expository passages include fewer goal-oriented conceptualizations than does narrative, the events and states in expository passages usually have intential, goal-oriented aspects. States and events are often created by virtue of the goals of animate beings. Man collectively manufactures the world with certain Goals in mind. States in the physical world are intentionally created so that man can satisfy goals more quickly and easily.

Wagons have wheels so that *man can pull his possessions more easily.*

Coaches have four wheels so that *the coach is better balanced when animals or men pull them.*

Events in the physical world unfold because individuals want these events to occur and they create the preconditions for such events to evolve.

The wagon was developed because *humans wanted some way to pull their possessions more easily and they thought of ways that this could be done.*

Facial expressions became more complicated because *apes wanted to communicate more things in order to avoid fighting.*

Much of the physical world is the way it is because animate beings wanted it to be this way.

Differences Between Narrative and Expository Prose

Although it is well acknowledged that prose may be classified into different genres, there is not an ironclad agreement on the most sensible categorization scheme. Brooks and Warren (1972) have found it convenient to segregate prose into four basic categories: narrative, expository, descriptive, and persuasive. For the present purposes, this categorization scheme is quite adequate. In Chapter 1 these four categories were described and some examples of each were presented.

There are several reasons for construing the four prose genres as fuzzy categories rather than discrete categories. First, some passages may have properties that are associated with more than one genre. A novel, for example, might have a lengthy description of the setting as well as the plot. Second, it may be difficult or impossible to strictly define the properties associated with any given genre. There may not be any properties of a given genre that all exemplars possess; any common property would end up being so abstract that it would be trivial. Instead of ascribing necessary properties to a given genre, it may be more sensible to delineate some typical properties that are not strictly necessary. Thus, the genres may be viewed as fuzzy sets, just as most categories of knowledge are (Gaines, 1976; Rosch, 1978; Zadeh, 1975). Although fuzzy, the genres are psychologically real. Adult subjects can categorize passages into different genres with a substantial degree of reliability and in a manner that makes sense according to analytical theories. Passages from the same genre have been found to cluster together when adults categorize passages (Munro, Lutz, and Gordon, 1979).

In this section some of the differences between narrative and expository prose will be enumerated. Each of these properties should be viewed as characteristic of one genre or the other rather than definitional. The motivation for comparing these two genres is primarily psychological. Specifically, several of the studies reported earlier in this book have demonstrated dramatic differences between narrative and expository prose regarding comprehension and retention. Compared to expository prose, narrative is read faster, easier to comprehend, and better retained in memory. Narrativity has consistently been the most robust predictor of reading times, comprehension scores, and recall. Why does narrative prose have such a privileged status in the information processing system? After a single exposure, we can easily comprehend a story and have impressive retention of it. It frequently doesn't matter whether the story is semantically well formed or whether it includes events that defy natural laws. The setting may be surrealistic. Inanimate objects may do things intentionally. Characters may solve problems with telekinesis, clairvoyance, or ESP. On the other hand, an expository passage that has sound logic, nontechnical terms, and a cohesive organization may require hours to be understood and be forgotten the next day. How does narrative differ from expository prose?

Suspension of Disbelief

The information in narrative prose is often fictitious, whereas the information conveyed in expository prose is supposed to be true. This constitutes an implicit pragmatic contract between the reader and writer, or speaker and listener. A reader of science fiction assumes that the writer has invented a fictitious, hypothetical world and plot. The reader does not constantly evaluate the truth or falsity of information in relation to the reader's general world knowledge.

Coleridge (1967) calls this "the willing suspension of disbelief." In contrast, a reader of the daily newspaper assumes that the writer has reported a real situation, problem, or event. The news reader may question whether the reporter gave a fair (true) account.

Temporal and Spatial Referents

The episodes in narrative prose have specific spatial and temporal indices. An episode takes place at a specific time and in a specific place. The temporal and spatial referents may be fictitious (e.g., *On July 1, 2001 the astronauts landed on Venus*) or semantically depleted (e.g., *Once upon a time in a far off land . . .*), but the time and space indices do have particular instantiations. In contrast, the temporal and spatial indices in expository prose are often generic. A statement in an expository passage would ordinarily be regarded as universally true at relevant places and times. The scope of the time and space indices tends to be generic in expository prose and specific in narrative prose.

Since the spatial and temporal indices are specific in narrative prose, other indices are also specific. The characters and objects in stories are referentially specific, whereas many objects and entities in expository prose are general. The wolf in *Little Red Riding Hood* is specific, whereas an encyclopedia article on wolves would refer to wolves in general. The comprehender may construct richer, more elaborate, and more vivid conceptualizations for the specific referents in narrative prose, compared to the general referents in expository prose. Why? Perhaps because the comprehender is more cautious when ascribing a property to a generic concept, compared to a specific referent.

Conceptual Structure

Narrative prose differs from expository prose along structural and conceptual dimensions. The sequences of episodes in narrative chronologically unfold in a causal and goal-oriented manner. The comprehender constructs chains of episodes, or what B. N. Colby (1973) calls *eidochronic sequences*. The episodes are linked by relationships that are causal or intentional. It is important to establish causal and intentional connectivity between episodes in narrative. According to many theories of narrative organization (Beaugrande and Colby, 1979; Black and Bower, 1980; Bruce, 1978b, 1980; Bruce and Newman, 1978; Lichtenstein and Brewer, 1980; Rumelhart, 1977c; Wilensky, 1978b), goal-oriented conceptualizations should be particularly prevalent in narrative prose—in fact, more prevalent than causally oriented conceptualizations. If this is correct, then the Reason arcs and Goal nodes would be quite prevalent in narrative prose.

The formation of eidochronic sequences is not an important feature of expository prose. Propositions in expository prose are frequently interrelated by referential linkages or what Kintsch has called *coherence graphs* (Kintsch, 1979; Kintsch and van Dijk, 1978). Coherence graphs are constructed on the basis of a very simple coherence rule: "connections are formed whenever two propositions share an argument" (Kintsch, 1979, p. 5). The *given-new* distinction (Clark, 1977; Clark and Haviland, 1977; Halliday, 1967; Halliday and Hasan, 1976; Haviland and Clark, 1974; MacWhinney and Bates, 1978) is also an important analytical component for forming expository structures. Each sentence in a passage contains both *given* information (a proposition or an argument of a proposition) and *new* information. When a sentence or clause is interpreted, the comprehender first searches the previous passage context for information that matches the given information. When a match is found, the new information is structurally appended to the old proposition or argument. From the perspective of the representational system discussed in this chapter, we would expect a large number of Property arcs in expository prose.

The analyses of the arc and node distributions presented in Table 4.6 are consistent with the above observations. First, goal-oriented conceptualizations are more prevalent in narrative than expository prose. Narrative passages have more Goal nodes and Reason arcs. Second, State nodes and Property arcs are more prevalent in expository than in narrative prose. Consequence arcs are also more prevalent in expository than narrative passages. The latter trend suggests that causally oriented conceptualizations occur more frequently in expository than narrative prose.

Narrative and expository prose may be compared on the basis of a second structural dimension. To what extent does the structure of a passage conform to a vertical organization versus a horizontal organization? The notions of vertical and horizontal organizations can be easily defined if we assumed that nodes are organized according to a strict hierarchy (Lehnert, 1980; Thorndyke, 1977). In a vertical organization there would be a great deal of embedding. Horizontal organizations have relatively flat structures. It has been proposed that narrative prose has a more vertical organization than expository prose (Munro, Gordon, Rigney, and Lutz, 1979; Munro, Lutz, and Gordon, 1979), whereas expository prose is more horizontal. Indeed, most of the passages examined by story grammars (Johnson and Mandler, 1980; Rumelhart, 1975, 1977c; Stein and Glenn, 1979; Thorndyke, 1977) are more vertical than horizontal; the expository passages that have been analyzed by Kintsch's coherence graphs (Kintsch and van Dijk, 1978) are more horizontal than vertical. However, more research is clearly needed before these generalizations can be defended more strongly.

Literate Prose Versus Mother Tongue

Converations normally fall under the rubric of the narrative rather than the expository genre (Olson, 1977). What do people talk about? People talk about their experiences. They gossip. They tell jokes. Most of this information conveys what happened. Suppose that your phone rang and you experienced one of the following two conversations.

> (A) Art [Jim! What's happening?] Gail's pregnant! [You've got to be kidding] No. One night last summer Gail stayed over at my house because it was raining. We talked for a couple of hours and had a few drinks. Then we

started talking about sex. Gail told me she was really unhappy with her marriage. About midnight we looked at each other and, well, then we went upstairs. What am I gonna do??

(B) Art [Jim! What's happening?] Gail's pregnant! [You've got to be kidding] No. Sometimes two people of the opposite sex are in the same house together because of extreme weather conditions. The two people usually talk and have a few drinks. The female may talk about sex and how unhappy she is in her marriage, even though the man in the house is not her husband. If the two obtain eye contact, they might have sex. This happened to Gail and me on a rainy night last summer. What am I gonna do??

The more typical conversation is clearly A rather than B. People who talk in the expository mode sound stilted or are indeed eggheads.

Olson (1977) has discussed some of the differences between literate language and language in the mother tongue. Language is spoken in the mother tongue, whereas literate language is reserved for textbooks and other written documents. The language of our mother tongue embodies common sense knowledge, is socially conceived and structured, makes use of illustrations and examples, and is specialized for particular, context-sensitive information. Literate language obeys Aristotelian logic, is academically conceived and structured, makes use of reasoning and deduction, and embodies generic truth. Literate language should have logical cohesion whereas the speaker can get away with logical inconsistencies in the mother tongue. Olson points out other differences, but these need not be discussed here. The important points to recognize are that (a) most of our experience with language is in the mother tongue and (b) the language of our mother tongue is embodied in narrative prose (passage A above) more than expository prose (passage B above).

Rhetorical Features

Writers must follow certain rhetorical rules when composing well-formed narrative. Many of these rules have been uncovered by researchers who have developed story grammars (Johnson and Mandler, 1980; Mandler and Johnson, 1977; Rumelhart, 1975, 1977c; Stein and Glenn, 1979; Thorndyke, 1977). For example, it is a good policy to include some information about the setting (time, location, certain characters) at the beginning of the story before the plot unfolds. It is a good policy to deliver the plot's episodes in the same order as they unfold chronologically. In fact, when the narrative passage deviates from chronological order, the comprehender tends to recall the episodes in the chronological order rather than the presentation order (Mandler, 1979; Mandler and Johnson, 1977; Stein and Nezworski, 1978). Of course, authors sometimes write narratives that include transformations from the chronological order, but even these transformations should follow certain constraints (Brewer and Lichtenstein, 1980). An author might start a novel with a dramatic sequence of episodes from the plot. However, the set of episodes that are preposed would be part of an important episodic sequence rather than a minor episodic sequence.

Just as there are certain rules for composing well-formed narrative, there are certain constraints that are characteristic of interesting narrative. The properties of interesting narrative have only recently interested researchers in the cognitive sciences (Beaugrande and Colby, 1979; Brewer and Lichtenstein, 1980; Bruce, 1978; Schank, 1979a; Wilensky, 1978c). Most of these researchers agree that an analysis of interesting narrative will require some understanding of the following elements:

(1) The characters' plans and goals.
(2) The way in which the plans and goals of the characters interact. Interactions may include goal conflicts, goal competition, goal concord, goal facilitation, and counterplanning.
(3) A certain level of uncertainty and suspense, at least until the turning point or climax. After the turning point, goals will be fulfilled and conflicts resolved. Of course, some characters end up getting hurt.

The enterprise is not developed enough to make specific recommendations on how to write award-winning narrative. Nevertheless, this is an interesting direction for future research.

The rhetorical devices for writing expository prose are different than those for narrative. For example, it would be inappropriate to write a journal article by giving a chronological rendition of how the investigator researched and conducted his study. Journal articles do not apply the uncertainty or suspense principle (point 3 above) and do not slowly build up to a turning point or climax. In fact, it is conventional to begin with an abstract that announces the highlights, critical ideas, and earth-shattering results. Writers should invoke the rhetorical devices that are appropriate for the genre, and different genres have different rhetorical devices (Collins and Gentner, 1980; Olson, Duffy, and Mack, 1980).

Consider some rhetorical rules for a prototypical expository passage, such as an encyclopedia article. The first paragraph is usually devoted to defining the topic. Subsequent paragraphs are devoted to important aspects or elements of the topic, and each paragraph embellishes the topic further and further. The rhetorical development could easily be summarized in an outline format (Meyer, 1975). In fact, English teachers encourage students to write an outline before writing the prose. The outline has a hierarchical organization that includes a list of main points; each main point has a set of subpoints, and subpoints may contain a set of subsubpoints, etc. It is difficult or awkward, however, to superimpose an outline on narrative prose.

Expository prose contains certain types of signaling devices to aid the reader in organizing the information (van Dijk, 1979). First, there may be typographical cues, such as titled subsections, which render more salient the main points of the underlying outline (Glynn, 1978; Glynn and DiVesta, 1980). Second, there are constraints and conventions in paragraph structure. The first sentence in a paragraph is supposed to announce the theme or main issue of the paragraph. If this convention is adhered to, then the paragraph structure serves as a signaling device. Comprehenders often regard the first sentence as the theme or topic of the paragraph even when it is not (Kieras, 1978). The theme of the paragraph is embellished with information in the subsequent sentences. This convention seems to provide the optimal conditions for the formation of the coherence graphs (Kieras, 1978; Kintsch, 1979; Kintsch and van Dijk, 1978) which were discussed earlier. The comprehender starts with the theme and then appends embellishing propositions to the propositions and arguments of the main theme (by virtue of referential coherence).

Transitional words or phrases are important signaling devices in expository prose (Grimes, 1975; Halliday and Hasan, 1976). An *additive* relation signals the reader that some information should be added to the previously acquired structure, e.g., *in addition, furthermore, moreover,* etc. A *temporal* relation signals the reader about sequential or temporal properties of the content, e.g., *then, next, soon.* A *causal* relation helps the reader keep track of the logical development of the content, e.g., *therefore, because, consequently,* etc. An *adversative* relation signals the reader that there is a contrast or comparison, e.g., *but, however, on the other hand,* etc. Most of these signaling relations are more characteristic of expository prose than narrative prose. In fact, the plot in narrative can be quite comprehensible with a semantically depleted temporal relation, *and then.*

This section has identified five major dimensions in which expository and narrative prose differ. Which of these dimensions are responsible for the fact that narrative prose has such a privileged status in the information processing system? Unfortunately, available research has not explored this question. Hopefully, future research will unravel the mystery of why narrative is to easy to comprehend and so easy to remember.

Conceptual Graph Structures for Schemas

The claim has been made throughout this book that schemas guide the comprehension of specific passages. Passages invoke schemas that correspond to different knowledge domains and levels of structure. When a schema is identified, it guides the interpretation of specific statements, the generation of inferences, and the generation of expectations. Given the importance of schemas in the comprehension process, a worthwhile project would be to map out the representations of various schemas. This is the goal of the present section.

One method of empirically extracting schema representations involves two phases. There is a free generation phase followed by a Q/A phase. Suppose that the investigator were interested in the conceptual representation of a schema for *catching a fish.* In the free generation phase, a group of subjects would be asked to list actions, events, and attributes that typically occur or exist when someone catches a fish. All items generated by at least two subjects would be included in this free generation set of nodes. In the second phase, extended Q/A protocols would be collected for each node in the free generation set. A *why* question and a *how* question could be asked for each node in the free generation set and subjects would be required to give some minimal amount of information (four lines) as an answer to each question. All items generated by at least two subjects in the Q/A task would be included in the set of Q/A nodes. The set of nodes for a schema would include both the free generation and the Q/A sets of nodes.

One semester I required students in a class at Rosemead Graduate School of Psychology to generate schema representations using the method described above. Each student was responsible for mapping out a schema of his or her choice. The students had 3 weeks of training in the representational system discussed in this chapter. The project served two functions above the educational benefits for the students. First, it was possible to explore how a variety of schemas were represented. Second, an informal assessment could be made of how readily the representational system could be used by investigators who were minimally trained in the representational system. How salient are the node categories? How easily and reliably can the nodes be interrelated by the different arc categories?

The graduate students generally had little difficulty in assigning nodes to the six categories. My judgments agreed with theirs for at least 90 percent of the nodes. In contrast, my intuitions often differed from the students' with regard to assigning arc categories and interrelating the nodes. About one-half of the students had little trouble interrelating the nodes, whereas the other half of the students did have substantial problems. Interrelating the nodes is clearly a challenging puzzle and interjudge discrepancies do arise.

Table 4.7 is a list of the schemas chosen by the students, along with the corresponding distributions of nodes and arcs for the categories. These distributions are based on the students' decisions rather than my own! The schemas for six of the students were eliminated because they had substantial problems in representing the schemas. Each of the schemas are based on protocols collected from only two to five subjects.

The schemas in Table 4.7 are segregated into three categories. There are 8 *person* schemas, which correspond to a role, a stereotype, or people in general. The 8 person schemas varied in abstractness, ranging from a specific student (John Doe) to people in general. The person schemas included 33 nodes and 34 arcs on the average. The second category of schemas is *common activities.* The 6 common activity schemas had an average of 33 nodes and 33 arcs. The third category of schemas involved *situations or social interactions among characters.* These 5 schemas had an average of 26 nodes and 27 arcs.

The distribution of nodes and arcs differed among the three categories of schemas. The proportion of nodes that were in Goal and Style categories was higher for common activity schemas (.87) then for person schemas (.34) and situational schemas (.50). Common activities also had a higher proportion of Reason, Initiate, and Manner arcs (.90) than did the person schemas (.43) and situational schemas (.55). Thus, common activities highlight goal-oriented conceptualizations. Person schemas and situational schemas contain predominately the causally oriented and static conceptualizations, which include (a) Event and State nodes and (b) Consequence and Property arcs. There was one difference

Table 4.7. Distribution of Nodes and Arcs in Various Schemas

	Nodes							Arcs					
Schemas	Fr.[a]	G	S	PS	PE	IS	IE	Fr.[a]	R	I	M	C	P
Person													
Theological liberal	45	.07	0	.04	.02	.80	.02	50	0	0	0	.70	.30
Woman	58	.69	.05	.12	.03	.09	.02	61	.57	.11	.10	.10	.11
Friend	32	.47	0	.03	.09	.13	.28	31	.45	.26	0	.13	.16
Girlfriend of a male	38	.39	.03	.08	0	.47	.03	38	.24	.16	.03	.55	.03
Male friend of female divorcee	45	.13	.20	.07	.16	.38	.07	46	.07	.22	.20	.43	.09
A person	11	.09	0	.09	.09	.55	.18	9	0	.33	0	.44	.22
Mentally ill person	26	.23	0	.08	.23	.15	.31	7	.11	.11	.11	.59	.08
John Doe	12	.42	0	0	0	.50	.08	12	.25	.08	0	.67	0
Mean	33	.31	.03	.06	.08	.39	.13	34	.21	.16	.06	.45	.12
Common activities													
Snow skiing	26	.88	.08	.04	0	0	0	26	.46	.12	.38	.04	0
Water skiing	58	.69	.19	0	.09	.03	0	61	.59	.08	.26	.08	0
Brushing teeth	26	.58	.35	.08	0	0	0	25	.44	.08	.40	.04	.04
Disciplining a child	29	.66	.21	.03	.07	.03	0	29	.45	.07	.34	.14	0
Throwing darts	22	.50	.23	.23	.04	0	0	21	.48	.10	.24	.05	.14
Starting a car	35	.77	.09	.03	.09	.03	0	33	.79	.03	.09	.09	0
Mean	33	.68	.19	.07	.05	.02	0	33	.54	.08	.28	.07	.03
Social interaction or situation													
Jealousy	28	.25	.11	0	.07	.14	.43	35	.06	.14	.09	.72	0
Dentist office	18	.50	.06	.11	.11	.17	.06	21	.48	.10	.05	.33	.05
Babysitting	28	.64	0	.25	.04	.07	0	31	.39	.19	.06	.32	.03
Grief	27	.19	.11	.04	.04	0	.67	26	.15	.08	.12	.50	.23
Prayer	27	.37	.26	.15	0	.14	.07	23	.22	.22	.39	.17	0
Mean	26	.39	.11	.11	.05	.10	.25	27	.26	.15	.14	.41	.06

[a]Fr.: Frequency.

between person schemas and situational schemas. Person schemas had a higher proportion of Internal State and Event nodes (.52) than did the situational schemas (.35).

Some example schemas are presented in Tables 4.8-4.10 and Figures 4.6-4.8. The schema for a *mentally ill person* (Table 4.8 and Figure 4.6) is a person schema, the *snow skiing* schema (Table 4.9 and Figure 4.7) is a common activity schema, and *jealousy* (Table 4.10 and Figure 4.8) is a situational schema. The

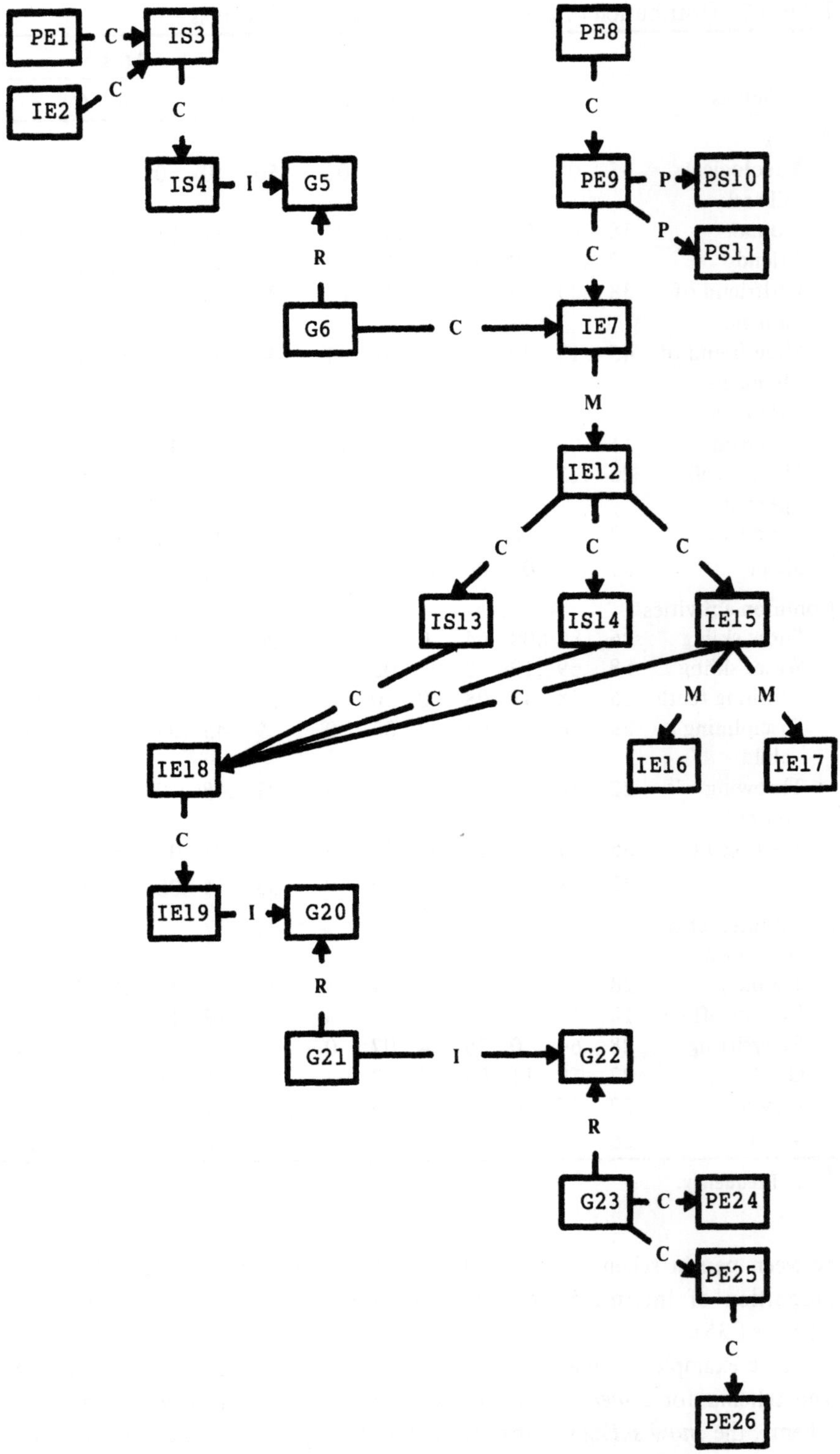

Figure 4.6. Nodal structure of the schema for a mentally ill person. (See Table 4.8 for identification of nodes.)

Table 4.8. Schema for a Mentally Ill Person

(1)	PE:	X[a] is hurt by people in the past
(2)	IE:	X perceives new people as people in the past
(3)	IS:	X is afraid that people will hurt X
(4)	IS:	X is afraid of talking to people
(5)	G:	X avoids talking to people
(6)	G:	X turns inside himself
(7)	IE:	X goes crazy
(8)	PE:	X is hit in the head
(9)	PE:	X's brain is damaged
(10)	PS:	X's sight is wrong
(11)	PS:	X's hearing is wrong
(12)	IE:	X loses track of outside world
(13)	IS:	X is not aware of people
(14)	IS:	X cannot take care of himself
(15)	IE:	X does not think properly
(16)	IE:	X hallucinates
(17)	IE:	X hears voices
(18)	IE:	People think X is unusual
(19)	IE:	People think X might be dangerous
(20)	G:	People avoid being around X
(21)	G:	People put X in hospital
(22)	G:	Doctors control X's behavior
(23)	G:	Doctors give X drugs
(24)	PE:	X acts more normal
(25)	PE:	X becomes doped up
(26)	PE:	X thinks slower

[a]X: mentally ill person.

differences in node and arc categories among these three types of schemas are quite apparent. The snow skiing schema has a hierarchical structure with primarily Goal nodes, Reason arcs, and Manner arcs. The mentally ill schema and jealousy schema have more structure loops with Event and State nodes and Consequence arcs; the structures approach network configurations rather than strict hierarchies.

Goal-oriented hierarchies may be identified in all three schemas. In the mentally ill schema there is a small hierarchical chain of goals.

The doctor controls X's behavior (G22).
The doctor gives X drugs (G23).

Goal G23 is subordinate to G22. In the skiing schema there is a larger hierarchical Goal stack.

X enjoys himself (G1).
X goes skiing (G2).
X goes to top of hill (G14).
X rides chair lift (G15).

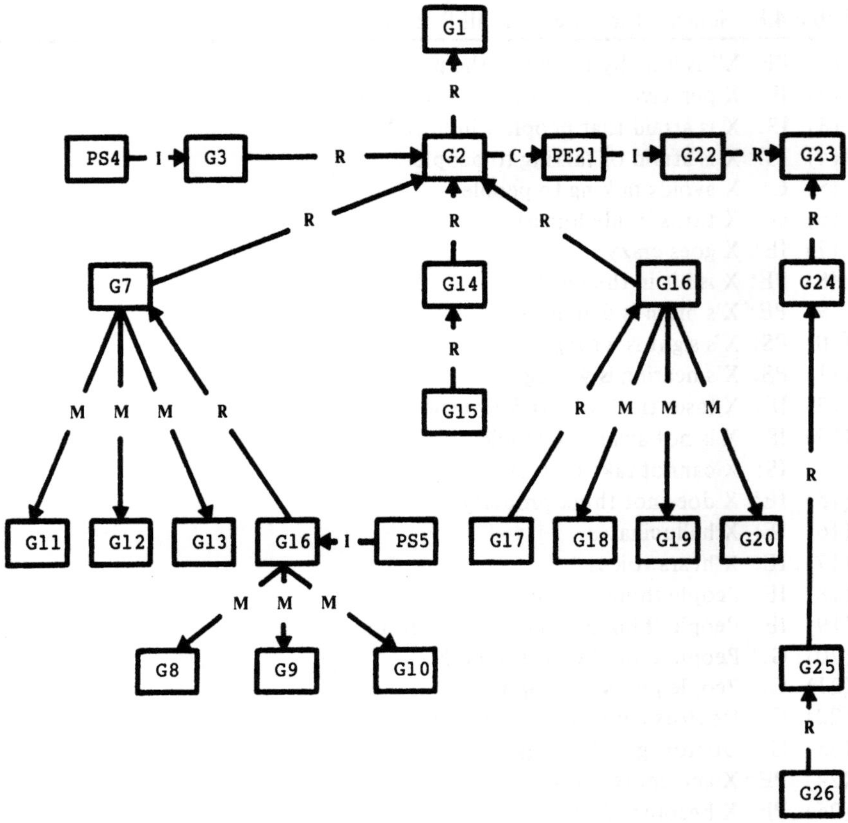

Figure 4.7. Nodal structure of the schema for snow skiing. (See Table 4.9 for identification of nodes.)

Goal G1 is the most superordinate node and G15 the most subordinate. In the jealousy schema, there also is a Goal hierarchy.

> *X have a relationship with someone* (G1).
> *X meets people* (G2).
> *X goes out* (G3).

Goal G1 is the most superordinate node and G13 the most subordinate. Thus, all schemas had hierarchical chains that involve planning on the part of a given character. However, there were more Goal hierarchies and longer Goal stacks in common activities than in person schemas and situational schemas.

A strict hierarchy exists when any given node has at most one mother node. A mother node of a node will be defined as follows.

> Node N is a mother node of node M if N is linked directly to M by a backward Reason arc or a forward Consequence, Manner, or Property arc.

Using this definition of a mother node (the mother node is superordinate to its daughter node), it is possible to assess the degree to which a graph structure devi-

Table 4.9. Schema for Snow Skiing

(1)	G:	X[a] enjoy himself
(2)	G:	X go skiing
(3)	G:	X go to ski resort
(4)	PS:	Snow-covered mountains are at ski resort
(5)	PS:	Proper equipment is needed for skiing
(6)	G:	X get equipment
(7)	G:	X put on equipment
(8)	G:	X get boots
(9)	G:	X get poles
(10)	G:	X get skiis
(11)	G:	X put on warm clothes
(12)	G:	X put boots on feet
(13)	G:	X step into bindings
(14)	G:	X go to top of hill
(15)	G:	X ride chair lift
(16)	G:	X go down hill
(17)	G:	X push off
(18)	G:	X keep knees bent
(19)	G:	X keep skis parallel
(20)	G:	X keep weight forward
(21)	PE:	X reaches bottom
(22)	G:	X stops
(23)	G:	X avoid injury
(24)	G:	X avoid losing control
(25)	G:	X avoid gaining too much speed
(26)	G:	X weaves

[a]X: skiier.

ates from a strict hierarchy. As more nodes have two or more mother nodes in their structures, the structure deviates from a strict hierarchy and approaches a nonhierarchical network structure with structural loops. None of the nodes in the snow skiing schema have multiple mother nodes, whereas six nodes have multiple mother nodes in the jealousy schema (IS11, IE13, IS17, IE23, IE27, and IE28) and three nodes have multiple mother nodes in the mentally ill schema (IS3, IE7, and IE18). Thus, there is a way to assess the degree to which a structure adheres to a strict hierarchy versus a nonhierarchical network.

It should be pointed out that a causal conceptualization is the beginning node in a causal chain; it is not the most abstract or general node. In contrast, a root node in a Goal hierarchy is the most superordinate and global node. It is somewhat awkward to discuss hierarchies in causally oriented conceptualizations.

Differences between narrative and expository passages can also be assessed by the degree to which the structures are stricitly hierarchical. The proportion of nodes that had multiple mother nodes was .07 for the four narrative passages in Table 4.3 and .22 for the four expository passages in Table 4.5. Thus, expository passages have more structural loops and deviate more from a strict hierarchy compared to narrative passages.

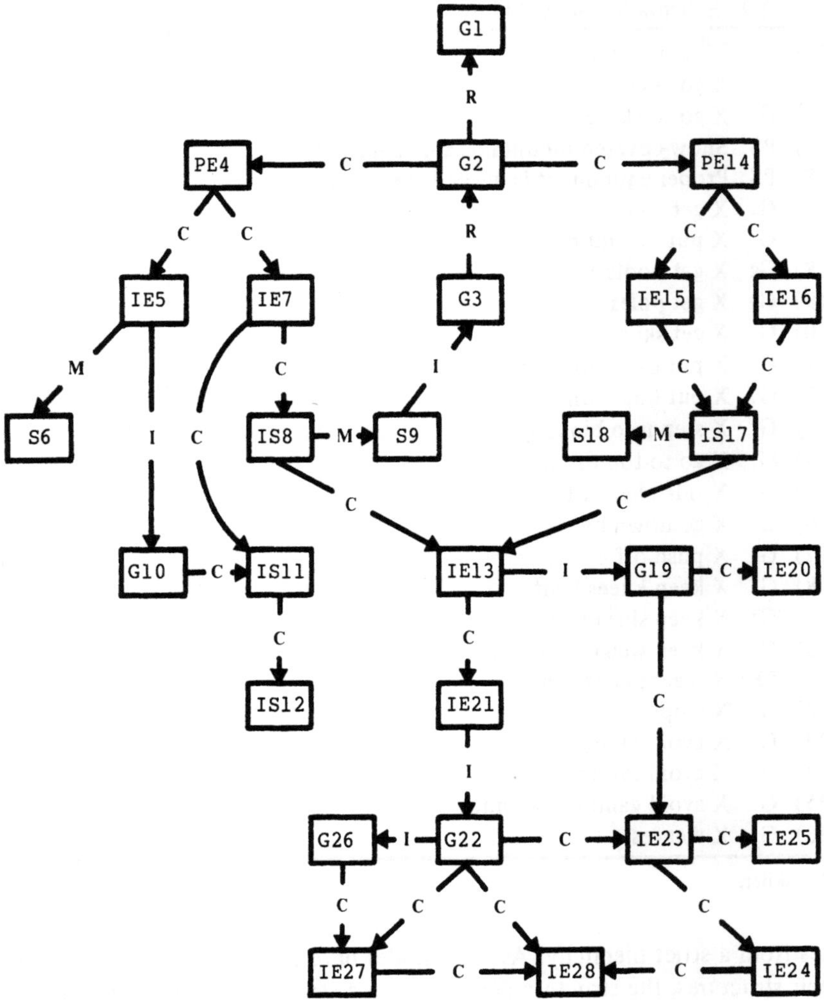

Figure 4.8. Nodal structure of the schema for jealousy. (See Table 4.10 for identification of nodes.)

Before this section ends, a few comments should be made about the "free generation plus Q/A" method of probing schematic knowledge structures. The major virtue of this method is that it is presently the only empirical technique for mapping out schematic knowledge structures. However, it is certainly not a perfect method. The method does not exhaust all the information that is known about a given schema. The method does expose nodes that are expected to be applicable to a large number of instantiations of a schema. However, the method does not usually expose knowledge that is related to a schema, but not frequently applicable to specific instantiations. In other words, the method does not expose nodes whose application is contingent on states of the world that do not exist very often. The following knowledge about an *eating at a restaurant* schema would probably not be exposed by the free generation plus Q/A method.

Table 4.10. Schema for Jealousy

(1)	G:	X[a] have relationship with someone
(2)	G:	X meet people
(3)	G:	X goes out
(4)	PE:	X meets Y
(5)	IE:	Y values X
(6)	S:	Y values X greatly
(7)	IE:	X values Y
(8)	IS:	X is satisfied with Y
(9)	S:	X is satisfied with Y somewhat
(10)	G:	Y wants X to value Y
(11)	IS:	Y is satisfied
(12)	IS:	Y is happy
(13)	IE:	X believes Z is better than Y
(14)	PE:	X meets Z
(15)	IE:	X values Z
(16)	IE:	Z values X
(17)	IS:	X is satisfied with Z
(18)	S:	X is satisfied with Z greatly
(19)	G:	X pays more attention to Z
(20)	IE:	Z believes Z is better than X
(21)	IE:	X values Y less
(22)	G:	X pays less attention to Y
(23)	IE:	Y believes Z is better than Y
(24)	IE:	Y feels put down
(25)	IE:	Y feels insecure
(26)	G:	Y wants more attention from X
(27)	IE:	Y gets frustrated
(28)	IE:	Y gets angry

[a]X, person loving Y and Z; Y, jealous person; Z, person X loves most.

The customer picks up the napkin off the floor.
The waiter sweeps up the glass.

These schema-relevant actions would occur, however, when a customer drops a napkin or a glass. The free generation plus Q/A method does not usually tap conventional aspects of a schema that are associated with infrequent states of the world, misfires, accidents, and correction mechanisms.

Additional Issues Concerning the Conceptual Graph Structures

The distinction between goal-oriented and causally oriented conceptualizations was natural and salient in the graph structures of passages and of schemas. The differences are summarized on the following page.

(1) The goal-oriented conceptualizations include Reason, Initiate, and Manner arcs, whereas causally oriented conceptualizations include Consequence and Property arcs.
(2) Goal-oriented conceptualizations tend to include Goal and Style nodes, whereas causally oriented conceptualizations tend to include Physical Event, Physical State, Internal Event, and Internal State nodes.
(3) Goal nodes tend to be ordered hierarchically in goal-oriented conceptualizations, whereas Event and State nodes tend to have a sequential chain or network structure in causally oriented conceptualizations.
(4) Actions are driven by *future*-directed goals in goal-oriented conceptualizations, whereas events and states are driven by *past* events and states in causally oriented conceptualizations.

Goals and Actions

In the proposed representational system actions are categorized as Goal nodes. A character may achieve a goal by executing behavior and the behavior may or may not be conveyed in the node descriptions. Goal+ nodes refer to actions that achieve goals and Goal– nodes refer to goals that were not achieved. The Goal– nodes occur when (a) the character does not even attempt to achieve the goal by executing the appropriate behavior or (b) the character executes behavior but the goal is blocked by another character or by events in the world. It is apparent from this analysis of actions that actions are defined primarily in terms of intentions and achieved goal states. However, the overt behaviors and events that achieve goals do have a significance with respect to physical-causal conceptualizations. Some consequences of actions are not intended by characters.

In order to illustrate the intentional versus behavioral aspects of actions, consider the following sentences.

(1) *The heroes killed the dragon.*
(2) *The heroes stabbed the dragon and it died.*
(3) *The heroes wanted the dragon to be stabbed in order for the dragon to be dead, so the heroes stabbed the dragon, which caused the dragon to die.*

Suppose that sentence 3 is the relevant interpretation of sentences 1 and 2. Sentence 1 is an action statement that captures the intentional aspect of the episode, but not the behavioral aspect. According to some theories in psychology (Norman and Rumelhart, 1975), action verbs are decomposed into do-cause-change frames that would produce the following representation of sentence 1:

The heroes did something which caused the dragon to change from being alive to being dead.

It should be noted that sentence 1 is semantically vacuous with respect to the specific behaviors that were executed (i.e., *the heroes did something*), whereas it is relatively explicit about the final desired state of the unspecified behavior (i.e., the event of *the dragon becoming dead*). Sentence 2 is somewhat more specific about the behaviors that were executed in the slaying episode: ***the heroes stabbed the dragon.*** However, even the predicate ***stab*** does not fully convey the behaviors that were executed in the episode. Action statements primarily convey information about intended events and states that are ultimately achieved (Schank, 1973). Action statements only weakly specify the behaviors that are executed in order to achieve the desired events and states. Nevertheless, the behaviors that are executed may be critical in determining what happens in physical-causal domains. The instrumental behavior takes time to accomplish and the achievement of the goal has a time span (Steedman, 1977; Vendler, 1967), which is important to consider when a character interacts with the physical or social world. Stabbing behabior has a number of physical consequences that may or may not be intended by the character.

In summary, it appears that action nodes involve certain components or aspects.

(1) **Goal.** The desired state that the agent wants to achieve by executing planned behavior.
(2) **Goal initiators.** States and events that initiate the goal in item 1.
(3) **Behavior.** Some planned behaviors or set of subgoals that are executed in order to lead to the goal in item 1.
(4) **Intended outcome.** The behavior in item 3 leads to a state or event that satisfies the goal state in item 1.
(5) **Unintended outcome.** The behavior in item 3 leads to a state or event that was not intended or not anticipated by the agent.

The example below includes nodes that fill each of the five components.

The bankrupt politician robbed the bank but was caught by the police.

The five aspects would be filled as follows.

Goal:	*Politician obtain money.*
Goal initiator:	*Politician was bankrupt.*
Behavior:	*Politician robbed bank.*
Intended outcome:	*Politician obtained money.*
Unintended outcome:	*Police caught politician.*

The five aspects of intentional actions could have been incorporated more explicitly or more saliently in the proposed system of representing intentional actions. However, all of these five aspects were not saliently segregated for some esoteric reasons. In the proposed system, only two of the five aspects of an action are segregated structurally: (a) goal initiators are structurally segregated from the Goal node by virtue of the Initiate arc, and (b) unintended actions are structurally segregated from the Goal node by virtue of a Consequence arc. As a result, the goal, the behavior, and the intended outcome aspects are amalgamated into a single Goal node. There was some rationale for this amalgamation (Searle, 1980). Consider the behavioral aspect of an action. The behavioral aspect is either semantically depleted (*character does X*) or embellished by subgoal and style information that would be captured by additional nodes. When the behavioral aspect of an action is semantically depleted, then there is no information about the behavior; when the behavioral aspect of an action is specified to some extent, this embellishment is captured by the subordinate Goal and Style nodes that are linked to the original Goal node by Reason and Manner arcs. Therefore, the representational system does capture the behavioral aspect of intentional actions. What about the goal and intended outcome aspects? If the intended outcome matches the goal state, then the Goal node is designated as a Goal+; if the intended outcome does not match the goal state, then the Goal node is designated as a Goal−. Therefore, the goal and intended outcome aspects are actually differentiated in the proposed system, but not by separate nodes. Ultimately, there is only one distinction that the proposed representational system would not capture.

(1) An agent attempting to achieve a goal by executing some unspecified behavior or plan, but ultimately failing. For example, *Nick tried to fix the sink, but he couldn't.*
(2) An agent not executing any behavior or plan, but still having a goal. For example, *Nick wanted to fix the sink, but he never got around to it.*

This subtle difference did not create a problem in applying the representational system because situation 1 never occurred in the passages that were analyzed. However, such a situation could potentially arise in certain passages. If so, then there would be some rationale for decomposing the goal and the intended outcome into two separate nodes.

Internal States and Events

Internal states and events provide the basis for characters' generating goals. A character's perceptions of physical events and states create the goals of characters. At the same time, physical behaviors are executed by characters in order to achieve the goals. Behavior results in causally driven sequences of physical events and states. This cycle continues throughout the narrative and creates the logical structure of the story (Beaugrande and Colby, 1979; Nicholas and Trabasso, 1980; Warren et al., 1979; Wilensky, 1978c). In most narrative passages the Goal configurations and the internal states and events of the characters must be continuously modified and updated from episode to episode. An updating is required because of (a) events occurring in the physical world, (b) actions executed by other characters, and (c) goals that are being achieved or interrupted by occurrences in the social and physical world.

The internal events and states of the characters are just as important as the physical states and events that unfold in narrative. The goals of the character are constructed on the basis of perceptions, knowledge states, sentiments, and emotions of the characters. Some comedies capitalize on situations in which various characters have different knowledge about what is happening in the story. The audience, of course, is fully aware of what is going on and chuckles at the fact that characters are lacking in full knowledge of the situation and foolishly displaying inappropriate actions and emotions. Detective stories involve the protagonist experiencing many episodes until a key fact is recognized, which ultimately is used to solve the case. An analysis of the characters' internal events and states is crucial for a satisfactory theory of narrative representation.

Internal Event nodes in the graphs were often critical in bridging the actions of one character to actions of another character. For example, consider the following conceptualization from *The Czar and His Daughters.*

The daughters cried for help. The heroes heard the cires and went to the dragon.

The heroes hearing the cries is an Internal Event that is caused by (a) *the daughters crying loudly,* (b) *the heroes being near the daughters,* and (c) *the heroes having the ability to hear noises.* The heroes would have never gone to the dragon and rescued the daughters without the prerequisite Internal Event of *the heroes hearing the cries.* The goals and predicaments of one character need to be perceived by another character before the other character facilitates or interrupts the goals of the first character.

Physical Event and States

The physical-causal conceptualizations in this chapter consisted of a network of Physical Event and Physical State nodes interrelated by Consequence arcs. It is possible to perform a more detailed analysis of causal conceptualizations by making further distinctions within the Consequence arc category. For example, it may be important to distinguish the following instances.

(1) **States enabling Events.** The State of *a faucet being on a sink* enables the Event of *water moving from the pipes to the sink.*
(2) **Events causing Events.** The Event of *the car hitting a pedestrian* directly caused the Event of *the pedestrian dying.*
(3) **Events leading to Events.** The Event of *the boy falling into the water* led to the Event of *the boy drowning.*
(4) **Events resulting in States.** The Event of *the dragon's dying* resulted in the State of *the daughters being eternally happy.*

These distinctions may ultimately be important for future research, but they were not adopted in the proposed representational theory.

Node Clusters

Many researchers have attempted to explain how statements cluster in a passage (Baggett, 1979; Black and Bower, 1979, 1980; Johnson and Scheidt, 1977; Lehnert, 1980; Pollard-Gott, McCloskey, and Todres, 1979). The underlying assumption is that a passage contains subclusters and the subclusters consist of packets of statements. To what degree do the graph structures demarcate these subclusters? Node clusters are in fact not always salient in the graph structures.

Node clusters are usually difficult to identify in the networks and hierarchies that represent passages. Instead, the cluster boundaries are probably better defined by the subschemas that are relevant to the passage.

On the other hand, there are some features of the graph structures that seem to isolate node clusters. In stories, a node cluster can be identified when a single character invokes a plan of action in the form of a Goal hierarchy. A juncture occurs between nodal clusters when the focus is shifted from one character (and his Goal hierarchy) to another character. The link between the two nodal clusters is often one character perceiving another character (and his plans). Thus, node clusters can be identified by shifts in character perspectives.

There is another property that serves to identify node clusters. In stories, much of the setting information often occurs at the beginning of the story and forms a natural node cluster. This setting information is often set apart from the plot by Property arcs. Thus, in the Czar story, nodes 0-20 convey setting information that is segregated from nodes 21-156 by a Property arc. Nodes 0-20 would be a natural setting cluster.

With the setting and shifting character focus criteria, one can go a long way in segregating a story into statement clusters. For example, the Czar story would have the following clusters.

Once there was a Czar who had three lovely daughters (cluster 1).

The three daughters went walking in the woods. They were enjoying themselves so much that they forgot the time and stayed too long (cluster 2).

A dragon kidnapped the three daughters and dragged them off (cluster 3).

The daughters cried for help (cluster 4).

Three heroes heard the cries and set off to rescue the daughters. The heroes came and fought the dragon and rescued the daughters. The heroes returned the daughters to their palace (cluster 5).

The Czar heard of the rescue and rewarded the heroes (cluster 6).

The six clusters form the essence of a story involving a saving theme. The six clusters may be summarized as follows.

Cluster 1: Setting.
Cluster 2: Victim violates a norm.
Cluster 3: Villain attacks victim.
Cluster 4: Victim pleads for help.
Cluster 5: Hero rescues victim.
Cluster 6: Hero gets rewarded.

These six basic components are part of most stories involving saving. In fact, Clusters 2, 3, 4, 5, and 6 are quite analogous to the *affect units* in Lehnert's theory of story organization (Lehnert, 1980). *Saving stories* vary according to how each component is embellished. Unfortunately, the graph structures do not saliently capture the global levels of structure. Instead, the clusters and global levels are identified by the content of relevant higher level schemas that are involved. These global levels of structure may be important in guiding the course of expressing the content of a graph structure (Lehnert, 1980).

The Process of Expressing the Content of Graph Structures

The process of expressing the content of the conceptual graph structures is believed to be guided by linguistics rules, rhetorical rules, and abstraction or summarization operators. The rules must solve two basic problems. First, they must specify the level of detail at which the representation will be articulated. Abstraction and summarization processes systematically delete nodes when a conceptualization is summarized or recalled. Second, the rules must determine the order in which the nodes are expressed. The problem of output order is relatively simple in causal chains with linear organizations. The nodes are produced in a chronological order, starting with the initial State or Event, following the forward Consequence arcs, and ending with the terminal node in the causal sequence. Hierarchical Goal structures are also relatively simple, but more complex than causal chains. The subordinate Goal nodes are usually produced before the more superordinate Goal nodes in a hierarchical path of Goal nodes; for Goal nodes that are directly dominated by the same mother node, the nodes are produced from left to right following the chronological order. The problem of output order is more complex when there are structural loops in network structures. In these cases the chronological sequence is more complicated.

The problems involved in articulating the graph structures are related to the utilization of prose representations. The utilization of the graph structures will be examined further in Chapter 5.

5

The Utilization of Prose Representations

In Chapter 4 a method was described for exposing the content of schemas and the cognitive representations of passages. A representational system was also presented in which it was assumed that the cognitive representations consist of conceptual graph structures. These graph structures contain labeled nodes that are interconnected by labeled, directed arcs. In Chapter 4 no experimental evidence was presented that tested how well the theoretical graph structures approximate the true cognitive representations of passages. One goal in this chapter is to present supporting data. If the representations can account for data in a variety of behavioral tasks, then the representational system approaches credibility. As more data can be explained, the representational system becomes more credible. The studies reported in this chapter will not prove that the representational system is correct or better than all alternative representational systems. The enterprise is too young and the data are too scant to arrive at any definitive or sweeping statements. The most that can be hoped for is that some readers will be convinced that the proposed framework is worthwhile to pursue.

A second goal in this chapter is to explore how the theoretical graph structures are utilized in a variety of experimental tasks. This question must be examined whenever a representational theory is tested by behavioral data. The representations themselves don't do anything. The representations are static. However, the representations do participate in guiding behavior whenever there is some process or procedure that operates on the representation and thereby produces some behavioral output. It is assumed that behavior is a product of two fundamentally different components: (a) *representations,* and (b) *procedures* that operate on representations. An explanation of behavior must specify both the nature of the representations and also the procedures that operate on the representations in specific tasks.

What is being advocated here is a *declarativist* position regarding the nature and use of knowledge representations (Norman and Rumelhart, 1975; Winograd, 1975). According to this position, individuals possess a large inventory of relatively static (declarative) knowledge structures. These knowledge structures may correspond to either generic conceptualizations (schemas) or specific memory traces. In contrast, there is a relatively small set of procedures that operate on the static conceptualizations. A specific behavioral task employs one or more of these procedures and psychologists attempt to identify these procedures.

The segregation of representations from procedures, or stored code from processes, has traditionally been adopted in cognitive theorizing. This orientation is summarized in Figure 5.1. Suppose that there are two different representations (X and Y) and two different behavioral tasks (A and B). Four sets of data would be collected from the two different behavior tasks and the two different representations: AX, BX, AY, and BY. In the course of accounting for the behavior in all four situations, the investigator makes a separate set of claims about the properties of the representations (structures X and Y) and the properties of the symbolic procedures (a, b, c, and d) that operate on the representations. If these claims are sound, then certain outcomes should occur. If the claims about representation are correct, then such properties should be detected (or accountable) in a variety of behavioral tasks (A and B) that involve different configurations of symbolic procedures. If the claims about the symbolic, computational procedures are correct, then these properties should apply to a wide variety of representations (X and Y). If the data are sufficiently rich and informative, then the investigator should be able to distinguish between properties of representations versus the symbolic procedures that operate on the representations.

An example should help clarify the approach. Suppose that a representation has been constructed for two passages, X and Y, and that Q/A protocols are collected for statements in these passages. Both *how* questions (A) and *why* questions (B) are answered. The two behavioral tasks involve different symbolic procedures. Task A includes procedures a, b, and c, whereas task B involves procedures b and d. A given set of procedures for a task is applied consistently to the different representations (X versus Y). If the symbolic procedures for *why* and *how* questions are understood theoretically, then the investigator should be able to predict the answers that are generated from a specific representation when the two different questions are asked. The answers would be different for the different questions. If the representations are understood theoretically, then the investigator should be able to predict output for many different questions.

Psychologists have often been squeamish about the possibility of forming a clean segregation of representations from procedures, of storage from retrieval, and of code from process. There are important reasons for this skepticism. One reason is that the data have usually not been rich enough to segregate the different components. The behavior is a product of some amalgamation of representation and process. The demarcation has been fuzzy because the behavioral data have usually been reduced to a handful of means that call for explanation. As long as there are just a handful of data points, the data are easier to communicate. However, the data are also less decisive and informative, and an amalgamation of representation and process is ensured. How does the psychologist circumvent this mess?

The data reported in this section are based on symbolic analyses that seem to be sufficiently rich and informative to arrive at a segregation of representations

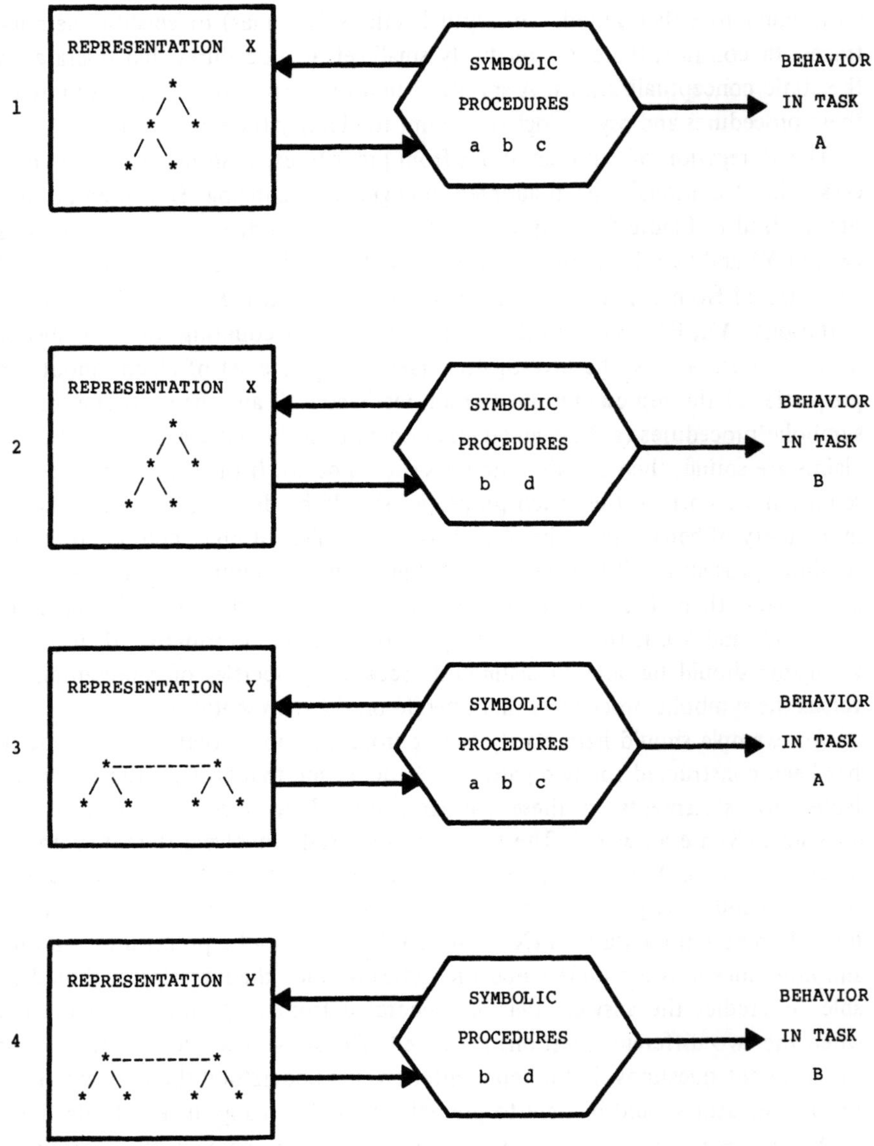

Figure 5.1. Distinctions between representations, symbolic procedures, and behavior.

from the symbolic procedures that operate on the representations. As long as there is a complicated array of data to be explained, there will be fewer alternative theories to consider. The analyses will either reveal salient patterns or be a complete mess. If a mess emerges from the data base, then we are at ground zero. However, if patterns systematically emerge, then we can be confident that we are onto something.

A representational theory and a method for empirically exposing these representations were described in Chapter 4. What is the nature of the symbolic procedures that operate on the representations in specific behavioral tasks? The symbolic procedures will be captured by production systems (Anderson, 1976; Collins, 1977; Hayes-Roth and Hayes-Roth, 1979; Hayes-Roth, Waterman, and Lenat, 1978; McDermott, 1978; McDermott and Forgy, 1978; Newell, 1973, 1980; Newell and Simon, 1972; Stevens and Collins, 1977). Production systems have been adopted in theories of problem solving, memory, and other areas in cognitive psychology. What is a production system?

A production system is much like a program that operates on a data base and ultimately generates output. In the present applications, the conceptual graph structures serve as the data base. When a production system is applied to a graph structure, certain nodes are produced and constitute the theoretically expected output. A production system is defined as an ordered set of if-then rules. Each production (if-then statement) specifies what action is applied when a specific state exists in the knowledge base.

(1) If ⟨state X1⟩ Then ⟨perform operation A1⟩.
(2) If ⟨state X2⟩ Then ⟨perform operation A2⟩.
(3) If ⟨state X3⟩ Then ⟨perform operation A3⟩.

The productions are applied in a specific order: 1, then 2, then 3. For each production, the graph representation is consulted to see if a particular state is applicable. If the state exists, then the operation is performed and then the next production in the sequence is evaluated. However, if the state does not exist, then the corresponding operation is not performed. For example, consider the situation in which state X1 and state X3 are present in the graph structure. Operation A1 would be executed and then operation A3; A2 would not be executed because state X2 was not present in the graph structure.

There are two other properties of production systems that should be briefly discussed. First, a production system often involves recycling when it is applied. After step 3 is evaluated, the system is recycled starting with step 1. Recycling might be prevalent when applied to the graph structures. As each node or arc in the structure is searched and evaluated, the relevant production system is recycled. A complete production system may be applied to each node or arc when checking whether certain states are relevant and applying operations if they are relevant. Then another arc or node is evaluated with the production system starting all over again.

A second property of production systems is that embedding may occur when more than one production system is used in a specific behavioral task. One production system is embedded in another production system.

(1) If ⟨state X1⟩ Then ⟨perform operation A1⟩.
(2) If ⟨state X2⟩ Then ⟨perform production system PS1⟩.
(3) If ⟨state X3⟩ Then ⟨perform production system PS2⟩.
(4) If ⟨state X4⟩ Then ⟨perform operation A2⟩.

It is convenient to refer to a *main* production system, within which other production systems are embedded. In fact, any specific behavioral task involves the construction of a main production system which is to be applied in generating the output. Sometimes these main production systems are difficult for subjects to construct or discover, but once a subject converges on a production system, the data are systematic, and the task is simplified for the subject. A goal for the psychologist is to specify in sufficient detail exactly what main and embedded production systems are used in specific behavioral tasks.

One objective in this chapter is to examine how prose representations are utilized in different behavioral tasks. The representations correspond to the conceptual graph structures that were discussed in Chapter 4. Production systems will be specified for each behavioral task that will be explored. The expected output in a given behavioral task is theoretically generated by applying the hypothetical production system to the empirically constructed graph structures discussed in Chapter 4. If the representations and production systems are good simulations of psychological mechanisms, then the expected output should match the obtained output.

As an example, suppose that a group of subjects read *The Czar and His Daughters* and 1 day later were asked to summarize the story. The graph structure in Table 4.4 would serve as the data base. What symbolic procedure (production system) would be applied to the knowledge structure in order to generate a summary? Consider a rather simple (but ultimately inadequate) symbolic procedure that generates all critical nodes. ***Critical nodes*** are defined as those nodes that have many arcs directly radiating from them (Lehnert, 1980; Schank, 1975). The symbolic procedure would generate all nodes that have at least *n* arcs radiating from them. The production system for this behavioral task is shown in Table 5.1.

The production system in Table 5.1 is not a perfect account of summarization, but it is an informative example of how a production system would be applied to a structure. The purpose of discussing this production system is to illustrate how a production system may be written and applied; the production system should not be construed as a serious proposal of how humans generate summaries. According to production 1, the subject needs to be motivated to give a summary. This trivial production would be executed by searching long-term memory for the graph structure. If the graph structure is accessed, then a node is sampled (production 2) and evaluated as to whether it should be included in the summary. If the node has at least *n* arcs radiating from it, it is

Table 5.1. Production System for Summarizing Prose

(1) If ⟨subject wants to give summary of passage⟩
 Then ⟨search memory for graph structure of passage⟩
(2) If ⟨graph structure of passage is accessed⟩
 Then ⟨find a node⟩
(3) If ⟨node has already been written down⟩
 Then ⟨recycle in the production system⟩
(4) If ⟨node has at least *n* arcs radiating from it⟩
 Then ⟨write down content of node⟩
(5) If ⟨subject wants to continue⟩
 Then ⟨recycle in the production system⟩

written down in the summary (production 4), and the production system is recycled if the subject wants to continue with more information (production 5). In order to avoid repeating nodes in the written protocol, production 3 checks to see if the node has already been written down before evaluating whether it is a critical node. If the subject is motivated, and recycling continues until all nodes are evaluated, then the following nodes would be generated when $n = 5$.

The daughters looked attractive (PS13).
The daughters enjoyed themselves (G+21).
The daughters walked in the woods (G+24).
A dragon kidnapped the daughters (G+61).
A dragon dragged off the daughters (G+75).
Some heroes went to the dragon (G+125).
Some heroes attacked the draon (G+116).
The dragon was defeated (PE107).
The daughters returned to the palace (G+105).
The Czar heard about the rescue (IE141).
The Czar rewarded the heroes (G+149).

A predicted summary protocol would include these nodes. If the nodes were produced in chronological order, the protocol would be as follows:

> Some attractive daughters were walking in the woods and enjoying themselves. A dragon dragged off the daughters in order to kidnap them. Some heroes went to the dragon and attacked it. The dragon was defeated and the daughters returned to the palace. The Czar heard about the rescue and rewarded the heroes.

This is not a bad summary. If the production system were applied with $n = 7$, then the summary protocol would be as follows:

> Some daughters were walking in the woods and enjoying themselves. A dragon was defeated. The Czar rewarded the heroes.

This is not a good summary. A good production system with the proper parameter specifications (critical number of arcs) might provide a reasonable match to the summaries that subjects generate.

The production system in Table 5.1 provides a prediction regarding the selection of *which* nodes are eventually included in the summary. Suppose it is assumed that the parameter n varies from subject to subject according to some distribution. Then a positive correlation is predicted between (a) the number of arcs that directly radiate from a given node and (b) the mean likelihood that the node is in the obtained summary protocols.

The production system in Table 5.1 has a number of deficiencies aside from the issue of whether the appropriate nodes are generated in the expected summary protocol. First, the nodes are randomly searched, which is inconsistent with the output order of humans. Subjects normally produce episodes in stories in a chronological order rather than in a random order (Mandler, 1979; McClure et al., 1979; Munro, Lutz, and Gordon, 1979; Stein and Nezworski, 1978). The production system would need to be modified in order to capture the regularities in output order. Second, there is no straightforward method of stopping the recycling of the production system; it continues until the subject "wants" to stop. However, subjects know directly when the summary is finished, again because the nodes are normally produced in a chronological order. The production system would need to be modified to capture the closing formula that humans use. A third and very serious shortcoming of the production system in Table 5.1 is that it makes no provisions for the categories or content of the nodes that are sampled. Previous studies suggest strongly that the production rules for summarizing text would need to be sensitive to the types of nodes that are involved (Black and Bower, 1980; Graesser, Robertson, Lovelace, and Swinehart, 1980; Johnson and Mandler, 1980; Lehnert, 1980; Rumelhart, 1977c).

A few comments need to be made about the production systems that will be adopted in this chapter. Some productions will not be conditional; they will directly specify what operations are executed without checking for conditions. It is not worth the effort and detail to check for trivial conditions, such as whether the subject is motivated or whether a graph structure has been accessed from memory. Whenever a production has no conditional description, the operation is automatically applied.

A second constraint addresses the search problem when nodes and arcs are examined. What assumptions will be made regarding the *likelihood* of accessing specific nodes and the *sequential order* in which nodes are accessed? In the past, search processes have been examined extensively in cognitive psychology (Anderson, 1976; Anderson and Bower, 1973; Pachella, 1974; Sternberg, 1970; Townsend, 1974; Wickelgren, 1974) and artificial intelligence (Charniak, Riesbeck, and McDermott, 1980; Feigenbaum, 1963; Hunt, 1975; Winograd, 1976). However research in cognitive psychology has been less than conclusive about how humans search information in memory, e.g., serial versus parallel, ordered versus random, and exhaustive versus self-terminating. In the analyses discussed in this chapter, the search problem will be circumvented by assuming that all nodes and arcs in the graph structure are automatically and equally available. It is just as if one were to look at a graph structure that is taped to a wall. This (over)simplification has important implications. In particular, the behavioral data will not be explained by special assertions about the order of sampling nodes and the likelihood of accessing those nodes that should be theoretically produced. Instead, there will only be claims as to which of the nodes among the total set of nodes in the graph structure are theoretically produced. Unfortunately, the subsequent analyses have nothing to contribute to the important, but challenging question of how the nodes are sampled (see Dyer and Lehnert, 1980; Lehnert, 1978a).

Three types of behavioral tasks will be examined in this chapter.

(1) **Question answering.** Is it possible to account for the specific answers that subjects give when they answer specific questions about a passage?

(2) **Verification of inferences.** Can verification ratings of statements (truth versus falsity) be predicted by structural properties of the conceptual graph structures?

(3) **Recall of stated information.** Can the recall of explicitly stated nodes be predicted by structural and conceptual properties of the conceptual graph structures?

Question Answering

The symbolic procedures involved in question answering have only recently been examined in the cognitive sciences (Collins, 1977; Dyer and Lehnert, 1980; Graesser, 1978a; Graesser et al., 1981; Graesser, Robertson, Lovelace, and Swinehart, 1980; Lehnert, 1977, 1978a; Norman and Rumelhart, 1975; Stein and Glenn, 1979). The most comprehensive and detailed analysis of question answering is in Lehnert's book *The Process of Question Answering* (1978a). Lehnert specified the symbolic procedures for 13 categories of questions that operate on a knowledge base represented by Schank's conceptual dependency theory. The book provided a comprehensive framework for investigating such a broad phenomenon as question answering. However, it was beyond the scope of her book to give supporting empirical data. Nevertheless, the data reported in this section indirectly provide empirical support for some of her invaluable insights.

Lehnert's 13 categories of questions are listed in Table 5.2. Each question category samples the relevant knowledge base according to a specific symbolic procedure. The result is an answer. According to Lehnert, a question passes through a number of levels of interpretive analysis before a memory search through the knowledge base is begun. From the present standpoint, an important level of interpretive analysis determines what question category is relevant. Thus, when a question is asked, the answerer first determines which of the 13 categories is involved and then searches the knowledge base according to the symbolic procedure of the question category.

Sometimes ambiguities arise when determining which question category is applicable. Consider the following excerpt and question.

The dragon dragged off the daughters. The daughters cried for help.
Why did the daughters cry?

In one sense, the daughters' crying may be construed as an automatic process that was causally elicited by antecedent events. In particular, *the dragon's dragging off the daughters caused the daughters to be frightened, and their fright automatically caused them to cry.* Answers that include this information indicate that a causal antecedent question has been selected. In another sense, the daughters' crying was a goal-driven action and a goal-oriented question may be selected to elicit the information that *the daughters cried so that someone would hear them and rescue them.* A question may invoke more than one of the 13 categories and ambiguities may arise as to which category is relevant. However, ambiguities become less frequent as more context is provided to the answerer. In normal conversations, the answerer usually knows why a question is being asked.

Table 5.2. Lehnert's 13 Categories of Questions

Question category	Description
(1) Causal antecedent	What states and events in some way caused the concept in question?
(2) Goal orientation	What are the motives or goals behind an action?
(3) Enablement	What act or state enabled the concept in question?
(4) Causal consequent	What states or events causally follow from the concept in question?
(5) Verification	Is the concept or question true or false?
(6) Disjunctive	What member of a set of concepts is relevant?
(7) Instrumental/procedural	What method or instrument was used in executing an action?
(8) Concept completion	Who? What? Where? When?
(9) Expectational	Why did some action not occur?
(10) Judgmental	What is the listener's judgment about something?
(11) Quantification	How much? How many?
(12) Feature specification	What properties does an object have?
(13) Requests	The questioner requests that a specific act be performed; these are indirect requests in the form of questions.

Adapted from Lehnert (1978a).

Whereas Lehnert's symbolic procedures were applied to knowledge bases represented by the conceptual dependency theory, the procedures that will be reported in this section are applied to the graph structures discussed in Chapter 4. Thus, the subsequent analyses will examine which nodes from the graph structure are produced as answers when a specific node is questioned by a specific type of question. Is it possible to account for the specific answers that subjects generate to specific questions? What symbolic procedures are involved when operating on the graph structures and selecting the appropriate nodes?

The goals of Lehnert's book are different from the objectives in this section. Lehnert provided a comprehensive theoretical analysis and model that accommodates all questions. However, there was no supporting empirical data. In this section supporting data will be presented, but the scope will be restricted to a handful of question categories. Specifically, the present focus will be on *how* and *why* questions.

The first set of analyses examined the Q/A protocols that were collected from the four narrative passages in Table 4.3 (Graesser et al., 1981). Subjects first read each passage and later answered a *how* question and a *why* question about each explicitly mentioned state, event, and action in the passage. The subjects were probed under both the standard and extended Q/A methods. Graph structures were constructed from the stated nodes and inference nodes that were generated from the various Q/A protocols *collectively*. The purpose of presenting the analyses in this section is to explain the *specific answers* to the *specific questions*.

At this point, an observant reader may wonder whether the proposed analyses are circular. The Q/A method was used to generate empirically the nodes in the conceptual graph structures (Chapter 4). Then the graph structures were used in part to explain the answers that are given to questions. It can be argued, however, that the supposed circularity is more apparent than real. The Q/A method was used to generate empirically a pool of inferences about a given passage. The resulting set of stated nodes and inference nodes were subsequently organized into a graph structure by judges who were not completely cognizant of how the graph structures would be analyzed. Moreover, the composition of each graph structure was partially determined by theoretical considerations that involved specific claims about how nodes are categorized and specific constraints on the arcs that interrelate nodes. From a mathematical perspective, the nodes could potentially be interrelated in an exponentially horrendous number of ways. However, only one or a few of these configurations would meet the constraints of the theory, e.g., the constraints on the arc categories. Had the nodes been interrelated in a more haphazard or random manner, the symbolic procedures for generating specific answers to specific questions would have been doomed to failure. Strictly speaking, the analyses reported in this section are not circular.

There is one other issue that needs to be clarified concerning the graph structures and Q/A procedures. Were the inference nodes in the graph structures truly part of the representations constructed during comprehension, or were the inference nodes derived only at question answering? The obvious answer to this question is that some inference nodes were generated during comprehension whereas others were derived at question answering on the basis of relevant generic schemas (see Chapter 4). At this point, there is no way of segregating which nodes are to be placed in either of these two categories. Moreover, it is conceivable that any given node could be generated during comprehension by some subjects, but derived during question answering by other subjects. Perhaps some future research will unveil some empirical and/or rational criteria for segregating nodes generated during comprehension from those generated during question answering. Nevertheless, this problem does not detract from the findings and conclusions discussed in this section. The proposed Q/A procedures should apply to the content of generic schema structures as well as to the content of specific passage representations.

Symbolic procedures were delineated for four types of questions.

(1) **Why ⟨action⟩**. Why did a specific action occur?
(2) **How ⟨action⟩**. How did a specific action occur?
(3) **Why ⟨event⟩**. Why did a specific event occur?
(4) **How ⟨event⟩**. How did a specific event occur?

The symbolic procedures for how ⟨state⟩ and why ⟨state⟩ questions will not be immediately examined here because there were very few state nodes that were explicitly stated in the narrative passages.

Generally speaking, the above four types of questions have a fairly direct correspondence to some of Lehnert's question categories (Table 5.2). Why ⟨action⟩ questions are goal orientation questions. How ⟨action⟩ questions are instrumental/procedural questions. Why ⟨event⟩ and how ⟨event⟩ questions are causal antecedent questions.

The symbolic procedures for answering the four different types of questions are presented in Table 5.3. The category and direction of the arcs are critical in determining which nodes are sampled when a specific type of question is asked. Why ⟨action⟩ questions sample nodes connected to the probed action by forward Reason arcs and backward Initiate arcs. How ⟨action⟩ questions pursue backward Reason arcs and foward Manner arcs. The symbolic procedures for why ⟨event⟩ and how ⟨event⟩ questions are very similar in that both sample nodes connected to the probed node by paths of backward Consequence arcs.

In order to provide a concrete example of the symbolic procedures, the graph structure for the following excerpt from *The Ant and the Dove* story is shown in Table 5.4 and Figure 5.2.

A thirsty ant went to a river and became carried away by the rush of the stream.

The graph structure contains 21 nodes, but only three nodes (1, 7, and 21) were explicitly stated in the passage; the other nodes were inferences derived empirically from the Q/A method.

The graph structure has examples of nearly all of the categories of arcs and nodes. The graph also contains both a goal-oriented structure and a causally oriented structure. The goal-oriented structure consists of (a) a set of Goal nodes that are related by Reason arcs in a hierarchical fashion (nodes 2, 3, 6, 7, 8, 9, and 11), (b) a set of State and Event nodes (nodes 1, 4, and 5) that are related to the Goal nodes by Initiate arcs, and (c) a Style node (node 10) that is directly related to a Goal node by a Manner arc. In contrast, the causally oriented conceptualization consists of a set of State and Event nodes (nodes 12-21) that are interrelated by a network of Consequence arcs.

The symbolic procedures in Table 5.3 operate on graph structures such as that in Table 5.4 and Figure 5.2. The symbolic procedures determine which nodes are generated as answers when a specific node is probed by a specific type of question. The why ⟨action⟩ questions are goal-orientation questions that sample superordinate Goal nodes and goal initiators. For example, the question *Why did the ant go to the river?* generates three superordinate Goal nodes that are connected to the probed node (G7) by forward Reason arcs.

In order to satisfy his thirst (G2).
In order to get water (G3).
In order to drink river water (G6).

State and Event nodes that initiate the probed node and the superordinate Goal nodes would also be generated.

Table 5.3. Symbolic Procedures for Generating Answers to Four Types of Questions

Why ⟨action⟩ (goal orientation)

(1) Output nodes radiating from the action node via $\overrightarrow{\mathrm{R}}*$.

(2) Output nodes radiating from the action node via $\overleftarrow{\mathrm{I}}$ and the nodes in step 1 via $\overleftarrow{\mathrm{I}}$

How ⟨action⟩ (instrumental/procedural)

(1) Output nodes radiating from the action node via $\overleftarrow{\mathrm{R}}*$.

(2) Output nodes radiating from the action node via $\overrightarrow{\mathrm{M}}*$ and the nodes in step 1 via $\overrightarrow{\mathrm{M}}*$.

Why ⟨event⟩ and how ⟨event⟩ (causal antecedent)

(1) Output nodes radiating from the event node via $\overleftarrow{\mathrm{C}}*$.

Adapted from Graesser, Robertson, and Anderson (1981).[a]

[a] An asterisk (*) signifies a path of links with the designated label.

Table 5.4. Node Descriptions for Excerpt from *The Ant and the Dove*

Node number	Node category	Node description
1[a]	PS	Ant was thirsty
2	G+	Ant satisfy thirst
3	G+	Ant get (ingest) water
4	IS	Ant liked fresh water
5	PS	River was closest place for water
6	G+	Ant drink river water
7[a]	G+	Ant go to river
8	G+	Ant crawl
9	G+	Ant walk
10	S	Ant's crawling was slow
11	G+	Ant go into river
12	PE	Ant became too close to stream
13	PE	Ant fell into stream
14	PE	Stream was rushing hard
15	PE	An accident occurred
16	PE	Ant slipped
17	PE	Stream overpowered ant
18	PS	Ant was small
19	PS	Ant was light
20	PS	Ant was unable to swim
21[a]	PE	Stream carried ant away

Adapted from Graesser, Robertson, and Anderson (1981).

Note: See structure in Figure 5.2.

[a] Stated node.

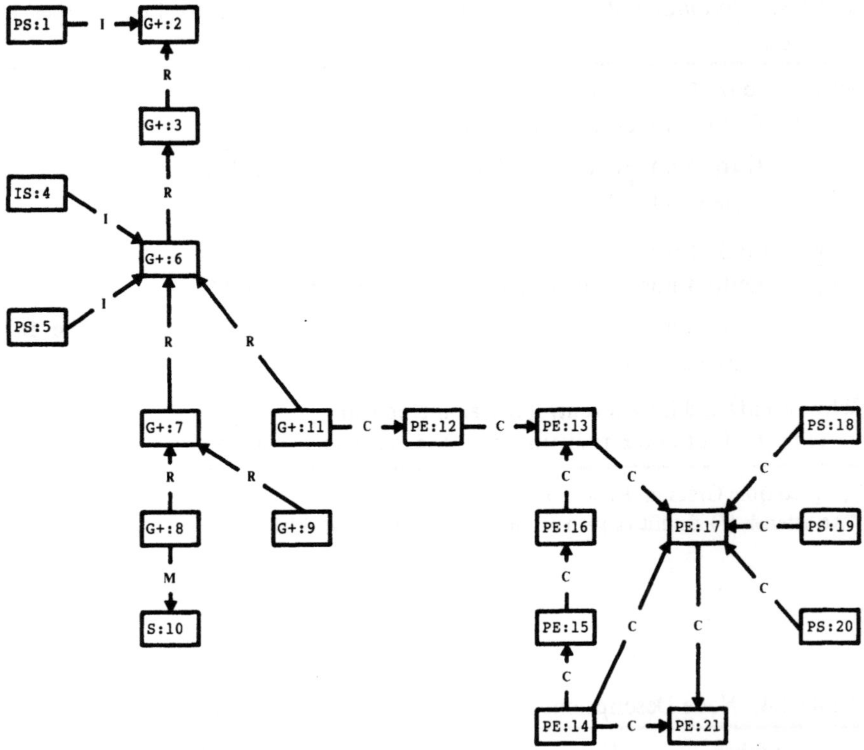

Figure 5.2. Nodal structure for *A thirsty ant went to a river and became carried away by the rush of the stream* (see Table 5.4 for identification of nodes). (Adapted from Graesser, Robertson, and Anderson, 1981.)

Because the ant was thirsty (PS1).
Because the ant liked fresh water (IS4).
Because the river was the closest place for water (PS5).

The how ⟨action⟩ questions are instrumental-procedure questions that sample information that is subordinate to the probed node. For example, suppose that node 7 was probed with the how ⟨action⟩ question *How did the ant go to the river?* The answers would sample subordinate Goal nodes that are linked to the probed actions by backward Reason arcs.

The ant crawled (G8).
The ant walked (G9).

Subordinate Style nodes would also be generated.

The ant's crawling was slow (S10).

In summary, when an action (Goal+) is probed in a goal-oriented structure, the answers to *why* questions sample superordinate information in the plan, whereas the answers to *how* questions sample subordinate information. It follows that there should be no overlap between answers to a why ⟨action⟩ and a how ⟨action⟩ question.

Answers to why ⟨event⟩ and how ⟨event⟩ questions are causal antecedent questions that tap into the causally oriented structures. If node 13 were probed, *Why did the ant fall into the stream?* then the answers would include nodes that are connected to node 13 via backward Consequence arcs.

Because the ant went to the river (G11).
Because the ant became too close to the stream (PE12).
Because the stream was rushing hard (PE14).
Because an accident occurred (PE15).
Because the ant slipped (PE16).

Is there empirical evidence that the symbolic procedures in Table 5.3 are good simulations of human thought processes? Four separate analyses consistly supported the proposed symbolic procedures. These analyses also indirectly validated the correctness of the graph structures that the symbolic procedures operate on.

The first analysis is a descriptive summary of which arcs were sampled in the course of generating the obtained (not expected) answers to specific questions. The sampling of arcs in the graph representations is summarized in Table 5.5 for the four types of questions. These analyses are based on the standard Q/A and the extended Q/A protocols collected on the four narrative passages. An arc was scored as sampled if it occurred in the path connecting the statement that was questioned and the answer to the question. There were sometimes alternative routes in causally oriented conceptualizations. In these instances the arcs were scored on the shortest path between the questioned node and the answer node. For example, the question *Why did the stream carry the ant away?* (node 21) generated the answer *Because the ant fell into the stream* (node 13). There are two paths of arcs between nodes 21 and 13. One path intersects node 17, while the other path intersects nodes 14, 15, and 16. The shortest path, which intersects node 17, was scored.

The distribution of arc categories in Table 5.5 corresponds closely to the categories that would be expected on the basis of the symbolic procedures in Table 5.3. The answers to why ⟨action⟩ questions followed the forward Reason arcs that lead to superordinate Goal nodes, along with the backward Initiate arcs that lead to nodes that initiate these Goals. The answers to how ⟨action⟩ questions followed the backward Reason arcs that lead to subordinate Goal nodes and also the forward Manner arcs that embellish the style of the action. Answers to why ⟨event⟩ questions followed similar routes as answers to how ⟨event⟩ questions. The backward Consequence arcs were pursued when these causal antecedent questions were answered. A minor difference between the latter two types of questions is that how ⟨event⟩ questions occasionally sampled forward Manner arcs, whereas this was not the case for why ⟨event⟩ questions. Among the four types of questions, 88% of the sampled arcs were in categories specified by the symbolic procedures in Table 5.3.

Table 5.5. Distribution of Arc Categories Sampled for Answers to Questions About Narrative Passages

	Sampled arc categories							
Question category	$\overrightarrow{R}$	$\overleftarrow{R}$	$\overrightarrow{M}$	$\overrightarrow{I}$	$\overleftarrow{I}$	$\overrightarrow{C}$	$\overleftarrow{C}$	Fr.[a]
Extended Q/A								
Why ⟨action⟩	.72	.00	.00	.00	.20	.01	.07	2182
How ⟨action⟩	.05	.66	.21	.01	.03	.02	.02	1595
Why ⟨event⟩	.04	.08	.00	.00	.09	.00	.78	1008
How ⟨event⟩	.03	.03	.06	.00	.05	.01	.83	673
Standard Q/A								
Why ⟨action⟩	.78	.00	.00	.00	.13	.01	.07	1009
How ⟨action⟩	.03	.67	.22	.01	.03	.02	.02	475
Why ⟨event⟩	.01	.05	.00	.00	.08	.00	.86	392
How ⟨event⟩	.03	.02	.03	.00	.05	.01	.87	218

Adapted from Graesser, Robertson, and Anderson (1981).
[a]Fr.: frequency.

The sampling of arc categories was equivalent for standard Q/A and extended Q/A responses. In fact, an overall chi-square test was not significant when arc distributions of the standard and extended Q/A tasks were compared, χ^2 (24) = 33.18, $p > .05$. Thus, the procedures of sampling arcs do not change when subjects are asked to give more detailed answers to questions.

The second analysis examined the degree to which answers were similar for *why* and *how* questions when a specific statement was probed. It is apparent from Table 5.3 that none of the nodes sampled by why ⟨action⟩ questions should overlap with nodes sampled by how ⟨action⟩ questions. However, there should be a high overlap in questions to why ⟨event⟩ and how ⟨event⟩ questions. Therefore, the obtained distributions of answers to *how* versus *why* questions should show a high degree of overlap for events, but there should be no overlap for actions. In order to test this prediction, *overlap scores* between answers to *how* and *why* questions were computed for each action and event. An overlap score was computed as the number of common answers (nodes) to *why* and *how* questions (adjusted by frequency) divided by the total number of answers to *why* and *how* questions. The mean overlap score was significantly higher for events than that for actions, .56 versus .05, respectively, $t(57) = 15.41, p < .01$. As predicted, the mean overlap score for actions did not differ significantly from 0. Also computed were overlap scores for seven probed statements that were ambiguous with regard to the action/event distinction. The mean overlap score for these items (.18) fell between the overlap scores for actions and for events.

A third set of analyses provided stronger confirmation of the symbolic procedures in Table 5.3. The theoretical symbolic procedures were applied to the graphs of the four passages in order to generate a set of permissible answers to each question. The proportions of obtained answers in the extended Q/A test that were accepted by the symbolic procedures in Table 5.3 were .97, .91, .88, and .89 for why ⟨action⟩, how ⟨action⟩, why ⟨event⟩, and how ⟨event⟩ questions, respectively; the corresponding proportions from the standard Q/A protocols were .94, .92, .86, and .90, respectively. Consequently, 91% of the obtained answers were accepted by the theoretical symbolic procedures when they were applied to the graph representations!

A fourth set of analyses provided perhaps the strongest support for the symbolic procedures in Table 5.3. Graesser et al. (1981) conducted an experiment in which 16 subjects rated the quality of specific answers to specific questions on a "goodness-of-answer" scale. Of course, the ratings were collected after the subjects read the passages. The answers were rated on the following 4-point scale.

4 = very good answer
3 = fairly good answer
2 = possibly an acceptable answer
1 = bad answer

A subset of the answers was expected to receive very low ratings because the *theoretical* symbolic procedures in Table 5.3 would not generate these answers when they were applied to the graph structures of the four narrative passages. Another subset of answers would be generated theoretically and therefore were expected to have very high ratings.

A set of 16 actions and 8 events were selected from the four narrative passages as items that were questioned. A *how* question and a *why* question was prepared for each action and event. The answers to be rated for a given item were the same for the *why* question and the *how* question. The answers were also inferences as opposed to being explicitly stated nodes. There were five classes of answers for each why ⟨action⟩ and how ⟨action⟩ question.

(1) **Superordinate goals.** These answers included Goal nodes radiating from the questioned action via the forward Reason arcs. These answers would in theory be generated by the why ⟨action⟩ questions but not the how ⟨action⟩ questions. There were 32 actions in this category that were selected randomly from the graph structures.
(2) **Subordinate goals.** These answers included 32 randomly selected answers that radiated from the questioned action via the backward Reason arcs. In theory these answers would be generated by how ⟨action⟩ questions but not why ⟨action⟩ questions.
(3) **Goal initiators.** These answers included 59 randomly selected answers that were linked to the questioned actions and their superordinate Goal nodes via the backward Initiate arc. In theory these would be acceptable answers to why ⟨action⟩, but not to how ⟨action⟩ questions.
(4) **Irrelevant goals.** These answers included 16 randomly selected Goal nodes that would not be accepted by either how ⟨action⟩ or why ⟨action⟩ questions.

(5) **Irrelevant goal initiators.** These answers were 16 randomly selected Events and States that would not in theory be generated by how ⟨action⟩ and why ⟨action⟩ questions.

There were three classes of answers for the eight questioned events.

(1) **Causal antecedents.** These answers were 16 randomly selected States and Events that would be theoretically generated by why ⟨event⟩ and how ⟨event⟩ questions. These answers radiated from the questioned event via the backward Consequence arc.
(2) **Consequences.** These answers were 16 randomly selected States and Events that would not in theory be generated by the why ⟨event⟩ and how ⟨event⟩ questions. The answers radiated from the questioned events via the forward Consequence arcs.
(3) **Irrelevant antecedents.** These answers were 16 randomly selected States and Events that would not in theory be generated by the *how* and *why* questions. These answers were not directly connected to the questioned event via a backward Consequence chain.

The mean goodness-of-answer ratings of the *how* and *why* questions are presented in Table 5.6. The mean ratings were uniformly high (2.95) for those classes of answers that were theoretically generated from the proposed symbolic procedures in question answering, and low (1.26) for those classes of answers that were not generated theoretically, $F(1, 422) = 1123.02, p < .01, MSe = .25$. These data are consistent with the belief that the proposed graph representations and symbolic procedures have a substantial degree of validity.

An alternative explanation of the data in Table 5.6 is that the ratings can be predicted simply by the empirical likelihood of producing a specific answer to a specific question. Those classes of answers that were theoretically generated by

Table 5.6. Goodness-of-Answer Ratings for the Different Classes of Answers

	Question type	
Class of answer	Why	How
Questioned actions		
Superordinate goals	3.20[a]	1.29
Subordinate goals	1.37	3.18[a]
Goal initiators	2.73[a]	1.39
Irrelevant goals	1.14	1.04
Irrelevant goal initiators	1.27	1.10
Questioned events		
Causal antecedents	2.99[a]	2.63[a]
Irrelevant antecedents	1.39	1.24
Consequences	1.23	1.21

Adapted from Graesser, Robertson, and Anderson (1981).
[a] Answers were theoretically generated by the graph representations and proposed symbolic procedures for question answering.

the graphs and Q/A procedures were also often empirically produced by subjects in the extended and standard Q/A protocols. However, the classes of answers that were not expected to be generated theoretically were in fact never empirically produced in the Q/A protocols for a particular question; the answers were produced from some other question. It is possible that (a) the empirical likelihood of producing a specific answer to a specific question, as assessed by the Q/A protocols, can completely account for the goodness-of-answer ratings, and (b) the graphs and proposed symbolic procedures of question answering have no additional predictive validity.

In order to test between the above two explanations of the data, answers were segregated into three groups.

(1) Those answers to a question that would be generated in theory and in fact were empirically generated in the standard or extended Q/A protocols for that specific question. For example, one of the obtained answers to *How was the ant carried away by the stream?* was *The ant slipped.* This answer would also be generated theoretically.
(2) Those answers to a question that would be generated in theory, but in fact were *not* empirically generated in the Q/A protocols of that specific question. These answers were empirically generated by some other question. For example, ***An accident occurred*** would be generated theoretically from the question *Why was the ant carried away by the stream?* However, this answer was not produced by the subjects as an answer to that question.
(3) Those answers to a question that would not in theory be generated, and in fact were not empirically generated in the Q/A protocols of that specific question. These answers were empirically generated by some other question. For example, *The ant became tired* was not empirically produced and would not theoretically be generated from the question *Why was the ant carried away by the stream?*

If the graph structures and symbolic procedures completely explained the goodness-of-answer ratings, then the following pattern of ratings would emerge: rating (1) = rating (2) > rating (3). If, however, the ratings can completely be explained by the empirical likelihood of generating specific answers to specific questions, then the following pattern of ratings would emerge: rating (1) > rating (2) = rating (3). The obtained means clearly supported the former alternative more than the latter. The means were 3.02, 2.76, and 1.26 for answer sets 1, 2, and 3, respectively. These means were all significantly different from each other, but it was clearly the case that rating (2) was quantitatively closer to rating (1) than to rating (3). Therefore, the goodness-of-answer ratings were robustly predicted by the conceptual graphs and theoretical Q/A procedures, whereas empirical generation likelihood only modestly predicted the ratings.

Analyses were also performed on the Q/A protocols that were collected on the four expository passages in Table 4.5. These analyses were informative for two reasons. First, it was possible to confirm the Q/A procedures for why ⟨action⟩, how ⟨action⟩, why ⟨event⟩, and how ⟨event⟩ questions. Second, it was possible to examine the symbolic procedures that are involved in why ⟨state⟩ and how ⟨state⟩ questions since expository passages have many static propositions.

Table 5.7 contains the distribution of arc categories that were sampled in the course of generating the obtained answers to specific questions. Separate distributions are reported for *why* versus *how* questions. Separate distributions are also reported for probed actions versus events versus states. The arc distributions for why ⟨action⟩, how ⟨action⟩, why ⟨event⟩, and how ⟨event⟩ questions essentially replicated the analyses for the four narrative passages and supported the proposed symbolic procedures in Table 5.3. Of the 2172 sampled arcs in these four question categories, 81% were in the categories specified by the symbolic procedures in Table 5.3.

The symbolic procedures that are applied for why ⟨state⟩ and how ⟨state⟩ questions are more complicated. According to the data in Table 5.7, 70% of the answers to why ⟨state⟩ questions pursue paths of forward and backward Consequence arcs. Thus, when questioned about why a state exists, the answerer pursues causal antecedent chains and also causal consequence chains. For how ⟨state⟩ questions, 80% of the answers followed backward Consequence arcs and forward and backward Property arcs. When questioned about how a state exists, the answerers pursued causal antecedent chains and Property arcs. What do these arc distributions reveal about the manner in which why ⟨state⟩ and how ⟨state⟩ questions are answered?

The fact that answers to why ⟨state⟩ questions follow causal antecedent paths (backward Consequence chains) is very much expected. Ongoing states are usually a result of chains of prior actions, events, and states. The answerer explains the existence of a given state by tracing the chain of occurrences that led up to it. This is illustrated in the following example.

Why do wagons have wheels?
Because someone put the wheels on the wagon.
Because someone attached wheels to the axle.

Table 5.7. Distribution of Arc Categories Sampled for Answers to Questions About Expository Passages

Question category	Sampled arc categories										
	→ R	← R	→ I	← I	→ C	← C	→ M	← M	→ P	← P	Fr.[a]
Why ⟨action⟩	.63	.01	.01	.25	.04	.04	.01	.02	.01		329
How ⟨action⟩	.13	.44		.05	.05	.01	.25	.01	.07		351
Why ⟨event⟩	.01			.05	.02	.85		.05	.02		698
How ⟨event⟩				.10	.01	.83	.01	.02	.03		794
Why ⟨state⟩	.06		.01	.03	.22	.48		.02	.06	.13	658
How ⟨state⟩	.02	.03			.11	.38	.03	.02	.22	.20	566

[a] Fr.: frequency.

The answerer also produces causal consequences when asked to explain why a certain state exists.

Why do wagons have wheels?
  So that the wagon moves more easily.
  To reduce friction.

There is an intentional flavor to answers that emanate from causal Consequence arcs. The probed state appears to exist for the benefit and facilitation of some future event. Ongoing states are often enabling states that are needed for some future events to unfold. Comprehenders are inclined to impose intentionality on strictly causally oriented mechanistic or natural systems (Brown, Collins, and Harris, 1978). The mechanism is believed to have a purpose and is functionally goal oriented.

Why does it rain?
  So that flowers can grow.
  So that humans do not die of thirst.

When animate beings use equipment, the static properties of the equipment are believed to serve a purpose for the user. In these instances, explanations of a state involve Consequence arcs.

Why is this knob on the television set?
  In order to turn the channel.

States of the world are often created by humans. When asked to explain why these states exist, the answerer may focus on either (a) the physical events that led up to the state by sampling causal antecedents (backward Consequence arcs) or (b) the intentional rationale for animate beings' creating the state by sampling causal consequences (forward Consequence arcs).

It is often awkward or unnatural to answer how ⟨state⟩ questions. For example, consider the following questions.

How is this knob on the television set?
How does the cup have a handle?
How are your eyes brown?

These questions are awkward and difficult to comprehend. It is fair to say that how ⟨state⟩ questions are rarely asked. When such a question is asked, the answerer may interpret the question in different ways. For example, *How are your eyes brown?* may be interpreted in the following ways:

How did your eyes come to be brown?
What properties are characteristic of brown eyes?

The answerer generates an answer either by (a) delineating the actions, events, and states that led up to the state (backward Consequence arcs) or (b) describing the properties associated with the state (forward or backward Property arcs).

Although how ⟨state⟩ questions are often awkward queries, the answerer does search and output nodes with some regularity.

In this section, the symbolic procedures have been delineated for a variety of question categories. The proposed symbolic procedures and the underlying graph structures can impressively account for the specific answers that are generated when specific statements are queried with specific types of questions. The symbolic procedures for each of the six categories of questions are summarized in Table 5.8. These Q/A procedures for each type of question were tested or discovered by observing the categories of arcs that were sampled in the conceptual chains that intervene between a questioned node and an answer node. The cells that are marked "+" in Table 5.8 are those cells in which an arc category was sampled at a proportion of .15 or higher (see Tables 5.5 and 5.7). The arcs in the + cells accounted for .86 of the sampled arcs.

Verification of Nodes

The nodes in the graph structures undoubtedly vary in the degree to which individuals perceive them to be true or false. The perceived truth of a statement is probably not discrete in the sense of being either true or false. Instead, truth values vary along a continuum. Statements may be perceived as possibly true, probably true, or definitely true. Subjects also may not agree on the truth value of specific nodes. The research reported in this section pertains to the truth values that subjects assign to nodes in the graph structures. What makes some nodes more true than others?

In one experiment by Graesser et al. (1981), 16 subjects gave verification ratings of the nodes in the graph structure of the four narrative passages in Table

Table 5.8. Summary of Arcs That Are Sampled When Specific Types of Questions Are Asked

	Sampled arc categories									
Question category	$\overrightarrow{R}$	$\overleftarrow{R}$	$\overrightarrow{I}$	$\overleftarrow{I}$	$\overrightarrow{C}$	$\overleftarrow{C}$	$\overrightarrow{M}$	$\overleftarrow{M}$	$\overrightarrow{P}$	$\overleftarrow{P}$
Why ⟨action⟩ (goal orientation)	+			+						
How ⟨action⟩ (instrumental/procedural)		+					+			
Why ⟨event⟩ (causal antecedent)						+				
How ⟨event⟩ (causal antecedent)						+				
Why ⟨state⟩					+	+				
How ⟨state⟩						+			+	+

4.3. After the subjects read each passage, each node in the graph structure was rated on the following 4-point scale.

4 = definitely true
3 = probably true
2 = possibly true
1 = not true

The test items included all statements in the passages plus all of the inferences except for those inferences in the Style category. The Style nodes were eliminated because there is a problem of focus for such items. For example, consider the Style item below.

The ant crawled slowly.

The *slow* nature of the action specifies the style of the action *the ant crawled.* The problem arises for such an item when subjects base their verification judgments on the modified proposition (*the ant crawled*) rather than the style (*slowly*).

A number of variables could conceivably predict verification ratings of the nodes. One obvious variable would be whether the node was an inference or whether it was explicitly stated in the passage. Stated nodes would be expected to receive higher verification ratings than inference nodes (Kintsch, 1974; Reder, 1979; Singer, 1979) when tested after a short retention interval. Whereas the subjects would automatically regard explicitly stated information as true, certain inferences may be perceived as erroneous by some subjects. In fact, this hypothesis was confirmed. The mean verification ratings for explicitly stated nodes was significantly higher than for the inferences, 3.46 versus 2.84, respectively, $F(1, 439) = 44.39, p < .01, MSe = .45$.

Although inferences received lower ratings, on the average they were rated as "probably true." This suggests that the inferences generated from the Q/A method are generally true rather than being erroneous fabrications that subjects invent in order to deal with the Q/A task. Furthermore, there was no significant difference in ratings between those inferences that were generated in the standard Q/A procedure (2.87) and those inferences that were generated only in the extended Q/A procedure (2.79). Thus, as subjects are probed further and further during question answering, the perceived truth of their answers does not decline.

Three variables were examined as likely predictors of the verification ratings of inference nodes.

(1) **Generation likelihood.** This variable is simply the likelihood that a given inference would be produced by the subjects in the Q/A procedure. Generation likelihood was measured as the proportion of subjects who included a specific inference in their extended Q/A protocols. The obvious prediction is that verification ratings will increase with generation likelihood. Inferences that were produced by many subjects in the Q/A task should be rated as more true than those inferences produced by relatively few subjects. This outcome should occur

if (a) there are substantial differences among comprehenders as to what inferences are plausible, and (b) the ability to produce information is a valid index of a comprehender's ability to understand a passage and draw inferences about it (Omanson, Warren, and Trabasso, 1978).

(2) **Converging evidence.** Some inferences were activated and reactivated by many statements in a passage, whereas other inferences were constructed on the basis of only a single passage statement. Converging evidence is an index of how many passage statements activate a given inference. This variable was measured by counting the number of statements in a passage that generated a specific inference in the extended Q/A protocols. Verification ratings would be expected to increase as converging evidence increases.

(3) **Structural centrality.** Some inferences are critical because they have many arcs that directly radiate from (or to) them. The critical inferences are at busy "intersections" in the graphs. The structural centrality of a node can be measured by counting the number of arcs that are directly connected to the node in the graph structure. Nodes with high structural centrality are critical (Lehnert, 1980; Reder, 1979; Schank, 1975) because they are pivotal concepts around which other nodes are organized. Some examples of nodes with high structural centrality are nodes 6 and 17 in Figure 5.2. These nodes have 5-6 radiating arcs. Nodes 1, 4, 5, 9, 10, 18, 19, and 20 are dead-end nodes with only one radiating arc. These nodes have low structural centrality. Verification ratings should increase with higher structural centrality.

A multiple regression analysis was performed in order to examine the extent to which generation likelihood, converging evidence, and structural centrality predicted the verification ratings of the inference nodes. It is informative to point out that the three predictor variables were only modestly intercorrelated with one another (r's $< .39$). The multiple regression analysis revealed that the most robust predictor of the verification ratings was structural centrality. The three predictor variables together accounted for a significant 23% of the variance (r^2) for Event/State inferences and a significant 21% of the variance for Goal nodes. Structural centrality accounted for almost all of this predicted variance. Structural centrality predicted a significant 19% of the variance for Event/State inferences, $F(1, 184) = 40.56$, $p < .01$, and 20% of the variance for Goal inferences, $F(1, 184) = 42.19$, $p < .01$. The converging evidence variable did not have a significant effect on verification ratings for Event/State inferences or Goal inferences. Surprisingly, generation likelihood also did not have a significant effect on Goal inferences, although it did have a significant effect on Event/State inferences, $F(1, 184) = 7.96$, $p < .01$. Consequently, structural centrality was the only variable that had a consistently significant effect on verification ratings.

The data presented in Table 5.9 show that verification ratings increased with structural centrality. Both the Goal inferences and the Event/State inferences showed an increase in verification ratings as a function of the number of arcs radiating from the nodes. The mean ratings were 2.48, 2.86, and 3.19 for nodes with 1, 2, and 3-5 radiating arcs, respectively. The graph structures are therefore substantial predictors of verification ratings.

Table 5.9. Influence of Structural Centrality on Verification Ratings

Inference category	Number of arcs directly radiating from the inference		
	1	2	3-5
Goals	2.42	2.91	3.11
Events/states	2.54	2.81	3.24

Adapted from Graesser, Robertson, and Anderson (1981).

An important question is whether the above findings generalize to passages other than the four stories in Table 4.3. In order to answer this question, an experiment was conducted that essentially replicated the procedures in the above verification study. The stimulus passages were the four expository passages in Table 4.5 instead of the four narrative passages in Table 4.3. The Q/A method described in Chapter 4 was used for empirically deriving inferences that subjects would presumably make when comprehending the expository prose. Conceptual graph structures were also constructed from the pool of inferences and stated nodes. Therefore, each node could be scaled along three dimensions: (1) generation likelihood, (2) converging evidence, and (3) structural centrality.

The verification study included two conditions. In the *read* condition, subjects first read a passage and then rated each of the nodes on the 4-point verification scale. Thus, the read condition followed the same procedure as the verification experiment in the Graesser et al. (1981) study and the above verification experiment. The second condition was a *no read* condition in which subjects rated the nodes but never read the passages. The no read condition served as an index of how true the nodes were judged to be, based on the subjects' prior knowledge about the subject matter discussed in the passages. A statement may be regarded as true based on general knowledge rather than the information discussed in the passages.

It is important to point out that verification ratings in the no read condition would be meaningful for expository passages but not particularly meaningful for narrative passages. Why? Because stories are fictitious. The significance of information in narrative fiction is restricted to the specific story and in stories there is a "suspension of disbelief" (Coleridge, 1967; van Dijk, 1976). It would be ridiculous to collect verification ratings for nodes from narrative passages without the subjects' having read the passages. Without knowledge of story context, the subjects would not have any basis for evaluating the truth of statements such as those below.

The ant went to the river.
The dragon kidnapped three daughters.
John's pocket was picked.
The rabbits gave the dog carrots.

These actions and events refer to specific characters who act in stories that are specific and fictitious. Expository passages, on the other hand, convey information that is regarded as generally or universally true (Munro, Gordon, Rigney, and Lutz, 1979; Olson, 1977). Of course, expository passages may embody episodes that have specific temporal or spatial references; however, the episodes are historical facts that are publicly acknowledged as true. A subject needs a general context, but not all the details of a passage in order to judge the truth values of the following statements.

Apes tried to defend their home base.
Blood flows from the umbilical cord to the embryo.
Wheels reduce friction.
Spectrum lines are split into different components.

The patterns of verification ratings for expository passages were quite similar to those for narrative passages. Stated nodes received higher ratings than inference nodes in the read condition, 3.25 and 2.98, respectively. This difference could not be explained by the preexperimental knowledge that subjects had about the topics, since the mean verification ratings were slightly higher for inference nodes than stated nodes in the no read condition, 3.10 versus 2.96, respectively. The ratings were impressively high in the no read condition. In fact, the ratings for inference nodes were slightly higher in the no read than in the read condition. Thus, the test items were generally perceived as true regardless of whether or not the subjects received the passages. Of course, this outcome would presumably be restricted to expository passages that embody generic knowledge.

A multiple regression analysis was performed in order to examine the extent to which four variables predict verification ratings of the inference items. The following four variables were entered as predictors of the ratings in the read condition: (a) generation likelihood, (b) converging evidence, (c) structural centrality, and (d) prior knowledge, as assessed by the verification ratings in the no read condition. The four variables together predicted a significant 45% of the variance (r^2). The most robust predictor of the verification ratings was prior knowledge [$r^2 = .32, F(1, 172) = 87.44, p < .05$], followed by structural centrality [$r^2 = .05, F(1, 172) = 5.70, p < .05$], and then generation likelihood [$r^2 = .02, F(1, 172) = 3.90, p < .05$]. Converging evidence did not significantly predict verification ratings [$F(1, 172) = 1.03, p > .25$]. The simple correlations between verification ratings and the four predictor variables showed the same pattern: .63, .32, .27, and .24 for prior knowledge, structural centrality, generation likelihood, and converging evidence, respectively.

The outcome of the multiple regression analysis confirmed the prediction that structural properties of the graphs explain verification ratings to some extent. Inference nodes are perceived as more true as there are more arcs that directly radiate from the nodes. The mean verification ratings were 2.79, 3.10, and 3.22 for inference nodes with 1, 2, and 3-5 radiating arcs, respectively. The critical nodes with many radiating arcs are perceived as more true than the dead-end nodes. This trend apparently is not confounded with some potential third variable, such as generation likelihood, prior knowledge, or converging evidence.

An interesting pattern emerged regarding the degree to which verification ratings are predicted by generation likelihood. Generation likelihood predicted verification ratings of inference nodes in expository passages. The effect was small but significant. However, generation likelihood did not consistently predict verification ratings of the nodes in the narrative passages. The Event and State nodes in narrative passages were significantly predicted by generation likelihood, but the Goal nodes were not. There is at least one plausible explanation of these outcomes:

(1) There is high intersubject agreement on how to understand goal-oriented structures, but relatively lower intersubject agreement on how to understand causally oriented structures.
(2) Generation likelihood is expected to predict verification ratings better as there is a decrease in intersubject agreement on how to understand prose.

It follows from points 1 and 2 that generation likelihood should predict verification ratings of inferences to a greater extent when the inferences are part of causally oriented structures than when inferences are part of goal-oriented structures.

In Chapter 4 it was reported that causally oriented structures are more prevalent in expository passages than in narrative passages. It is also the case that expository prose is more difficult to comprehend. Not only do subjects require more time to read expository text than narrative (Graesser, Hoffman, and Clark, 1980), but also a smaller amount of information is recalled from expository text than from narrative prose (Cohen and Graesser, 1980; Graesser, Hauft-Smith, Cohen, and Pyles, 1980; Munro, Gordon, Rigney, and Lutz, 1979; Munro, Lutz, and Gordon, 1979). Comprehension scores are also lower when subjects read expository prose than narrative prose (Graesser, Hauft-Smith, Cohen, and Pyles, 1980). Since expository prose is more difficult, it is not surprising that there are more differences among individuals in comprehending the material. Moreover, as prose is more difficult to comprehend, generation likelihood would be expected to have increasing predictive validity in explaining verification ratings of the inference nodes.

A production system that generates verification ratings for inferences and stated nodes is presented in Table 5.10. The production system captures the important trends that have been reported in this section as well as some additional data that have not yet been reported. The production system explicitly delineates the symbolic procedures that are applied to the conceptual graph structures when humans give verification judgments. The proposed production system probably does not perfectly explain the way humans generate verification ratings, but it is a reasonable start. The proposed system could be expanded and modified as more data are collected. Such modifications would involve the introduction of new productions and a reordering of the productions in Table 5.10.

According to the proposed production system, subjects initially search the graph structure to see whether there is a node that matches the test item. If no

Table 5.10. Symbolic Procedure for Generating Verification Ratings

(1) If ⟨test node does not match a node in the graph structure⟩
Then ⟨embellish the graph structure by applying relevant schemas⟩
(2) If ⟨test node does not match a node in the graph structure⟩
Then ⟨respond FALSE⟩
(3) If ⟨test node matches a node in the graph structure⟩
Then ⟨evaluate whether node was stated in the passage⟩
(4) If ⟨graph node was stated in the passage⟩
Then ⟨respond DEFINITELY TRUE⟩
(5) If ⟨graph node was not stated in passage⟩
Then ⟨compute how many arcs radiate from it⟩
(6) If ⟨number of radiating arcs is greater than or equal to m⟩
Then ⟨respond DEFINITELY TRUE⟩
(7) If ⟨number of radiating arcs is less than m and greater than or equal to n⟩
Then ⟨respond PROBABLY TRUE⟩
(8) If ⟨number of radiating arcs is less than n⟩
Then ⟨respond POSSIBLY TRUE⟩

match is found, the subject embellishes the relevant region of the graph structure by consulting relevant schemas (production 1). If a match is still not found, then the subject responds **FALSE** (production 2). If a match is found, then the subject evaluates whether the node has been explicitly stated in the passage (production 3). If the subject decides that the node was explicitly stated, then the subject responds **DEFINITELY TRUE** (production 4). If the subject decides that the node was not stated explicitly in the passage, then the subject evaluates how many arcs radiate from the node (in either direction) in the graph structure (production 5). If the number of radiating arcs is greater than or equal to m, the subject responds **DEFINITELY TRUE** (production 6). If the number of radiating arcs is less than m, but greater than or equal to n, then the subject responds **PROBABLY TRUE** (production 7). If the number of arcs is less than n, then the subject responds **POSSIBLY TRUE**. Of course, the threshold values n and m would vary from subject to subject and perhaps from passage to passage.

It is important to point out how the production system accounts for verification ratings. Production 1 captures the distinction between inferences that comprehenders draw during comprehension and inferences that are derived only at test time. If a match is found between the test item and a node in the conceptual graph structure that was constructed during comprehension, then production 1 would not be executed. If, however, a match is not found between the test item and a node in the conceptual graph structure, then production 1 is executed. When production 1 is executed, the subject may embellish the graph structure by adding new nodes. The subject evaluates which region of the graph structure is relevant to the test item and attempts to "fit in" the test node by consulting relevant schemas. When the test node can be fit into the graph structure, the graph structure is expanded (enriched) by the additional node along with any additional inferences that bridge the additional node to the old graph structure. The subject presumably would not expand the graph structure without consulting the relevant schemas.

There are two empirical outcomes that would be predicted by virtue of production 1. The first prediction is that verification ratings should be higher for inferences generated during comprehension than inferences derived only at test time whenever (a) there are correct inferences that are *not* drawn during comprehension and (b) the subject sometimes fails to fit these correct inferences into the graph structure at test time by consulting relevant schemas and embellishing the graph structure. The second prediction pertains to verification latencies for plausible inferences. Verification latencies should be faster for those inferences that were generated during comprehension than those inferences derive at test time. The latter inferences would require more processing time because of the additional time needed to embellish the conceptual graph structure. Unfortunately, there was no way of testing these predictions with the present data because verification latencies were not collected and there were no criteria for segregating inferences generated during comprehension from those inferences derived at test time. Nevertheless, psychologists have examined or discussed these predictions in other studies (Harris and Monaco, 1978; Keenan, 1978).

According to production 2, a **FALSE** response is generated whenever the test item does not match any of the nodes that are available in the conceptual graph structure. Productions 1 and 2 together capture some empirical trends if it is assumed that there are some fluctuations from subject to subject with regard to which nodes are incorporated in the graph structure either during comprehension or at test time (after executing production 1). One trend involves the positive correlation between verification ratings and generation likelihood. Specifically, it explains two outcomes that were discussed. Some analyses revealed that the mean verification ratings of inference items increased as a function of the proportion of subjects that generated specific inferences in the Q/A task. Those inference items that had higher generation likelihoods would have (a) a higher likelihood of being included in the graph structures of subjects and therefore (b) a lower likelihood of receiving a **FALSE** verification rating by virtue of production 2.

Subjects do not substantially differ in how they interpret some types of knowledge structures. For goal-oriented conceptualizations in simple narratives, the conceptual structures were apparently the same for all college students. For the inferences in these goal-oriented structures, the generation likelihood of an inference did not reflect the true likelihood that a given inference was included in the subject's graph structure; there was *not* a significant positive correlation between verification ratings and generation likelihoods for the Goal inferences in the simple short stories in Table 4.3. In contrast, the more difficult expository passages did show a significant but modest correlation between generation likelihoods and verification ratings. There was also a positive correlation for causally oriented conceptualizations in narrative prose. It appears, therefore, that some of the expository inference nodes (and particularly the nodes of causally oriented conceptualizations) were not constructed by all of the subjects. For inferences in causally oriented structures, the generation likelihoods did reflect the likelihood that subjects would include a given inference node in the causally oriented structure.

A second trend is also accommodated by the assumption that there are fluctuations (among subjects) as to which inference nodes are included in a conceptual graph structure. The verification ratings of expository inferences were robustly predicted by the verification ratings in the no read condition. The verification ratings in the no read condition served as an index of a generic truth judgment based on prior knowledge. It is plausible to assume that those items that have higher truth ratings based on prior knowledge would also be more likely to have been included in the conceptual graph structure.

To summarize, two empirical trends regarding verification ratings have been accommodated by productions 1 and 2 along with the assumption that there are fluctuations between subjects as to which nodes are constructed and available in the conceptual graph structures. Verification ratings of inference nodes increase with (a) truth judgments based on prior knowledge and (b) the likelihood of subjects generating specific inferences in the Q/A task.

Productions 1 and 2 together provide one prediction about the verification latencies of implausible inferences. Latencies should be shorter for test items that are obviously false or not relevant to the passage than test items that initially appear to be relevant and plausible but are eventually judged to be implausible after careful examination. Latencies should be shorter for irrelevant items because the graph structures would not be embellished and carefully examined during the execution of production 1. This prediction has been supported by previous research (Lovelace and Graesser, 1978).

According to productions 3 and 4, when subjects find a match between the test node and a node in the graph, they evaluate whether or not the node was explicitly stated in the passage. It should be pointed out that the conceptual graph structures do not intrinsically distinguish between explicitly stated nodes and inference nodes except for the fact that explicitly stated nodes are flagged with asterisks. For the present purposes, the asterisk notation is quite adequate. Subjects have some likelihood of remembering the wording, syntax, and other surface structure characteristics of those nodes that have asterisks beside them. Moreover, as the retention interval increases between comprehension and test, there is a lower likelihood of retaining the surface structure code and there will be poor discrimination between explicit nodes and inference nodes (Bower et al., 1979; Graesser, Woll, Kowalski, and Smith, 1980; Kintsch, 1974; Kintsch and van Dijk, 1978). The verification data reported in this section involved a relatively short retention interval (5 minutes), so subjects should have been able to discriminate between explicit nodes and inferences nodes to some extent. Of course, subjects differ in their ability to remember whether a node was explicitly stated.

Production 3 yields a decision as to whether the test item was or was not explicitly stated in the passage. According to production 4, subjects respond **DEFINITELY TRUE** if they decide that the test item was explicitly stated. If they decide that the test item was not explicitly stated in the passage, then the test item is evaluated by productions 5, 6, 7, and 8. The inclusion of productions 3 and 4, and their order of occurrence in the production system, have a number of implications for the verification data. Three implications will be discussed.

The first and most obvious prediction of this production system is that mean verification ratings should be higher for the set of nodes that were explicitly stated in the passages than for the set of nodes that were inferred. Explicit nodes would have a higher likelihood than inference nodes of being judged as **DEFINITELY TRUE** by virtue of production 4. Inference nodes would receive lower ratings because the decision would frequently be based on productions 7 and 8; productions 7 and 8 generate **POSSIBLY TRUE** and **PROBABLY TRUE** responses. The experiments reported in this section uniformly confirmed this prediction. Explicit nodes had significantly higher verification ratings than the inference nodes for both narrative and expository prose. Other studies (Bacon, 1979; Hasher, Goldstein, and Toppino, 1977; Hayes-Roth and Walker, 1979; Kintsch, 1974; Singer, 1979) have also shown that the truth ratings increase simply as a consequence of the information having been explicitly mentioned at some point in time.

A second prediction of the proposed production system is that structural centrality will not substantially predict verification ratings of explicitly stated nodes. Explicit nodes are normally evaluated by productions 3 and 4 when items are tested after short retention intervals. Productions 3 and 4 occur prior to the productions that evaluate nodes according to structural criteria (productions 5-8). This prediction was in fact found to be correct. The mean verification ratings of explicit nodes in the four expository passages were 3.26, 3.20, and 3.28 for nodes with 1-2, 3-4, and 5-6 radiating arcs, respectively. In the four narrative passages, the mean verification ratings were 3.45, 3.49, and 3.45 for nodes with 1-2, 3-4, and 5-9 radiating arcs, respectively. Thus, verification ratings of explicit nodes did not increase with structural centrality.

A third prediction could be derived from the production system, although this prediction was not examined in the data reported in this section. The likelihood of evaluating an explicit node via productions 3 and 4 should be influenced by the interval between the time the passages are comprehended and the time that the verification ratings are collected. Previous research has repeatedly demonstrated that subjects have increasing difficulty in discriminating explicit nodes from inference nodes as the retention interval increases (Graesser, Woll, Kowalski, and Smith, 1980; Kintsch, 1974; Kintsch and van Dijk, 1978). Surface structure code decays with an increasing retention interval. A consequence of this process is that it would be more difficult to judge test items via productions 3 and 4 under delayed testing conditions. The explicit nodes and inference nodes should show increasingly similar patterns as the retention interval increases. In fact, such a trend has been found in studies by Kintsch (Kintsch, 1974) in which latencies were collected. Whereas in immediate testing conditions the verification latencies are shorter for verbatim than inference items, such differences disappear as the retention interval increases. An interesting prediction follows from the assumption that decisions via productions 3 and 4 are less prevalent as the retention interval increases. Structural centrality should predict the verification ratings of verbatim items under delayed testing conditions but not in immediate testing conditions. Unfortunately, this prediction could not be tested on the present data because verification ratings were not collected after long retention intervals.

According to productions 5-8, the verification ratings of inferences should increase with structural centrality. This prediction was uniformly confirmed for both narrative and expository prose. These data support Schank's prediction that nodes are more critical as more arcs radiate from them (Schank, 1975).

The ordering of productions 6, 7, and 8 is not completely arbitrary. Lovelace and Graesser (1978) collected verification latencies for inference nodes and found that **DEFINITELY TRUE** judgments had shorter latencies than **PROBABLY TRUE** judgments, which in turn had shorter latencies than **POSSIBLY TRUE** answers. This trend could perhaps be captured by the analogous ordering of productions in the production system. On the other hand, the obtained verification latencies might also be captured by processes that occur in earlier productions (productions 1 and/or 5). Further research is clearly needed in order to explain the verification latencies of the inference nodes.

The production system in Table 5.10, along with the conceptual graph structures, can account for a large number of trends when verification ratings are collected for inference nodes and explicit nodes. The proposed production system is undoubtedly imperfect and incomplete. However, it could be revised by adding, deleting, and reordering the productions as new findings accumulate. It is believed that the framework and procedures outlined in this section offer a promising approach to exploring how humans decide whether information about a passage is true or false.

Recall of Prose

The most popular test of theories of prose representation has been whether the theories can explain the recall of stated information. A psychological theory should explain why certain sentences, statements, or propositions in a passage tend to be recalled. Recall protocols are easy to collect. The comprehender reads or listens to the passage and later recalls it. Recall protocols are more challenging to explain. To what extent does a theory of prose representation predict recall of individual statements?

Cognitive psychologists have identified at least three dimensions in which recall of passage statements can be predicted by properties of the representation.

(1) Structural properties of the representation.
(2) Categories of statements.
(3) Typicality of statements with respect to the background schemas.

The third approach to predicting recall has already been discussed in detail in Chapter 3. After short retention intervals recall is better for statements that are atypical of a schema than for statements that are typical. This conclusion must be qualified somewhat. First, it is based on recall measures that control for guessing biases. When guessing is ignored, the likelihood of recalling typical items normally exceeds that of atypical items. Second, it is restricted to short retention intervals. As the retention interval increases, there is better recall of schema-consistent information than information that is unrelated to a schema. Third, it seems to be restricted to shorter passages (see Spilich et al., 1979). When subjects are faced with the challenge of recalling a very long passage, there apparently is a "summarization-and-abstraction editor" that filters out potentially recallable atypical information.

The second approach to predicting prose recall involves the assignment of statements to representational categories and an explanation of why some categories show better recall than others. For example, J. M. Mandler has reported that statements that refer to certain properties of settings and the beginnings, attempts, and outcomes of episodes in stories tend to be recalled more often than statements referring to the internal reactions of characters and the endings of episodes (Mandler, 1978; Mandler and Johnson, 1977; Mandler et al., 1980). One explanation of this finding is that reactions and endings can readily be inferred from the other statements in the episode (Black and Bower, 1980; Graesser, Robertson, Lovelace, and Swinehart, 1980; Johnson and Mandler, 1980). Since certain categories of nodes are inferrable, they could be deleted from a recall protocol without a substantial loss in information.

The first approach to predicting recall is to correlate recall with structural dimensions of the representation. This approach has received the most attention. Studies have frequently demonstrated that recall decreases as statements become more subordinate in the underlying structural hierarchies (Black and Bower, 1980; Dawes, 1966; Graesser, 1978a; Graesser, Robertson, Lovelace, and Swinehart, 1980; Kintsch, 1974; Meyer, 1975; Rumelhart, 1977c; Thorndyke, 1977). A variety of other structural dimensions may also predict recall. Recall for certain nodes increases as the nodes are embellished by an increasing number of subordinate nodes (Black and Bower, 1979; Kintsch, 1974). Recall for a node has been shown to increase with relational density, i.e., the extent to which it is conceptually related to other passage statements (Graesser, 1978a; Graesser, Robertson, Lovelace, and Swinehart, 1980). Relational density is analogous to the structural centrality variable discussed in the previous section.

The relationship between recall and hierarchical level has been reexamined in recent studies. The hierarchical orderings generated by Kintsch's (1974) theory of prose microstructure and Schank's conceptual dependency theory (Schank and Abelson, 1977) apparently predict recall with impressive consistency (Black and Bower, 1980). However, the hierarchies generated by story grammars are not found to predict substantially the recall of statements when a diverse set of stories is sampled (Black and Bower, 1980; Johnson and Mandler, 1980). Black and Bower used multiple regression analyses to assess the degree to which recall could be predicted by the hierarchical orderings of Kintsch's theory, Schank's theory, and several story grammars. The story grammar predicted a modest 1-7% of the recall variance among the passages tested. In contrast, Kintsch's and Schank's theories *together* predicted an impressive amount of recall variance (roughly 40-50%). Prediction of recall for story statements has been shown to be even better in Black's hierarchical state transition theory (Black and Bower, 1980) and Omanson's narrative analysis theory (Omanson, 1979). The predictive power of the latter two theories is based on a combination of structural properties and categorical (semantic) properties of the nodes.

There is one subset of statements in narrative that shows a reliable relationship between recall and hierarchical level. When a character in a passage enacts a planned sequence of intentional actions, and the actions successfully achieve the intended goals, then recall of the actions tends to decrease as the actions are progressively more subordinate in the hierarchy (Black and Bower, 1980; Graesser, 1978a; Graesser et al., 1981; Graesser, Robertson, Lovelace, and Swinehart, 1980; Johnson and Mandler, 1980; Rumelhart, 1977c). A relatively subordinate subgoal can be deleted from a recall protocol "since its outcome is inferrable from subsequent actions which will be expressed" (Rumelhart, 1977c, p. 279). For example, actions 1, 2, and 3 are hierarchically ordered, with action 1 being most superordinate and action 3 being most subordinate.

(1) *The heroes rescued the daughters.*
(2) *The heroes fought the dragon.*
(3) *The heroes went to the daughters.*

Recall is predicted to be highest for action 1 and lowest for action 3. The more subordinate actions can be deleted without a substantial loss of information. Since the heroes' going to the dragon is a necessary precondition for the heroes' fighting the dragon, action 3 can be deleted.

As predicted, recall of the actions systematically varied as a function of the goal hierarchies in the graph structures of the four narrative passages examined in this chapter. In the Graesser et al. (1981) study, 32 subjects recalled the four short narrative passages in Table 4.3 about .5 hour after hearing them. Among the four stories, there were four triads of actions that followed a hierarchical ordering (as in actions 1, 2, and 3 above). Each of the four triads provided three binary predictions with regard to recall: action 1 > action 2, action 2 > action 3, and action 1 > action 3. Altogether, there were 12 binary predictions from the four triads. In addition, there were 8 dyads of actions, which provided 8 more binary predictions. Of the 20 binary predictions, 19 were in the directions predicted by the theoretical orderings. This outcome is significant according to a sign test, $p < .01$. The mean recall proportions were .38, .52, and .75 for the sub-, mid-, and superordinate nodes in the triads, respectively. In the dyads, the mean recall proportions were .30 and .68 for the subordinate and superordinate nodes, respectively.

A study by Graesser (1978a) focused on memory for actions in passages that were organized according to goal-oriented knowledge structures. The passages were descriptions of common procedures, such as *catching a fish, washing a car,* and *making an egg salad sandwich.* The acquisition passages were constructed on the basis of a free generation group of subjects. Each common procedure included all actions that were produced by at least two subjects in the free generation group. Another group of subjects was asked to recall the acquisition passages 1 hour after the passages were presented from a tape recorder. Three measures were collected for each action in the common procedures, based on the recall group and the free generation group. For each action the following measures were computed.

(1) **Free generation proportion.** The proportion of subjects that mentioned the action in the free generation group.
(2) **Recall proportion.** The proportion of subjects that recalled the action in the recall group.
(3) **Improvement score.** A measure of recall memory that corrects for guessing: improvement score = p (recall) − p (free generation).

The central question of the Graesser (1978a) study was whether memory improvement scores could be predicted by structural properties of the underlying Goal hierarchies.

Two dimensions of structure were scaled by the distribution of answers collected from a Q/A group of subjects. The subjects answered *why* questions for each action in the common procedures after the passages were read to them. Each action was scaled on two structural dimensions on the basis of the distribution of answers. The first structural dimension was hierarchical level. Given a hierarchy of Goal nodes and the symbolic procedures for why ⟨action⟩ questions in Table 5.3, the hierarchical level of an action could be scaled by counting the number of distinct answers generated from a questioned action. Specifically, as an action is more superordinate in the Goal hierarchy, there should be fewer distinct answers. Why? The symbolic procedure for why ⟨action⟩ questions is known to sample nodes that are superordinate to the probed actions. Since fewer nodes are superordinate to a superordinate action than to a subordinate action, fewer distinct answers should be generated when questions concern superordinate actions. Thus, the hierarchical level of an action was scaled simply by counting the number of unique answers that the Q/A subjects generated for a given action that was probed. An action is scored as more subordinate as there are more distinct answers.

The second structural dimension was relational density. Relational density is analogous to structural centrality. The relational density of an explicitly mentioned action corresponds to the degree to which the action is related to other explicitly stated actions in a passage by virtue of sharing common answers to the *why* questions. The relational density of an action increases as answers about an action overlap more and more with answers about other actions that are probed. Unlike the structural centrality variable, the computation of relational density does not require the investigator to construct conceptual graph structures for passages. Relational density is scaled simply by computing the number of answers that a particular action has in common with other actions that are questioned. The formula for computing relational density is reported in Graesser (1978a).

In order to assess the effects of relational density and hierarchical level on recall, a median split criterion was used to segregate superordinate from subordinate actions and high relational density actions from low relational density actions. The pattern of recall improvement scores supported the predicted trend that superordinate actions would be recalled better than subordinate actions. High relational density statements were also found to be recalled better than low relational density statements. There was no significant interaction between relational density and hierarchical level. The means from two experiments in the Graesser (1978a) study are shown in Table 5.11.

The finding that recall for intentional actions increases with relational density and decreases with hierarchical level is not restricted to passages that describe common activities. A study by Graesser, Robertson, Lovelace, and Swinehart (1980) showed that the same trends are found in long familiar stories. Just as in the Graesser (1978a) study, free generation, recall, and Q/A groups of subjects were tested with three familiar stories: *Hansel and Gretel* (H & G), *Jack and the Beanstalk* (J & B), and *Little Red Riding Hood* (LRRH). Median splits served as the criteria for segregating high from low relational density statements for each story separately. Actions were also segregated into super- (1-3 distinct answers), mid- (4 answers), and subordinate items (5-8 answers). A recall improvement score was computed for each action as a measure of memory that corrects for guessing. In Table 5.12 the mean recall improvement scores are shown as a function of hierarchical level and relational density. Recall significantly increased with relational density and decreased with hierarchical level. Thus, the same trends were found for actions in stories and actions in common activities.

Stories include many statements that are not intentional actions. An interesting outcome of the Graesser, Robertson, Lovelace, and Swinehart (1980) study was that the scaled dimensions of relational density and number of answers did not predict recall for other categories of statements. Specifically, three other categories were examined.

(1) **Communications.** Statements that convey one character speaking to another character.
(2) **Events.** Statements that convey an internal or physical event.
(3) **States.** Statements that convey an internal or physical state.

Table 5.11. Recall Improvement Scores for Actions in Common Activities as a Function of Relational Density and Hierarchical Level

Experiment number	High relational density		Low relational density	
	Superordinate	Subordinate	Superordinate	Subordinate
1	.22	.10	.07	−.01
2	.36	.29	.30	.22

Adapted from Graesser (1978a).

Communications had the same patterns of correlations as those for intentional actions but the trends were not significant. Recall for states and events tended to decrease with the number of answers but the trends were not significant. Recall for states and events also decreased, rather than increased with relational density, but again the trends were not significant. Thus, it is clear that the influence of hierarchical level and relational density on recall is restricted to intentional actions that are part of goal-oriented conceptualizations. The trends did not emerge for causally oriented conceptualizations.

It is not surprising that recall for events was *not* influenced by relational density and number of answers. Recall for events was not predicted by the number of distinct answers because event sequences are not organized hierarchically. At best, event sequences are sequential chains. Consider the following events.

(1) *The stream began to rush swiftly.*
(2) *The child fell into the water.*
(3) *The child drowned.*

The three events formed a causal chain. Event 1 has the consequence of Event 2, which in turn has the consequence of Event 3. Given that why ⟨event⟩ questions follow backward Consequence arcs, Events 1 and 2 would be produced when Event 3 is probed with a *why* question. When Event 2 is probed, a possible answer is Event 1 but not Event 3. It follows that terminal events in a causal chain would generate more answers to *why* questions than events that are at the beginning of a chain. However, there are no theories that predict whether beginning, middle, or final events of a chain are recalled best. Thus, the number of answers in a Q/A task would not be expected to predict recall of events on any theoretical basis.

Recall of states and communications were also not expected to be predicted theoretically by the number of distinct answers generated in the Q/A task. State statements often referred to setting information that was not organized hierarchically. These States were simply loosely organized nodes referring to attributes of

Table 5.12. Recall Improvement Scores for Actions in Stories as a Function of Relational Density and Hierarchical Level

	Story[a]			
Statement category	LRRH	J&B	H&G	Mean
High relational density				
Superordinate	.63	.68	.70	.67
Midordinate	.39	.53	.42	.44
Subordinate	.33	.38	.41	.37
Low relational density				
Superordinate	.43	.34	.53	.43
Midordinate	.34	.14	.32	.27
Subordinate	.29	.17	.25	.25

Adapted from Graesser, Robertson, Lovelace, and Swinehart (1980).
[a]LRRH, *Little Red Riding Hood*; J&B, *Jack and the Beanstalk*; H&G, *Hansel and Gretel.*

objects or characters, to time information, or to location information. Communications were intentionally executed, but unfortunately the answers to the *why* questions were often not particularly informative. The answers generated for communications often referred to general properties of communicative acts rather than the specific content of what a character said. For example, consider the following answers to *Why did Gretel tell Hansel that the witch was nearly blind?*

Gretel had noticed that the witch was nearly blind.
The witch was nearly blind.
Gretel wanted Hansel to know that the witch was nearly blind.

It is generally true for all sincere speech acts in which X is expressed by a character that (a) the speaker knows X, (b) that X exists, and (c) the speaker wants the listener to know X (Searle, 1969). The answers did not reveal much about the significance of what specifically was stated by the characters.

How are the above recall data to be explained? Two points should be acknowledged when considering an adequate explanation of recall for statements in prose. One point to recognize is that the patterns of recall are complex. The variables that predict recall are different for different categories of nodes (actions, states, and events). Structural properties predict recall for statements in some categories of nodes but not in others; the underlying structural configurations are different for nodes in different categories. Actions are believed to be interrelated by underlying Goal hierarchies. Event sequences are believed to be interrelated by nonhierarchical chains of events and enabling states. The states in static descriptions are often not interrelated in a hierarchical fashion or by conceptual chains. These complexities that are involved in predicting prose recall lead up to the second point. Recall for statements in prose will probably not be adequately explained by a simple, elegant, parsimonious theory.

In this section a *summarization-abstraction model* will be examined in order to explain the recall data. Researchers have proposed that recall of text does not always entail an exact reproduction of what was stated. Instead there are abstraction and summarization processes (Cofer et al., 1976; van Dijk, 1977; Gomulicki, 1956; Kintsch and van Dijk, 1978; Rumelhart, 1977c; Zangwill, 1972) that delete certain statements and preserve others. In the extreme form of a summarization-abstraction model, patterns of recall are entirely explained by processes that occur during the course of retrieving information in text rather than the course of acquiring information in text. According to this extreme position, all of the nodes are available and accessible during retrieval. However, the recall of these nodes is edited by abstraction and summarization operators. Consequently, patterns of recall would be entirely explained by production mechanisms during recall and not at all explained by acquisition mechanisms during comprehension. This extreme form of an abstraction-summarization model is undoubtedly implausible; recall of statements is certainly to some extent determined by processes occurring at acquisition (Bower et al., 1979; Kintsch and van Dijk, 1978; Miller and Kintsch, 1980). A weaker form of an abstraction-summarization model would assert the following.

(1) Recall of statements in prose is to some extent determined by processes occurring at acquisition, to some extent by processes occurring during memory retrieval, and to some extent by abstraction and summarization operators.
(2) Abstraction and summarization operators are particularly important determinants of recall for prose content.

The weaker form of the abstraction-summarization model will be adopted in this section. The emphasis in this section is on how recall is predicted by specific abstraction and summarization rules.

There are two general deletion rules that can be used to explain which statements are deleted and which statements are preserved.

Deletion Rule 1. A statement tends to be deleted if it can be inferred from another statement that is stated.

Deletion Rule 2. A statement does not tend to be deleted if it is needed for a sensible interpretation of another statement that is stated.

Deletion Rule 2 has been directly proposed by Kintsch and van Dijk (1978), whereas Deletion Rule 1 has been directly or indirectly assumed by several investigators (Johnson and Mandler, 1980; Rumelhart, 1977c).

The fact that recall for intentional actions decreases with hierarchical level can be explained by Deletion Rule 1. The completion of a subgoal can always be inferred if some statement is mentioned that conveys the accomplishment of a more superordinate goal. For example, *the dragon's carrying off the daughters* (superordinate goal) implies that *the dragon must have gone to the daughters* (subordinate goal). Since states and events are not organized hierarchically, the deletion rule would not apply in the same way as for goal-oriented conceptualizations.

The effect of relational density on recall was significantly positive for intentional actions and nonsignificantly negative for states and events. It is plausible that relational density would be influenced by both Deletion Rules 1 and 2. On the one hand, statements with high relational density might be deleted by virtue of Deletion Rule 1 because statements that are related to many other statements would have a higher likelihood of being inferred from other statements. On the other hand, statements with high relational density might not be deleted by virtue of Deletion Rule 2 because such statements would have a higher likelihood of being interpretation conditions for other statements; failure to interpret a statement with high relational density may have drastic repercussions on the interpretation of other statements. The obtained recall data indicate that Deletion Rule 2 is more prevalent than Deletion Rule 1 for intentional actions, because recall increases with relational density for actions. However, Deletion Rule 1 is slightly more prevalent than Deletion Rule 2 for events and states; recall for events and states tends to decrease as a function of relational density (although not significantly).

Again, it should be apparent that the relationship between recall and representation is hardly simple. An elegant production system for recall is not presently in sight. The production system would need to be sensitive to the types of nodes that are involved (actions versus states versus events), the structural properties of the graph (hierarchical level and relational density), and the conceptual relationship between the statement and the relevant background schemas (typical versus atypical information). Nevertheless, a few hypotheses can be offered that should be incorporated in an adequate production system for recall. Such a production system would operate on the conceptual graph structure for a passage.

(1) Recall of a passage is critically affected by abstraction and summarization procedures. These presumably unconscious procedures delete some nodes that were explicitly stated and insert other nodes that are inferences (rather than explicit passage statements). Important questions address the productions that are included in the *summarization-abstraction editor.* This component will be called the *Editor.*
(2) An important determinant of which nodes are deleted by the editor is whether a given node can be inferred from other nodes. Nodes that can be inferred from other nodes tend to be deleted.
(3) An important determinant of which nodes are deleted by the editor is whether a given node is an interpretation condition for other nodes. A given node is not deleted if it is required for the interpretation of other nodes.

The above hypotheses are general in the sense that they do not depend on the content and structure of the representations. More informative hypotheses would provide special productions or rules that operate on specific domains of knowledge in the passage, as well as specific node and arc categories. Some of these esoteric editing rules will now be described.

(1) **Goal hierarchies that involve a single agent successfully enacting a planned action sequence.** Whenever a single agent or character in a passage enacts a sequence of actions (Goal+) that embody a script or a plan, the action sequence is organized by a hierarchy of goal nodes. In some instances, the goals in a plan are not interrupted by occurrences of the physical or social world (other characters). In other words, the world is cooperative. In these cases, the necessary subgoals of a given Goal node can be deleted by the editor, provided that the Goal node is stated in the recall protocol. The subgoals can be deleted because they can be inferred from the more superordinate Goal nodes. Suppose the following two statements were included in a passage.

(1) *The heroes fought the dragon.*
(2) *The heroes went to the dragon.*

Statement 2 can be deleted if statement 1 is mentioned in the recall protocol. Several studies have provided data that support this editing rule (Black and Bower, 1980; Graesser, 1978a; Graesser et al., 1981; Graesser, Robertson, Lovelace, and Swinehart, 1980; Johnson and Mandler, 1980; Lichtenstein and Brewer, 1980; Rumelhart, 1977c).

(2) **Goal hierarchies that involve an action (goal) being interrupted by world events.** Sometimes characters attempt to achieve goals and subgoals but are interrupted by other characters or physical events.

While the heroes were going to the dragon they were ambushed by bandits. However, the heroes managed to escape the bandits. Then the heroes fought the dragon . . .

The fact that an action (Goal) is interrupted by world events influences the likelihood of recalling the action. The action tends to be recalled if the superordinate goal is eventually achieved and if the interrupting event is important, i.e., structurally related to many other statements in a passage. However, the interrupted action tends to be deleted if the action or goal is abandoned or the interrupting event is not particularly important in the story (Black and Bower, 1980).

(3) **A Goal node that is embellished by many subordinate nodes.** Consider the following two descriptions of an episode.

(1) *The heroes fought the dragon.*
(2) *The heroes fought the dragon. They ran after the dragon and stabbed it several times.*

The likelihood of recalling *the heroes fought the dragon* would be higher with description 2 than 1. Similarly, the relational density of this statement would be higher in 2 than 1. When a node is highly embellished in a passage, the listener perhaps assumes that the node is important and therefore will include it in the protocol. Data from a number of studies support this editing rule (Black and Bower, 1979; Graesser, 1978a; Graesser, Robertson, Lovelace, and Swinehart, 1980).

(4) **Internal events that are driven by physical events and actions.** Internal events can often be deleted because they can be inferred from physical events and actions. Perceptual events can be inferred when some physical event or action occurs and a character is spatially near the occurrence.

(1) *The daughters cried for help.*
(2) *The heroes were near the daughters.*
(3) *The heroes heard the cries.*

If these three statements were stated in a passage, then statement 3 could be deleted because it can be inferred from statements 1 and 2. Perceptual events usually involve the following components.

(1) *A physical occurrence X.*
(2) *A character C being near X.*
(3) *Character C being able to perceive.*
(4) *Character C perceiving X.*

If some subset of these components is expressedly in a passage, then the comprehender normally infers the other components. Characters are assumed not to have perceptual problems, unless the passage explicitly states that a character has a perceptual defect.

Emotional events may also be inferred from physical events when they are predictable. When this is the case, the emotional events may be deleted by the editor:

(1) *The boy lost his dog.*
(2) *The boy was sad.*

Whenever a character loses a valued object, the character becomes sad. The recall protocol can delete mention of sadness. This editing rule has been supported by recall data in several studies (Johnson and Mandler, 1980; Mandler, 1978; Mandler and Johnson, 1977).

(5) **An enabling state that is a precondition for an event or action.** States can be deleted by the editor when they necessarily enable an event (or action) and the event is stated in the protocol. Consider the following statements.

(1) *The daughters cried.*
(2) *The heroes were nearby.*
(3) *The heroes ran to the daughters.*

Statement 2 can be deleted because it is inferrable from statements 1 and 3. The heroes must have heard the cries in order to go to the daughters. *Hearing the daughters' cries* implies that *the heroes were near the daughters.* In this example, the state (2) can be inferred from the action (3). In a similar fashion, events can entail enabling states. Unfortunately, there presently is no behavioral evidence for this plausible editing rule.

(6) **Intermediate events in causally driven event chains.** Whenever a causally driven event chain is stated in a passage, the events that intervene between the beginning and final events may be deleted. This is especially true when the event chain follows a typical course.

(1) *The child fell into the stream.*
(2) *The stream pulled the child under water.*
(3) *The child drowned.*

Statement 2 can be inferred from statements 1 and 3 and therefore can be deleted. Lehnert (1979) has suggested this editing rule in a theoretical context but there presently are no behavioral data to support it.

(7) **Static properties of arguments.** Sometimes an argument of a node is embellished or modified by a description of its static properties. In these instances, the modifying State node is connected with the primary node (which contains the argument in question) by a Property arc. For example, consider the following excerpt.

The attractive daughter went into the woods.

The primary node is the Goal node *The daughter went into the woods.* The *daughter* argument is modified by the State node *daughter is attractive.*

Previous studies (Kintsch, 1974; Kintsch and Keenan, 1973; Manelis, 1980; Meyer, 1975, 1977a, 1977b) have shown that recall for propositions decreases as the propositions are more subordinate in the underlying hierarchies. According to these hierarchies, the primary propositions are more superordinate than the State nodes that modify arguments of the more superordinate propositions. Thus, it appears that State nodes tend to be deleted by the editor when these nodes ascribe static properties to arguments, i.e., characters, objects, locations, etc. Moreover, the study by Black and Bower (1980) supports the conclusion that the State nodes tend to be deleted if they are not needed to interpret the actions and events in the plot.

Most of the above rules (1-7) cannot be applied unless the comprehender recognizes the underlying schemas that are involved. In other words, the rules are based on an interaction between incoming statements and the foregrounded schemas. When a statement fits a foregrounded schema, it can often be deleted, provided that some statement invokes the schema in the recall protocol. However, some incoming statements convey information that does not fit the schema. This leads to the next rule.

(8) **Incoming statements that are inconsistent with or unrelated to the foregrounded schemas in a passage.** In Chapter 3 it was shown that memory is better for information that is atypical of the prevailing schema in a passage. When atypical information is available in memory, it tends not to be deleted by the editor. Why? Because it is often informative, particularly when an atypical state, event, or action is needed for interpreting later information in the passage. When an atypical statement is not needed as an interpretation condition for later statements, it may still be informative. Why would the speaker or writer include an atypical statement unless there was an important point to be made by it? The pragmatic interaction between speaker and listener or reader and writer must be considered as well as the more literal content and representation of a passage (van Dijk, 1979). On the other hand, if the comprehender perceives that the atypical information is unimportant or irrelevant to the rest of the passage, it tends to be deleted by the editor (Black and Bower, 1980; Bower et al. 1979; Kintsch and van Dijk, 1978; Spilich et al., 1979).

In this section, a summarization-abstraction editor has been proposed as an important predictor of which passage statements tend to be recalled. An interesting direction for future research would be to examine the productions or symbolic rules that are included in the editor. Of course, there are other aspects of recall that have not been addressed in this section. What about those statements that tend to capture the theme of a passage or subthemes that capture an excerpt in a passage? What about recall intrusions? What about the order in which statements are produced in the recall protocol? Answers to these questions await future research. Although recall of prose has been vigorously examined in recent years, there still is no comprehensive explanation of recall. It is hoped that the proposed rules and the notion of a summarization-abstraction editor has shed new light on an old paradigm.

Conceptual Graph Structures Revisited

Are the proposed conceptual graph structures good approximations to the prose representations that humans construct. Obviously, there is no absolute answer to this question. The proposed representational system and the conceptual graph structures do provide some explanation of behavior in diverse experimental tasks. The structures and the theory provide a foundation for making sense out of some detailed patterns of data. It is fair to say that we at least have a better understanding of question answering, truth verification, and recall.

At this point it would be premature to evaluate how well the graph structures correspond to the true cognitive representations that are constructed when humans comprehend prose. It is also too early to assess how well the proposed conceptual graph structures compare to representations that would be constructed by other theories. Other theories in psychology have not been developed to the point of solving all three of the following goals (which were discussed in Chapter 4).

(1) To develop a representational system that can be applied to passages in different prose genres.
(2) To develop a representational system that can explain behavioral data in tasks that involve question answering, verification ratings, and recall.
(3) To develop a representational system that incorporates pragmatic inferences as well as explicit information and propositional (necessary) inferences.

The proposed representational system is presently the only candidate that has attempted to meet these objectives. To what extent can other representational theories be expanded and modified to meet the above goals? How well would alternative theories compare to the present representational system? It was beyond the scope of this chapter to examine these very important questions. The answers await further research.

We are now ready to explore the complex question of how prose representations are constructed during comprehension. It has been argued that comprehension proceeds by identifying and applying schemas. More will be said about this matter in the next chapter.

6

The Construction of Prose Representations

How is the conceptual representation of a passage constructed during comprehension? How are inferences and expectations generated? How are erroneous inferences and expectations disconfirmed? A psychological theory of discourse processing must eventually address these questions. The question of how conceptual graph structures are constructed on-line during comprehension will be explored in this chapter.

Available psychological research and theory has made a rather modest contribution to our understanding of how prose is comprehended on-line. The studies discussed in earlier chapters have specified in detail how prose is represented after comprehension is completed. In contrast, the on-line construction of these representations is still a mystery. Psychologists have only recently acknowledged the importance of exploring the on-line construction of prose structures (Black and Bower, 1980; Collins et al., 1980; Graesser, Robertson, and Clark, 1980; Kintsch, 1977a; Kintsch and van Dijk, 1978; Lesgold et al., 1979; Miller and Kintsch, 1980; Olson, Mack, and Duffy, 1980; Rumelhart, 1979), so the enterprise is very much in its infancy.

A number of investigators have tested specific hypotheses about comprehension processes, but very few of these hypotheses have focused on the conceptual levels that were examined in Chapters 4 and 5. These hypotheses were derived theoretically and have been tested in experiments in which simple response measures were collected during comprehension. Researchers have collected reading times for sentences and sentence sets (Black et al., 1979; Clark, 1977; Clark and Haviland, 1977; Garrod and Sanford, 1977; Graesser, Hoffman, and Clark, 1980; Haberlandt, 1980; Haberlandt and Bingham, 1978; Haviland and Clark, 1974; Kieras, 1978; Lesgold et al., 1979; Miller and Kintsch, 1980; Ortony, Schallert, Reynolds, and Antos, 1978; Yekovich and Walker, 1978). Other measures include the duration and patterns of eye movements during reading (Carpenter and Just, 1977b; Just and Carpenter, 1978, 1980; McConkie, Hogaboam, Wolverton, Zola, and Lucas, 1979; Rayner, 1977; Rayner et al., 1978) and latencies in responding to a secondary task during comprehension (Britton,

Meyer, Simpson, Holdredge, and Curry, 1979). Stimulus materials in these studies were systematically varied in a way that tested a given hypothesis or a set of alternative hypotheses. The contributions of some of these studies were discussed in earlier chapters. They have indeed confirmed a number of plausible hypotheses about what goes on during comprehension. When an investigator has a reasonably good understanding of some processing component, these measures are available for testing alternative theories.

Reading times, eye movements, and other simple response measures will probably continue to provide the critical data that convince psychologists which hypotheses, models, and theories are plausible. For lack of a better term, such an approach to conducting research will be called the *simple response measure approach.* It can be argued that there are certain shortcomings to such an approach to investigating comprehension. The following shortcomings readily come to mind.

One shortcoming of the simple response measure approach pertains to the discovery problem. The data that investigators collect are often not sufficiently rich and distinctive for the investigator to discover new aspects of the comprehension mechanism. The experiments are designed to test hypotheses, theories, or theoretical frameworks that have already been developed. Thus, progress critically depends on advancements in theory, and advancements in theory are often not facilitated by observed patterns in the data. Without a theoretical foundation, the investigator may be at a loss in making sense out of sets of reading times or of the frequencies, durations and loci of eye fixations. It is relatively difficult for an investigator to perceive unexpected processes and structures from a list of numbers. The simple response measure approach is useful when a fairly sophisticated understanding of a mechanism has been achieved. Unfortunately, we do not have an impressive understanding of comprehension. The simple response measure approach alone will probably *not* uncover new parts of the comprehension puzzle.

A second shortcoming of the simple response measure approach is that it has not adequately dealt with the problem of inference. Reading times, eye movements, and latencies in secondary tasks have not led researchers to identify the vast panorama of inferences, expectations, and tacit knowledge structures that are intimately involved in the comprehension process. The simple response measure approach has not unveiled how such inferences and expectations are generated, preserved, or disconfirmed. This approach focuses primarily on the measurement and explanation of the processing time for explicitly presented stimulus material and has not contributed substantially to an understanding of inference processing in all its complexity. Available psychological models of online comprehension (Just and Carpenter, 1980; Kintsch, 1979; Kintsch and van Dijk, 1978; Kintsch and Vipond, 1979; Miller and Kintsch, 1980; Perfetti and Lesgold, 1977; Spilich et al., 1979) have deemphasized or postponed the problem of inference.

To be fair, there are some reading time studies that have been designed to test hypotheses about inference processing (Clark, 1977; Clark and Haviland,

1977; Garrod and Sanford, 1977; Lesgold et al., 1979; Miller and Kintsch, 1980; Vipond, 1980). Many of these studies have directly or indirectly involved the construct of *bridging*. Sometimes explicit propositions or statements in text are conceptually related by virtue of *bridging inferences*. Without intermediate bridging inferences, the explicit propositions would be difficult or impossible to relate semantically. The phenomenon of bridging can be illustrated by situations involving definite reference. Consider the two excerpts below.

(1) *John left the beer in the car. The beer was too warm to drink.*
(2) *John left the picnic supplies in the car. The beer was too warm to drink.*

In excerpt 1 *the beer* in the second sentence directly corresponds to *the beer* in the first sentence. The same referential index is captured by identical noun-phrase descriptions: *the beer.* In excerpt 2, however, *the beer* in the second sentence does not have a direct match to any noun-phrase in the first sentence. Instead, a bridging inference must be made: *picnic supplies include beer.* Once the bridging inference is made, a direct match can be made between *the beer* in the second sentence and *beer* in the bridging inference. The studies cited above have shown that additional processing time is needed to construct the bridging inference. For example, the second sentence in excerpt 2 requires more time to read than the second sentence in excerpt 1, despite the fact the two sentences are identical. Such an outcome supports the hypothesis that the construction of bridging inferences requires additional processing time. The notion of bridging is an important construct that needs to be incorporated into our theories of comprehension.

Most of the research exploring bridging inferences has been theory driven. For example, in Clark's research, reading times were measured to test specific hypotheses about direct and indirect references, presuppositions, implicatures, and "invited inferences" (Clark, 1977, 1979; Clark and Clark, 1977; Clark and Haviland, 1977; Clark and Lucy, 1975). These studies were inspired by certain advancements in semantics and linguistic theory (Gordon and Lakoff, 1971; Halliday, 1967; Halliday and Hasan, 1976). These studies have had an important impact on the field because (a) they have established the importance of examining inference processes and (b) they have demonstrated that these hypotheses can be tested experimentally by simple reading time measures. Nevertheless, studies such as these require some theory or hypothesis to guide the experimental research. Inferences that are not incorporated in the prevailing theories have received little or no attention. Specifically, in Chapter 4 it was demonstrated that most inferences that are constructed during comprehension are schema-based, pragmatic inferences and are not within the scope of existing linguistic or logical theories of inference. As a result, most schema-based inferences have been ignored in psychological research.

A third shortcoming of the simple response measure approach is that the investigators usually select or invent the stimulus items that are used to test the proposed hypothesis or alternative hypotheses. There is a question of whether the stimulus sentences or excerpts are representative of the input that comprehenders normally receive. There are several traps that may seduce researchers who select or invent their own stimulus items. First, the investigator may have followed some unintended rule or criterion when generating the stimulus items; the unintended systematicity may be responsible for the data rather than the variable or hypothesis that the researcher proposes. Second, the investigator may unintentionally be guided by private and unanalyzed intuitions about processing time when selecting the items. The investigator may reject candidate tiems that do not fit the investigator's intuitions about processing time and accept items that conform to intuition. Third, the investigator may inflate the importance or prevalence of his pet process or phenomenon. When normal prose is analyzed, the investigator's pet phenomenon may prove to be rare. As a consequence, the investigator may devote years to exploring a very rare phenomenon and overlook a more prevalent phenomenon in comprehension. It appears that despite its virtues, the simple response measure approach has serious shortcomings.

There is an alternative approach to exploring on-line comprehension mechanisms. The alternative method will be called the *complex protocol analysis approach.* This method sacrifices some purity and ease in operationally defining variables in order to arrive at a richer data base for discovering and explaining properties of on-line comprehension. The data base for complex protocol analyses consists of verbal protocols. Subjects verbally describe what they are thinking about or what they can say about prose segments at different points in the passage. For example, in *think aloud* protocols, subjects are stopped at various points while listening to a passage. When they are stopped, they are asked to describe what is happening in the passage (Collins et al., 1980; Olson, Mack, and Duffy, 1980; Rumelhart, 1979). Alternatively, subjects may be probed with specific questions at different points in the passage (Graesser, Robertson, and Clark, 1980; Olson, Mack, and Duffy, 1980; Rumelhart, 1979). The answers and verbal protocols of subjects provide insights about the development of information structures that are constructed during comprehension.

Think aloud protocols and Q/A protocols obviously do not perfectly reflect the process of constructing prose representations. In fact, there is some controversy over the usefulness of verbal protocols in uncovering the underlying cognitive processes (Ericsson and Simon, 1979; Nisbett and Wilson, 1977). Nisbett and Wilson (1977) have concluded that subjects have "little or no direct introspective access to higher order cognitive processes" (p. 231) and suggest that subjects' verbal reports are based on apriori, implicit causal theories about how their cognitions should work. This conclusion may be limited, however, to particular types of materials and probing conditions. Ericsson and Simon (1979) have gathered together an impressive number of studies that speak in favor of using verbal protocols as data, and have even offered a model of subject verbalizations. Ericsson and Simon have concluded that "verbal protocols reflect very closely the internal structure of the cognitive processes that occur during task performance" (p. 43). Although there is some controversy over the role of verbal protocols in uncovering cognitive processes, there is less controversy about their usefulness in uncovering cognitive representations and content. Verbal protocols may impressively reveal *what* the comprehender is thinking about even though there is some question as to whether the comprehender can articulate *how* he came to think it. Moreover, the *how* may be inferred by the investigator after analyzing patterns of data that emerge from the *what*.

The complex protocol analysis approach requires the investigator to examine verbal reports of subjects. The analyses are qualitative or symbolic. The investigator typically segments protocols into propositions and interrelates these propositions conceptually and structurally. The analyses are generally less straightforward than the simple response measure approach. For the most part, no one disputes how latencies are measured when investigators collect reading times, eye movements, or reaction times in secondary tasks. However, some quibbles may evolve over (a) how verbal protocols are to be segmented into information units, (b) whether two information units capture the same meaning, and (c) how information units are interrelated. In terms of measurement error and the operational definitions of variables, there is no doubt that the simple response measure approach has advantages over the complex protocol analysis approach.

What does the complex protocol analysis approach have to offer researchers? One advantage is that the data are qualitatively rich and distinctive. Consequently, the investigator can identify informative patterns and discover phenomena that are outside the scope of available theories. Second, the complex protocol analysis approach provides a method of exposing inferences that comprehenders generate. Third, researchers can apply the method to virtually any prose passage. Instead of selecting or inventing stimulus passage that fulfill dozens of design constraints, the investigator can preserve a healthy respect for ecologically valid prose if so desired. In short, the complex protocol analysis approach fills the gaps and shortcomings of the simple response measure approach.

The point of this discussion is not that the simple response measure approach should be abandoned. Rather, it is believed that comprehension research will progress optimally when there is a balance between the simple response measure approach and the complex protocol analysis approach. Nearly all of the studies in experimental psychology have fixated on collecting simple response measures. However, the complex protocol analysis approach has not been duly appreciated.

In this chapter there will be a focus on research that has adopted the complex protocol analysis approach. These studies have unveiled some intriguing insights about on-line comprehension. Many of these insights have not been apparent or emphasized by theorists and have not been discovered by researchers that collect simple response measures. Unfortunately, most of the findings reported in this chapter have not been tested further by collecting reading times, eye movements, or other simple behavioral measures. A more rigorous test of these insights awaits future research.

A few comments should be made about the theoretical perspective that lurks in the background of the studies to be discussed. The theoretical framework throughout this book has been that schemas guide the interpretation of input, generation of inferences, and expectations. Schemas are identified at different levels of analysis and capture different knowledge domains. However, little is known about how these different knowledge domains interact, how they are synchronized, and what information in schemas is ultimately passed to the passage representation. In order to examine these weighty questions, the investigator ultimately needs to examine the following:

(1) The schemas that comprehenders identify during comprehension.
(2) The representations of the identified schemas.
(3) The representation of the passage that is finally constructed after comprehension is completed.
(4) The representations of passage excerpts at intermediate points during the course of comprehension.

The discussion in this chapter will focus primarily on the third and fourth issues.

A Question-Answering Method of Exploring the Construction of Prose Representations

In Chapter 4 some studies were reported that used a Q/A method for examining the inferences and cognitive representations that are constructed when adults comprehend passages. After the subjects read a passage, they were probed with *why* questions and *how* questions. Each statement in the passage was probed with both types of questions. The answers that subjects gave to the questions uncovered a large number of inferences. In Chapter 4 a representational system was presented that (a) segmented the inferences and explicit information into statement nodes, (b) assigned each node to one of six node categories (Physical State, Physical Event, Internal State, Internal Event, Goal, and Style), and (c) interrelated the nodes by labeled, directed arcs (Reason, Initiate, Manner, Consequence, and Property). The empirically derived representations were called *conceptual graph structures.* The conceptual graph structures depicted the memory representations that individuals have available *after* a passage is finished being comprehended. The studies in Chapter 4 were not designed to explore how the conceptual graph structures are constructed *during* comprehension.

In the studies reported in this chapter a Q/A method was used to examine on-line comprehension. Statements in passages were probed in different context conditions. Such contextual manipulations provide the basis for identifying the informational sources from which inferences and expectations are generated. Target statements were probed with different types of questions. *Why* questions and *how* questions provided a profile of the reasons and causes that are involved in the interpretations of target statements. *What happened next* (WHN) questions provided a profile of expectations.

A variety of context conditions may be implemented in order to explore constructive processes. Three conditions to explore initially are *no context, prior context,* and *full context.* These manipulations are depicted in Table 6.1. In the no context condition, subjects are presented a target statement in isolation and then the statement is probed with questions. In the prior context condition, the target statement is probed after the subject receives the target statement plus the passage information before the target statement; the subject is not exposed to passage information that occurs after the target statement. In the full context condition, the subject receives the entire passage before any given target statement is probed. The answers that are extracted in the full context condition consist of nodes that are *preserved* in the final representation of a passage. The representations that are probed in the no context and prior context conditions do not include all the information that is eventually constructed. The answers that are generated in incomplete context conditions are sometimes in error and do not exhaust the nodes that are constructed in the final passage representation.

The answers generated in the no context condition include inferences and expectations that were generated on the basis of the target statements in isolation.

Table 6.1. Three Context Conditions Imposed for Examining the Construction of Prose Representations

(1) No context

Presented information:

The dove plucked a leaf.

Questions:

Why did the dove pluck a leaf?
How did the dove pluck a leaf?
What happened next?

(2) Prior context

Presented information:

A thirsty ant went to a river. He became carried away by the rush of the stream and was about to drown. A dove was sitting in a tree overhanging the water. The dove plucked a leaf.

Questions:

Why did the dove pluck a leaf?
How did the dove pluck a leaf?
What happened next?

(3) Full context

Presented information:

A thirsty ant went to a river. He became carried away by the rush of the stream and was about to drown. A dove was sitting in a tree overhanging the water. The dove plucked a leaf and let it fall. The leaf fell into the stream close to the ant and the ant climbed onto it. The ant floated safely to the bank. Shortly afterward, a birdcatcher came and laid a trap in the tree. The ant saw his plan and stung him on the foot. In pain the birdcatcher threw down his trap. The noise made the bird fly away.

Questions:

Why did the dove pluck a leaf?
How did the dove pluck a leaf?
What happened next (after the dove plucked a leaf)?

These answers are called ***statement-driven*** nodes. In the prior context condition subjects generate both (a) statement-driven nodes that are based on the target statement and (b) nodes that are generated on the basis of the target statement together with the context prior to the target statement, i.e., ***prior-context–driven*** nodes. The answers generated in the full context condition include statement-driven nodes, prior-context-driven nodes, and nodes that are generated on the basis of information that occurs ***after*** the target statement, i.e., ***subsequent-context-driven*** nodes. Thus, there are three types of nodes that are related to a target statement.

(1) Statement-driven nodes
(2) Prior-context–driven nodes
(3) Subsequent-context–driven nodes

The distribution of nodes collected from the Q/A protocols in the no context, prior context, and full context conditions provides the data for examining the course of constructing prose representations. It is possible to identify the sources of inferences and expectations that are ultimately ***preserved*** in the final passage representations, and also the course of ***disconfirming*** incorrect inferences and expectations.

A disconfirmed inference or expectation is one that disappears with the addition of context. For example, the nodes produced in the prior context condition include information that is either statement-driven or prior-context-driven. For any given target statement, only some of the nodes that were statement driven (appearing in the no context condition) will appear also in the prior context condition. Those statement-driven nodes that are absent when prior passage content is introduced must have been blocked or somehow disconfirmed. Similarly, when subsequent passage context is introduced, some of the statement-driven nodes and prior-context–driven nodes may drop out of the subjects' protocols. Disconfirmed inferences and expectations consist of nodes that never make it into the final representation of a passage but may reveal some conceptual processes that occurred during comprehension.

Six categories of nodes can be identified from the way in which an answer node is distributed among the three context conditions (Table 6.2). A plus (+) in Table 6.2 signifies that a particular node was included as an answer to a particular questioned statement in a specific context condition. A minus (–) signifies that a particular node was not an answer in the specific context condition. For example, one of the answers to ***Why did the dove pluck a leaf?*** was ***In order to save the ant.*** This Goal node, ***dove save ant,*** was not generated as an answer to the question in the no context and prior context conditions, but was generated as an answer in the full context condition. According to the distribution chart in Table 6.2, this node would be classified as a subsequent-context–driven node. Once the answer nodes are classified into the six categories shown in Table 6.2, a variety of analyses can be performed to examine constructive processes.

After the distinct answer nodes are assigned to the six categories, the investigator prepares a frequency distribution. For example, if 200 distinct nodes were

Table 6.2. Criteria for Identifying Six Categories of Inferences and Expectations

Category of Answer	Context condition		
	None	Prior	Full
(A) Statement-driven nodes that are preserved	+	+/−	+
(B) Statement-driven nodes that are disconfirmed by prior context	+	−	−
(C) Statement-driven nodes that are disconfirmed by subsequent context	+	+	−
(D) Prior-context–driven nodes that are preserved	−	+	+
(E) Prior-context–driven nodes that are disconfirmed by subsequent context	−	+	−
(F) Subsequent-context–driven nodes	−	−	+

Symbols: +, answer is present in Q/A protocols; −, answer is not present in Q/A protocols.

generated in the Q/A task, these 200 distinct nodes would be distributed among the six node categories (A, B, C, D, E, and F) in some manner that produces six frequency scores. *Conditional probabilities* can be computed from these six frequency scores.

Some nodes are ultimately *preserved* in the final representation that is established after comprehension of a passage is finished. Categories A, D, and F are preserved nodes. Notice that these three categories have plus values in the full context condition (Table 6.2). Some of these preserved nodes were generated by the target statement (A), others were generated by virtue of prior passage context (D), and others were generated by virtue of subsequent passage context (F). From where do preserved nodes tend to be generated? From the target statement, from prior context, or from future context? The following conditional probabilities can be computed in order to answer this question. *A, D,* and *F* consist of frequency scores.

$$p(\text{statement-driven node/preserved}) = A/(A+D+F) \quad (6.1)$$

$$p(\text{prior-context–driven node/preserved}) = D/(A+D+F) \quad (6.2)$$

$$p(\text{subsequent-context-driven node/preserved}) = F/(A+D+F) \quad (6.3)$$

These three conditional probabilities reveal the developmental process of constructing the nodes in the conceptual graph structure that is ultimately preserved.

Another set of conditional probabilities assesses the disconfirmation of inferences and expectations. For example, what is the likelihood that a statement-driven node or a prior-context–driven node will be disconfirmed? The conditional probabilities below permit assessment of these questions (*A, B, C, D,* and *E* are the frequency scores for their respective categories).

$$p(\text{node is disconfirmed/statement-driven}) = (B+C)(A+B+C) \quad (6.4)$$

$$p(\text{node is disconfirmed/prior-context-driven}) = E/(D+E) \quad (6.5)$$

It should be noted that subsequent-context-driven nodes are never disconfirmed.

Statement-driven nodes that are disconfirmed may be pruned out either by information in prior context or by information in subsequent context. The following conditional probabilities assess the disconfirmation of these statement-driven nodes.

$$p(\text{node is disconfirmed by prior context/statement-driven and disconfirmed}) = B/(B+C) \qquad (6.6)$$

$$p(\text{node is disconfirmed by subsequent context/statement-driven and disconfirmed}) = C/(B+C). \qquad (6.7)$$

Those prior-context-driven nodes that are disconfirmed are always pruned out by virtue of subsequent context.

To summarize, the conditional probabilities in Formulas 6.1-6.7 provide the foundation for exploring the process of constructing prose representations. These conditional probabilities may be computed for individual target statements.

A second type of analysis measures *overlap scores* between sets of answers that are generated from a target statement in different context conditions. The set of distinct answers that are generated from a specific target statement is called an *answer distribution.* An overlap score computes the proportion of answers that are common to any two answer distributions (Table 6.3). An overlap score of 1.0 means that there is perfect overlap in the answers of two distributions. An overlap score of 0 means that there is no overlap.

The pattern of overlap scores between conditions provides some estimates of what proportions of preserved answers are driven by the statement, by prior context, and by subsequent context. Such an estimate requires the inclusion of a full context comparison condition that is identical to the full context condition. The comparison condition is needed in order to arrive at an empirical maximum value for overlap scores. The magnitude of an overlap score (OS) is to some extent sensitive to sampling error and the number of observations collected. The comparison condition provides a standard against which to compare the no context, prior context, and full context conditions.

(1) OS (no context, comparison)
(2) OS (prior context, comparison)
(3) OS (full context, comparison)

If there were no sampling error, then the third overlap score would be 1.0.

The informational sources of preserved nodes can be derived from the above three overlap scores as shown below.

$$p(\text{statement-driven node/preserved}) = \frac{\text{OS (no context, comparison)}}{\text{OS (full context, comparison)}} \qquad (6.8)$$

$$p(\text{prior-context-driven nodes/preserved}) = \frac{\text{OS (prior context, comparison)} - \text{OS (no context, comparison)}}{\text{OS (full context, comparison)}} \qquad (6.9)$$

$$p(\text{subsequent-context-driven nodes/preserved}) = \frac{\text{OS (full context, comparison)} - \text{OS (prior context, comparison)}}{\text{OS (full context, comparison)}} \quad (6.10)$$

Formulas 6.8, 6.9, and 6.10 are comparable to Formulas 6.1, 6.2, and 6.3, respectively, except that the former computations are based on the distribution of answers among the six types of nodes in Table 6.2, while the latter are based on overlap scores. The two sets of computations are expected to agree. The purpose of both sets of computations is to estimate the proportion of preserved nodes in the graph structures that are statement-driven, versus prior-context-driven, versus subsequent-context-driven. These properties can be obtained for individual target statements.

Table 6.3. Computation of an Overlap Score Between Two Distributions of Answers

Let: (1) A_{xy} be the number of times that a particular answer y occurs in answer distribution x.

(2) n be the number of particular answers that occur in either of the two distributions of answers.

$$\text{Overlap score} = \frac{\sum_{k=1}^{2} \sum_{j=1}^{n} A_{kj} - \sum_{j=1}^{n} \left| A_{1j} - A_{2j} \right|}{\sum_{k=1}^{2} \sum_{j=1}^{n} A_{kj}}$$

Example

	A_{x1}	A_{x2}	A_{x3}	A_{x4}	A_{x5}
A_{1y}	8	3	4	2	0
A_{2y}	6	1	4	0	4

$$\text{Overlap score} = \frac{8+3+4+2+0+6+1+4+4-2-2-0-2-4}{8+3+4+2+0+6+1+4+0+4}$$

$$= \frac{22}{32}$$

$$= .69$$

The relative proportions of preserved nodes that are statement-driven, versus prior-context-driven, versus subsequent-context-driven would have implications about the difficulty of comprehending passages and statements in a passage. If the relative proportions were .10, .10, and .80, respectively, for statement-driven, prior-context-driven, and subsequent-context-driven inferences, then a given statement would not be fully interpreted until subsequent context is received. If most of the statements had such relative proportions, then a passage might be difficult to comprehend. As statements would be received, previous statements would need to be extensively elaborated and reinterpreted. Comprehension would be complex in the sense that very little could be concluded about a given statement until the entire passage is known. Consider a different set of proportions for statement-driven, prior-context-driven, and subsequent-context-driven nodes that are preserved: .10, .80, and .10, respectively. In this distribution, prior context is primarily responsible for the interpretation of an incoming statement. A statement would not be embellished very much by future context. The on-line representation of a statement would for the most part characterize the final representation of the statement and comprehension would be simplified. In a .80, .10, and .10 distribution of statement-driven, prior-context-driven, and subsequent-context-driven nodes, the statement itself would for the most part characterize the interpretation of the statement; prior and subsequent context would have only a residual influence on interpretation. The latter distribution of nodes would suggest a building-block analogy of prose comprehension and lead one to conclude that a passage is little more than the sum of its explicitly stated nodes. A passage with a .80, .10, and .10 distribution would lack cohesion.

There is still another set of analyses that is particularly informative about the comprehension process. Which nodes in the preserved conceptual graph structures were statement driven, which were prior context driven, and which were subsequent context driven? Analysis of the processing history of the nodes in the final passage structure provides invaluable insights, as will be seen in the analyses to follow. There are other related questions. For example, the on-line representation of a statement and the surrounding inferences can be represented in terms of a conceptual graph structure. Which nodes are pruned out of a temporary structure when later passage information is encountered? Structural analyses can be performed when tracing the creation and pruning of nodes during comprehension.

It is ultimately possible to manipulate finer gradations of context in order to examine comprehension processes in more detail. Thus, there could be conditions in which subjects receive the target statement plus (a) one statement of prior context, (b) two statements of prior context, (c) three statements of prior context, (d) one statement of subsequent context, (e) two statements of subsequent context, and so on. Before attaining this level of detail, however, the most informative initial study would include the three context conditions in Table 6.1.

The proposed method uses a Q/A task to probe the comprehenders' conceptual representations at different points in the passage. The Q/A task does indeed elicit an impressive amount of implicit information. However, a critical question has been raised about the inferences and expectations that are exposed in the Q/A protocols. Was the information truly constructed during the comprehension process or was the information dredged out only by the Q/A task? Is there any way of segregating nodes that were truly constructed at comprehension from those nodes that were derived during question answering?

At present there is no way of determining which inferences or expectations were generated at comprehension and which were generated only during question answering. It is plausible to assume that a proportion of the nodes were generated at comprehension and the rest of the nodes were derived at question answering. Hopefully, the proportion of nodes generated at comprehension is sufficiently high so that findings and conclusions will be reliable and valid. Moreover, the proportion may be more or less constant for different categories of nodes, for different types of questions, and for the different classification categories in Table 6.2. To the extent that the proportion is reasonably high and remains constant, the analyses in this chapter will lead to valid conclusions about on-line comprehension processes. In other words, the proposed Q/A analyses do not require that all of the nodes be constructed during comprehension. Furthermore, the generation of an answer to a question about a target statement implies the development of enough of the underlying conceptual structure to compute a plausible inference or expectation. Whether each and every answer maps directly onto a node in actual memory is not known. However, each node in the graph structure (that is built from subjects' answers) represents the potential to compute an answer. Comparisons of answers across the different context conditions are illustrative of changes in the underlying structure. These changes cannot be seen directly, but they are reflected by the subjects' answers.

Effects of Prior Context on the Interpretation of Statements

The study reported in this section shows how a simple application of the Q/A method can be used to explore certain questions about on-line comprehension. A more complex and complete application of the Q/A method will be reported in the next section. The data in this section were reported in a study by Graesser, Robertson, and Clark (1980). The study was designed to examine a very fundamental question: To what extent does prior context influence the interpretation of a target statement in a passage? The question may be posed somewhat differently. To what extent is the on-line interpretation of a target statement determined or constrained by (1) the target statement itself, (2) local context (such as the sentence prior to the target statement), or (3) global context (such as a paragraph or set of sentences prior to the target statement)?

In order to examine the above questions Graesser, Robertson, and Clark (1980) probed target statements with *why* questions after receiving excerpts in *three different context conditions.*

No context
Sentence context
Paragraph context

These three conditions are summarized in Table 6.4. In the no context condition the subjects received only the target statement, followed by a *why* question about that statement. In the sentence context condition, the subjects answered the *why* question after reading the target statement plus the sentence that occurred immediately prior to the target statement. Thus, a local context was provided in the sentence context condition. In the paragraph context condition, subjects were probed with the *why* question after reading the target sentence plus all of the prior context that led up to the target statement. The paragraph context condition provided a global context for the target statement.

Table 6.5 contains the six categories of nodes that can be identified by the distribution of answers in the three conditions. Answer nodes are divided into statement-driven, local-context-driven, and global-context-driven. If an answer is statement-driven, it was either preserved in the on-line representation or was disconfirmed by local context or by global context. Local-context-driven nodes may or may not be disconfirmed by global context.

A few details about the study should be mentioned. Forty subjects answered *why* questions about target statements after the statements were read in the three different context conditions. Thirty of the subjects were probed on 27 target statements, with 9 items per context condition. There were three groups

Table 6.4. Study on Effects of Prior Context: Context Conditions

(1) No context condition
Presented information:
The dove plucked a leaf.
Question:
Why did the dove pluck a leaf?

(2) Sentence context condition
Presented information:
A dove was sitting in a tree overhanging the river. The dove plucked a leaf.
Question:
Why did the dove pluck a leaf?

(3) Paragraph context condition
Presented information:
A thirsty ant went to a river. He became carried away by the rush of a stream and was about to drown. A dove was sitting in a tree overhanging the water. The dove plucked a leaf.
Question:
Why did the dove pluck a leaf?

Adapted from Graesser, Robertson, and Clark (1980).

of 10 subjects that received different booklets. The net effect was that each target statement was assigned to the no context condition for 10 subjects, to the sentence context condition for 10 subjects, and to the paragraph context condition for 10 subjects. Ten additional subjects were assigned to the comparison condition, in which all 27 target statements were preceded by a paragraph of context. As was mentioned in the previous section, this comparison condition is needed for a meaningful analysis of the overlap scores.

The paragraphs covered a variety of topics and ranged from roughly 100 to 200 words. The passages were selected from magazines and collections of short stories. Among the 27 passages, 9 passages were in the narrative genre, 9 were in the expository genre, and 9 were in the persuasive genre. Among the 27 target statements, 9 statements were intentional actions, 9 were physical or internal events, and 9 were physical or internal states. Proper counterbalancing was incorporated in the design so that all subjects received 3 items in each target statement category (action, event, state), each genre category (expository, persuasive, narrative), and each context condition. Every target statement was probed an equal number of times in each context condition.

Subjects read the items and answered the *why* questions that were presented in the booklets. They completed the Q/A task at their own pace. Subjects were instructed to write down whatever reasons and causes came to mind when answering the *why* questions.

Table 6.6 is a summary of the outcome of the categorization analysis presented in Table 6.5. An answer was included in this analysis only if it was generated by at least 3 of the 30 subjects who received booklets with items in different context conditions. Altogether, 146 distinct answers were generated among the 27 items. Of these answers, .86 were inferences and .14 were nodes explicitly

Table 6.5. Study on Effects of Prior Context: Categorization of Nodes Based on Distribution of Answers

	Context condition		
Node category	None	Sentence	Paragraph
(A) Statement-driven nodes that are preserved	+	+/−	+
(B) Statement-driven nodes that are disconfirmed by local context	+	−	−
(C) Statement-driven nodes that are disconfirmed by global context	+	+	−
(D) Local-context–driven nodes that are preserved	−	+	+
(E) Local-context–driven nodes that are disconfirmed by global context	−	+	−
(F) Global-context–driven nodes	−	−	+

Adapted from Graesser, Robertson, and Clark (1980).

Symbols: +, answer is present in Q/A protocols; −, answer is not present in Q/A protocols.

Table 6.6. Study on Effects of Prior Context: Number of Answers in Each Node Category

Node category	Number of answers
(A) Statement driven, preserved	33
(B) Statement driven, disconfirmed by local context	26
(C) Statement driven, disconfirmed by global context	17
(D) Local context driven, preserved	20
(E) Local context driven, disconfirmed by global context	17
(F) Global context driven	33

Adapted from Graesser, Robertson, and Clark (1980).

stated in the paragraphs. An answer was scored as appearing in a specific context condition if it appeared in at least one of the 10 subjects' protocols.

Conditional probabilities were computed on the data in Table 6.6 in order to examine the process of creating and disconfirming nodes at comprehension. A number of conclusions could be drawn from the conditional probabilities.

> **Observation 1.** The on-line interpretation of a statement critically depends on previous passage context.

This observation would not surprise anyone. The comprehender often requires some context in order to understand why an action or event occurs, or why a state exists. What analyses and data support Observation 1? An analysis of overlap scores and the frequency scores in Table 6.6 support the first observation. Of the 86 answers that were preserved in the on-line representation (categories A, D, and F in Table 6.6), .38 were statement-driven, .23 were local-context-driven, and .38 were global-context-driven.

An analysis of overlap scores confirmed the above estimates. It should be noted that overlap scores were computed from all distinct answers that subjects gave, whereas the frequency scores in Table 6.6 include only those answer nodes that were generated by at least 3 of 30 subjects. When overlap scores were computed, answers in the comparison group were compared to answers in the no context, sentence context, and paragraph context conditions. Overlap scores were computed for each of the target statements. When averaging over the 27 target statements, there were the following mean overlap scores (OS).

OS (no context with comparison) = .20

OS (sentence context with comparison) = .29

OS (paragraph context with comparison) = .49.

These three overlap scores were all significantly different when variability between target statements was used as an error term. It is important to point out that there was a modest overlap score (.49) between the paragraph context and comparison conditions. Since these were identical conditions, the overlap score would be 1.0 in the best of all possible worlds. However, the obtained overlap score was much lower because of sampling error and differences among subjects.

On the basis of the above three overlap scores, it is possible to estimate the proportion of preserved nodes that are statement-driven, local-context-driven, and global-context-driven (see Formulas 6.8, 6.9, and 6.10):

$$p(\text{statement-driven node/preserved}) = .20/.49 = .41$$

$$p(\text{local-context-driven node/preserved}) = (.29 - .20)/.49 = .18$$

$$p(\text{global-context-driven node/preserved}) = (.49 - .29)/.49 = .41$$

These estimates are quantitatively similar to the estimates derived from the category analysis in Table 6.6. It appears that prior context is important in guiding the interpretation of a target statement. More of the inference nodes were generated by local and global context than were generated by information in the target statement per se. This difference was significant when the 53 statements in categories D and F in Table 6.6 were compared with the 33 statements in category A, χ^2 (1) = 5, $p < .05$. Of course, these frequencies are averaged over many target statements and therefore disguise the potential differences between different categories of statements.

A second conclusion can be drawn from the above quantitative estimates of the proportion of preserved nodes that are statement-driven, versus local-context-driven, versus global-context-driven.

Observation 2. The on-line interpretation of a target statement is determined by global context (e.g., prior set of sentences) more than by the local context (e.g., the prior sentence).

Observation 2 is supported by the fact that roughly twice as many preserved nodes were global-context-driven (.38-.41) than local-context-driven (.18-.23). This difference was marginally significant when the 20 items in category D were compared with the 33 items in category F, χ^2 (1) = 3.4, $p < .10$. This observation would lead to the rejection of a simple chaining hypothesis of constructing prose structure. According to a simple chaining hypothesis, an incoming statement is directly associated to the previous statement (which is presumably in short-term memory) by either a direct link or a set of bridging inferences. Instead, an incoming statement is linked to information that is constructed from several prevous statements.

To what extent do the above conclusions generalize to different passages and different types of statements? In Table 6.7 overlap scores are given for target statements that were actions, versus events, versus states. Target statements were also segregated according to whether they appeared in narrative, expository, or persuasive prose. When statistical analyses were performed on the overlap scores in Table 6.7 (using the variability between target statements as an error

Table 6.7. Study on Effects of Prior Context: Overlap Scores

Classification of target statement	Context condition		
	None	Sentence	Paragraph
Text genre			
Narrative	.23	.29	.48
Expository	.19	.28	.46
Persuasive	.17	.31	.54
Type			
Intentional action	.24	.29	.52
Event	.16	.27	.48
State	.19	.32	.46

Adapted from Graesser, Robertson, and Clark (1980).

term), there were no significant differences among the types of target statements and the passage genres. Thus, the above conclusions apparently generalize to virtually all stimulus materials. These data support the following observation.

Observation 3. Observations 1 and 2 generalize to different types of statements (actions, events, states) and different genres of prose (narrative, expository, persuasive).

The previous observations pertained to inference nodes that are preserved in the on-line interpretation of a target statement. What can be said about the process of disconfirming inferences that potentially could be made? The following observations can be made about the disconfirmation of statement-driven and local-context–driven nodes.

Observation 4. Statement-driven inferences have a higher likelihood of being disconfirmed than do local-context–driven inferences.

Conditional probabilities support Observation 4. Of the 76 statement-driven nodes (categories A, B, and C in Table 6.6), .43 were preserved in the on-line interpretation of a target statement. The other statement-driven nodes were disconfirmed by virtue of local or global context. Of the 37 local-context-driven nodes (categories D and E), .54 were preserved, whereas the other local-context–driven nodes were disconfirmed by virtue of global context. Unfortunately, a statistical test could not be performed on this comparison.

From one perspective, local-context–driven inferences would be expected to be preserved more often than would statement-driven inferences. Local-context-driven inferences are generated on the basis of more information than are statement-driven inferences. Local-context–driven inferences are invoked by the target statement plus the previous sentence, whereas statement-driven inferences are invoked by only the target statement. Inferences that are based on more information are expected to have a higher likelihood of being preserved.

Observation 5. The disconfirmation of potential statement-driven inferences is more often governed by local context than by global context.

Observation 5 is also supported by conditional probabilities. Of those 43 statement-driven nodes that were disconfirmed (categories B and C in Table 6.6), .60 were disconfirmed on the basis of local context, whereas .40 were disconfirmed on the basis of global context. It appears that a small amount of context is sufficient to block most of the statement-driven inferences that potentially could be generated. A statistical test was not performed on these frequencies, however, due to the small number of observations.

The analyses reported in this section have supported five observations about the on-line interpretation of statements in prose. Some of the observations would be obvious to many researchers, whereas others are not particularly obvious. It is important to point out that support for some of the observations rested on relatively few observations. Some of the conditional probabilities were not submitted to statistical analyses because they were based on a relatively small frequency of nodes (less than 100). At the same time, it is important to mention that Observations 4 and 5 are based on data that average over nodes. These observations gloss over differences that might exist between different classes of target statements and passages.

The analyses reported in this section hopefully conveyed how the Q/A method can be used to examine the on-line construction of prose representations. The reader has been introduced to overlap scores, the criteria for tracing the processing history of inference nodes (Tables 6.2 and 6.5), and the significance of specific conditional probabilities. However, there are several issues that this study never addressed. How is the on-line representation of a target statement influenced by subsequent passage context? What happens when target statements are probed by other types of questions, e.g., *how* and *what happened next?* What about the role of expectations? These and other questions will be examined in the next section.

Generation and Disconfirmation of Inferences and Expectations

The on-line construction of narrative representations will be explored in this section. The analyses reported here are based on a study conducted by Patricia Anderson and Brian Ronk. In this study the Q/A method was used to examine the on-line comprehension of four short narrative passages: *John at Leone's, The Czar and His Daughters, The Ant and the Dove,* and *The Boy and His Dog.* These were the same four narrative passages that were used in the Graesser et al. (1981) study and in Chapters 4 and 5. Since all four passages were in the narrative genre, it is unknown whether the subsequent observations would apply to passages in other prose genres.

Three context conditions were imposed in order to examine the on-line comprehension of the narrative passages: no context, prior context, and full context (Table 6.1). Separate groups of subjects participated in the three different context conditions. In each condition, each action and event in a passage was probed with three questions. Answers to *why* questions exposed the causes and reasons for a target action or event occurring. Answers to *how* questions exposed (a) the causes of target events and (b) the procedure, plan, or style of executing intentional actions. Answers to *what happened next* questions exposed expectations about future occurrences that subjects were able to generate during comprehension. Some details need to be mentioned about the methods employed in the three context conditions.

(1) **Full context condition.** Subjects first read the entire passage. Then they answered a *why* question, a *how* question, and a *what happened next* question for each action and event that was explicitly mentioned in the passage. The statements were probed with all three types of questions in the order that the statements appeared in the passage. The subjects wrote down their answers to these questions in a response booklet. The subjects were required to write down at least four lines of information for each question. Thus, an extended Q/A procedure was imposed in this condition. An extended Q/A procedure was also imposed in the no context and prior context conditions. Forty college students participated as subjects in the full context condition. Ten subjects were randomly assigned to each of the four stimulus passages; thus, any given subject was tested on only one passage.

The answers in the full context condition were assumed to include information that is preserved in the final story representation. The subjects had knowledge of the entire story before they answered any of the questions. The answers to questions about any given target statement could be formulated on the basis of (a) information in the target statement itself, (b) information from statements prior to the target statement, and (c) information from statements subsequent to the target statement. Note that in the full context condition the answers to the *what happened next* questions were not expectations because the subjects knew the entire story before being questioned.

(2) **Prior context condition**. Subjects answered the *why* questions, *how* questions, and *what happened next* questions *during* the course of reading the passage. The subjects started by reading an excerpt that included the first statement. The subjects then wrote down answers to the three types of questions for the first target action or event. After they finished the Q/A protocols for the first target item, they were presented an excerpt that included the second target action or event and wrote down answers to the three types of questions about the second target statement. After these Q/A protocols were collected, the subjects read the third action or event in the story and were subsequently probed with questions about this third target action or event. The procedure continued in this manner until all of the passage statements were presented and probed. Of course, the subjects were fully informed that the sequence of excerpts that they read formed a story. Forty subjects participated in the prior context condition. Just as in the full context condition, 10 subjects were randomly assigned to each of the four passages and any given subject was tested on only one passage.

The prior context condition probed the subjects' on-line representations of a passage at different points in the passage. The subjects always knew about information that occurred prior to a target statement in the passage, but they never knew about actions and events that would occur after the target statement. Therefore, the answers to the questions were based on (a) information in the target statement itself and (b) information from statements prior to the target statement.

(3) **No context condition.** The target actions and events were probed out of context. Each target statement was presented and probed with a *why* question, a *how* question, and a *what happened next* question. A target statement was presented and probed without the subjects' receiving either a prior passage context or a subsequent passage context. Therefore, the answers to the questions were based on information in the target statement itself. Forty subjects participated in the no context condition. The 40 subjects were randomly divided into four groups of 10 subjects, and each group received received a different sample of target actions and events. For any given group, approximately one-fourth of the target statements were from *The Czar and His Daughters,* one-fourth from *The Ant and the Dove,* one-fourth from *The Boy and His Dog,* and one-fourth from *John at Leone's.* The target statements within a group were randomly presented and probed with the constraint that a successive pair of target statements was never from the same story. Each statement in the stories was administered to 10 subjects in the no context condition.

As a consequence of the design in this study, each event and action in a story was probed by 10 subjects in the no context condition, 10 subjects in the prior context condition, and 10 subjects in the full context condition.

An answer node was included in the subsequent analyses if it was generated by at least two subjects for any given question. For example, one of the answers to *Why did the dog break the leash?* was *Because the dog saw an animal.* This answer was given by one subject in the no context condition, no subject in the prior context condition, and one subject in the full context condition. The answer node *dog saw animal* would be scored because two subjects generated the answer. Altogether, 30 subjects (10 in each context condition) answered each specific question. Thus, a node was scored in subsequent analyses if it was generated by at least 2 of the 30 subjects.

In the next step of the analysis a listing was prepared that contained each distinct node that was either explicitly stated in the passage or generated in the Q/A protocols. Any given answer node may have been generated by more than one target statement and more than one type of question (*why, how,* and *what happened next*). However, it would only be counted once in this listing. Thus, the final listing included all of the unique nodes that were ever generated in the Q/A task. The segmentation of answer protocols into nodes followed the representational system discussed in Chapter 4.

Table 6.8 includes some summary data for the nodes that were generated in the four short narrative passages. There were 1858 uniques nodes in the four stories combined. There were 68 statement nodes that were explicitly stated in the passages and 1790 unstated nodes that were exposed by the Q/A task. Therefore, approximately 26 unique inference or expectation nodes were gener-

Table 6.8. Summary Data for Nodes Generated in the Narrative Passages

	Story				
	Czar and Daughters	John at Leone's	Ant and Dove	Boy and Dog	Stories combined
Number of explicitly states nodes (target statements)	14	18	15	21	68
Number of inference or expectation nodes	286	453	437	614	1790
Ratio of inference or expectation nodes to explicit node	20.4	25.2	29.1	29.2	26.3
Number of inference or expectation nodes that were ultimately preserved in story representation	175	266	257	340	1038
Ratio of preserved inference or expectation nodes to explicit node	12.5	14.8	17.1	16.2	15.3
Number of inference or expectation nodes that were disconfirmed	111	187	180	274	752
Ratio of disconfirmed inference or expectation nodes to explicit node	7.9	10.4	12.0	13.0	11.1

ated for every action and event that was stated in a passage. On the average, 58% of the inference and expectation nodes were ultimately preserved in the final narrative representations, whereas 42% were eventually disconfirmed.

It is possible to trace the history of how specific nodes are generated, preserved, and possibly disconfirmed. Table 6.9 is a chart that depicts the constructive history of the node *The daughters became frightened.* This node was never explicitly stated in the story of *The Czar and His Daughters.* However, it was ultimately preserved in the final story representation because it was generated by at least one question in the full context condition. The chart specifies how many subjects (out of 10) generated the specific node when segregating (a) the three context conditions, (b) the three types of questions, and (c) the set of target statements that were explicitly mentioned in the story. Each of the target statements had been probed with questions. *The daughters became frightened* was an answer generated by four different questions.

Table 6.9. Constructive History of the Inference Node *The Daughters became frightened*

Target statements	Type of question and context condition								
	Why			How			What happened next		
	No	Prior	Full	No	Prior	Full	No	Prior	Full
Daughters walked in woods									
Daughters enjoyed themselves									
Daughters forgot time									
Daughters stayed too long									
Dragon kidnapped daughters							2	1	2
Dragon dragged off daughters							1	10	1
Daughters cried	2	9	6	1	2	2			
Heroes heard cries									
Heroes went to the daughters									
Heroes fought dragon									
Heroes rescued daughters									
Heroes returned daughters to palace									
Czar heard of rescue									
Czar rewarded heroes									

The dragon kidnapped the daughters–what happened next?
The dragon dragged off the daughters–what happened next?
Why did the daughters cry?
How did the daughters cry?

For each of these questions, *The daughters became frightened* was a statement-driven answer that was ultimately preserved (category A in Table 6.2); that is, the node was generated by at least one subject in each context condition (this distribution defines an item as a preserved statement-driven node).

Table 6.10 is a chart that traces the constructive history of the node *The daughters slept.* This node was generated by the following questions.

The daughters enjoyed themselves–what happened next?
How did the daughters forget the time?
The daughters stayed too long–what happened next?

The daughters slept was not explicitly stated in the passage and was not ultimately preserved in the final story representation. The node was initially generated as a statement-driven expectation based on the target statement *The daughters enjoyed themselves.* This statement-driven expectation was eventually disconfirmed by subsequent passage context and would be placed in category C in Table 6.2 because the expectation node was generated by at least 1 subject (out of 10) in the no context condition and in the prior context condition, but it was never generated in the full context condition (this distribution defines a node as being statement-driven and disconfirmed by subsequent context.

Sometimes a specific answer node is generated by more than one target statement. For example, *The daughters became frightened* and *The daughters slept* were both generated by three different target statements. Among the 1790 inference and expectation nodes, there were 1466, 193, 69, 24, 19, 11, 3, 3, and 2 nodes that were generated from 1, 2, 3, 4, 5, 6, 7, 8, and 10 target statements, respectively. Therefore, .81 of the inference and expectation nodes were generated from only one target statement. On the average, each node was generated by 1.33 target statements. Of course, a target statement occasionally generated a specific node by virtue of more than one type of question.

For each distinct node, a chart was prepared tracing the history of its generation, its preservation, and possibly its disconfirmation. From these charts a number of observations could be made about the on-line construction of prose structures. These charts will hereafter be called the *construction charts.*

Where are inferences generated from that are ultimately preserved in the final story representation? The construction chart for each inference node was examined in order to answer this question. A node was scored as a preserved inference in this analysis if it satisfied the following constraints.

(1) The node was not explicitly mentioned in the passage.
(2) The node was generated by a *why* question or a *how* question from any of the target statements. Nodes that were generated only by *what happened next* questions were excluded.

Table 6.10. Constructive History of the Inference Node *The daughters slept*

	Type of question and context condition								
	Why			How			What happened next		
Target statement	No	Prior	Full	No	Prior	Full	No	Prior	Full
Daughters walked in woods									
Daughters enjoyed themselves							1	1	0
Daughters forgot time				2	0	0			
Daughters stayed too long							1	1	0
Dragon kidnapped daughters									
Dragon dragged off daughters									
Daughters cried									
Heroes heard cries									
Heroes went to daughters									
Heroes fought dragon									
Heroes rescued daughters									
Heroes returned daughters to palace									
Czar heard of rescue									
Czar rewarded heroes									

(3) The node was generated in the full context condition by at least one target statement.

The preserved inference nodes were subsequently classified into the following four categories.

Statement driven
Prior context driven
Prior expectation driven
Subsequent context driven

When a node was generated by only one statement, it was quite obvious how the node would be classified. The classification followed the scheme in Table 6.2. However, when a node was generated by more than one target statement it was classified on the basis of the first target statement in the story that generated the node via a *why* question or a *how* question. A node was occasionally generated by two questions for a target statement. For example, the construction chart in Table 6.9 shows that the inference node *The daughters became frightened* was generated by both *Why did the daughters cry?* and *How did the daughters cry?* In these instances the inference node was scored in the analyses of both the *how* questions and the *why* questions.

An observant reader may have noticed that an additional category has been introduced into the analysis, namely *prior-expectation-driven nodes.* What is a prior-expectation-driven node? In many instances an inference node was generated by a target statement via a *why* or *how* question. However, prior to this target statement, the inference node was generated as an expectation by virtue of a previous target statement. For example, in Table 6.9 the inference node *The daughters became frightened* was first generated as an inference from the questions *Why did the daughters cry?* and *How did the daughters cry?* However, previous to this target statement (*daughters cried*) the inference node was generated as an expectation by virtue of the target statement *A dragon kidnapped the daughters.* The inference node *The daughters became frightened* would be categorized as a prior-expectation-driven inference. In contrast, prior-context-driven inferences were never expectation nodes generated by target statements that occurred prior to the target statement in question. Instead, the prior-context-driven inferences were generated on the basis of previous passage context together with the target statement.

The number of preserved inference nodes that were statement-driven, prior-context-driven, prior-expectation-driven, and subsequent-context-driven is shown in Table 6.11. The inference nodes were segregated according to four node categories: Goal, Style, Event, and State. The reader may want to refer to Table 4.1 for descriptions of the different node categories. Internal Events and Physical Events were combined into a more general Event category in this analysis. Similarly, the State category included both Internal States and Physical States. The inference nodes were also segregated according to the type of question and category of target statement that generated the inference node as shown on the next page.

Table 6.11. Number of Inference Nodes That Are Preserved in the Final Story Representation

Source of generation	Category of inference node	Statement driven	Prior context driven	Prior expectation driven	Subsequent context driven
Inferences that are	Goal	37	49	32	10
generated by	Event	11	24	8	5
why ⟨action⟩	State	79	30	3	13
questions					
Inferences that are	Goal	96	41	10	11
generated by	Style	134	22	0	10
how ⟨action⟩	Event	2	13	2	1
questions	State	29	2	1	1
Inferences that are	Goal	8	13	5	1
generated by	Event	13	21	8	1
why ⟨event⟩	State	34	14	1	7
questions					
Inferences that are	Goal	21	11	5	2
generated by	Style	40	10	0	0
how ⟨event⟩	Event	21	17	8	1
questions	State	15	5	1	0

(1) **Why ⟨action⟩.** The inference node was generated by a target statement that was an action (Goal+). A *why* question produced the inference node.
(2) **How ⟨action⟩.** The inference node was generated by a target statement that was an action (Goal+). A *how* question produced the inference node.
(3) **Why ⟨event⟩.** The inference node was generated by a target statement that was an event. A *why* question produced the inference node.
(4) **How ⟨event⟩.** The inference node was generated by a target statement that was an event. A *how* question produced the inference node.

The frequency scores in Table 6.11 correspond to the number of Goal, Style, Event, and State nodes that were generated from one of the question ⟨target statement⟩ categories listed above. On the basis of the data in Table 6.11, a number of observations can be made about how preserved inferences are generated on-line. It should be reemphasized that the subsequent observations reflect general trends that average over the target statements in the four passages.

> **Observation 6.** The preserved inferences that are associated with a target statement are rarely generated by information subsequent to the target statement.

The data in Table 6.11 indicate that only 7% (63/959) of the preserved inference nodes were subsequent context driven. The inferences associated with a target statement were normally generated by information in the target statement itself and the passage information that occurred prior to the target statement.

Observation 6 has some interesting implications regarding on-line comprehension. The inferences that are established in the on-line representation of a statement include virtually all of the inferences that will ever be associated with that statement. Stated differently, an incoming passage statement rarely embellishes previous statements by appending additional inference nodes to the previous structures that have already been constructed. In order to construct inferences about a statement in a narrative passage, the comprehender usually does not need to know the entire story. The comprehender needs to know the previous passage context, but not the subsequent passage context. Generally speaking, the construction of inference nodes is guided by past and present information, not future information.

Given that very few preserved inference nodes are subsequent context driven, the next question to ask is Where do most of the inferences come from? Are most of the inferences generated by information in the target statement alone or by the target statement together with prior context? There is no simple answer to this question. The answer depends on the category of inference node (Goal, State, Event, or Style). It also sometimes depends on whether the inference embellish *how* versus *why* a target action or event occurs. The following observations address the extent to which preserved inference nodes are driven by the target statement versus prior passage context.

Observation 7. Preserved Goal inferences are usually driven by prior passage context when they are generated as explanations of *why* a target action or event occurred.

Altogether there were 155 preserved Goal inferences that were generated by *why* questions. Of these 155 Goal inferences, 45 were statement-driven and 99 were driven by virtue of the target statements together with prior context (prior-context-driven or prior-expectation-driven). Therefore, roughly twice as many of the Goal nodes were generated by virtue of prior context as were generated by the information in the target statement alone. This difference is statistically significant, χ^2 (1) = 20, $p < .01$. Prior passage context is critically important for explaining the underlying goals that motivate actions in a story and also the implicit actions that led up to story events; the information that is carried in the target action or event is not as critical.

Observation 8. Preserved Goal and Style inferences are usually driven by the target statement when the inferences are generated as explanations of *how* the target action or event occurred.

Altogether, there were 413 preserved Goal and Style inferences that were generated by *how* questions. Of these 413 nodes, 291 were statement-driven and 99 were either prior-context–driven or prior-expectation-driven. The difference between 291 and 99 was statistically significant, χ^2 (1) = 95, $p < .01$. Thus, 70% of these Goal and Style inference nodes were generated by the information in the target statement alone. The target action or event alone carries the major burden of determining *how* the action or event occurs; prior passage context imposes only modest constraints.

Observations 7 and 8 together have interesting implications concerning the construction of goal-oriented conceptualizations. When an action (Goal+) is comprehended in a passage, the comprehender constructs a hierarchical structure of Goal nodes that are superordinate to the action. The superordinate Goal nodes explain *why* the action was executed. Many of these superordinate Goal nodes are inferences and prior passage context has a major impact on guiding the construction of these inferences. The comprehender also constructs Goal and Style inferences that are subordinate to the target action. These subordinate Goal and Style inferences specify how the target action was executed. These subordinate inferences are generated primarily by information in the target statement itself. Prior context does not have a major impact on the construction of Goal and Style inferences that are subordinate to the target action.

Observation 9. Event inferences that are preserved in the final story representation are usually driven by prior passage context.

Altogether, there were 156 preserved Event inferences. Of these 156 nodes, 47 were statement-driven and 101 were generated on the basis of the information in the target statement plus prior context (prior-context-driven and prior-expectation-driven). Thus, roughly twice as many of these inference nodes were generated by virtue of prior context as were generated on the basis of the target statement alone. This difference is statistically significant [χ^2 (1) = 20, $p < .01$] and was quite consistent (Table 6.11). Prior context is clearly important for constructing Event inferences.

Observation 10. State inferences that are preserved in the final story representation are usually statement-driven.

Altogether, there were 235 preserved State inferences. Of these 235 nodes, 157 were statement-driven and 57 were generated on the basis of the target statement plus prior context. The difference between 157 and 57 is statistically significant [χ^2 (1) = 47, $p < .01$] and was quite consistent (Table 6.11). Thus, 67% of the State inferences were statement driven. It appears that State inferences are driven primarily by information in the target statements, whereas prior context carries the burden of generating Event inferences.

Observation 11. The inference nodes that are associated with a given target statement are rarely generated as expectations from previous target statements.

Only 9% of the 959 nodes in Table 6.11 were prior-expectation-driven. When an inference was generated by virtue of prior context, the previous passage statements did not usually produce the inference in the form of an expectation (as in Tables 6.9 and 6.10). Instead, the inferences were usually generated by the information in the target statement together with the prior context. All 14 rows of data in Table 6.11 showed higher frequencies in the prior-context-driven column than in the prior-expectation-driven column. It appears, therefore, that most inferences in prose passages are not confirmed expectations. The inferences are usually generated in a bottom-up fashion, rather than being expectation-driven in a top-down fashion.

The next set of analyses is focused on inference nodes that are ultimately disconfirmed. Just as in the previous set of analyses, a node was scored as an inference if it was generated by either a *why* or a *how* question. Whenever an inference node was generated by more than one target statement, the node was classified according to its first occurrence in its construction chart.

The frequency data for those nodes that were disconfirmed are given in Table 6.12. The nodes are segregated according to (a) node category (Goal, Style, Event, State), (b) the type of target statement and question that generated the inference, and (c) the three subcategories listed below (see also Table 6.2).

(B) Statement-driven and disconfirmed by prior context.
(C) Statement-driven and disconfirmed by subsequent context.
(E) Prior-context–driven and disconfirmed by subsequent context.

There is one primary observation about the frequency data in Table 6.12.

> **Observation 12.** Statement-driven nodes are disconfirmed more often by subsequent passage context than by prior passage context.

There was a total of 414 disconfirmed statement-driven nodes. Of these 414 nodes, 165 were disconfirmed by prior context, whereas 249 were disconfirmed by subsequent context. This difference is significant $[\chi^2(1) = 17, p < .01]$ and the trend is quite consistent. Among the 14 comparisons in Table 6.12, 12 show higher frequencies in category C than category B.

Table 6.12. Number of Inference Nodes That Are Eventually Disconfirmed

		Statement driven, disconfirmed by		Prior context driven, disfirmed by subsequent context
Source of generation	Category of inference	Prior context	Subsequent context	
Inferences that are generated by why ⟨action⟩ questions	Goal	32	41	11
	Event	13	12	5
	State	17	32	18
Inferences that are generated by how ⟨action⟩ questions	Goal	22	35	12
	Style	30	64	15
	Event	4	5	2
	State	4	9	0
Inferences that are generated by why ⟨event⟩ questions	Goal	2	4	3
	Event	6	2	3
	State	12	14	3
Inferences that are generated by how ⟨event⟩ questions	Goal	5	6	2
	Style	10	13	2
	Event	4	7	4
	State	4	5	1

According to Observation 12, the passage context that occurs after a target statement plays a critical role in pruning out incorrect inference nodes that had been constructed. This finding is particularly interesting when it is contrasted with Observations 6, 7, and 9. Compared to subsequent context, prior context has a substantially greater impact on the *construction* of inference nodes. However, subsequent context has a greater impact than prior context on the *disconfirmation* of statement-driven inferences. In other words, prior context directs most of the construction of inference nodes, whereas subsequent context tends to direct the process of pruning out erroneous information.

Expectation nodes were examined in the next set of analyses. A node was scored as an expectation if it fulfilled the following constraints.

(1) The node was generated from a *what happened next* question.
(2) The expectation node was either statement-driven or prior-context-driven. Nodes that were exclusively subsequent-context-driven were eliminated because they were not really expectations; the comprehenders knew the entire story.
(3) According to the construction chart, the node was never generated by a *how* or *why* question from a previous target statement. Thus, the node was generated as an expectation before it was ever generated as an inference.

Sometimes an expectation node was generated from more than one target statement; in these instances the node was scored according to its first occurrence in the construction chart.

The frequency data for the expectation nodes are presented in Table 6.13. The nodes were segregated according to (a) whether they were preserved or disconfirmed, (b) node category (Goal, Event, State), and (c) whether the node was generated by a target action or a target event. A number of conclusions can be made from the pattern of frequency scores in Table 6.13.

Observation 13. Roughly the same number of confirmed expectations are statement-driven and prior-context–driven.

According to Table 6.13, 177 expectations were ultimately confirmed. Of these 177 nodes, 99 were statement driven and 78 were prior context driven. This difference was not statistically significant, χ^2 (1) = 2.5, $p > .10$.

Observation 14. Statement-driven expectations are disconfirmed by information in subsequent context more often than by information in prior context.

Altogether, there were 219 statement-driven expectations that were disconfirmed. Of these 219 nodes, 89 were disconfirmed by prior context, whereas 130 were disconfirmed by subsequent passage context. This difference is statistically significant, χ^2 (1) = 8, $p < .01$. Thus, statement-driven expectations are pruned out by subsequent context more often than being blocked by information in prior passage context. An observant reader may have noticed that the trend in Observation 14 is analogous to the trend in Observation 12.

Table 6.13. Number of Expectations That Are Confirmed Versus Disconfirmed

Source of generation	Category of node	Expectations that are confirmed: Statement driven	Expectations that are confirmed: Prior context driven	Expectations that are disconfirmed: Statement driven, disconfirmed by Prior context	Expectations that are disconfirmed: Statement driven, disconfirmed by Subsequent context	Expectations that are disconfirmed: Prior context driven
Expectations that are generated by actions	Goal	40	31	40	53	34
	Event	21	15	16	28	15
	State	7	2	5	2	1
Expectations that are generated by events	Goal	19	16	16	28	16
	Event	10	13	9	18	11
	State	2	1	3	1	2

What is the likelihood that a generated node is ultimately preserved in the final story representation? A set of conditional probabilities was computed in order to examine this question. The frequency scores in Tables 6.11, 6.12, and 6.13 provided the data for computing these conditional probabilities. For each category of node in these tables, three different conditional probabilities were computed.

(1) Probability of a node being preserved given that it is statement-driven: p(preserved/statement-driven).
(2) Probability of a node being preserved given that it is statement-driven and not disconfirmed by prior context: p(preserved/statement-driven and preserved on-line).
(3) Probability of a node being preserved given that it is prior-context-driven: p(preserved/prior-context-driven).

The Goal nodes that were generated by why ⟨action⟩ questions will be used as an example of how the conditional probabilities are computed. According to Table 6.11, there were 37 preserved nodes that were statement-driven and 49 preserved nodes that were prior-context-driven. According to Table 6.12, there were 32 statement-driven nodes that were disconfirmed by prior context, 41 statement-driven nodes that were disconfirmed by subsequent context, and 11 disconfirmed prior-context-driven nodes. The three conditional probabilities for these Goal nodes are computed below.

p(preserved/statement-driven) = 37/(37+32+41) = .34

p(preserved/statement-driven and preserved on-line) = 37/(37+41) = .47

p(preserved/prior-context-driven) = 49/(49+11) = .82

The three conditional probabilities for various categories of nodes are shown in Table 6.14. The nodes were segregated according to (a) category of node

(Goal, Style, Event, State), (b) type of question that generated the node (*why, how, what happened next*), and (c) the category of target statement that generated the node. These data supported some additional conclusions.

Observation 15. Prior-context–driven nodes have a higher likelihood of being preserved than do statement-driven nodes. This is true for both inference and expectation nodes.

The data in Table 6.14 uniformly support Observation 15. For all 20 categories of nodes in Table 6.14, the conditional probabilities were higher for prior-context–driven nodes than statement-driven nodes. This is statistically significant when a sign test is computed, $p < .01$. Altogether, there were 1272 statement-driven nodes and 510 prior-context–driven nodes in Tables 6.11, 6.12, and 6.13. Whereas 50% of the statement-driven nodes were preserved, 70% of the prior-context–driven nodes were preserved. Statement-driven nodes that are preserved on-line (i.e., not disconfirmed by prior context) also have a lower likelihood of being preserved in the final story representation than do prior-context–driven inferences. Of the 1018 statement-driven nodes that are preserved on-line, 63% are ultimately preserved. A chi-square test indicated that the 63% value is significantly lower than 70%, χ^2 (1) = 8, $p < .01$. The trend is also rather consistent. Of the 20 node categories in Table 6.14, 16 have higher conditional probabilities for prior-context–driven nodes than for the statement-driven nodes that were preserved on-line.

The thrust of Observation 15 is quite similar to Observations 2 and 4 in the previous section. Statement-driven nodes are generated from less information than are prior-context–driven nodes. As a result, the statement-driven inferences and expectations have a lower likelihood of being preserved in the final story representation. Observations 2, 4, and 15 support a rather simple generalization: the likelihood of a node being preserved increases as a function of the amount of information that generates it. This generalization is also supported by the next observation:

Observation 16. Prior-context–driven nodes have an increasing likelihood of being preserved as their corresponding target statements occur later in the passage.

For target statements that appear later in a passage, there is a more extensive backlog of prior context. Therefore, the prior-context–driven nodes generated by these target statements should have a higher likelihood of being preserved than nodes generated by target statements appearing early in a passage. Analyses support Observation 16. Inference and expectation nodes were segregated into two groups: (a) nodes that were generated by target statements appearing in the first half of a passage, and (b) nodes that were generated by target statements appearing in the second half of the passage. The likelihood of a prior-context-driven node being preserved was uniformly lower in the first half than the second half: .76 versus .84 for nodes generated by *why* questions; .77 versus .82 for nodes generated by *how* questions; and .40 versus .61 for nodes generated by

Table 6.14. Likelihood of a Generated Node Being Preserved in the Final Story Representation

Source of generation	Category of node	Statement driven	Statement driven and preserved on-line	Prior context driven
Nodes that are generated by why ⟨action⟩ questions	Goal	.34	.47	.82
	Event	.31	.48	.83
	State	.62	.71	.63
Nodes that are generated by how ⟨action⟩ questions	Goal	.63	.73	.77
	Style	.59	.68	.60
	Event	.18	.29	.87
	State	.69	.76	1.00
Nodes that are generated by why ⟨event⟩ questions	Goal	.57	.67	.81
	Event	.62	.87	.88
	State	.57	.71	.82
Nodes that are generated by how ⟨event⟩ questions	Goal	.66	.78	.85
	Style	.63	.75	.83
	Event	.66	.75	.81
	State	.63	.75	.83
Nodes that are generated by WHN ⟨action⟩ questions	Goal	.30	.43	.48
	Event	.32	.43	.50
	State	.50	.78	.66
Nodes that are generated by WHN ⟨event⟩ questions	Goal	.30	.40	.50
	Event	.27	.36	.54
	State	.33	.66	.33

what happened next questions. These differences could not be attributed to special differences between the target statements in the first half and the second half. Why? Because the likelihood of statement-driven nodes being preserved did not differ between the first half and the second half: .50 and .50 for nodes generated by *why* questions; .62 and .61 for nodes generated by *how* questions; and .31 versus .32 for nodes generated by *what happened next* questions.

The studies reported in this section and the previous section have established 16 observations about the on-line construction of prose representations. Some of these observations are not particularly surprising, whereas others would probably not be discovered on a rational or intuitive basis. In the next section some structural and conceptual aspects of constructing narrative representations are explored. These analyses will give rise to further observations.

A Structural-Conceptual Analysis of On-line Comprehension

In this section, we will examine how the graph structures are constructed during the course of comprehending a passage. The representational system discussed in Chapter 4 was adopted in these analyses. It is possible to trace the development of a graph structure as each statement is interpreted on-line. When an incoming statement is interpreted, additional nodes are appended to the available structure and some nodes in the available structure are pruned out. Nodes can also be restructured. The purpose of the following analyses is to trace the evolution of constructing prose structures. If a set of n statements produces some structure S, then structure S is modified when statement n+1 is interpreted. The statements 1 to n+1 together produce a new modified structure, S′. How do structures S and S′ differ?

The diagrams in Figure 6.1 show five ways that a structure S may be transformed to structure S′ after an additional statement is comprehended. New nodes are added to the structure by either appending or inserting transformations. Appending is a simpler transformation than inserting. *Appending* occurs when a new node is adjoined (by an arc) to some node in structure S. *Inserting* occurs when a new node is adjoined in between two nodes in structure S. Analogously, there are two ways that nodes are removed from structure S. *Pruning* occurs when there is a removal of some node m in structure S; when applicable, all nodes that radiate from node m (away from the main structure) are removed as well. *Deleting plus restacking* involves a more complex structural change. A node r is removed from structure S, and then the nodes that were directly connected to r are joined together (restacked). The inserting and the deleting plus restacking modifications involve a restructuring of a graph, whereas the appending and the pruning modifications simply involve adding or removing nodes from structure S. There is a fifth type of modification that involves a *reordering* of the nodes in structure S. However, recording will not be discussed any further in this section becaues such a modification virtually never occurred in the passages that were examined. There were clearly enough semantic constraints on the nodes to eliminate the possibility of nodes in structure S being reordered.

The Q/A protocols of the narrative passages were examined in order to assess the frequency of appending, inserting, pruning, and deleting plus restacking modifications. The first set of analyses traced the entire evolution of each passage structure, starting with the first statement and incrementing statement by statement. Thus, the first structural comparison was between (a) the structure generated from statement 1, S(1), and (b) the structure generated on the basis of statements 1 and 2, S(1,2). The next comparison was between S(1,2) and S(1,2,3). The next comparison was between S(1,2,3) and S(1,2,3,4), and so on. For each increment, the nodes generated by *why, how,* and *what happened next* questions were included in the structure.

The first analysis focused entirely on the course of adding nodes to prior structures as incoming statements are comprehended. Thus, this analysis com-

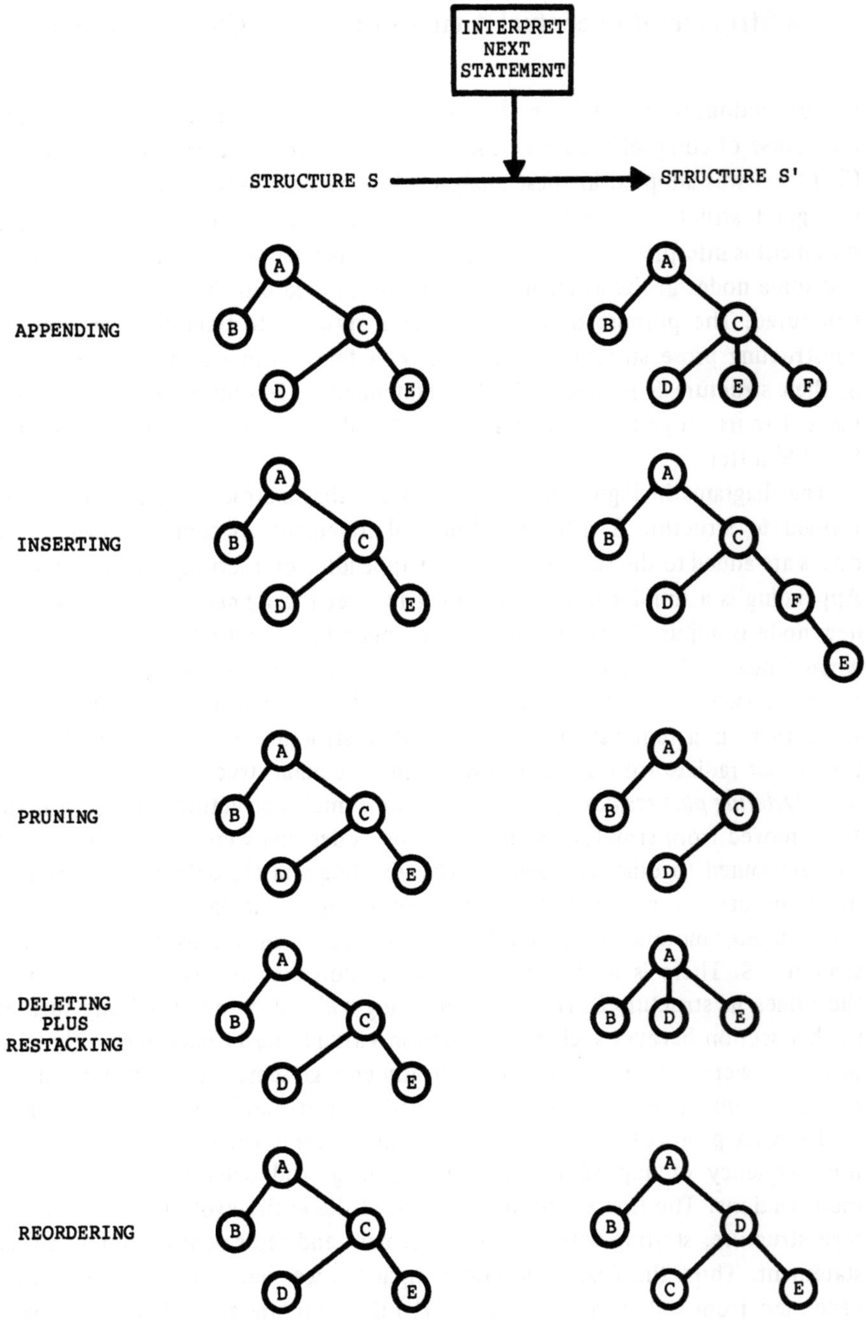

Figure 6.1. Five types of structural changes.

puted the frequencies of appending nodes and inserting nodes, but not the removal of nodes (i.e., pruning and deleting plus restacking). The set of nodes that were included in this analysis consisted of preserved nodes that were statement-driven and prior-context-driven. Unfortunately, it was impossible to isolate the exact statement that generated a subsequent-context-driven node because there were several nodes after the target statement that could have produced a subsequent-context–driven inference. The fact that subsequent-context–driven inferences were not included in this analysis was not a very serious problem because less than 7% of the preserved nodes (categories A, D, and F in Table 6.2) were subsequent-context–driven (see Observation 6).

Observation 17. As narrative structures are built during on-line comprehension, new nodes tend to be appended to previous structures rather than being inserted. Stated differently, the incoming information does *not* substantially impose a reorganization of previous structures.

Evidence for Observation 17 is based on the proportion of added nodes that are appended versus inserted into previous structures. Among the preserved inferences and expectations, 89% were appended to previous structures, whereas 11% were inserted into previous structures. Within the set of inserted nodes, 72% embellished previous expectations, whereas only 28% were inserted into structures involved in the interpretation of previous actions and events. Only 3% of the new nodes were inserted into previous structures that captured the interpretation of prior information (i.e., not prior expectations). In other words, most of the restructuring (inserting) that did occur, involved the restructuring of previous expectations rather than the interpretations of previous statements.

Observation 18. Three layers of nodes radiated from target statement nodes that are preserved in the narrative structure. Statement-driven nodes form the inner layer, which is nearest to the target statement. Prior-context–driven nodes form the middle layer. Subsequent-context–driven nodes form the outer layer, which is farthest from the target statement. This layering phenomenon will be called the *lamination effect.*

A number of analyses support Observation 18 and the lamination effect. For each target statement, a structure was created from the set of preserved nodes (categories A, D, and F) that were empirically generated from the target statement. The nodes included answers to *why, how,* and *what happened next* questions. An example structure for the target statement *The heroes fought the dragon* in the story of *The Czar and His Daughters* is presented in Figure 6.2. There were 15 preserved nodes in this structure in addition to the target statement. Ten nodes were statement-driven from the target statement (category A), 5 nodes were prior-context–driven (category D), and 0 nodes were subsequent-context–driven (category F).

The pattern of nodes in Figure 6.2 shows that statement-driven nodes were closer to the target statement than were prior-context-driven nodes. On the average, prior-context–driven nodes were 2.60 arcs away from the target statement, whereas statement-driven nodes were only 1.20 arcs away. Thus, Observation 18 is supported by a simple computation of the number of arcs that intervene between a target statement and an answer node. There is stronger evidence for the lamination effect when the categories of nodes on paths that radiate from the target statement are examined. For all paths or chains of nodes that radiate from the target statement in Figure 6.2, the set of prior-context–driven nodes is more distant than the set of statement-driven nodes.

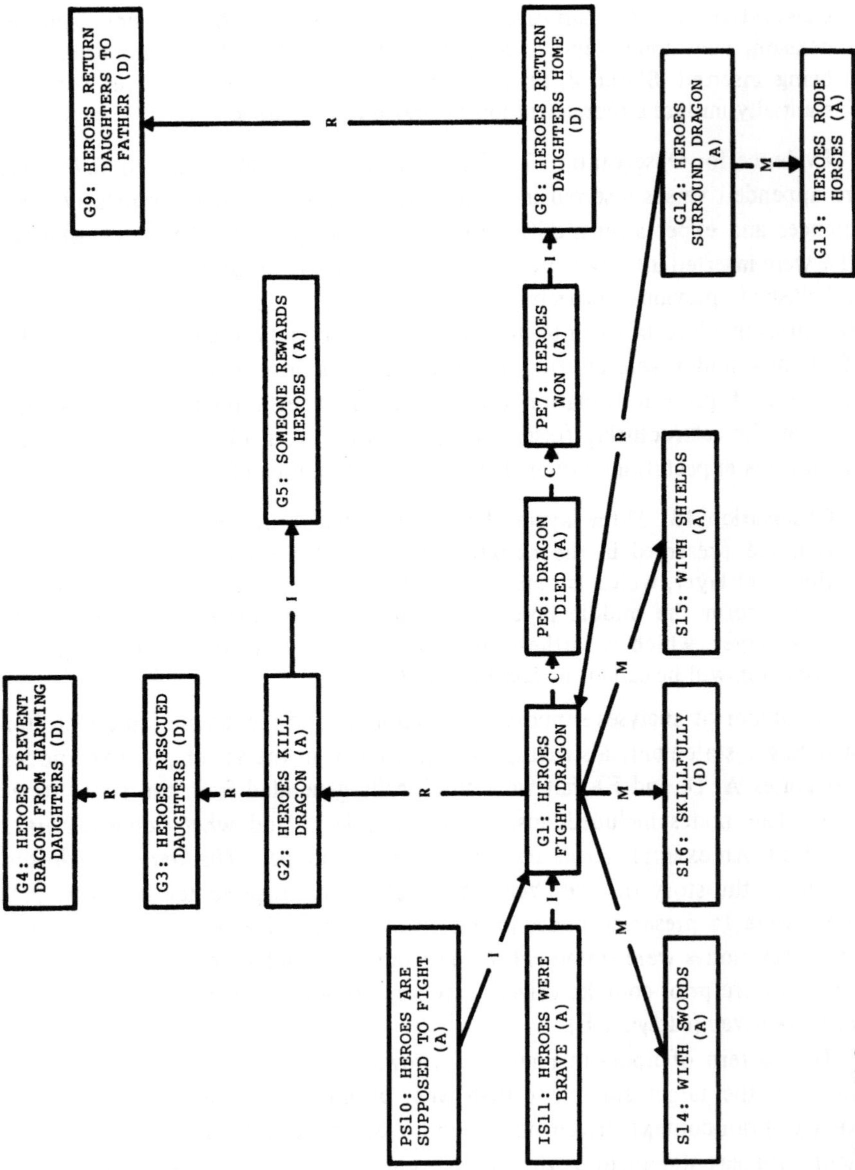
G9: HEROES RETURN DAUGHTERS TO FATHER (D)
R
G8: HEROES RETURN DAUGHTERS HOME (D)
G12: HEROES SURROUND DRAGON (A)
M
G13: HEROES RODE HORSES (A)
G5: SOMEONE REWARDS HEROES (A)
I
PE7: HEROES WON (A)
I
C
PE6: DRAGON DIED (A)
C
R
S15: WITH SHIELDS (A)
G4: HEROES PREVENT DRAGON FROM HARMING DAUGHTERS (D)
R
G3: HEROES RESCUED DAUGHTERS (D)
R
G2: HEROES KILL DRAGON (A)
R
G1: HEROES FIGHT DRAGON
M
M
S16: SKILLFULLY (D)
M
PS10: HEROES ARE SUPPOSED TO FIGHT (A)
I
IS11: HEROES WERE BRAVE (A)
I
S14: WITH SWORDS (A)

Figure 6.2

In other words, a prior-context–driven node never occurred in a path between a statement-driven node and the target statement.

The pattern of nodes in Figure 6.2 is representative of the structures generated for all of the target statements. Structures were constructed for all of the target statements in the four narrative stories. On the average, the statement-driven nodes were 1.71 arcs away from the target statement, prior-context–driven nodes were 2.66 arcs away, and subsequent-context-driven nodes were 3.72 arcs away. These differences are statistically significant and have been replicated in the study by Graesser, Robertson, and Clark (1980). An analysis was also performed on the paths radiating from each target statement. Only 2% of the subsequent-context–driven nodes occurred in a path between a target statement node and a statement-driven or a prior-context-driven node; 98% of the subsequent-context–driven nodes were layered on top of the statement-driven and prior-context–driven nodes. Similarly, only 9% of the prior-context-driven nodes occurred in a path between a target statement and a statement-driven node. In summary, there appears to be a strict ordering of nodes that radiate on a path from a target statement: statement-driven nodes, then prior-context-driven nodes, and then subsequent-context-driven nodes.

Observations 17 and 18 pertain to the construction of nodes that are ultimately preserved in the final narrative representation. What about the disconfirmation of erroneous nodes? In the next set of analyses pruning and deleting plus restacking modifications are examined.

Observation 19. During the on-line comprehension of narrative, incoming information removes nodes from structures that were constructed earlier in the passage. The removal of nodes virtually always involves pruning rather than deleting plus restacking transformations. Stated differently, incoming information does *not* substantially impose a reorganization of previous structures.

On-line passage structures were composed for each statement increment, i.e., S(1), S(1,2), S(1,2,3), etc. The structure of each increment included statement-driven and prior-context–driven nodes that were preserved in the on-line representations of excerpts in a passage (categories A, C, D, and E in Table 6.2). Nodes in categories C and E were removed from the on-line structures by virtue of subsequent context. Among these erroneous nodes, 98% involved pruning and 2% involved deleting plus restacking. Thus, nodes are pruned out of the previous structure; when a node is removed, the previous structure is not reorganized.

Observation 20. Statement-driven nodes have a higher likelihood of being disconfirmed as they radiate further from the target statement.

For each target statement, a graph structure was prepared of the statement-driven nodes (categories A, B, and C in Table 6.2). Figure 6.3 is a graph structure

---

Figure 6.2. Structure of preserved nodes associated with the target statement *The heroes fought the dragon.*

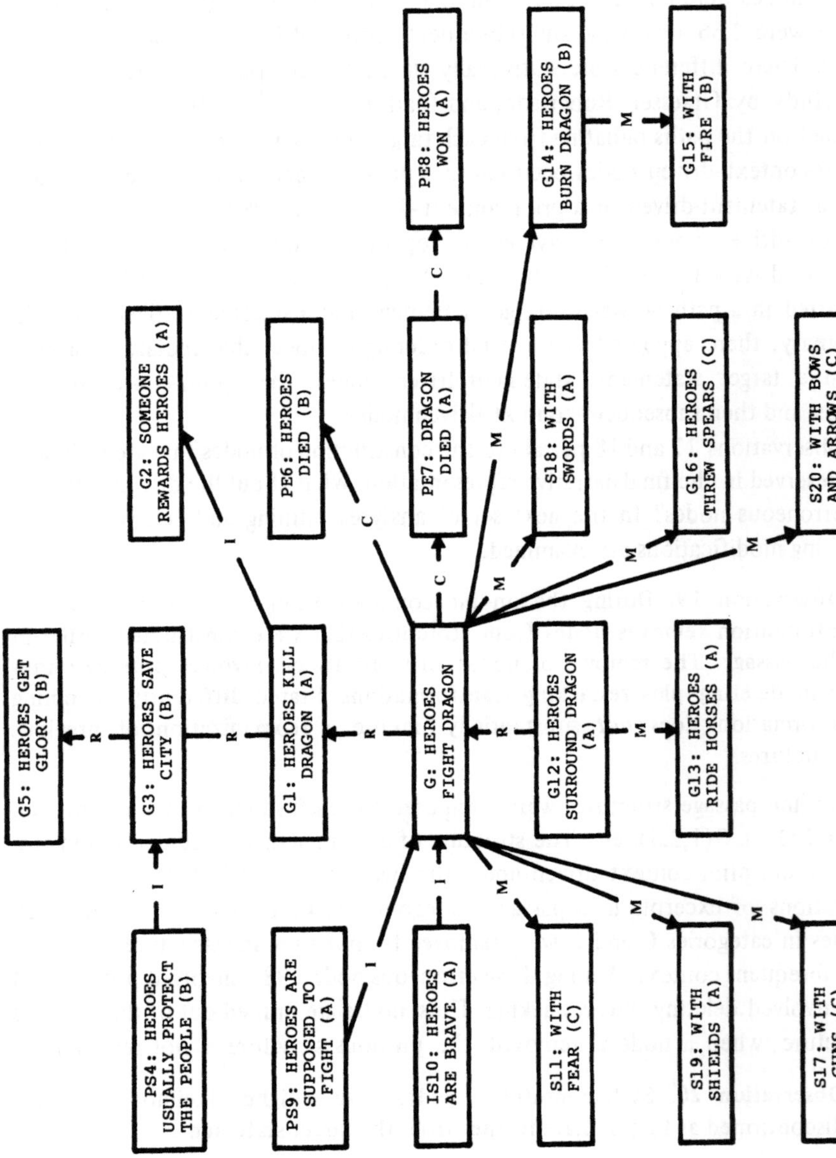
G5: HEROES GET GLORY (B)
G3: HEROES SAVE CITY (B)
G1: HEROES KILL DRAGON (A)
G: HEROES FIGHT DRAGON
G12: HEROES SURROUND DRAGON (A)
G13: HEROES RIDE HORSES (A)
G2: SOMEONE REWARDS HEROES (A)
PE6: HEROES DIED (B)
PE7: DRAGON DIED (A)
PE8: HEROES WON (A)
S18: WITH SWORDS (A)
G14: HEROES BURN DRAGON (B)
G15: WITH FIRE (B)
G16: HEROES THREW SPEARS (C)
S20: WITH BOWS AND ARROWS (C)
PS4: HEROES USUALLY PROTECT THE PEOPLE (B)
PS9: HEROES ARE SUPPOSED TO FIGHT (A)
IS10: HEROES ARE BRAVE (A)
S11: WITH FEAR (C)
S19: WITH SHIELDS (A)
S17: WITH GUNS (C)
R
R
R
R
I
I
I
I
I
C
C
C
M
M
M
M
M
M
M
M
M
M

Figure 6.3

for the target statement *The heroes fought the dragon.* There were 20 statement-driven nodes that were generated by *why, how,* or *what happened next* questions. There were 10 preserved nodes (category A), 6 nodes that were blocked by prior context (category B), and 4 nodes that were disconfirmed by subsequent context (category C). On the average, the preserved nodes were 1.20 arcs away from the target statement, whereas the disconfirmed nodes (B and C) were 1.50 arcs away. The trend can be captured somewhat differently. The likelihood of a node being preserved was .54 for nodes that were one arc away from the target statement and .43 for nodes that were 2 or 3 arcs away. The pattern of node categories (A, B, C) in Figure 6.3 is also interesting. A disconfirmed node (B or C) was never in a path between a target statement and a preserved node (A).

The structure in Figure 6.3 is representative of statement-driven structures. When all target statements were analyzed, the preserved statement-driven nodes were fewer arcs away from the target statement than were disconfirmed statement-driven nodes, 1.52 versus 2.02, respectively [$F(1, 1236) = 41.37, p < .05$]. The likelihood of a statement-driven node being preserved was .52, .41, and .13 for nodes that were 1, 2, and 3-5 arcs away from the target statement, respectively. In addition, only 3% of the disconfirmed nodes were on a path between a target statement and a preserved statement-driven node. Thus, erroneous statement-driven nodes are virtually always removed by pruning rather than deleting plus restacking.

In many of the previous analyses a distinction has been made between structures involving expectations and structures involving the interpretation of previous actions and events. When a target statement is comprehended on-line, the following types of structures are evaluated or constructed.

(1) Verbatim and inference nodes that are involved in the interpretation of information prior to the target statement.
(2) Expectation nodes that are created by information prior to the target statement.
(3) Additional inference nodes that are added during the on-line interpretation of a target statement.
(4) Additional expectation nodes that are added during the on-line interpretation of a target statement.

Sometimes the nodes in the above four types of structures are mutually exclusive; expectation nodes are not inference nodes. However, in other instances there is an overlap between expectation and inference nodes; a node may be both an inference and an expectation. The next set of analyses will show that such an overlap is quite predictable.

Consider a target statement that is an intentional action. In order to understand *why* an action (Goal+) occurred, the comprehender evaluates and constructs potential Goal nodes that are superordinate to the target action. For ex-

---

Figure 6.3. Structure of statement-driven nodes associated with the target statement *The heroes fought the dragon.*

ample, suppose that the comprehender listened to *The Czar and His Daughters* up through the action *The heroes fought the dragon* and then was asked to answer a *why* question about the fighting episode. A typical Q/A protocol is shown below.

Why did the heroes fight the dragon?
In order to kill the dragon.
In order to rescue the daughters.

According to Figure 6.2, the *killing* and *rescuing* Goal nodes are superordinate to the *fighting* Goal node. An important property of a superordinate Goal node is that it is achieved or potentially achieved *after* the target action. In other words, actions are executed in order to achieve desired states in the future. This, of course, is the essence of planning. It follows that the Goal nodes that are generated from why⟨action⟩ questions should have high overlap with the expected future actions that are generated from WHN⟨action⟩ questions. The answers in the following Q/A protocol are quite sensible.

The heroes fought the dragon. What happened next?
The heroes killed the dragon.
The heroes rescued the daughters.

In contrast to the target actions, there should be no overlap between answers to why⟨event⟩ questions and WHN⟨event⟩ questions. Similarly, there should be no overlap between answers to how⟨event⟩ and WHN⟨event⟩ questions. When a target event is probed with a *why* question or a *how* question, the answerer generates past actions, events, and states that led up to target event. When a target event is probed with a *what happened next* question, the answerer generates expected or actual actions and events that occur in the future. Stated differently, answers to why⟨event⟩ questions sample backward Consequence arcs, whereas answers to WHN⟨event⟩ questions sample forward Consequence arcs. Therefore, the nodes generated by the two types of questions should be entirely different.

Analyses supported the outcomes anticipated in the above discussion. Overlap scores (OS) were computed on the answer distributions of *why, how,* and *what happened next* questions. The following overlap scores were computed.

OS (why and what happened next)
OS (why and how)
OS (how and what happened next)

When the overlap scores were computed (see Table 6.3), target events were segregated from target actions and overlap scores were assessed separately for answers in the no context, prior context, and full context conditions. The outcome of the overlap score analyses is shown in Table 6.15.

The mean overlap scores in Table 6.15 show no differences among the three context conditions. However, there were striking differences between probed actions and events. The overlap scores between *why* and WHN questions were

Table 6.15. Overlap Scores for Answers to Different Types of Questions

	Context condition		
	None	Prior	Full
Overlap between answers to *why* questions and *what happened next* questions			
Actions	.26	.26	.23
Events	.04	.01	.02
Overlap between answers to *why* questions and *how* questions			
Actions	.02	.01	.04
Events	.30	.41	.40
Overlap between answers to *how* questions and *what happenen next* questions			
Actions	.02	.03	.02
Events	.01	.01	.01

quite high for target actions (mean .25) but were essentially zero for target events (mean .02). Additional analyses revealed that overlapping Goal nodes were responsible for the relatively high overlap between answers to why⟨action⟩ and WHN⟨action⟩ questions. In fact, 94% of the overlapping nodes were Goal nodes. These data support the following observations.

Observation 21. The procedure of constructing expectations from target actions is shown below.

(1) Construct likely superordinate Goal nodes. These Goal nodes are connected to the target action by forward Reason arcs.

(2) Construct likely consequences of the (achieved) Goal nodes in step 1. These consequence nodes are connected to the nodes in step 1 by forward Consequence arcs.

Observation 22. The procedure of constructing reasons for why a target action occurs is shown below.

(1) Construct likely superordinate Goal nodes. These Goal nodes are connected to the target action by forward Reason arcs.

(2) Construct likely states, events, and actions that initiate the Goal nodes in step 1. These goal initiators are usually connected to the Goal nodes in step 1 via backward Initiate arcs.

The overlap scores between *why* and *how* questions show an informative and expected pattern. There is a high overlap score between answers to how⟨event⟩ questions and why⟨event⟩ questions (mean .37), but there is essentially no overlap between answers to why⟨action⟩ and how⟨action⟩ questions (mean .02). These overlap scores are consistent with the symbolic procedures for answering *how* and *why* questions, which were summarized in Table 5.3. Answers to both why⟨event⟩ questions and how⟨event⟩ questions are for the most part *causal antecedent* questions. Causal antecedent questions pursue nodes that are connected to target events by backward Consequence arcs. Answers to why⟨action⟩ questions pursue superordinate Goal nodes and goal initiators, following forward Reason arcs and backward Initiate arcs. In contrast, answers to how⟨action⟩ questions pursue subordinate Goal and Style nodes, following backward Reason arcs and forward Manner arcs.

For both actions and events, there was no overlap between answers to *how* and WHN questions. Table 6.12 shows that there was a .02 mean overlap score for actions and a .01 mean overlap score for events. This outcome is quite expected. Answers to WHN⟨event⟩ questions are products of forward Consequence arcs, whereas answers to how⟨event⟩ questions are products of backward Consequence arcs. Answers to WHN⟨action⟩ questions are products of forward Reason arcs and forward Consequence arcs, whereas answers to how⟨action⟩ questions are products of backward Reason arcs and forward Manner arcs. Analyses of the Q/A protocols generally support the following observations.

Observation 23. The procedure of constructing expectations from target events is shown below.

(1) Construct likely consequences of the target event, plus supporting states and events of the resulting events. These consequence nodes are connected to the target event (and/or supporting nodes) by forward Consequence arcs.

(2) Construct likely goal-oriented conceptualizations that may be initiated by the nodes in step 1. The nodes in these goal-oriented conceptualizations are connected to the nodes in step 1 by forward Initiate arcs and the resulting Goal nodes are connected to other Goal nodes by forward or backward Reason arcs.

(3) Go to step 1 and recycle the resulting set of nodes.

Observation 24. The procedure of constructing reasons for why a target event occurs is shown below.

Construct likely causal antecedents of the target event. The causal antecedents are connected to the target event by backward Consequence arcs.

Observation 25. The procedure of constructing explanations of how a target event occurs is shown below.

(1) Construct likely causal antecedents of the target event. The causal antecedents are connected to the target event by backward Consequence arcs.

(2) Construct likely nodes that embellish the style in which the nodes in step 1 occur. These nodes are connected to the nodes in step 1 by forward Manner arcs.

Observation 26. The procedure of specifying how a target action occurs is shown below.

(1) Construct likely subordinate Goal nodes. These Goal nodes are connected to the target statement by backward Reason arcs.

(2) Construct likely Style or Goal nodes that embellish the nodes in step 1. These nodes are connected to the nodes in step 1 by forward Manner arcs.

(3) Go to step 1 and recycle the resulting set of nodes.

Observations 21-26 specify how new expectation and inference nodes are constructed when a target action or event is comprehended on-line. A critical process has not yet been specified, however. How are the new nodes that are generated from a target statement synchronized or interfaced with the old structures? Certain procedures and structures need to be considered in order to answer this question:

(1) A procedure that prunes out erroneous nodes in the previous structure S.
(2) A procedure that appends new nodes to the previous structure S.
(3) A procedure that consults relevant schemas for guiding procedures 1 and 2 above.
(4) A procedure for recognizing that a particular node in structure S is sufficiently similar to a particular new node that is constructed by the target statement (this is called the *binding process*).

Whereas procedures 1 and 2 have been addressed to some extent in previous observations (Observations 17-20), procedures 3 and 4 have not been dealt with in this chapter. The process of accomplishing procedure 3 is, quite frankly, a mystery. Informative comments about procedure 3 cannot be made unless there is knowledge of (a) which schemas are foregrounded and (b) the conceptual structures of the foregrounded schemas. A few comments can be made about procedure 4, the process of binding new nodes to nodes in the previously established structure.

In many cases a new node was bound to a node in the previous structure by a direct match. For example, consider the story of *The Czar and His Daughters.* When the statement *The daughters were enjoying themselves* was comprehended on-line, the subjects generated the expectation that *The daughters would forget the time.* In fact, the next statement in the passage was *The daughters forgot the time.* When the statement *The heroes went to the daughters* was comprehended on-line, the subjects generated the expectation that *The heroes would fight the dragon.* In fact, the next statement in the passage was *The heroes fought the dragon.* Moreover, there often was a match between a new inference node (created from an incoming statement) and some node in the previous structure. For example, when the statement *The dragon dragged off the daughters* was comprehended on-line, the subjects generated the expectation that *The daughters would become frightened.* In fact, one of the statement-driven inferences from *The daughters cried* was *The daughters became frightened.* In summary, the new nodes generated from an incoming statement may directly match nodes in the old structure created from previous information in the passage.

Sometimes there is not a direct match when nodes bind to one another. For example, when *The daughters cried* was comprehended on-line, the subjects generated the expectation that *Someone heard the cries.* The next statement in the passage was *The heroes heard the cries.* In this example, the expectation node has a semantically depleted argument, *someone.* Subsequent information confirmed this expectation and the *someone* turned out to be *the heroes.* Thus, the argument is semantically embellished in this example of node binding. Analyses revealed that 21% of the node bindings involved argument embellishment, whereas 79% involved direct matches.

> **Observation 27.** Nodes are constructed from an incoming statement during on-line comprehension. Some of these nodes match nodes that have already been constructed by previous passage context. Most of the node matches are exact matches; in other matches, an argument in the old node is semantically embellished by the new information.

The final analysis traces the accumulation of new nodes as a function of incoming passage statements. The computation in this analysis is simply the number of new nodes that a given target statement generates. An inference or expectation is scored as a new node if it is generated by a target statement for the first time in the passage. This analysis includes only preserved nodes that were constructed on-line (categories A and D in Table 6.2). These frequency scores for each of the target statements in *The Czar and His Daughters* are given in Table 6.16.

The frequency scores in Table 6.16 show some informative trends. The most salient pattern is that successive target statements form subclusters. The first statement of a subcluster generates many new nodes, while subsequent nodes within a subcluster generate fewer and fewer new nodes. For example, statements 1, 2, 3, and 4 form a subcluster; the frequency scores are 29, 14, 8, and 2, respectively. Statements 5, 6, and 7 form a second subcluster, with frequencies of 22, 9, and 7, respectively. When a statement begins a new subcluster, many new nodes are generated. Nodes that occur later in a subcluster generate fewer

Table 6.16. Construction of New Nodes by Statements in *The Czar and His Daughters*

Target statement	Number of new nodes that are preserved
(1) The daughters walked in the woods	29
(2) The daughters enjoyed themselves	14
(3) The daughters forgot the time	8
(4) The daughters stayed too long	2
(5) The dragon kidnapped the daughters	22
(6) The dragon dragged off the daughters	9
(7) The daughters cried	7
(8) The heroes heard the cries	14
(9) The heroes went to the daughters	11
(10) The heroes fought the dragon	8
(11) The heroes rescued the daughters	6
(12) The heroes returned the daughters to the palace	10
(13) The Czar heard of the rescue	8
(14) The Czar rewarded the heroes	7

nodes. It is perhaps possible to identify the beginning of a subcluster by observing which nodes show an increase in frequency (above the frequency score of the previous statement). Using this definition, the following groups of statements form subclusters: (1, 2, 3, 4), (5, 6, 7), (8, 9, 10, 11), and (12, 13, 14).

An interesting aspect of the subclusters defined above is that they make sense intuitively and theoretically. The first subcluster involves *the daughters walking in the woods, enjoying themselves,* and *staying too long.* The second subcluster involves *the dragon kidnapping the daughters* and the *daughters crying.* The third subcluster involves *the heroes hearing the cries* and *rescuing the daughters.* The fourth subcluster involves *the heroes returning the daughters to the palace* and *being rewarded by the Czar.* It is quite apparent that a new subcluster emerges when a new character is introduced in the passage for the first time. The introduction of the new character requires the comprehender to generated likely motives of the character and expectations about what the character will do. The first three subclusters emerged when a new character was first introduced in the passage: *the daughters* (statement 1), *the dragon* (statement 5), and *the heroes* (statement 8). A subcluster also begins when the focus shifts to a new setting or spatial scenario. Of course, characters' motives may also change when they are in a new scene. The fourth cluster, for example, begins when the scene shifts to the palace. In summary, the beginning of a subcluster tends to occur when a new character is introduced or a new spatial setting is foregrounded. At these points in a passage, many new nodes are generated. It is also informative to point out that previous studies have shown that reading times are longer for sentences that foreground new characters or concepts (Graesser, Hoffman, and Clark, 1980; Kintsch, 1974; Yekovich and Walker, 1978) and shifts in character perspectives (Black et al., 1979). Perhaps one explanation for the increase in reading time is that the comprehender must generate more new inference and expectation nodes (Miller and Kintsch, 1980; Olson, Mack, and Duffy, 1980).

Observation 28. Narrative passages contain subclusters of statements. These subclusters are consistent with intuitions about story segments. A new subcluster often begins when a new character or spatial setting is introduced in the story for the first time. Many new nodes are constructed from statements marking the beginning of a subcluster, and successively fewer new nodes are generated from statements that occur later and later in the subcluster.

There is another trend that emerges from the frequency scores in Table 6.16. Fewer new nodes are constructed from statements that occur later in a narrative passage. Consider the first statement of each episode: statements 1, 5, 8, and 12. The frequency scores for these statements were 29, 22, 14, 10, respectively. The same trend occurs when all statements are considered. The statements in the first half of the four passages generated 16 nodes per statement, whereas only 12 nodes per statement were generated from statements in the second half. This trend is interesting in conjunction with Observation 16. As the narrative progresses, subjects generate fewer inference and expectation nodes per statement, but the nodes have a higher likelihood of being preserved.

Observation 29. Fewer new nodes are generated from statements that occur later in narrative passages.

It should be apparent by now that many interesting observations can be made by analyzing the Q/A protocols in the different context conditions. Some of the 29 observations would be quite obvious from rational, intuitive, and theoretical perspectives; however, other observations are not very obvious. The analyses and observations discussed thus far provide only a preliminary "peek" at the mysteries of on-line comprehension. There is still much work to be done. More context conditions may be introduced in order to pinpoint further the process of generating, preserving, and disconfirming inference and expectation nodes. More detailed symbolic analyses may be performed, and passages in other prose genres may be examined. Applications of the Q/A procedures are clearly unlimited and have only begun to be explored. Nevertheless, the available analyses on narrative passages provide an informative data base for sketching an on-line model of prose comprehension. Some plausible constraints on a model of on-line comprehension will be discussed in the next section.

Some Considerations for a Model of On-line Prose Comprehension

It is too early to proposed a model of on-line comprehension that is precisely articulated and that accommodates all prose genres. However, the 29 observations in this chapter do suggest some constraints or properties that such a model would probably have. This section will be organized along three different levels. The most general level is a sketch of a model of on-line comprehension. The second level will provide evidence by referring to the 29 observations as well as other research. The question as to what makes some passages more difficult to comprehend than other passages will be considered at the third level. To some extent, comprehension difficulty may be explained by certain properties of the proposed sketch of on-line comprehension.

Conceptual Structure

Conceptual structures are constructed when passages are comprehended and they interrelate the statements that are explicitly stated in prose. An on-line model of comprehension has two basic problems to deal with: How are the conceptual structures represented? How are the conceptual structures constructed on-line during the course of comprehension?

The research reported in this book hopefully has provided some contribution to the question of how conceptual structures are represented. One point that has consistently been emphasized is that statements in text are interrelated by conceptualizations that contain a large number of inferences. For example, a typical statement in a narrative passage generates 15 distinct inferences, on the average. The position here departs from previous psychological models of on-line comprehension, which have focused primarily or exclusively on explicitly stated information.

A representational system was proposed in Chapter 4 that interrelates the inferences and stated information. The conceptual structure of text is believed to consist of a set labeled nodes that are interrelated by labeled, directed arcs. In Chapter 5 data were reported that lend credence to the proposed representational system and the validity of the conceptual graph structures. The proposed representational system is undoubtedly not perfect, but it probably provides a fair approximation to the conceptual structures that comprehenders construct.

A number of predictions may be made regarding the relationship between comprehension difficulty and the conceptual structure of text. One obvious prediction is that passages will be difficult to comprehend when it is difficult or impossible to conceptually relate successive passage statements. In easy passages there is little challenge in forming conceptual structures that provide causal connectivity or conceptual coherence between and among passage statements. A second prediction involves structural properties of the graphic representations. It is believed that comprehension is easier for passages that are organized in a hierarchical fashion than those that are organized in a nonhierarchical network fashion (see Chapters 4 and 5). A third prediction involves the number of inferences that are invoked from the explicitly stated nodes. Easy passages have conceptual structures with a high ratio of inference nodes to explicitly stated nodes. Difficult passages have a lower inference to stated node ratio; the comprehender barely manages to make sense of and remember what is explicitly stated, let alone to construct inferences. This prediction clearly requires more research to be substantiated. Available supporting evidence resides in the observations that (a) the ratio is roughly four times as high for narrative passages as for expository passages and (b) narrative passages are easier to comprehend and remember (see Chapter 4). There are more esoteric properties of the conceptual structures that may prove to predict comprehension difficulty. However, more research is needed to uncover more specific relationships between comprehension difficulty and properties of conceptual structures.

Schemas

On the basis of explicitly stated information, the comprehender identifies relevant schemas that correspond to different knowledge domains and levels of structure. The schemas provide the tacit background knowledge that is required for the construction of conceptual structures. Without this tacit knowledge, it would literally be impossible to interpret sentences, to generate inferences and expectations, and to interrelate all the information (Adams and Collins, 1979).

It is convenient to isolate three levels of schemas. *Statement schemas* are identified by virtue of the information that spans a particular target statement. Statement schemas are identified when a statement is comprehended out of context. Statement-driven inferences and expectations are generated by the information provided in the target statement together with the identified statement schemas. *Local schemas* are identified by information that spans a group of statements. For example, a local schema might span a subcluster of statements in a passage (see Observation 28). *Global schemas* span many statements in a passage, if not the entire passage. Thus, when a target statement is comprehended on-line, inferences and expectations are constructed on the basis of statement schemas, local schemas, and global schemas (see Observations 1, 2, and 3). Of course, there may be a number of intermediate levels of schemas between the statement and global levels. These local, intermediate, and global levels of schemas presumably correspond to the different types of knowledge structures that have been introduced and discussed in schema-based theories, i.e., scripts (Abelson, 1980b; Schank and Abelson, 1977), plans (McDermott, 1978; Miller et al., 1960; Wilensky, 1978b, 1978c), frames (Minsky, 1975), themes (Agar, 1979; Halliday and Hasan, 1976; Schank and Abelson, 1977), memory organization packets (Schank, 1979b), and complex affect units (Lehnert, 1980). Categorizing schemas into only three levels (statement, local, and global) is suggested here in order to simplify matters.

Passages are easier to comprehend when there are global schemas that successfully integrate most of the passage statements (Bransford and Johnson, 1973). The comprehension and organization of more difficult passages is guided by local schemas and statement schemas. In very difficult passages, the comprehension of statements is confined to statement schemas. Without higher level schemas, the constructed conceptual structures lack coherence and connectivity. Higher level schemas also provide knowledge sources for generating more inferences and expectations.

Amount of Information

Inferences and expectations are generated on the basis of the stated information together with the relevant schemas that have been identified. Of the inferences and expectations that are generated on-line, some are confirmed and preserved in the conceptual structure. Other inferences and expectations are disconfirmed by subsequent context. The likelihood that a generated node will be preserved increases with the amount of information in the knowledge source that generated the node. This relationship provides some interesting predictions. It predicts that nodes that are generated by more global schemas will be confirmed more often than are nodes generated by less global schemas. It predicts that a node will have a higher likelihood of being confirmed when it is based on more passage statements.

Several observations support the above relationship between amount of information and the likelihood that a node will be preserved in the final conceptual structure. Nodes that are generated by local and global schemas are preserved more often than nodes that are generated by statement schemas (Observations 4 and 15). This trend occurs both for inferences and expectations. Prior-context-driven nodes have a higher likelihood of being preserved when the nodes occur later in a passage (Observation 16). Of course, more information has accrued for statements that occur later in a passage. Once again, this trend occurs both for inferences and expectations. To summarize, the likelihood that inferences and expectations will be preserved follows a basic Bayesian principle: the likelihood that generated nodes will be correct increases as they are based on more information.

The above trends have a number of implications regarding comprehension difficulty. One obvious implication is that a statement will be easier to comprehend and more correctly interpreted when it is preceded by more passage context. An isolated sentence is generally more difficult to comprehend than the same sentence embedded in context. A second implication addresses the role of expectations in comprehension. Almost everyone would agree that a passage is easier to comprehend to the extent that there are more expectations that are confirmed. Since local and global schemas generate additional expectations and these expectations have a relatively high likelihood of being correct, it should be relatively difficult to comprehend passages with statements that cannot be accommodated by global schemas, and even more difficult to comprehend statements that cannot be organized by local schemas.

Impact of Prior Context and Subsequent Context

The on-line comprehension of a target statement is influenced by prior passage context and subsequent passage context. This conclusion is rather obvious and analyses support it. What is less obvious about the analyses and outcomes, however, is the way in which the comprehension of a target statement is influenced by prior context and subsequent context. Consider the development of the preserved inferences that are closely associated with a given target statement. Whereas prior context is critical in generating these inferences, subsequent context constructs very few of the inferences that are associated with a target statement (Observation 6). The course of disconfirming erroneous nodes show a much different pattern. Consider the process of disconfirming erroneous statement-driven nodes. Erroneous statement-driven nodes are disconfirmed by subsequent context more often than they are blocked by prior context (Observations 12 and 14). This trend emerges for both inferences and expectations. It appears, then, that prior context carries the burden of generating nodes, whereas subsequent context carries the burden of disconfirming erroneous nodes.

The fact that subsequent context plays a minor role in constructing inferences has one implication concerning comprehension difficulty. A statement should be difficult to comprehend if its significance is not understood until subsequent information is received. In easy passages, the comprehender does not need to know the entire passage before inferences can be made about a specific statement. Instead, the on-line representation of a statement carries the lion's share of the inferences that will ultimately be associated with the statement.

Restructuring

When a statement is comprehended on-line, the comprehender identifies new schemas (statement, local, or global) and these schemas modify the previous conceptual structure that was available just before the statement was received; thus, new information modifies the previously established structure. The modification of old structures normally involves two relatively simple processes: (a) pruning out erroneous old nodes (Observations 19 and 20), and (b) appending new nodes to the old structure (Observation 17). The old structure is rarely reorganized when it is modified by new information. New nodes are rarely inserted in between two or more old nodes. When an old node is removed, it rarely involves a deletion plus restacking transformation.

Passages would be difficult to comprehend if each new statement required a reorganization of the nodes in the previous structures. A passage with a higher ratio of inserting to appending transformations should be more difficult to comprehend than a passage with a lower ratio. Similarly, comprehension difficulty should increase as more nodes are removed by deleting plus restacking than by pruning transformations. Some passages may indeed require restructuring. For example, restructuring may occur in narrative passages in which the episodes are not presented in chronological order. Difficult passages about a scientific mechanism may require a reorganization of old structures as new statements are received (Collins et al., 1980). This restructuring may be particularly challenging for comprehenders to accomplish when reading a passage on-line. The comprehender may find it easier to reread excerpts from the passage with the different organizational framework in mind. In other words, restructuring may require rereading.

Knowledge Sources of Preserved Inferences and Expectations

Where do preserved inferences come from? Do they come from statement schemas or more global schemas? The answer to this question depends on the category of inference node and sometimes on the structural relationship between the inference node and the target node. Goal nodes that are superordinate to a target action (Goal+) tend to be generated by local and global schemas rather than by statement schemas (Observation 7). However, Goal nodes and Style nodes that are subordinate to a target action tend to be generated by statement schemas rather than by local and global schemas (Observation 8). Stated differently, more global schemas and context are important for understanding why a goal is established, whereas the statement schemas carry the burden of conveying how a goal is achieved. The genesis of Event and State nodes is not particularly dependent on the category of target statement. Event inferences tend to be generated by more global schemas and contexts (Observation 9), whereas State inferences tend to be statement driven (Observation 10).

The implications the above findings have for comprehension difficulty are not altogether clear, however, a few speculations may be suggested. Sometimes comprehenders might find it difficult to acquire (a) important enabling states for causally oriented event chains or (b) important aspects of the procedure of achieving a goal. If such difficulties in comprehension arise, it would be worthwhile to appropriately embellish or modify the wording of the statements in the passage. In other instances, comprehenders may find it difficult to acquire (a) critical event links in causally oriented event chains or (b) reasons or motives for actions being performed. In these instances, a modification of the wording of statements should have a minor impact on comprehension difficulty. Instead, a more profitable solution would be to modify the sets of nodes that are explicitly articulated in the passage.

Another generalization can be made about the source of inferences that are ultimately preserved. The inferences that are associated with a particular target statement are rarely generated as expectations from prior passage information (Observation 11). Instead, most inferences are activated by the target statement together with prior context. It is somewhat surprising that expectations contribute so little to the development of the narrative structures, in light of the fact that schema-based theories have attributed a great deal of importance to the role of expectations in comprehension processes (Bobrow and Norman, 1975; Rumelhart and Ortony, 1977; Schank and Abelson, 1977; Tannen, 1979). The outcome is especially surprising since expectations are believed to be more prevalent and to be confirmed more often in narrative prose than in other prose genres that have less well-formed rhetorical rules and archetypical patterns. It appears, nevertheless, that schemas normally guide constructive processes by accommodating input rather than expecting or predicting input.

Lamination Effect

According to Observation 18, the preserved nodes that radiate from a target statement are layered, much like an onion. Statement-driven nodes form the inner layer, which is closest to the target statement; prior-context-driven nodes form the middle layer; and subsequent-context-driven nodes form the outer layer. Violations of this lamination effect are rare (less than 6% of the nodes in the analyses reported here).

The lamination effect is observed in the final conceptual structure that is achieved after comprehension is finished. It would be informative to speculate how this lamination effect is achieved during on-line comprehension. What does the lamination effect reveal about the process of on-line comprehension? It is possible to specify a processing mechanism that generates a lamination effect? Consider the following mechanism. When a target statement is comprehended on-line, the following sequentially ordered processes occur.

(1) Statement schemas are identified by the information in the target statement.
(2) The statement schemas generate inferences and expectation nodes (statement-driven nodes).
(3) Some erroneous statement-driven nodes are blocked or disconfirmed by prior context. Prior context includes a constructed conceptual structure, plus local and global schemas.

(4) New local and global schemas may be identified by virtue of (a) the remaining (unblocked) statement-driven nodes in step 3 together with (b) the conceptual structure and schemas that were constructed or identified from prior context.
(5) The new local and global schemas prune out the erroneous nodes and the erroneous schemas that were available in prior context.
(6) The new local and global schemas append new nodes to the remaining (unpruned) statement-driven nodes and the nodes in the conceptual structure of prior context.

These steps must be ordered properly in order to generate the lamination effect. At this time there are not enough data to argue strongly for the above processing mechanism. The above mechanism is merely proposed as one mechanism that would produce a lamination effect. It is interesting to point out that the mechanism offers a number of plausible predictions. First, the preserved statement-driven nodes should be constructed or activated more quickly than the preserved prior-context–driven nodes. Second, erroneous statement-driven expectations should be disconfirmed more quickly than erroneous prior-context–driven expectations.

The lamination effect has implications regarding comprehension difficulty. Passages should be easier to comprehend to the extent that the nodes are arranged in a laminated fashion, as opposed to a more random fashion. When statements in a passage engender a strictly laminated composition, the process of on-line comprehension is simplified because the interfacing of new nodes with old nodes involves pruning and appending modifications, but not inserting and deleting plus restacking modifications. Deviations from a laminated composition would involve more complicated processes. There would not only be the pruning of incorrect nodes and the appending of new nodes, but also the resulting set of nodes would need to be reordered and restructured. This restructuring would place additional demands on processing resources.

Causally Oriented Versus Goal-Oriented Conceptualizations

The on-line construction of inferences and expectations is quite different for goal-oriented than for causally oriented conceptualizations. Consider goal-oriented conceptualizations. Figure 6.4 shows a prototypical example of the nodes and arcs that would be generated during the on-line comprehension of a target action. When a target action is comprehended on-line, the following inferences and expectations are constructed (Observations 21, 22, and 26):

(1) Superordinate Goal nodes are linked to the target action by paths of forward Reason arcs.
(2) State and Event nodes initiate the target Goal node and the superordinate Goal nodes via backward Initiate arcs.
(3) Subordinate Goal nodes and Style nodes are linked to the target Goal node by paths of backward Reason arcs and forward Manner arcs.

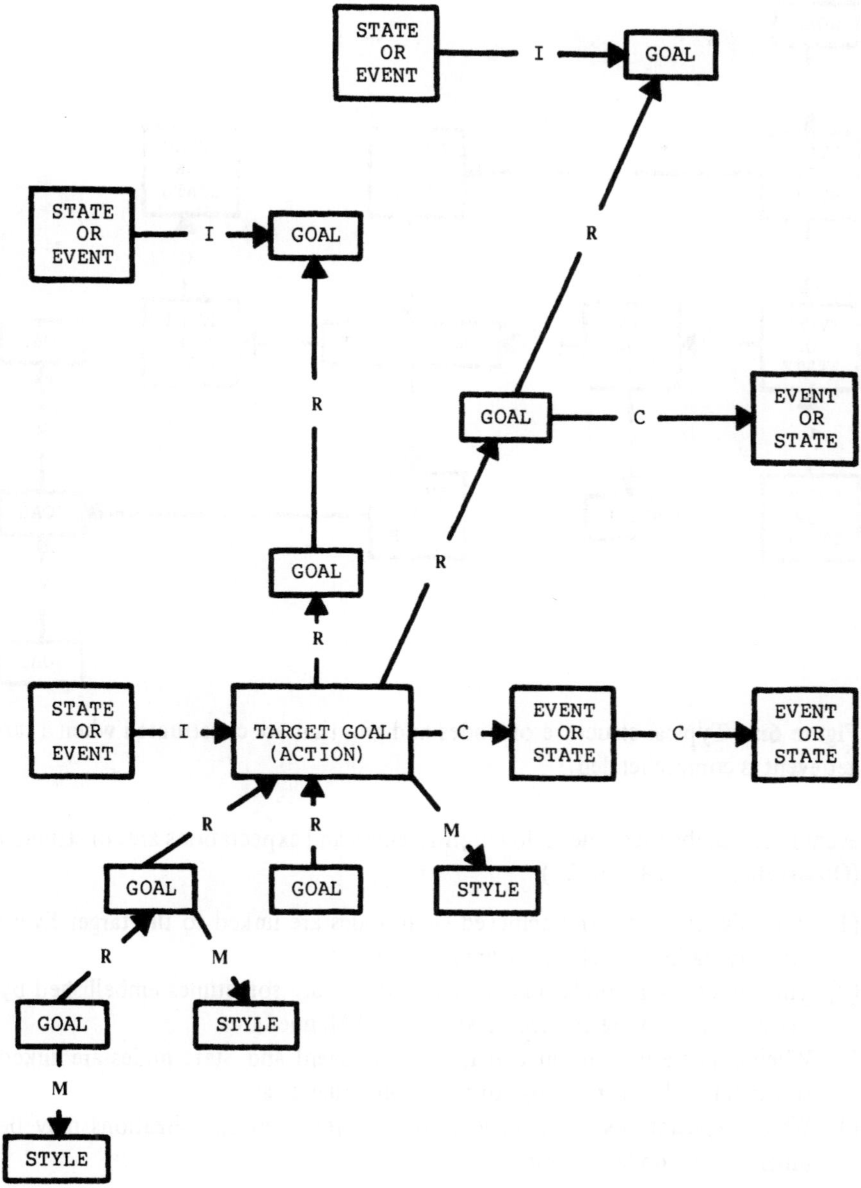

Figure 6.4. Typical structure of nodes and arcs that are constructed when a target action is comprehended.

(4) When expectations are involved (as opposed to inferences), there may be State and Event nodes that are linked to the target Goal node and superordinate Goal nodes by paths of forward Consequence arcs.

Causally driven conceptualizations involve different patterns of nodes and arcs. Figure 6.5 shows a prototypical example of the nodes and arcs that would be generated during the on-line comprehension of a target event. When a target

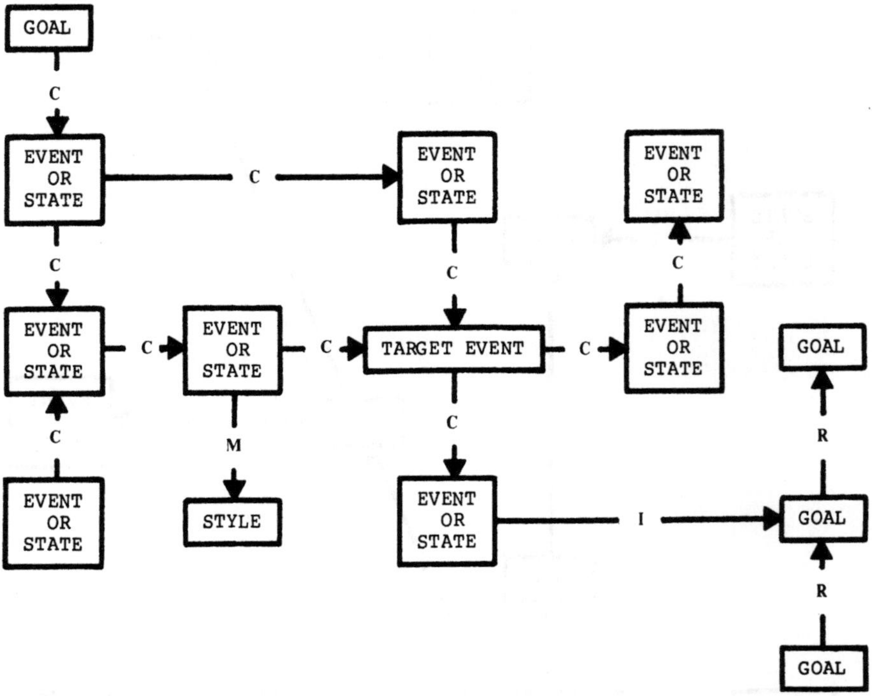

Figure 6.5. Typical structure of nodes and arcs that are constructed when a target event is comprehended.

event is comprehended, the following inferences and expectations are constructed (Observations 23, 24, and 25):

(1) Prior Event, State, and achieved Goal nodes are linked to the target Event node by paths of backward Consequence arcs.
(2) The target Event node and nodes in step 1 are sometimes embellished by Style nodes that are connected via forward Manner arcs.
(3) When expectations are involved, paths of Event and State nodes are linked to the target Event node by forward Consequence arcs.
(4) When expectations are involved, goal-oriented conceptualizations may be linked to the nodes in step 3.

There are salient differences between Figures 6.4 and 6.5. Target actions tend to generate Goal hierarchies with Goal nodes and Style nodes connected by Reason and Manner arcs. These Goal hierarchies are initiated by states and events; the goal initiators are connected to the Goal nodes by Initiate arcs. When expectations are involved, then sometimes states and events are expected to occur as a consequence of the Goal hierarchy being achieved. Target events generate a much different pattern of nodes and arcs. Target events generate causal chains and networks with Event and State nodes being connected by Consequence arcs. When expectations are involved, goal-oriented conceptualizations may occasionally spin off from events in the causal chain or network.

As argued in previous chapters, comprehension would be expected to become more difficult to the extent that causally oriented conceptualizations are constructed, as opposed to goal-oriented conceptualizations. It is computationally simpler to prune out nodes and append nodes to hierarchies than network structures that deviate from a strict hierarchy. Of course, there may be other reasons that causally oriented conceptualizations are more difficult to comprehend than goal-oriented conceptualizations.

Binding of New Nodes to Old Nodes

Some new nodes (that are generated by an incoming target statement) are more or less equivalent to old nodes that are part of the conceptual structure that was available before the target statement was received. An equivalent pair of nodes (old and new) would obviously be bound together. This binding process provides the foundation for synchronizing new and old information. The match between new and old nodes is usually an exact match (Observation 27). However, there occasionally is not a perfect match. The old node may have a semantically depleted argument (*someone* or *something*), whereas the new node has a particular argument that is elaborated semantically (*daughter* or *knife*). Comprehension difficulty should increase for passages under the following conditions.

(1) If, when new and old nodes are bound together, there is a low incidence of exact matches and a high incidence of nodal arguments at different levels of abstraction.
(2) If nodal arguments are at different levels of abstraction and the reader does not have the lexical knowledge to identify the functional equivalence of the arguments.

Questions for Future Research

The analyses and observations in this chapter have unraveled some of the mysteries of how prose representations are constructed during comprehension. However, there are still many issues that are presently unsettled and many questions that have not been explored. Do the observations and conclusions generalize to other narrative passages? Are there interesting differences among passages of different prose genres? To what extent can comprehension difficulty be explained by the factors discussed in this section? Which inference and expectation nodes are constructed during comprehension versus at question answering? Answers to these questions should be uncovered by applying the Q/A method and the analytical procedures discussed in this chapter. Hypotheses will be more rigorously tested, confirmed, or disconfirmed by experiments that involve the collection of simple response measures, such as recall protocols, summary protocols, verification ratings, reading times, ratings of comprehension difficulty, and other measures that experimental psychologists are familiar with (Olson, Mack, and Duffy, 1980).

There is one direction for future research that should be quite suited for the Q/A technique. Throughout this book the point has consistently been made that schemas guide comprehension. However, we have not explored the nitty-gritty details of how specific, relevant schemas guide the construction of the conceptual graph structures. It is much too easy to claim that schemas fill in the gaps between what is stated and what is constructed in memory. It is easy to claim that inference and expectation nodes are constructed by virtue of schematic knowledge structures that correspond to different domains of knowledge and levels of structure. However, it is a very difficult challenge to examine in detail how the schemas perform these magical deeds. How are the relevant schemas represented? How do the various schemas communicate with each other during the course of constructing prose structures? In order to explore these questions it may be fruitful to expose the representations of specific schemas that are relevant to the interpretation of specific passages. The Q/A method is available as an empirical tool for exposing the content of these schemas (see Chapter 4). As was mentioned earlier in this chapter, some of the fundamental puzzles of comprehension may be discovered and solved by examining the following four questions.

(1) How are specific passages represented in memory after comprehension is completed?
(2) How are passage segments represented at different points during on-line comprehension?
(3) What is the representation of those schemas that are relevant to the comprehension of specific passages?
(4) How do the relevant schemas communicate with one another in guiding the construction of a passage representation?

The Q/A procedure has been somewhat successful in examining the first two questions. Perhaps the Q/A method might also unravel some of the mysteries of the last two questions.

Final Comments

One of the major goals of this book was to help to bridge the gap between (a) the methods and research in experimental psychology and (b) contributions in cognitive science that do not have roots in the methodologies of experimental psychology. Researchers in artificial intelligence, linguistics, and other areas in the cognitive sciences have had much to say about prose comprehension. However, many of their insights have not been fully appreciated by many experimental psychologists because they have not been tested by methods that are acceptable in experimental psychology. A cognitive scientist writes a computer program that demonstrates the plausibility of some mechanism or principle of comprehension. The experimental psychologist immediately becomes skeptical. The mechanism or principle may work computationally, but does it correspond to human thought processes?

It is a very challenging enterprise to interface the contributions of two or more disciplines that have different goals and methodologies. In this book data and analyses have been presented that should be of interest to both experimental psychologists and researchers in other disciplines within cognitive science. In order to promote a cross-fertilization of ideas, the experimental methods in this book have often differed from the standard methods that experimental psychologists use and righteously defend. Experimental psychologists just might have to change their perspective in conducting research if they intend to test the plausibility of contributions from the sister sciences. Much of the research reported in this book has been inspired by four basic attitudes that are not universally shared and appreciated by experimental psychologists.

The first attitude involves a profound acknowledgment that there will never be a direct translation between theories in psychology and theories in the sister sciences. The goals of the linguist are different than the goals of researchers in artificial intelligence or experimental psychology. Since the goals vary among disciplines, it is unlikely that the mechanisms and devices proposed in one discipline will be perfectly translated into analogous mechanisms and devices of another discipline. Consequently, the job of the experimental psychologist is not to test or assess directly whether specific computer systems or linguistic theories can explain behavioral data. Instead, the experimental psychologist develops his own models and theories. The psychological models and theories incorporate indirectly some of the ideas in the sister sciences. Good ideas survive the test of time and are incorporated into the theories of many subdisciplines of cognitive science.

A second attitude involves an appreciation of the virtues of complex protocol analysis. An analysis of free generation protocols, think aloud protocols, and question-answering protocols provides a rich data base for discovering new aspects of comprehension mechanisms. It is also possible to test theories, ideas, and hypotheses by conducting well-designed experiments that collect complex verbal protocols. The only fundamental difference between simple response measures and complex verbal protocols lies in the complexity or richness of the comprehender's output. Simple response measures may be easier to collect, but the resulting data base is often uninformative or ambiguous when it comes to discovering new ideas and testing alternative models.

A third attitude involves a fascination with symbolic mechanisms and representations. The most plausible symbolic systems contain several specialized components that interact with each other in complex, but interesting ways. Some psychologists are bored or alienated by this approach to examining comprehension. Other psychologists are intensely absorbed with the symbolic mechanisms of human thought.

The fourth attitude involves a strong motivation to explore how input and world knowledge is cognitively represented, constructed, and utilized at the "deeper" conceptual levels of analysis. Many experimental psychologists have shied away from some challenging questions about comprehension. For example, many researchers have studied the representation and memory of explicit content, but relatively few researchers have tried to investigate how inferences are incorporated into memory representations. Ironically, most of the mysteries, mechanisms, and marvels of prose comprehension reside in the tacit knowledge that exists beyond the word. A risky journey into the deep conceptual jungles may be preferable to a safe sojourn so skittishly skirting the borders.

References

Aaronson, D., & Scarborough, H. S. Performance theories for sentence coding: Some quantitative models. *Journal of Verbal Learning and Verbal Behavior*, 1977, *16*, 277-304.

Abbott, V., & Black, J.B. *Representations of scripts in memory.* (Cognitive Science Tech. Rep. No. 5). New Haven: Yale University, Cognitive Science Program, 1980.

Abelson, R. P. The structure of belief systems. In R. C. Schank & K. M. Colby (Eds.), *Computer models of thought and language*. San Francisco: Freeman, 1973.

Abelson, R. P. Concepts for representing mundane reality in plans. In D. G. Bobrow & A. Collins (Eds.), *Representation and understanding*. New York: Academic Press, 1975.

Abelson, R. P. *Differences between belief and knowledge systems* (Cognitive Science Tech. Rep. No. 1), New Haven: Yale University, Cognitive Science Program, 1980. (a)

Abelson, R. P. *The psychological status of the script concept* (Cognitive Science Tech. Rep. No. 2), New Haven: Yale University, Cognitive Science Program, 1980. (b)

Adams, M. J., & Collins, A. A schema-theoretic view of reading. In R. O. Freedle (Ed.), *New directions in discourse processing* (Vol. 2). Norwood, N.J.: Ablex, 1979.

Agar, M. Themes revisited: Some problems in cognitive anthropology. *Discourse Processes*, 1979, *2*, 11-31.

Anderson, J. R. *Language, memory, and thought*. Hillsdale, N.J.: Erlbaum, 1976.

Anderson, J. R. Induction of augmented transition networks. *Cognitive Science,* 1977, *1*, 125-157.

Anderson, J. R. Arguments concerning representation for mental imagery. *Psychological Review*, 1978, *85*, 249-277.

Anderson, J. R., & Bower, G. H. Recognition and retrieval processes in free recall. *Psychological Review*, 1972, *79*, 97-123.

Anderson, J. R., & Bower, G. H. *Human associative memory*. Washington, D.C.: Winston, 1973.

Anderson, J. R., & Paulson, R. Representation and retention of verbatim information. *Journal of Verbal Learning and Verbal Behavior*, 1977, *16*, 439-451.

Anderson, R. C., & Pichert, J. W. Recall of previously unrecallable information following a shift in perspective. *Journal of Verbal Learning and Verbal Behavior*, 1978, *17*, 1-12.

Atkinson, R. C., & Juola J. F. Factors influencing speed and accuracy in word recognition. In S. Kornblum (Ed.), *Attention and performance IV*. New York: Academic Press, 1973.

Atkinson, R. C., & Juola, J. F. Search and decision processes in recognition memory. In D. H. Krantz, R. C. Atkinson, R. D. Luce, & P. Suppes (Eds.), *Contemporary developments in mathematical psychology* (Vol. 1). San Francisco: Freeman, 1974.

Atkinson, R. C., & Shiffrin, R. M. Human memory: A proposed system and its control processes. In K. W. Spence & J. T. Spence (Eds.), *The psychology of learning and motivation: Advances in research and theory* (Vol. 2). New York: Academic Press, 1968.

Austin, J. L. *How to do things with words*. Oxford: Oxford University Press, 1962.

Bach, E. Nouns and noun phrases. In E. Bach & R. T. Harms (Eds.), *Universals in linguistic theory*. New York: Holt, Rinehart & Winston, 1968.

Bacon, F. T. Credibility of repeated statements: Memory for trivia. *Journal of Experimental Psychology: Human Learning and Memory*, 1979, *5*, 241-252.

Baggett, P. Structurally equivalent stories in movie and text and the effects of medium on recall. *Journal of Verbal Learning and Verbal Behavior*, 1979, *18*, 333-356.

Baron, J. Phonemic stage not necessary for reading. *Quarterly Journal of Experimental Psychology*, 1973, *25*, 241-246.

Bartlett, F. C. *Remembering*. Cambridge, Mass.: Cambridge University Press, 1932.

Bates, E. *Language and context: The acquisition of pragmatics*. New York: Academic Press, 1976.

Bates, E., Masling, M., & Kintsch, W. Recognition memory for aspects of dialogue. *Journal of Experimental Psychology: Human Learning and Memory*, 1978, *4*, 187-197.

Beaugrande, R., & Colby, B. N. Narrative models of action and interraction. *Cognitive Science*, 1979, *3*, 43-66.

Becker, J. D. Reflections on the formal description of behavior. In D. G. Bobrow & A. Collins (Eds.), *Representation and understanding*. New York: Academic Press, 1975.

Bever, T. G. The cognitive basis for linguistic structures. In J. R. Hayes (Ed.), *Cognition and the development of language*. New York: Wiley, 1970.

Bever, T. G., Garrett, M. F., & Hurtig, R. R. The interaction of perceptual processes and ambiguous sentences. *Memory and Cognition*, 1973, *1*, 277-286.

Black, J. B., & Bern, H. *Causal coherence and memory for narrative* (Cognitive Science Tech. Rep. No. 3), New Haven: Yale University, Cognitive Science Program, 1980.

Black, J. B., & Bower, G. H. Episodes as chunks in narrative memory. *Journal of Verbal Learning and Verbal Behavior*, 1979, *18*, 309-318.

Black, J. B., & Bower, G. H. Story understanding and problem solving. *Poetics*, 1980, *9*, 223-250.

Black, J. B., Turner, T. J., & Bower, G. H. Point of view in narrative comprehension, memory, and production. *Journal of Verbal Learning and Verbal Behavior*, 1979, *18*, 187-198.

Black, J. B., & Wilensky, R. An evaluation of story grammars. *Cognitive Science*, 1979, *3*, 213-230.

Blank, M. A., & Foss, D. J. Semantic facilitation and lexical access during sentence processing. *Memory and Cognition*, 1978, *6*, 644-652.

Bobrow, D. G., & Norman, D. A. Some principles of memory schemata. In D. G. Bobrow & A. Collins (Eds.), *Representation and understanding*. New York: Academic Press, 1975.

Bower, G. H. Imagery as a relational organizer in associative learning. *Journal of Verbal Learning and Verbal Behavior*, 1970, *9*, 529-533.

Bower, G. H. Experiments on story comprehension and recall. *Discourse Processes*, 1978, *1*, 211-232.

Bower, G. H., Black, J. B., & Turner, T. J. Scripts in memory for text. *Cognitive Psychology*, 1979, *11*, 177-220.

Bower, G. H., & Clark, M. C. Narrative stories as mediators for serial learning. *Psychonomic Science*, 1969, *14*, 181-182.

Bransford, J. D. *Human cognition: Learning, understanding, and remembering*. Belmont, Calif.: Wadsworth, 1979.

Bransford, J. D., & Johnson, M. K. Contextual prerequisites for understanding: Some investigations of comprehension and recall. *Journal of Verbal Learning and Verbal Behavior*, 1972, *11*, 717-726.

Bransford, J. D., & Johnson, M. K. Considerations of some problems of comprehension. In W. G. Chase (Ed.), *Visual information processing*. New York: Academic Press, 1973.

Bransford, J. D., & McCarrell, N. S. A sketch of a cognitive approach to comprehension: Some thoughts about understanding what it means to comprehend. In W. B. Weiner & D. S. Palermo (Eds.), *Cognition and the symbolic processes*. Hillsdale, N.J.: Erlbaum, 1974.

Bregman, A. S. Perception and behavior as compositions of ideals. *Cognitive Psychology*, 1977, *9*, 250-292.

Brewer, W. F. Memory for the pragmatic implications of sentences. *Memory and Cognition*, 1977, *5*, 673-684.

Brewer, W. F., & Harris, R. J. Memory for deictic elements in sentences. *Journal of Verbal Learning and Verbal Behavior*, 1974, *13*, 321-327.

Brewer, W. F. & Lichtenstein, E. H. Event schemas, story schemas, and story grammars. Paper presented at the Attention and Performance Conference IX, Jesus College, Cambridge, England, 1980.

Britton, B. K. Use of cognitive capacity in reading: Effects of processing information from text for immediate recall and retention. *Journal of Reading Behavior*, 1980.

Britton, B. K., Glynn, S., Meyer, B. J. F., & Penland, M. *Use of cognitive capacity in reading text: Effects of variations in surface features of text with underlying meaning held constant*. Unpublished manuscript, University of Georgia, 1980.

Britton, B. K., Hamilton, T., Graesser, A. C., & Penland, M. *Use of cognitive capacity in reading: Effects of content features of text*. Unpublished manuscript, University of Georgia, 1980.

Britton, B. K., Holdredge, T. S., Curry, C., & Westbrook, R. D. Cognitive capacity usage in reading identical texts with different amounts of discourse level meaning. *Journal of Experimental Psychology: Human Learning and Memory*, 1979, *5*, 262-270.

Britton, B. K., Meyer, B. J. F., Hodge, M. H., & Glynn, S. Effects of the organization of text on memory: Tests of retrieval and response criterion hypotheses. *Journal of Experimental Psychology, Human Learning and Memory*, 1980, *6*, 620-629.

Britton, B. K., Meyer, B. J. F., Simpson, R., Holdredge, T. S., & Curry, C. Effects of the organization of text on memory: Tests of the implications of a selective attention hypothesis. *Journal of Experimental Psychology: Human Learning and Memory*, 1979, *5*, 496-506.

Britton, B. K., Piha, A., Davis, J., & Wehausen, E. Reading and cognitive capacity usage: Adjunct question effects. *Memory and Cognition*, 1978, *6*, 266-273.

Britton, B. K., & Price, K. *Use of cognitive capacity in reading: A performance operating characteristic*. Unpublished manuscript, University of Georgia, 1980.

Britton, B. K., Westbrook, R. D., & Holdredge, T. S. Reading and cognitive capacity usage: Effects of text difficulty. *Journal of Experimental Psychology: Human Learning and Memory*, 1978, *4*, 582-591.

Britton, B. K., Zeigler, R., & Westbrook, R. Use of cognitive capacity in reading easy and difficult text: Two tests of an allocation of attention hypothesis. *Journal of Reading Behavior*, 1980, in press.

Broadbent, D. E. *Perception and communication*. New York: Pergamon Press, 1958.

Brooks, C., & Warren, R. P. *Modern rhetoric*. New York: Harcourt Brace Jovanovich, 1972.

Brown, A. L. Semantic integration in children's reconstruction of narrative sequences. *Cognitive Psychology*, 1976, *8*, 247-262.

Brown, J. S., Collins, A., & Harris, G. Artificial intelligence and learning strategies. In H. O'Neill (Ed.), *Learning strategies*. New York: Academic Press, 1978.

Bruce, B. C. What makes a good story? *Language Arts,* 1978, *55*, 460-466.

Bruce, B. C. Analysis of interacting plans as a guide to the understanding of story structure. *Poetics,* 1980, *9*, 295-311.

Bruce, B. C., & Newman, D. Interacting plans. *Cognitive Science*, 1978, *2*, 195-233.

Bruce, D., & Gaines, M. T. Tests of an organizational hypothesis of isolation effects in free recall. *Journal of Verbal Learning and Verbal Behavior*, 1976, *15*, 59-72.

Buschke, H., & Schaier, A. H. Memory units, ideas, and propositions in semantic remembering. *Journal of Verbal Learning and Verbal Behavior*, 1979, *18*, 549-564.

Cairns, H. S., & Kamerman, J. Lexical information processing during sentence comprehension. *Journal of Verbal Learning and Verbal Behavior*, 1975, *14*, 170-179.

Calfee, R. C. Assessment of independent reading skills: Basic research and practical applications. In A. S. Reber & D. L. Scarborough (Eds.), *Toward a psychology of reading.* Hillsdale, N.J.: Erlbaum, 1977.

Cantor, N. *Prototypicality and personality judgments.* Unpublished doctorial dissertation, Stanford University, 1978.

Cantor, N., & Mischel, W. Traits as prototypes: Effects on recognition memory. *Journal of Personality and Social Psychology*, 1977, *35*, 38-48.

Caramazza, A., Grober, E., Garvey, C., & Yates, J. Comprehension of anaphoric pronouns. *Journal of Verbal Learning and Verbal Behavior*, 1977, *16*, 601-610.

Carbonell, J. G. *POLITICS*: Automated ideological reasoning. *Cognitive Science,* 1978, *2*, 27-51.

Carpenter, P. A., & Just, M. A. Sentence comprehension: A psycholinguistic processing model of verification. *Psychological Review*, 1975, *82*, 45-73.

Carpenter, P. A., & Just, M. A. Integrative processes in comprehension. In D. La-Berge & S. J. Samuels (Eds.), *Basic processes in reading: Perception and comprehension*. Hillsdale, N.J.: Erlbaum, 1977. (a)

Carpenter, P. A., & Just, M. A. Reading comprehension as the eye sees it. In M. A. Just & P. A. Carpenter (Eds.), *Cognitive processes in comprehension.* Hillsdale, N.J.: Erlbaum, 1977. (b)

Carpenter, P. A., & Just, M. A. Cognitive processes in reading: Models based on readers' eye fixations. In A. M. Lesgold & C. A. Perfetti (Eds.), *Interactive processes in reading*. Hillsdale, N.J.: Erlbaum, 1980.

Chafe, W. L. Discourse structure and human knowledge. In J. B. Carroll & R. O. Freedle (Eds.), *Language comprehension and the acquisition of knowledge*. Washington, D.C.: Winston, 1972.

Chaffin, R. Knowledge of language and knowledge about world: A reaction time study of invited and necessary inferences. *Cognitive Science*, 1979, *3*, 311-328.

Charniak, E. A framed *PAINTING*: The representation of a common sense knowledge fragment. *Cognitive Science*, 1977, *1*, 355-394.

Charniak, E., Riesbeck, C. K., & McDermott, D. V. *Artificial intelligence programming*. Hillsdale, N.J.: Erlbaum, 1980.

Chomsky, N. *Aspects of the theory of syntax*. Cambridge, Mass.: M.I.T. Press, 1965.

Chomsky, N., & Halle, M. *The sound pattern of English*. New York: Harper & Row, 1968.

Clark, H. H. Space, time, semantics and the child. In T. E. Moore (Ed.), *Cognitive development and the acquisition of language*. New York: Academic Press, 1973.

Clark, H. H. Inferences in comprehension. In D. LaBerge & S. J. Samuels (Eds.), *Basic processes in reading: Perception and comprehension*. Hillsdale, N.J.: Erlbaum, 1977.

Clark, H. H. Responding to indirect speech acts. *Cognitive Psychology*, 1979, *11*, 430-477.

Clark, H. H., & Clark, E. V. *Psychology and language*. New York: Harcourt Brace Jovanovich, 1977.

Clark, H. H., & Haviland, S. E. Comprehension and the given-new contract. In R. O. Freedle (Ed.), *Discourse production and comprehension* (Vol. 1). Norwood, N.J.: Ablex, 1977.

Clark, H. H., & Lucy, P. Understanding what is meant from what is said: A study in conversationally conveyed requests. *Journal of Verbal Learning and Verbal Behavior*, 1975, *14*, 56-72.

Clark, H. H., & Sengul, C. J. In search of referents for nouns and pronouns. *Memory and Cognition*, 1979, *7*, 35-41.

Cofer, C. N., Chmielewski, D. L., & Brockway, J. F. Constructive processes and the structure of human memory. In C. N. Cofer (Ed.), *The structure of human memory*. San Francisco: Freeman, 1976.

Cohen, A. D., & Graesser, A. C. The influence of advanced outlines on the free recall of prose. *Psychonomic Society*, 1980, *15*, 348-350.

Cohen, C. *Cognitive basis of stereotyping*. Paper presented at the meeting of the American Psychological Association, San Francisco, August, 1977.

Cohen, M. E., & Carr, W. J. Facial recognition and the von Restorff effect. *Psychonomic Society*, 1975, *6*, 383-384.

Cohen, P. R., & Perrault, C. R. Elements of a plan-based theory of speech acts. *Cognitive Science*, 1979, *3*, 177-212.

Colby, B. N. A partial grammar of Eskimo folktales. *American Anthropologist*, 1973, *25*, 645-662.

Colby, K. M. Simulations of belief systems. In R. C. Schank & K. M. Colby (Eds.), *Computer models of thought and language*. San Francisco: Freeman, 1973.

Cole, R. A., & Perfetti, C. A. Listening for mispronunciations in a children's story: The use of context by children and adults. *Journal of Verbal Learning and Verbal Behavior*, 1980, *19*, 297-315.

Coleridge, S. T. Biographia literaria. In D. Perkins (Ed.), *English romantic writers*. New York: Harcourt, Brace, & World, 1967.

Collins, A. M. Processes in acquiring knowledge. In R. C. Anderson, R. J. Spiro, & W. E. Montague (Eds.), *Schooling and the acquisition of knowledge*. Hillsdale, N.J.: Erlbaum, 1977.

Collins, A. M., Brown, J. S., & Larkin, K. M. Inference in text understanding. In J. Spiro, B. C. Bruce, & W. F. Brewer (Eds.), *Theoretical issues in reading comprehension*. Hillsdale, N.J.: Erlbaum, 1980.

Collins, A. M., & Gentner, D. A framework for a cognitive theory of writing. In L. W. Gregg & E. Steinberg (Eds.), *Cognitive processes in writing: An interdisciplinary approach*. Hillsdale, N.J.: Erlbaum, 1980.

Collins, A. M. & Loftus, E. F. A spreading activation theory of semantic processing. *Psychological Review*, 1975, *82*, 407-428.

Collins, A. M. & Quillian, M. R. Retrieval from semantic memory. *Journal of Verbal Learning and Verbal Behavior*, 1969, *8*, 240-247.

Coltheart, M., Davelaar, E., Jonasson, J., & Besner, D. Access to the internal lexicon. In S. Dornic (Ed.), *Attention and performance VI*. Hillsdale, N.J.: Erlbaum, 1977.

Corbett, A. T., & Dosher, B. A. Instrument inferences in sentence encoding. *Journal of Verbal Learning and Verbal Behavior*, 1978, *17*, 479-491.

Crothers, E. J. Memory structure and the recall of discourse. In J. B. Carroll & R. O. Freedle (Eds.), *Language comprehension and the acquisition of knowledge*. Washington, D.C.: Winston, 1972.

Crothers, E. J. Inference and coherence. *Discourse Processes*, 1978, *1*, 51-71.

Crothers, E. J. *Paragraph structure inference*. Norwood, N.J.: Ablex, 1979.

Cullingford, R. E. Pattern-matching and inference in story understanding. *Discourse Processing*, 1979, *2*, 319-334.

Curtis, M. E. Development of components of reading skill. *Journal of Educational Psychology*, 1980, in press.

D'Andrade, R. G. Memory and the assessment of behavior. In H. Blalock (Ed.), *Measurement in the social sciences*. Chicago: Aldine, 1974.

Danks, J. H., & Glucksberg, S. Experimental psycholinguistics. *Annual Review of Psychology*, 1980, *31*, 391-417.

Davelaar, E., Coltheart, M., Besner, D., & Jonasson, J. T. Phonological recoding and lexical access. *Memory and Cognition*, 1978, *6*, 391-402.

Dawes, R. M. Memory and the distortion of meaningful written material. *British Journal of Psychology*, 1966, *57*, 77-86.

Dawes, S. Shallow psychology. In J. S. Carroll & J. W. Payne (Eds.), *Cognition and social behavior*. Hillsdale, N.J.: Erlbaum, 1976.

DeJong, G. Prediction and substantiation: A new approach to natural language processing. *Cognitive Science*, 1979, *3*, 251-273.

van Dijk, T. A. *Some aspects of text grammars*. The Hague: Mouton, 1972.

van Dijk, T. A. Text grammar and text logic. In J. A. Petofi & H. Rieser (Eds.), *Studies in text grammar*. Dordrecht: Reidel, 1973.

van Dijk, T. A. Pragmatics and poetics. In T. van Dijk (Ed.), *Pragmatics of language and literature*. Amsterdam: North-Holland, 1976.

van Dijk, T. A. Semantic macro-structures and knowledge frames in discourse comprehension. In M. A. Just & P. A. Carpenter (Eds.), *Cognitive processes in comprehension*. Hillsdale, N.J.: Erlbaum, 1977.

van Dijk, T. A. Relevance assignment in discourse comprehension. *Discourse Processes* 1979, *2*, 113-126.

Dooling, D. J., & Christiaansen, R. E. Episodic and semantic aspects of memory for prose. *Journal of Experimental Psychology: Human Learning and Memory*, 1977, *3*, 428-436.

Dooling, D. J., & Lachman, R. Effects of comprehension on the retention of prose. *Journal of Experimental Psychology*, 1971, *88*, 216-222.

Dosher, B. A. The retention of sentences from memory: A speed-accuracy study. *Cognitive Psychology*, 1976, *8*, 291-310.

Drewnowski, A., & Healy, A. F. Detention errors on *the* and *and:* Evidence for reading units larger than the word. *Memory and Cognition*, 1977, *5*, 636-647.

Dyer, M. G., & Lehnert, W. G. *Memory organization and search processes for narratives* (Res. Rep. No. 175), New Haven: Yale University, Department of Computer Science, 1980.

Ericsson, K. A., & Simon, H. A. *Thinking-aloud protocols as data* (C.I.P. Working paper No. 397). Pittsburgh, Pa.: Carnegie-Mellon University, 1979.

Faught, W. S., Colby, K. M., & Parkison, R. C. Inferences, affects, and intentions in a model of paranoia. *Cognitive Psychology*, 1979, *9*, 153-187.

Feigenbaum, E. A. The simulation of verbal learning behavior. In E. A. Feigenbaum & J. A. Feldman (Eds.), *Computers and thought*. New York: McGraw-Hill, 1963.

Fetler, M. E. Methods for the analysis of two-party question and answer dialogues. *Discourse Processes*, 1979, *2*, 127-144.

Fillmore, C. J. The case for case. In E. Bach & R. T. Harms (Eds.), *Universals in linguistic theory*. New York: Holt, Rinehart & Winston, 1968.

Fine, J. Conversation, cohesion, and themetic patterning in children's dialogues. *Discourse Processes*, 1978, *1*, 247-266.

Flavell, J. H. *The developmental psychology of Jean Piaget*. New York: Van Nostrand, 1963.

Fodor, J. A., Bever, T. G., & Garrett, M. *The psychology of language*. New York: McGraw-Hill, 1974.

Forster, K. I. Accessing the mental lexicon. In R. J. Wales & E. Walker (Eds.), *New approaches to language mechanisms*. Amsterdam: North-Holland, 1976.

Foss, D. J. Some effects of ambiguity upon sentence comprehension. *Journal of Verbal Learning and Verbal Behavior*, 1970, *9*, 699-706.

Foss, D. J., & Blank, M. A. Identifying the speech codes. *Cognitive Psychology*, 1980, *12*, 1-31.

Foss, D. J., Cirilo, R. K., & Blank, M. A. Semantic facilitation and lexical access during sentence processing: An investigation of individual differences. *Memory and Cognition*, 1979, 7, 346-353.

Foss, D. J., & Jenkins, C. J. Some effects of context on the comprehension of ambiguous sentences. *Journal of Verbal Learning and Verbal Behavior*, 1973, *12*, 577-589.

Frase, L. T. Inference and reading. In R. Revlin & R. E. Mayer (Eds.), *Human reasoning*. New York: Wiley, 1978.

Frederiksen, C. H. Effects of context-induced processing operations on semantic information acquired from discourse. *Cognitive Psychology*, 1975, *7*, 139-166.

Frederiksen, C. H. Semantic processing units in understanding text. In R. O. Freedle (Ed.), *Discourse processes: Advances in research and theory* (Vol. 1). Norwood, N.J.: Ablex, 1977.

Frederiksen, J. R., & Kroll, J. F. Spelling and sound: Approaches to the internal lexicon. *Journal of Experimental Psychology: Human Perception and Performance*, 1976, *2*, 361-379.

Gagne, E. D. Long-term retention of information following learning from prose. *Review of Educational Research*, 1978, *48*, 629-665.

Gaines, B. R. Foundations of fuzzy reasoning. *International Journal of Man-Machine Studies*, 1976, *8*, 623-668.

Garrod, S., & Sanford, A. Interpreting anaphoric relations: The integration of semantic information while reading. *Journal of Verbal Learning and Verbal Behavior*, 1977, *16*, 77-90.

Gibbs, R. W. Contextual effects in understanding indirect requests. *Discourse Processes*, 1979, *2*, 1-10.

Gibson, E. J., & Levin, H. *The psychology of reading*. Cambridge, Mass.: M.I.T. Press, 1975.

Gilbert, L. Speed of processing visual stimuli and its relation to reading. *Journal of Educational Psychology*, 1959, *55*, 8-14.

Glynn, S. M. Capturing reader's attention by means of typographical cuing strategies. *Educational Technology*, 1978, 7-12.

Glynn, S. M., & DiVesta, F. J. Control of prose processing via instructional and typographical cues. *Journal of Educational Psychology*, 1980, *71*, 595-603.

Goetz, E. T. Inferring from text: Some factors influencing which inferences will be made. *Discourse Processes*, 1979, *2*, 179-195.

Goffman, E. *Frame analysis*. New York: Harper & Row, 1974.

Going, M., & Read, J. D. Effects of uniqueness, sex of subject, and sex of photograph on facial recognition. *Perceptual and Motor Skills*, 1974, *39*, 109-110.

Goldin, S. E. Memory for the ordinary: Typicality effects in chess memory. *Journal of Experimental Psychology: Human Learning and Memory*, 1978, *4*, 605-616.

Gomulicki, B. R. Recall as an abstractive process. *Acta Psychologica*, 1956, *12*, 77-94.

Goodenough, D. R., & Weiner, S. L. The role of conversational passing moves in the management of topical transitions. *Discourse Processes*, 1978, *1*, 395-404.

Goodman, G. S. Memory for high- and low-relevant information in pictures. Paper presented at the meeting of the Psychonomic Society, San Antonio, Texas, 1978.

Goodman, K. S. Reading: A psycholinguistic guessing game. *Journal of the Reading Specialist*, 1966, *6*, 126-135.

Gordon, D., & Lakoff, G. Conversational postulates. *Papers from the seventh regional meeting, Chicago Linguistics Society*, 1971, 7, 63-84.

Gough, P. B. One second of reading. In J. F. Kavanagh & J. G. Mattingly (Eds.), *Language by ear and by eye*. Cambridge, Mass.: M.I.T. Press, 1972.

Graesser, A. C. Study times for sentences in stories. Paper presented at the meetings of the Western Psychological Association, Sacramento, Calif., April, 1975.

Graesser, A. C. *Sentence memory and representation*. Unpublished doctorial dissertation, University of California, San Diego, 1977.

Graesser, A. C. How to catch a fish: The representation and memory of common procedures. *Discourse Processes*, 1978, *1*, 72-89. (a)

Graesser, A. C. Tests of a holistic chunking model of sentence memory through analyses of noun intrusions. *Memory and Cognition*, 1978, *6*, 527-536. (b)

Graesser, A. C., Gordon, S. E., & Sawyer, J. D. Memory for typical and atypical actions in scripted activities: Test of a script pointer + tag hypothesis. *Journal of Verbal Learning and Verbal Behavior*, 1979, *18*, 319-332.

Graesser, A. C., Hauft-Smith, K., Cohen, A. D., & Pyles, L. D. Advanced outlines, familiarity, text genre, and retention of prose. *Journal of Experimental Education*, 1980, *48*, 209-220.

Graesser, A. C., Higginbotham, M. W., Robertson, S. P., & Smith, W. R. A natural inquiry into the *National Enquirer*: Self-induced versus task-induced reading comprehension. *Discourse Processes*, 1978, *1*, 355-372.

Graesser, A. C., Hoffman, N. L., & Clark, L. F. Structural components of reading time. *Journal of Verbal Learning and Verbal Behavior*, 1980, *19*, 131-151.

Graesser, A. C., & Mandler, G. Recognition memory for the meaning and surface structure of sentences. *Journal of Experimental Psychology: Human Learning and Memory*, 1975, *104*, 238-248.

Graesser, A. C., Robertson, S. P., & Anderson, P. A. Incorporating inferences in narrative representations: A study of how and why. *Cognitive Psychology*, 1981, *13*, 1-26.

Graesser, A. C., Robertson, S. P., & Clark, L. F. *A look at on-line constructions of prose representations: A method and a model*. Unpublished manuscript, California State University, Fullerton, 1980.

Graesser, A. C., Robertson, S. P., Lovelace, E., & Swinehart, D. Answers to why-questions expose the organization of story plot and predict recall of actions. *Journal of Verbal Learning and Verbal Behavior*, 1980, *19*, 110-119.

Graesser, A. C., Woll, S. B., Kowalski, D. J., & Smith, D. A. Memory for typical and atypical actions in scripted activities. *Journal of Experimental Psychology: Human Learning and Memory*, 1980, *6*, 503-515.

Green, D. M., & Swets, J. A. *Signal detection theory and psychophysics*. New York: Wiley, 1966.

Grice, H. P. Logic and conversation. In P. Cole & J. L. Morgan (Eds.), *Syntax and semantics* (Vol. 3): *Speech acts*. New York: Seminar Press, 1975.

Griggs, R. A. Drawing inferences from set inclusion information given in text. In R. Revlin & R. E. Mayer (Eds.), *Human reasoning*. New York: Wiley, 1978.

Grimes, J. *The thread of discourse*. The Hague: Mouton, 1975.

Haberlandt, C. Story grammar and reading time of story constituents. *Poetics*, 1980, *9*, 99-116.

Haberlandt, K., & Bingham, G. Verbs contribute to the coherence of brief narratives: Reading related and unrelated sentence triplets. *Journal of Verbal Learning and Verbal Behavior*, 1978, *17*, 419-425.

Halliday, M. A. Notes on transitivity and theme in English: II. *Journal of Linguistics*, 1967, *3*, 199-244.

Halliday, M. A., & Hasan, R. *Cohesion in English*. London: Longman, 1976.

Harris, R. J., & Monaco, G. E. Psychology of pragmatic implication: Information processing between the lines. *Journal of Experimental Psychology: General*, 1978, *107*, 1-22.

Hasher, L., Goldstein, D., & Toppino, T. Frequency and the conference of referential validity. *Journal of Verbal Learning and Verbal Behavior*, 1977, *16*, 107-112.

Hastie, R. Memory for behavioral information that confirms a personality impression. In R. Hastie, T. M. Ostrom, E. B. Ebbesen, R. S. Wyer, D. L. Hamilton, & D. E. Carlston (Eds.), *Person memory: The cognitive basis of social perception*. Hillsdale, N.J.: Erlbaum, 1980.

Hastie, R., & Kumar, A. P. Person memory: Personality traits as organizing principles in memory for behaviors. *Journal of Personality and Social Psychology*, 1979, *37*, 25-38.

Haviland, S. E., & Clark, H. H. What's new? Acquiring new information as a process in comprehension. *Journal of Verbal Learning and Verbal Behavior*, 1974, *13*, 515-521.

Hayes-Roth, B., & Hayes-Roth, F. A cognitive model of planning. *Cognitive Science*, 1979, *3*, 275-310.

Hayes-Roth, B., & Walker, C. Configural effects in human memory: The superiority of memory over external information sources as a basis for inference verification. *Cognitive Science*, 1979, *3*, 119-140.

Hayes-Roth, F., Waterman, D. A., & Lenat, D. E. Principles of pattern-directed inference systems. In D. A. Waterman & F. Hayes-Roth (Eds.), *Pattern-directed inference systems*. New York: Academic Press, 1978.

Hildyard, A. Children's production of inferences from oral texts. *Discourse Processes*, 1979, *2*, 33-56.

Hildyard, A., & Olson, D. R. Memory and inference in the comprehension of oral and written discourse. *Discourse Processes*, 1978, *1*, 91-117.

Hobbs, J. R. Coherence and coreference. *Cognitive Science*, 1979, *3*, 67-90.

Hobbs, J. R., & Robinson, J. J. Why ask? *Discourse Processes*, 1979, *2*, 311-318.

Hochberg, J. Components of literacy: Speculations and exploratory research. In H. Levin & J. P. Williams (Eds.), *Basic studies on reading*. New York: Basic Books, 1970.

Hoffman, K., Hoffman, N. L., & Graesser, A. C. *Can reading time and comprehension be predicted by specific components of reading*? Paper presented at the meeting of the Western Psychological Association, Honolulu, Hawaii, 1980.

Huey, E. B. *The psychology and pedagogy of reading*. Published by Cambridge, Mass.: M.I.T. Press, 1968. (Originally published, 1908.)

Hunt, E. G. *Artificial intelligence*. New York: Academic Press, 1975.

Hunt, E., Lunneborg, C., & Lewis, J. What does it mean to be high verbal. *Cognitive Psychology*, 1975, *7*, 194-227.

Hurtig, R. The validity of clausal processing strategies at the discourse level. *Discourse Processes*, 1978, *1*, 195-202.

Jackson, M. D., & McClelland, J. L. Sensory and cognitive determinants of reading speed. *Journal of Verbal Learning and Verbal Behavior*, 1975, *14*, 565-574.

Jackson, M. D., & McClelland, J. L. Processing determinants of reading speed. *Journal of Experimental Psychology: General*, 1979, *108*, 151-181.

Jarvella, R. J. Syntactic processing of connected speech. *Journal of Verbal Learning and Verbal Behavior*, 1971, *10*, 409-416.

Jarvella, R. J., & Herman, S. J. Clause structure of sentences and speech processing. *Perception and Psychophysics*, 1972, *11*, 381-384.

Jebousek, S. E. *Recognition memory for typical and atypical actions in distorted versus prototypical scripts*. Unpublished masters thesis, California State University, Fullerton, 1978.

Johnson, N. F. On the function of letters in word identification: Some data and a preliminary model. *Journal of Verbal Learning and Verbal Behavior*, 1975, *14*, 17-29.

Johnson, N. F. A pattern-unit model of word identification. In D. LaBerge & S. J. Samuels (Eds.), *Basic processing in reading: Perception and comprehension*. Hillsdale, N.J.: Erlbaum, 1977.

Johnson, N. F. The role of letters in word identification: A test of the pattern-unit model. *Memory and Cognition*, 1979, *7*, 496-504.

Johnson, N. S., & Mandler, J. M. A tale of two structures: Underlying and surface forms in stories. *Poetics*, 1980, *9*, 51-86.

Johnson, R. E. Recall of prose as a function of the structural importance of the linguistic units. *Journal of Verbal Learning and Verbal Behavior*, 1970, *9*, 12-20.

Johnson, R. E., & Scheidt, B. J. Organizational encodings in the serial learning of prose. *Journal of Verbal Learning and Verbal Behavior*, 1977, *16*, 575-588.

Johnston, J. C. A test of the sophisticated guessing theory of word perception. *Cognitive Psychology*, 1978, *10*, 123-154.

Just, M. A., & Carpenter, P. A. Inference processes during reading: Reflections from eye fixations. In J. W. Senders, D. F. Fisher, & R. A. Monty (Eds.), *Eye movements and higher psychological functions*. Hillsdale, N.J.: Erlbaum, 1978.

Just, M. A., & Carpenter, P. A. A theory of reading: From eye fixations to comprehension. *Psychological Review*, 1980, *87*, 329-354.

Kahneman, D. *Attention and effort*. Englewood Cliffs, N.J.: Prentice Hall, 1973.

Kahneman, D., & Tversky, A. On the psychology of prediction. *Psychological Review*, 1973, *80*, 237-251.

Kaplan, R. M. On process models for sentence analysis. In D. A. Norman & D. E. Rumelhart, *Explorations in cognition*. San Francisco: Freeman, 1975.

Keele, S. W. *Attention and human performance*. Pacific Palisades, Calif.: Goodyear, 1973.

Keenan, J. M. Psychological issues concerning implication: Comments on "Psychology of pragmatic implication: Information processing between the lines" by Harris and Monaco. *Journal of Experimental Psychology: General*, 1978, *107*, 23-27.

Keenan, J. M., MacWhinney, B., & Mayhew, D. Pragmatics in memory: A study of natural conversation. *Journal of Verbal Learning and Verbal Behavior*, 1977, *16*, 549-560.

Kerr, B. Processing demands during mental operations. *Memory and Cognition*, 1973, *1*, 401-412.

Kieras, D. E. Good and bad structure in simple paragraphs: Effects on apparent theme, reading time, and recall. *Journal of Verbal Learning and Verbal Behavior*, 1978, *17*, 13-28.

Kintsch, W. *Learning, memory, and conceptual processes*. New York: Wiley, 1970.

Kintsch, W. *The representation of meaning in memory*. Hillsdale, N.J.: Erlbaum, 1974.

Kintsch, W. *Memory and cognition*. New York: Wiley, 1977. (a)

Kintsch, W. On comprehending stories. In M. A. Just & P. A. Carpenter (Eds.), *Cognitive processes in comprehension*. Hillsdale, N.J.: Erlbaum, 1977. (b)

Kintsch, W. On modeling comprehension. *Educational Psychologist*, 1979, *14*, 3-14.

Kintsch, W., & van Dijk, T. A. Toward a model of text comprehension and production. *Psychological Review*, 1978, *85*, 363-394.

Kintsch, W., & Keenan, J. Reading rate and retention as a function of the number of propositions in the base structure of sentences. *Cognitive Psychology*, 1973, *5*, 257-274.

Kintsch, W., Kozminsky, E., Streby, W. J., McKoon, G., & Keenan, J. M. Comprehension and recall of text as a function of content variables. *Journal of Verbal Learning and Verbal Behavior*, 1975, *14*, 196-214.

Kintsch, W., Mandel, T. S., & Kozminsky, E. Summarizing scrambled stories. *Memory and Cognition*, 1977, *5*, 547-552.

Kintsch, W., & Vipond, D. Reading comprehension and readability in educational practice and psychological theory. In L. G. Nilsson (Ed.), *Perspectives on memory research*. Hillsdale, N.J.: Erlbaum, 1979.

Kleiman, G. M. Speech recoding in reading. *Journal of Verbal Learning and Verbal Behavior*, 1975, *14*, 323-339.

Kolers, P. A. Three stages in reading. In H. Levin & J. P. Williams (Eds.), *Basic studies in reading*. New York: Basic Books, 1970.

Kosslyn, S. M. Scanning visual images: Some structural implications. *Perception and Psychophysics*, 1973, *14*, 90-94.

Kosslyn, S. M. Information representation in mental images. *Cognitive Psychology*, 1975, *7*, 341-370.

Kosslyn, S. M., & Pomerantz, J. R. Imagery, propositions, and the form of internal representation. *Cognitive Psychology*, 1977, *9*, 52-76.

Kosslyn, S. M., & Schwartz, S. P. A simulation of visual imagery. *Cognitive Science*, 1977, *1*, 235-264.

Kowalski, D. J., & Graesser, A. C. *Memory for passages describing scripted activities*. Paper presented at the meeting of the Western Psychological Association, San Diego, Calif., 1979.

Kozminsky, E. Altering comprehension: The effect of biasing titles on text comprehension. *Memory and Cognition*, 1977, *5*, 482-490.

Kuipers, B. J. Modeling spatial knowledge. *Cognitive Science*, 1978, *2*, 129-155.

LaBerge, D. Acquisition of automatic processing in perceptual and associative learning. In P. M. A. Rabbitt & S. Dornic (Eds.), *Attention and performance V*. New York: Academic Press, 1975.

LaBerge, D., & Samuels, S. J. Toward a theory of automatic information processing in reading. *Cognitive Psychology*, 1974, *6*, 293-323.

Lakoff, G. Linguistic and natural logic. In D. Donaldson & G. Harmon (Eds.), *Semantics and natural language*. Boston: Reidel, 1972.

Lea, G. Chronometric analysis of the method of loci. *Journal of Experimental Psychology: Human Perception and Performance*, 1975, *104*, 94-104.

Lehnert, W. Human and computational question-answering. *Cognitive Science*, 1977, *1*, 47-73.

Lehnert, W. *The process of question answering*. Hillsdale, N.J.: Erlbaum, 1978. (a)

Lehnert, W. *Representing physical objects in memory* (Res. Rep. No. 131). New Haven: Yale University, Department of Computer Science, 1978. (b)

Lehnert, W. *Text processing effects recall memory* (Res. Rep. No. 157). New Haven: Yale University, Department of Computer Science, 1979.

Lehnert, W. G. *Affect units and narrative summarization* (Res. Rep. No. 179), New Haven: Yale University, Department of Computer Science, 1980.

Lehnert, W., & Burstein, M. H. *The role of object primitives in natural language processing* (Res. Rep. No. 162). New Haven: Yale University, Department of Computer Science, 1979.

Lesgold, A. M., & Curtis, M. E. Learning to read words efficiently. In A. M. Lesgold & C. A. Perfetti (Eds.), *Interactive processes in reading*. Hillsdale, N.J.: Erlbaum, 1980.

Lesgold, A. M., & Perfetti, C. A. Interactive processes in reading comprehension. *Discourse Processes*, 1978, *1*, 323-336.

Lesgold, A. M., Perfetti, C. A. *Interactive processes in reading*. Hillsdale, N.J.: Erlbaum, 1980.

Lesgold, A. M., Roth, S. F., & Curtis, M. E. Foregrounding effects in discourse comprehension. *Journal of Verbal Learning and Verbal Behavior*, 1979, *18*, 291-308.

Levin, H., & Turner, A. Sentence structure and the eye-voice span. In H. Levin, E. J. Gibson, & J. J. Gibson (Eds.), *The analysis of reading skill* (Final Report Project No. 5-1213, U.S. Office of Education), Ithaca, N.Y.: Cornell University, 1968.

Levin, I. P., Ims, J. R., Simpson, J. C., & Kim, K. J. The processing of deviant information in prediction and evaluation. *Memory and Cognition*, 1977, *5*, 679-684.

Levin, J. A., & Moore, J. A. Dialogue-games: Metacommunication structures for natural language. *Cognitive Science*, 1977, *1*, 395-420.

Levin, J. R., & Pressley, M. *Improving children's prose comprehension: Selected strategies that seem to succeed.* Madison, Wisc.: University of Wisconsin, Wisconsin Research and Development Center for Individualized Schooling, 1978.

Lewis, D. General semantics. In D. Donaldson & G. Harmon (Eds.), *Semantics in natural language*. Boston: Reidel, 1972.

Lichtenstein, E. H., & Brewer, W. F. Memory for goal-directed events. *Cognitive Psychology*, 1980, *12*, 412-445.

Light, L. L., Kayra-Stuart, F., & Hollander, S. Recognition memory for typical and unusual faces. *Journal of Experimental Psychology: Human Learning and Memory*, 1979, *5*, 212-228.

Lindsay, P. H., & Norman, D. A. *Human information processing*. New York: Academic Press, 1977.

Loftus, E. F. Leading questions and the eye witness report. *Cognitive Psychology*, 1975, *7*, 560-572.

Loftus, G. R., & Mackworth, N. H. Cognitive determinants of fixation location during picture viewing. *Journal of Experimental Psychology: Human Perception and Performance*, 1978, *4*, 565-572.

Lovelace, E. R., & Graesser, A. C. *Verification of inferences in text material.* Paper presented at the meeting of the Western Psychological Association, San Francisco, Calif., 1978.

Mackworth, J. Some models of the reading process: Learners and skilled readers. *Reading Research Quarterly*, 1972, *7*, 701-733.

Mackworth, N. H., & Morandi, A. J. The gaze selects informative details within pictures. *Perception and Psychophysics*, 1967, *2*, 547-552.

Macnamara, J., Baker, E., & Olson, C. L. Four-year-olds' understanding of Pretend, Forget, and Know: Evidence for propositional operations. *Child Development*, 1976, *47*, 62-70.

MacWhinney, B., & Bates, E. Sentential devices for conveying giveness and newness. A cross-cultural developmental study. *Journal of Verbal Learning and Verbal Behavior*, 1978, *17*, 539-558.

Mandler, G. Organization and recognition. In E. Tulving & W. Donaldson (Eds.), *Organization and memory*. New York: Academic Press, 1972.

Mandler, G. *Mind and emotion*. New York: Wiley, 1976.

Mandler, G. Recognizing: The judgment of previous occurrence. *Psychological Review*, 1980, *87*, 252-271.

Mandler, G., & Graesser, A. C. Analyse dimensionelle et le "locus" de l'organization. In S. Ehrlich & E. Tulving (Eds.), *La memoire semantique*. Paris: *Bulletin de Psychologie*, 1976.

Mandler, J. M. A code in the node: The use of a story schema in retrieval. *Discourse Processes*, 1978, *1*, 14-35.

Mandler, J. M. Categorical and schematic organization in memory. In C. R. Puff (Ed.), *Memory organization and structure*. New York: Academic Press, 1979.

Mandler, J. M., & DeForest, M. Is there more than one way to recall a story? *Child Development*, 1979, *50*, 886-889.

Mandler, J. M., & Johnson, N. S. Remembrance of things parsed: Story structure and recall. *Cognitive Psychology*, 1977, *9*, 111-151.

Mandler, J. M., & Johnson, N. S. On throwing out the baby with the bathwater: A reply to Black and Wilensky's evaluation of story grammars. *Cognitive Science*, 1980, *4*, 305-312.

Mandler, J. M., & Ritchey, G. H. Long-term memory for pictures. *Journal of Experimental Psychology: Human Learning and Memory*, 1977, *3*, 386-396.

Mandler, J. M., Scribner, S., Cole, M., & DeForest, M. Cross-cultural invariance in story recall. *Child Development*, 1980, *51*, 19-26.

Manelis, L. Determinants of processing for a propositional structure. *Memory and Cognition*, 1980, *8*, 49-57.

Manelis, L., & Yekovich, F. R. Repetitions of propositional arguments in sentences. *Journal of Verbal Learning and Verbal Behavior*, 1976, *15*, 301-312.

Marslen-Wilson, W. D., & Welsh, A. Processing interactions and lexical access during word recognition. *Cognitive Psychology*, 1978, *10*, 29-63.

Mason, M. From print to sound in mature readers as a function of reader ability and two forms of orthographic regularity. *Memory and Cognition*, 1978, *6*, 569-581.

Massaro, D. W. *Understanding language: An information processing analysis of speech perception, reading, and psycholinguistics*. New York: Academic Press, 1975.

Masson, M. E. J., & Sala, L. S. Interactive processes in sentence comprehension and recognition. *Cognitive Psychology*, 1978, *10*, 244-270.

McCawley, J. D. Where do noun-phrases come from? In R. A. Jacobs & P. S. Rosenbaum (Eds.), *Readings in English transformational grammar*. Waltham, Mass.: Ginn, 1970.

McClelland, J. L. Letter and configuration information in word identification. *Journal of Verbal Learning and Verbal Behavior*, 1977, *16*, 137-150.

McClelland, J. L. On the time relations of mental processes. *Psychological Review*, 1979, *86*, 287-330.

McClure, E., Mason, J., & Barnitz, J. C. An exploratory study of story structure and age effects on children's ability to sequence stories. *Discourse Processes*, 1979, *2*, 213-249.

McConkie, G. W., Hogaboam, T. W., Wolverton, G. S., Zola, D., & Lucas, P. A. Toward the use of eye movements in the study of language processing. *Discourse Processes*, 1979, *2*, 157-178.

McDermott, D. Planning and acting. *Cognitive Science*, 1978, *2*, 71-109.

McDermott, D., & Forgy, C. Production system conflict resolution strategies. In D. A. Waterman & F. Hayes-Roth (Eds.), *Pattern-directed inference systems*. New York: Academic Press, 1978.

Meehan, J. R. *TALESPIN*, an interactive program that writes stories. *Proceedings from the Fifth International Joint Conference of Artificial Intelligence*, 1977, pp. 91-98.

Meyer, B. J. F. *The organization of prose and its effects on memory*. New York: American Elsevier, 1975.

Meyer, B. J. F. The structure of prose: Effects on learning and memory and implications for educational practice. In R. C. Anderson, R. J. Spiro, & W. E. Montague (Eds.), *Schooling and the acquisition of knowledge*. Hillsdale, N.J.: Erlbaum, 1977. (a)

Meyer, B. J. F. What is remembered from prose: A function of passage structure. In R. O. Freedle (Ed.), *Discourse processes: Advances in research and theory* (Vol. 1). Norwood, N.J.: Ablex, 1977. (b)

Meyer, D., & Schvaneveldt, R. Facilitation in recognizing pairs of words: Evidence of a dependence between retrieval operations. *Journal of Experimental Psychology*, 1971, *90*, 227-234.

Miller, G. A., Galanter, E., & Pribram, K. H. *Plans and the structure of behavior*. New York: Holt, Rinehart & Winston, 1960.

Miller, G. A., & Johnson-Laird, P. N. *Language and perception*. Cambridge, Mass.: Harvard University Press, 1976.

Miller, J. R., & Kintsch, W. Readability and recall of short prose passages: A theoretical analysis. *Journal of Experimental Psychology: Human Learning and Memory*, 1980, *6*, 335-354.

Minsky, M. A framework for representing knowledge. In P. H. Winston (Ed.), *The psychology of computer vision*. New York: McGraw-Hill, 1975.

Mitchell, D. C., & Green, D. W. The effects of content on immediate processing in reading. *Quarterly Journal of Experimental Psychology*, 1978, *30*, 609-636.

Miyake, N., & Norman, D. A. To ask a question, one must know enough to know what is not known. *Journal of Verbal Learning and Verbal Behavior*, 1979, *18*, 357-364.

Morton, J. The interaction of information in word recognition. *Psychological Review*, 1969, *76*, 165-178.

Munro, A., Gordon, L., Rigney, J. W., & Lutz, K. A. *Memory for three types of text*. Unpublished manuscript, University of Southern California, 1979.

Munro, A., Lutz, K. A., & Gordon, L. *On the psychological reality of text types*. Unpublished manuscript, University of Southern California, 1979.

Neely, J. H. Semantic priming and retrieval from lexical memory: Roles of inhibitionless spreading activation and limited-capacity attention. *Journal of Experimental Psychology: General*, 1977, *106*, 226-254.

Neisser, U. *Cognitive Psychology*. New York: Appleton-Century Crofts, 1967.

Neisser, U. *Cognition and reality*. San Francisco: Freeman, 1976.

Neisser, U., & Becklen, R. Selective looking: Attending to visually specific events. *Cognitive Psychology*, 1975, *7*, 480-494.

Nelson, K. Concept, word, and sentence: Interrelations in acquisition and development. *Psychological Review*, 1974, *81*, 267-285.

Nelson, K. Cognitive development and the acquisition of concepts. In R. C. Anderson, R. J. Spiro, & W. E. Montague (Eds.), *Schooling and the acquisition of knowledge*. Hillsdale, N.J.: Erlbaum, 1977.

Newell, A. Production systems: Models of control structures. In W. G. Chase (Ed.), *Visual information processing*. New York: Academic Press, 1973.

Newell, A. Harpy, production systems and human cognition. In R. Cole (Ed.), *Perception and production of fluent speech*. Hillsdale, N.J.: Erlbaum, 1980.

Newell, A., & Simon, H. A. *Human problem solving*. Englewood Cliffs, N.J.: Prentice-Hall, 1972.

Nicholas, D. W., & Trabasso, T. Towards a taxonomy of inferences. In F. Wilkening, J. Becker, & T. Trabasso (Eds.), *Information integration by children*. Hillsdale, N.J.: Erlbaum, 1980.

Nickerson, R. S., & Adams, M. J. Long-term memory for a common object. *Cognitive Psychology*, 1979, *11*, 287-307.

Nilsson, N. J. *Problem-solving methods in artificial intelligence*. New York: McGraw-Hill, 1971.

Nisbett, R. E., & Wilson, T. D. Telling more than we can know: Verbal reports on mental processes. *Psychological Review*, 1977, *84*, 231-259.

Noordman-Vonk, W. *Retrieval from semantic memory*. New York: Springer, 1979.

Norman, D. A. *Memory and attention*. New York: Wiley, 1976.

Norman, D. A. *Slips of the mind and an outline for a theory of action* (Tech. Rep. No. 88), San Diego: University of California, Center for Human Information Processing, 1979.

Norman, D. A. What goes on in the mind of the learner. In W. J. McKeachie (Ed.), *Cognition, college teaching, and student learning*. San Francisco: Jossey-Bass, 1980.

Norman, D., & Bobrow, D. On data-limited and resource-limited processes. *Cognitive Psychology*, 1975, *7*, 44-64.

Norman, D. A., & Bobrow, D. G. On the role of active memory processes in perception and cognition. In C. N. Cofer (Ed.), *The structure of human memory*. San Francisco: Freeman, 1976.

Norman, D. A., & Bobrow, D. G. Descriptions: An intermediate stage in memory retrieval. *Cognitive Psychology*, 1979, *11*, 107-123.

Norman, D. A., Gentner, D. R., & Stevens, A. L. Comments on learning: Schemata and memory representation. In D. Klahr (Ed.), *Cognition and instruction*. Hillsdale, N.J.: Erlbaum, 1976.

Norman, D. A., & Rumelhart, D. E. *Explorations in cognition*. San Francisco: Freeman, 1975.

Oden, G. C. Fuzziness in semantic memory: Choosing exemplars of subjective categories. *Memory and Cognition*, 1977, *5*, 198-204.

Oden, G. C. A fuzzy logical model of letter identification. *Journal of Experimental Psychology: Human Perception and Performance*, 1979, *5*, 336-352.

Olson, D. R. The languages of instruction: On the literate bias of schooling. In R. C. Anderson, R. J. Spiro, & W. E. Montague (Eds.), *Schooling and the acquisition of knowledge*. Hillsdale, N.J.: Erlbaum, 1977.

Olson, G. M., Duffy, S. A. & Mack, R. L. Knowledge of writing conventions in prose comprehension. In W. J. McKeachie & K. Eble (Eds.), *Learning, cognition, and college teaching*. San Francisco: Jossey-Bass, 1980.

Olson, G. M., Mack, R., & Duffy, S. *Strategies for story understanding*. Paper presented at the meeting of the Cognitive Science Society, Yale University, New Haven, 1980.

Omanson, R. C. *The narrative analysis*. Unpublished doctorial dissertation, University of Minnesota, 1979.

Omanson, R. C., Warren, W. H., & Trabasso, T. Goals, inferential comprehension, and recall of stories by children. *Discourse Processes*, 1978, *1*, 337-354.

Ortony, A. Remembering, understanding, and representation. *Cognitive Science*, 1978, *2*, 53-69.

Ortony, A., Schallert, D. L., Reynolds, R. E., & Antos, S. J. Interpreting metaphors and idioms: Some effects of context on comprehension. *Journal of Verbal Learning and Verbal Behavior*, 1978, *17*, 465-478.

Owens, J., Bower, G. H., & Black, J. B. The "soap opera" effect in story recall. *Memory and Cognition*, 1979, 7, 185-191.

Pachella, R. G. The interpretation of reaction time in information processing research. In B. H. Kantowitz (Ed.), *Human information processing: Tutorials in performance and cognition*. Hillsdale, N.J.: Erlbaum, 1974.

Paivio, A. *Imagery and verbal processes*. New York: Holt, 1971.

Palmer, S. E. Hierarchical structure in perceptual representation. *Cognitive Psychology*, 1977, *9*, 441-474.

Patberg, J. P., & Yonas, A. The effects of the reader's skill and difficulty of the text on the perceptual span in reading. *Journal of Experimental Psychology: Human Perception and Performance*, 1978, *4*, 545-552.

Perfetti, C. A. Levels of language and levels of process. In F. I. M. Craik & L. Cermak (Eds.), *Levels of processing in human memory*. Hillsdale, N.J.: Erlbaum, 1979.

Perfetti, C. A. Verbal coding efficiency, conceptual guided reading, and reading failure. *Bulletin of the Orton Society*, 1980, in press.

Perfetti, C. A., & Goldman, S. R. Discourse memory and reading comprehension skill. *Journal of Verbal Learning and Verbal Behavior*, 1976, *15*, 33-42.

Perfetti, C. A., Goldman, S. R., & Hogaboam, T. W. Reading skill and the identification of words in discourse context. *Memory and Cognition*, 1979, 7, 273-282.

Perfetti, C. A., & Hogaboam, T. The relationship between single word decoding and reading comprehension skill. *Journal of Educational Psychology*, 1975, *67*, 461-469.

Perfetti, C. A., & Lesgold, A. M. Discourse comprehension and sources of individual differences. In M. A. Just & P. A. Carpenter (Eds.), *Cognitive processes in comprehension*. Hillsdale, N.J.: Erlbaum, 1977.

Perfetti, C. A., & Lesgold, A. M. Coding and comprehension in skilled reading and implications for reading instruction. In L. B. Resnick & P. Weaver (Eds.), *Theory and practice in early reading*. Hillsdale, N.J.: Erlbaum, 1979.

Perfetti, C. A., & Roth, S. Some of the interactive processes in reading and their role in reading skill. In A. M. Lesgold & C. A. Perfetti (Eds.), *Interactive processing in reading*. Hillsdale, N.J.: Erlbaum, 1980.

Pew, R. W. Human perceptual-motor performance. In B. H. Kantowitz (Ed.), *Human information processing: Tutorials in performance and cognition*. Hillsdale, N.J.: Erlbaum, 1974.

Piaget, J. *The origins of intelligence in the child*. London: Routledge & Kegan Paul, 1953.

Pollard-Gott, L., McCloskey, M., & Todres, A. K. Subjective story structure. *Discourse Processes*, 1979, *2*, 251-281.

Posner, M. I., & Snyder, C. R. Attention and cognitive control. In R. L. Solso (Ed.), *Information processing and cognition: The Loyola symposium*. Hillsdale, N.J.: Erlbaum, 1975.

Posner, M. I., & Warren, R. E. Traces, concepts, and conscious constructions. In A. W. Melton & E. Martin (Eds.), *Coding processes in human memory*. Washington, D.C.: Winston, 1972.

Potts, G. R. Storing and retrieving information about ordered relationships. *Journal of Experimental Psychology*, 1974, *103*, 431-439.

Potts, G. R. Integrating new and old information. *Journal of Verbal Learning and Verbal Behavior*, 1977, *16*, 305-320.

Potts, G. R., & Scholz, K. W. The internal representation of a three-term series problem. *Journal of Verbal Learning and Verbal Behavior*, 1975, *14*, 439-452.

Poulton, E. C. Peripheral vision, refractoriness and eye movements in fast oral reading. *British Journal of Psychology*, 1962, *53*, 409-419.

Pylyshyn, Z. What the mind's eye tells the mind's brain: A critique of mental imagery. *Psychological Bulletin*, 1973, *80*, 1-24.

Rabinowitz, J. C., Mandler, G., & Patterson, K. E. Determinants of recognition and recall: Accessibility and generation. *Journal of Experimental Psychology: General*, 1977, *106*, 302-329.

Rapoport, A. *Human aspects of urban form*. Oxford, England: Pergamon Press, 1977.

Ratcliff, R., & McKoon, G. Priming in item recognition: Evidence for the propositional structure of sentences. *Journal of Verbal Learning and Verbal Behavior*, 1978, *17*, 403-419.

Rayner, K. The perceptual span and peripheral cues in reading. *Cognitive Psychology*, 1975, 7, 65-81.

Rayner, K. Visual attention in reading: Eye movements reflect cognitive processes. *Memory and Cognition*, 1977, *5*, 443-448.

Rayner, K., & McConkie, G. W. Perceptual processes in reading: The perceptual spans. In A. S. Reber & D. L. Scarborough (Eds.), *Toward a psychology of reading*. Hillsdale, N.J.: Erlbaum, 1977.

Rayner, K., McConkie, G. W., & Ehrlich, S. Eye movements and integrating information across fixations. *Journal of Experimental Psychology: Human Perception and Performance*, 1978, *4*, 529-544.

Reder, L. M. The role of elaborations in memory for prose. *Cognitive Psychology*, 1979, *11*, 221-234.

Reichenbach, H. *Elements of symbolic logic*. New York: Free Press, 1947.

Reicher, G. M. Perceptual recognition as a function of meaningfulness of stimulus material. *Journal of Experimental Psychology*, 1969, *81*, 275-280.

Reichman, R. Conversational coherency. *Cognitive Science*, 1979, *2*, 283-327.

von Restorff, H. Über die Wirkung von Bereichsbildung im Spurenfeld. *Psychologische Forschung*, 1937, *18*, 297-342.

Revlin, R., & Mayer, R. E. (Eds.), *Human reasoning*. New York: Wiley, 1978.

Rieger, C. Conceptual memory. In R. C. Schank (Ed.), *Conceptual information processing*. New York: American Elsevier, 1975.

Rieger, C. Spontaneous computation in cognitive models. *Cognitive Science*, 1977, *1*, 315-354.

Rieger, C. *GRIND*-1 First report on the Magic Grinder Story comprehension project. *Discourse Processes*, 1978, *1*, 267-303.

Rommetveit, R. *On message structure*. New York: Wiley, 1974.

Rosch, E. Principles of categorization. In E. Rosch and B. B. Lloyd (Eds.), *Cognition and categorization*. Hillsdale, N.J.: Erlbaum, 1978.

Rosch, E., & Mervis, C. B. Family resemblences: Studies in the internal structure of categories. *Cognitive Psychology*, 1975, 7, 573-605.

Rothkopf, E. Z. Structural text features and the control processes in learning from written materials. In J. B. Carroll & R. O. Freedle (Eds.), *Language comprehension and the acquisition of knowledge*. Washington, D.C.: Winston, 1972.

Rubenstein, H., Lewis, S. S., & Rubenstein, M. A. Evidence for phonemic recoding in visual word recognition. *Journal of Verbal Learning and Verbal Behavior*, 1971, *10*, 645-657.

Rumelhart, D. E. A multicomponent theory of the perception of briefly exposed visual displays. *Journal of Mathematical Psychology*, 1970, 7, 191-218.

Rumelhart, D. E. Notes on a schema for stories. In D. G. Bobrow & A. Collins (Eds.), *Representation and understanding*. New York: Academic Press, 1975.

Rumelhart, D. E. *Introduction to human information processing*. New York: Wiley, 1977. (a)

Rumelhart, D. E. Toward an interactive model of reading. In S. Dornic (Ed.), *Attention and performance VI*. Hillsdale, N.J.: Erlbaum, 1977. (b)

Rumelhart, D. E. Understanding and summarizing brief stories. In D. LaBerge & S. J. Samuels (Eds.), *Basic processes in reading: Perception and comprehension*. Hillsdale, N.J.: Erlbaum, 1977. (c)

Rumelhart, D. E. *Explorations in cognitive psychology from the Center for Human Information Processing*. Paper presented at the meeting of the Western Psychological Association, San Diego, Calif., 1979.

Rumelhart, D. E. & Norman, D. A. Accretion, tuning, and restructuring: Three models of learning. In J. W. Cotton & R. Klatzky (Eds.), *Semantic factors in cognition*. Hillsdale, N.J.: Erlbaum, 1978.

Rumelhart, D. E., & Ortony, A. The representation of knowledge in memory. In R. C. Anderson, R. J. Spiro, & W. E. Montague (Eds.), *Schooling and the acquisition of knowledge*. Hillsdale, N.J.: Erlbaum, 1977.

Sachs, J. S. Recognition memory for syntactic and semantic aspects of connected discourse. *Perception and Psychophysics*, 1967, *2*, 437-442.

Sachs, J. S. Memory in reading or listening to discourse. *Memory and cognition*, 1974, *2*, 95-100.

Sacks, H., Schegloff, E., & Jefferson, G. A simplest systematics of the organization of turn-taking for conversation. *Language*, 1974, *50*, 696-735.

Schank, R. C. Conceptual dependency: A theory of natural language understanding. *Cognitive Psychology*, 1972, *3*, 552-631.

Schank, R. C. Identification of conceptualizations underlying natural language. In R. C. Schank & K. M. Colby (Eds.), *Computer models of thought and language*. San Francisco: Freeman, 1973.

Schank, R. C. The structure of episodes in memory. In D. G. Bobrow & A. Collins (Eds.), *Representation and understanding*. New York: Academic Press, 1975.

Schank, R. C. Roles and topics in conversation. *Cognitive Science*, 1977, *1*, 421-442.

Schank, R. C. Interestingness: Controlling inferences. *Artificial intelligence*, 1979, *12*, 273-297. (a)

Schank, R. C. Reminding and memory organization: An introduction to *MOPS* (Tech. Rep. No. 170). New Haven: Yale University, Department of Computer Science, 1979. (b)

Schank, R. C., & Abelson, R. *Scripts, plans, goals, and understanding*. Hillsdale, N.J.: Erlbaum, 1977.

Schank, R. C., & Lehnert, W. G. The conceptual content of conversation (Res. Rep. No. 160), New Haven: Yale University, Department of Computer Science, 1979.

Schank, R. C., Wilensky, R., Carbonell, J. G., Kolodner, J. L., & Hendler, J. A. Representing attitudes: Some primitive states (Res. Rep. No. 128), New Haven: Yale University, Department of Computer Science, 1978.

Schmidt, C. F. Understanding human action: Recognizing the plans and motives of other persons. In J. S. Carroll and J. W. Payne (Eds.), *Cognition and social behavior*. Hillsdale, N.J.: Erlbaum, 1976.

Schmidt, C. F., Sridharan, N. S., & Goodson, J. L. The plan recognition problem: An intersection of psychology and artificial intelligence. *Artificial Intelligence*, 1978, *11*, 45-83.

Schmidt, R. A. A schema theory of discrete motor skill learning. *Psychological Review*, 1975, *82*, 225-260.

Schneider, W., & Shiffrin, R. M. Controlled and automatic human information processing: Detection, search and attention. *Psychological Review*, 1977, *84*, 1-66.

Schnur, P. Testing the encoding elaboration hypothesis: The effects of exemplar ranking on recognition and recall. *Memory and Cognition*, 1977, *5*, 666-672.

Schulman, H. G., Hornak, R., & Sanders, E. The effects of graphemic, phonetic, and semantic relationships on access to lexical structures. *Memory and Cognition*, 1978, *6*, 115-123.

Schweller, K. G., Brewer, W. F., & Dahl, D. A. Memory for illocutionary effects of utterances. *Journal of Verbal Learning and Verbal Behavior*, 1976, *15*, 325-334.

Searle, J. R. *Speech acts*. London: Cambridge University Press, 1969.

Searle, J. R. The intentionality of intention and action. *Cognitive Science*, 1980, *4*, 47-70.

Shaffer, W. O., & LaBerge, D. Automatic semantic processing of unattended words. *Journal of Verbal Learning and Verbal Behavior*, 1979, *18*, 413-426.

Shankweiler, D., Liberman, I. Y., Mark, L. S., Fowler, C. A., & Fischer, F. W. The speech code and learning to read. *Journal of Experimental Psychology: Human Learning and Memory*, 1979, *5*, 531-545.

Shiffrin, R. M., & Schneider, W. Controlled and automatic human information processing: II. Perceptual learning, automatic attending, and a general theory. *Psychological Review*, 1977, *84*, 127-190.

Simmons, R. F. Semantic networks: Their computation and use for understanding English sentences. In R. C. Schank & K. M. Colby (Eds.), *Computer models of thought and language*. San Francisco: Freeman, 1973.

Singer, M. Processes of inference during sentence encoding. *Memory and Cognition*, 1979, *7*, 192-200.

Smets, G. Pleasingness versus interestingness of visual stimuli with controlled complexity: Their relationship to looking time as a function of exposure time. *Perceptual and Motor Skills*, 1971, *40*, 3-10.

Smith, D. A., & Graesser, A. C. *Memory for actions in scripted activities as a function of typicality, retention interval, and retrieval task*. Unpublished manuscript, California State University, Fullerton, 1980.

Smith, D. A., Kinney, D., & Graesser, A. C. *The effect of story analogies on the acquisition of passages describing scientific mechanisms*. Paper presented at the meeting of the Western Psychological Association, Honolulu, Hawaii, 1980.

Smith, E. E., Shoben, E. J., & Rips, L. J. Structure and process in semantic memory: A feature model for semantic decisions. *Psychological Review*, 1974, *81*, 214-241.

Smith, E. E., & Spoehr, K. T. The perception of printed English: A theoretical perspective. In B. H. Kantowitz (Ed.), *Human information processing: Tutorials in performance and cognition*. Hillsdale, N.J.: Erlbaum, 1974.

Spilich, G. J., Vesonder, G. T., Chiesi, H. L., & Voss, J. F. Text processing of domain related information for individuals with high and low domain knowledge. *Journal of Verbal Learning and Verbal Behavior*, 1979, *18*, 275-290.

Spiro, R. J. Remembering information from text: Theoretical and empirical issues concerning the "state of schema" reconstruction hypothesis. In R. C. Anderson, R. J. Spiro, & W. E. Montague (Eds.), *Schooling and the acquisition of knowledge*. Hillsdale, N.J.: Erlbaum, 1977.

Stanovich, K. E., & West, R. F. Mechanisms of sentence context effects in reading: Automatic activation versus conscious attention. *Memory and Cognition*, 1979, *7*, 77-85.

Steedman, M. J. Verbs, time, and modality. *Cognitive Science*, 1977, *1*, 216-234.

Stein, N. L., & Glenn, G. G. An analysis of story comprehension in elementary school children. In R. O. Freedle (Eds.), *New directions in discourse processing* (Vol. 2). Norwood, N.J.: Ablex, 1979.

Stein, N. L., & Nezworski, T. The effects of organization and instructional set on story memory. *Discourse Processes*, 1978, *1*, 177-193.

Sternberg, S. Memory scanning: Mental processes revealed by reaction time experiments. In J. Antrobus (Ed.), *Cognition and affect*. Boston: Little, Brown, 1970.

Stevens, A. L., & Collins, A. The goal structure of a Socratic tutor (Report No. 3518), Cambridge, Mass.: Bolt, Beranek, and Newman, 1977.

Stevens, A. L., & Collins, A. Multiple conceptual models of a complex system. In R. E. Snow, P. A. Frederico, & W. E. Montague (Eds.), *Aptitude, learning, and instruction: Cognitive process analyses*. Hillsdale, N.J.: Erlbaum, 1979.

Stevens, A., Collins, A., & Goldin, S. E. Misconceptions in student's understanding. *International Journal of Man-Machine Studies*, 1979, *11*, 145-156.

Stevens, A., & Coupe, P. Distortions in judged spatial relations. *Cognitive Psychology*, 1978, *10*, 422-437.

Stevens, A., & Rumelhart, D. E. Errors in reading: Analyses using an augmented transition network model of grammar. In D. A. Norman & D. E. Rumelhart (Eds.), *Explorations in cognition*. San Francisco: Freeman, 1975.

Stillings, N. A. Meaning rules and systems of inference for verbs of transfer and possession. *Journal of Verbal Learning and Verbal Behavior*, 1975, *14*, 453-470.

Stockwell, R. P., Schachter, P., & Partee, H. *The major syntactic structures of English*. New York: Holt, Rinehart, & Winston, 1973.

Swinney, D. A. Lexical access during sentence comprehension: Reconsideration of context effects. *Journal of Verbal Learning and Verbal Behavior*, 1979, *18*, 645-659.

Swinney, D. A., & Hakes, D. T. Effects of prior context upon lexical access during sentence comprehension. *Journal of Verbal Learning and Verbal Behavior*, 1976, *15*, 681-690.

Tanenhaus, M. K., Leiman, J. M., & Seidenberg, M. S. Evidence for multiple stages in the processing of ambiguous words in syntactic contexts. *Journal of Verbal Learning and Verbal Behavior*, 1979, *18*, 427-440.

Tannen, D. What's in a frame? Surface evidence for underlying expectations. In R. O. Freedle (Ed.), *New directions in discourse processing* (Vol. 2). Norwood, N.J.: Ablex, 1979.

Taylor, S. Eye movements in reading: Facts and fallacies. *American Educational Research Journal*, 1965, *2*, 187-202.

Taylor, S. E., & Crocker, J. Schematic bases of social information processing. In E. T. Higgins, P. Herman, & M. P. Zanna (Eds.), *The Ontario Symposium on personality and social psychology*, 1980.

Taylor, S. E., Crocker, J., & D'Agostino, J. Schematic bases of social problem-solving. *Personality and Social Psychology Bulletin*, 1978, *4*, 447-451.

Tesser, A. Self-generated attitude change. In L. Berkowitz (Ed.), *Advances in experimental social psychology* (Vol. 11). New York: Academic Press, 1978.

Tesser, A., & Leone, C. Cognitive schemas and thought as determinants of attitude change. *Journal of Experimental Social Psychology*, 1977, *13*, 340-356.

Thorndyke, P. W. Cognitive structures in comprehension and memory of narrative discourse. *Cognitive Psychology*, 1977, *9*, 77-110.

Thorndyke, P. W. Knowledge acquisition from newspaper stories. *Discourse Processes*, 1979, *2*, 95-112.

Thorndyke, P. W., & Hayes-Roth, B. The use of schemata in the acquisition and transfer of knowledge. *Cognitive Psychology*, 1979, *11*, 82-106.

Tinker, M. A. *Bases for effective reading*. Minneapolis: University of Minnesota Press, 1965.

Townsend, D. J., & Bever, T. G. Interclause relations and clausal processing. *Journal of Verbal Learning and Verbal Behavior*, 1978, *17*, 509-522.

Townsend, J. T. Issues and models concerning the processing of a finite number of inputs. In B. H. Kantowitz (Ed.), *Human information processing: Tutorials in performance and cognition*. Hillsdale, N.J.: Erlbaum, 1974.

Treisman, A. Selective attention in man. *British Medical Bulletin*, 1964, *20*, 12-16.

Tulving, E. Episodic and semantic memory. In E. Tulving and W. Donaldson (Eds.), *Organization and memory*. New York: Academic Press, 1972.

Tulving, E., & Gold, C. Stimulus information as determinants of tachistoscopic recognition of words. *Journal of Experimental Psychology*, 1963, *66*, 319-327.

Tulving, E., Mandler, G., & Baumal, R. Interaction of two sources of information in tachistoscopic word recognition. *Canadian Journal of Psychology*, 1964, *18*, 62-71.

Tyler, L. K., & Marslen-Wilson, W. D. The on-line effects of semantic context on syntactic processing. *Journal of Verbal Learning and Verbal Behavior*, 1977, *16*, 683-692.

Vendler, Z. *Linguistics in philosophy*. Ithaca, N.Y.: Cornell University Press, 1967.

Verbrugge, R. R., & McCarrell, N. S. Metaphoric comprehension: Studies in reminding and resembling. *Cognitive Psychology*, 1977, *9*, 494-533.

Vipond, D. Micro- and macroprocesses in text comprehension. *Journal of Verbal Learning and Verbal Behavior*, 1980, *19*, 276-296.

Walker, C. H., & Meyer, B. J. F. Integrating different types of information in text. *Journal of Verbal Learning and Verbal Behavior*, 1980, *19*, 263-275.

Wallace, W. P. Review of the historical, empirical, and theoretical status of the von Restorff phenomenon. *Psychological Bulletin*, 1965, *63*, 410-424.

Wanner, E. *On remembering, forgetting, and understanding sentences*. The Hague: Mouton, 1974.

Wanner, E., & Maratsos, M. *An augmented transition network model of relative clause comprehension*. Unpublished paper, Harvard University, 1974.

Warren, W. H., Nicholas, D. W., & Trabasso, T. Event chains and inferences in understanding narratives. In R. O. Freedle (Ed.), *New directions in discourse processing* (Vol. 2). Norwood, N.J.: Ablex, 1979.

Waugh, N.C., & Norman, D. A. Primary memory. *Psychological Review*, 1965, *72*, 89-104.

Wegner, D. M., & Vallacher, R. R. *Implicit psychology: An introduction to social cognition*. New York: Oxford University Press, 1977.

Weinreich, U. On the semantic structure of language. In J. H. Greenberg (Ed.), *Universals of language*. Cambridge, Mass.: M.I.T. Press, 1963.

Wheeler, D. Processes in word recognition. *Cognitive Psychology*, 1970, *1*, 59-85.

Wickelgren, W. A. *How to solve problems: Elements of a theory of problems and problem solving*. San Francisco: Freeman, 1974.

Wilensky, R. A conceptual analysis of the verbs want and need. *Cognitive Science*, 1978, *2*, 391-396. (a)

Wilensky, R. Understanding goal-based stories (Res. Rep. No. 140), New Haven: Yale University, Department of Computer Science, 1978. (b)

Wilensky, R. Why John married Mary: Understanding stories involving recurring goals. *Cognitive Science*, 1978, *2*, 235-266. (c)

Wilks, Y. What sort of taxonomy of causation do we need for language understanding. *Cognitive Science*, 1977, *1*, 235-264.

Winograd, T. Frame representations and the declarative-procedural controversy. In D. G. Bobrow & A. Collins (Eds.), *Representation and understanding*. New York: Academic Press, 1975.

Winograd, T. Computer memories: A metaphor for memory organization. In C. N. Cofer (Ed.), *The structure of human memory*. San Francisco: Freeman, 1976.

Woll, S. B., & Graesser, A. C. *Memory discrimination for information typical or atypical of person schemata*. Unpublished manuscript, California State University, Fullerton, 1980.

Woods, W. Transition network grammars for natural language analysis. *Communications of the Association for Computing Machinery*, 1970, *13*, 591-606.

Woodworth, R. S. *Dynamics of behavior*. New York: Holt, 1958.

Woodworth, R. S., & Schlosberg, H. *Experimental Psychology*. New York: Holt, Rinehart & Winston, 1954.

vonWright, G. H. *Norm and action*. New York: Humanities Press, 1971.

Wulff, F. Uber die Veranderung von Vorstellungen. *Psychologische Forschung*, 1922, *1*, 333-373.

Wyer, R. S., & Carlston, D. E. *Social cognition, inference, and attribution*. Hillsdale, N.J.: Erlbaum, 1979.

Yekovich, F. R., & Walker, C. H. Identifying and using referents in sentence comprehension. *Journal of Verbal Learning and Verbal Behavior*, 1978, *17*, 265-278.

Yngve, V. H. A model and a hypothesis for language structure. *Proceedings of the American Philosophical Society*, 1960, *104*, 444-466.

Zadeh, L. A. Calculus of fuzzy restrictions. In L. A. Zadeh, K. Fu, K. Tanaka, & M. Shimura (Eds.), *Fuzzy sets and their applications to cognitive and decision processes*. New York: Academic Press, 1975.

Zangwill, O. L. Remembering revisited. *Quarterly Journal of Experimental Psychology*, 1972, *24*, 123-138.

Author Index

Aaronson, D. 52–53
Abbott, V. 23, 124
Abelson, R. P. 20, 29–34, 71, 111–16, 124, 136, 203, 264–67
Adams, M. J. 29, 33, 114, 263
Agar, M. 264
Anderson, J. R. 6, 43, 74, 110, 131, 175–80, 184–88, 192
Anderson, P. A. 23–25, 179, 183, 195, 204, 210
Anderson, R.C. 28
Antos, S. J. 215
Atkinson, R. C. 36, 74, 88–89
Austin, J. L. 10–13, 114

Bach, E. 11
Bacon, F. T. 201
Baggett, P. 169
Baker, E. 112
Barnitz, J. 18, 177
Baron, J. 60
Bartlett, F. C. 71, 95
Bates, E. 6, 12, 113, 154
Baumal, R. 61
Beaugrande, R. 15, 25, 115, 153–56, 168
Becker, J. D. 23, 124
Becklen, R. 34
Bern, H. 20
Besner, D. 60
Bever, T. G. 6, 42, 50–53
Bingham, G. 61, 215
Black, J. B. 16–27, 61, 70–75, 114–15, 124, 153, 169, 178, 200–4, 208–11, 215, 261
Blank, M.A. 60
Bobrow, D.G. 30–36, 72, 90, 105, 267
Bower, G. H. 6, 17–18, 24–28, 67–75, 114–15, 124, 153, 169, 178, 200–4, 208–11, 215, 261
Bransford, J. D. 29, 61, 69, 114, 264
Bregman, A. S. 27, 33, 72
Brewer, W. F. 13–15, 24–29, 114–15, 124, 153–55, 210
Britton, B. K. 53–55, 67, 215–16
Broadbent, D. E. 36
Brockway, J. F. 79, 95, 208
Brooks, C. 14, 151
Brown, J. S. 20–21, 70, 191, 215–17, 266
Bruce, B. C. 15, 23–25, 71, 106, 124, 153–56
Burstein, M. H. 29
Buschke, H. 6

Cairns, H. S. 60
Calfee, R. C. 53
Cantor, N. 28, 69, 81
Caramazza, A. 53
Carbonell, J. G. 29
Carlston, D. E. 28
Carpenter, P. A. 6, 42–44, 53, 215–16

Carr, W. J. 107
Chafe, W. L. 44
Charniak, E. 23, 124, 178
Chiesi, H. L. 53, 69, 79, 115, 203, 213–16
Chmielewski, D. L. 79, 95, 208
Chomsky, N. 6, 42, 50
Christiaansen, R. E. 29, 95
Cirilo, R. K. 60–61
Clark, E. V. 6, 11, 42
Clark, H. H. 6, 11, 13, 27, 42, 53, 61, 113–15, 154, 215–17
Clark, L. F. 40–41, 45, 50–56, 61, 67, 197, 215–18, 227–33, 253, 261
Clark, M. C. 18, 67
Cofer, C. N. 79, 95, 208
Cohen, A. D. 18, 44, 54–56, 67, 107, 197
Cohen, C. 81, 95
Cohen, M. E. 107
Cohen, P. R. 29
Colby, B. N. 15, 25, 115, 153–56, 168
Colby, K. M. 29
Cole, M. 17, 203
Cole, R. A. 61
Coleridge, S. T. 153, 195
Collins, A. M. 20–21, 29, 33, 114, 156, 175, 179, 191, 215–18, 263–66
Coltheart, M. 60
Corbett, A. T. 114–15
Coupe, P. 27
Crocker, J. 28, 69, 81
Crothers, E. J. 112–15
Cullingford, R. E. 111, 114
Curry, C. 54–55, 215–16
Curtis, M. E. 44, 56, 215–17

D'Andrade, R. G. 95
D'Agostino, J. 28
Dahl, D. A. 114–15
Danks, J. H. 60
Davelaar, E. 60
Davis, J. 54
Dawes, R. M. 108
Dawes, S. 203
DeForest, M. 17–18, 203
DeJong, G. 61
van Dijk, T. A. 9, 14, 36, 53, 69, 95, 104, 113–15, 153–57, 195, 200–201, 208–9, 213–6
DiVesta, F. J. 156
Dooling, D. J. 29, 95
Dosher, B. A. 6, 114–15
Drewnowski, A. 61
Duffy, S. A. 18, 48, 156, 215–18, 261, 271
Dyer, M. G. 178–79

Ehrlich, S. 49, 215
Ericsson, K. A. 218

Faught, W. S. 29
Feigenbaum, E. A. 178
Fetler, M. E. 29
Fillmore, C. J. 6, 9, 11, 42
Fine, J. 29
Fischer, F. W. 52
Flavell, J. H. 35
Fodor, J. A. 6, 42, 49–50
Forgy, C. 175
Forster, K. I. 60
Foss, D. J. 50, 60–61
Fowler, C. A. 52
Frase, L. T. 113
Frederiksen, C. H. 6, 60, 115

Galanter, E. 23, 124, 264
Gagne, E. D. 107
Gaines, B. R. 32
Gaines, M. T. 71, 106
Garrett, M. F. 6, 53, 152
Garrod, S. 215–17
Garrey, C. 53
Gentner, D. A. 20–21, 33
Gentner, D. R. 33, 156
Gibbs, R. W. 13, 61
Gibson, E. J. 42, 52
Gilbert, L. 52
Glenn, G. G. 14–15, 24, 111, 154–56, 179
Glynn, S. 54–55
Glucksberg, S. 60
Goetz, E. T. 115
Goffman, E. 29
Going, M. 70, 107
Gold, C. 61
Goldin, S. E. 20–21, 69
Goldman, S. R. 49, 53, 61
Goldstein, D. 201
Gomulicki, B. R. 79, 208
Goodenough, D. R. 29
Goodman, G. S. 108
Goodman, K. S. 61
Goodson, J. L. 25, 124
Gorden, L. 18, 152–54, 177, 196–97, 217
Gorden, S. E. 55–56, 70–79, 105–6, 114
Gordon, D. 12–13, 42, 217
Gough, P. B. 59–62
Graesser, A. C. 6, 18–27, 36, 40–45, 50–56, 61–79, 83–87, 93–99, 102–7, 114, 124, 128–31, 178–88, 192–211, 215–18, 227–33, 253, 261
Green, D. M. 94

Green, D. W. 53
Grice, H. P. 10–12, 113
Griggs, R. A. 113
Grimes, J. 112, 157
Grober, E. 53

Haberlandt, K. 61, 215
Hakes, D. T. 60
Halle, M. 6
Halliday, M.A. 112, 154–57, 217, 264
Hamilton, T. 54, 67
Harris, G. 20, 191
Harris, R. J. 27, 112–15, 199
Hasan, R. 112, 154–57, 217, 264
Hasher, L. 201
Hastie, R. 70, 81, 105
Hauft-Smith, K. 18, 44, 54–56, 67, 107, 197
Haviland, S. E. 61, 154, 215–17
Hayes-Roth, B. 72, 115, 175, 201
Hayes-Roth, F. 175
Healy, A. F. 61
Hendler, J. A. 29
Herman, S. J. 53
Higginbotham, M. W. 64–67
Hildyard, A. 112–15
Hobbs, J. R. 29, 61
Hochberg, J. 61
Hodge, M. H. 55
Hoffman, K. 56
Hoffman, N. L. 40–41, 45, 50–51, 55–56, 67, 197, 215, 261
Hogaboam, T. 52, 61, 215
Holdredge, T. S. 54–55, 215–16
Hollander, S. 70, 107
Hornak, R. 60
Huey, E. B. 52
Hunt, E. G. 52, 178
Hurtig, R. 53

Ims, J. R. 108

Jackson, M. D. 52, 56
Jarvella, R. J. 53
Jebousek, S. E. 76, 105
Jefferson, G. 29
Jenkins, C. J. 60
Johnson, M. K. 29, 264
Johnson, N. F. 61
Johnson, N. S. 14–18, 24, 111, 136, 154–55, 178, 203–4, 209–12
Johnson, R. E. 56, 169
Johnson-Laird, P. N. 6
Johnston, J. C. 61
Jonasson, J. 60

Juola, J. F. 74, 88–89
Just, M. A. 6, 42–44, 53, 215–16

Kahneman, D. 36–38, 54, 108
Kammerman, J. 60
Kaplan, R. M. 43, 49
Kayra-Stuart, F. 70, 107
Keele, S. W. 36
Keenan, J. M. 6, 11, 42–47, 55, 115, 199, 213
Kerr, B. 54
Kieras, D. E. 18, 61, 157, 215
Kim, K. J. 108
Kinney, D. 20
Kintsch, W. 6, 9–11, 19, 25, 36, 42–48, 53–55, 69, 74, 95–100, 112–15, 136, 153–57, 193, 200–204, 208–9, 213–17, 261
Kleiman, G. M. 61
Kolers, P. A. 60–61
Kolodner, J. L. 29
Kosslyn, S. M. 27
Kowalski, D. J. 56, 70–79, 83, 87, 93–97, 105, 200–201
Kozminsky, E. 18–19, 44, 67
Kroll, J. F. 60
Kuipers, B. J. 27
Kumer, A. P. 70, 81, 105

LaBerge, D. 36–37, 53, 61
Lachman, R. 29
Lakoff, G. 12–13, 42, 217
Larkin, K. M. 20–21, 215–18, 266
Lea, G. 27
Lehnert, W. G. 25, 29, 116, 120, 154, 169–70, 175–82, 194, 264
Leiman, J. M. 60
Lenat, D. E. 175
Leone, C. 29
Lesgold, A. M. 36, 44, 52–56, 60–61, 215–17
Levin, H. 42, 49–52
Levin, I. P. 108
Levin, J. A. 29
Levin, J. R. 27
Lewis, D. 10
Lewis, J. 52
Lewis, S. S. 60
Liberman, I. Y. 52
Lichtenstein, E. H. 15, 24, 29, 124, 153–56, 210
Light, L. L. 70, 107
Lindsay, P. H. 33
Loftus, E. F. 29, 113

Loftus, G. R. 34, 105
Lovelace, E. R. 23, 79, 128–31, 178–79, 200–11
Lucas, P. A. 215
Lucy, P. 13, 53, 217
Lunneborg, C. 52
Lutz, K. A. 18, 152–54, 177, 196–97

Mack, R. 18, 48, 156, 215–18, 261, 271
Mackworth, J. 34, 59, 105
Macnamara, J. 112
MacWhinney, B. 6, 113, 154
Mandel, T. S. 19
Mandler, G. 6, 29, 36, 61, 88–90, 107
Mandler, J. M. 14–8, 24, 95, 108, 111, 136, 154–55, 177–78, 203–4, 209–12
Manelis, L. 11, 44, 213
Maratsos, M. 49
Mark, L. S. 52
Marslen-Wilson, W. D. 60–61
Masling, M. 6
Mason, J. 18, 177
Mason, M. 60
Massaro, D. W. 6
Masson, M. E. J. 61
Mayer, R. E. 113
Mayhew, D. 6
McCarrell, N. S. 10, 29, 61, 114
McCawley, J. D. 11
McClelland, J. L. 52, 56, 61
McCloskey, M. 169
McClure, E. 18, 177
McConkie, G. W. 49, 215
McDermott, D. V. 124, 175–78, 264
McKoon, G. 6, 44
Meehan, J. R. 136
Mervis, C. B. 32
Meyer, B. J. F. 11, 54–55, 61, 112–15, 156, 203, 213–16
Miller, G. A. 6, 23, 264
Miller, J. R. 124, 208, 215–17, 261
Minsky, M. 27, 33, 72, 264
Mischel, W. 28, 69–70, 81
Mitchell, D. C. 53
Miyake, N. 29
Monaco, G. E. 112–15, 199
Moore, J. A. 29
Morandi, A. J. 34, 105
Morton, J. 61
Munro, A. 18, 152–54, 177, 196–97

Neely, J. H. 36
Neisser, U. 2, 33–34
Nelson, K. 29, 35, 67
Newell, A. 24, 124, 175
Newman, D. 15, 25, 124, 153
Nezworski, T. 18, 155, 177
Nicholas, D. W. 20, 24–25, 115, 132, 168
Nickerson, R. S. 29
Nilsson, N. J. 24
Nisbett, R. E. 218
Noordman-Vonk, W. 29
Norman, D. A. 6, 12, 20–21, 29–36, 72, 90, 105, 113–15, 124, 166, 172, 179, 267

Oden, G. C. 32
Olson, C. L. 112
Olson, D. R. 112–15, 153–55, 196
Olson, G. M. 18, 48, 156, 215–18, 261, 271
Omanson, R. C. 24, 194, 204
Ortony, A. 29–33, 115, 215, 267
Owens, J. 25

Pachella, R. G. 178
Paivio, A. 27
Palmer, S. E. 27
Parkison, R. C. 29
Partee, H. 6, 9–11
Patburg, J. P. 52
Patterson, K. E. 107
Paulson, R. 6
Penland, M. 54
Perfetti, C. A. 36–37, 49, 52–35, 59–61, 216
Perrault, C. R. 29
Pew, R. W. 23
Piaget, J. 35
Pichert, J. W. 28
Piha, A. 54
Pollard-Gott, L. 169
Pomerantz, J. R. 27
Posner, M. I. 36–37, 53–54
Potts, G. R. 113
Poulton, E. C. 49
Pressley, M. 27
Pribram, K. H. 23, 124, 264
Price, K. 54
Pyles, L. D. 18, 44, 54–56, 67, 107, 197
Pylyshyn, Z. 27

Quillian, M. R. 29

Rabinowitz, J. C. 107
Rapoport, A. 108
Ratcliff, R. 6
Rayner, K. 49, 215
Read, J. D. 70, 107
Reder, L. M. 115, 193–94

Reichenbach, H. 11
Reicher, G. M. 61
Reichman, R. 29
von Restorff, H. 70, 106
Revlin, R. 113
Reynolds, R. E. 215
Rieger, C. 61, 115
Riesbeck, C. K. 178
Rigney, J. W. 154, 196–97
Rips, L. J. 29
Ritchey, G. H. 95
Robertson, S. P. 23–25, 61–67, 128–31, 178–88, 192–95, 203–11, 215–18, 227–33, 253
Robinson, J. J. 29
Rommetueit, R. 12
Rosch, E. 32, 152
Roth, S. F. 37, 44, 52, 215–17
Rothkopf, E. Z. 19
Rubenstein, H. 60
Rubenstein, M. A. 60
Rumelhart, D. E. 6, 12–20, 24, 29–36, 42–43, 49, 61–62, 79, 111–16, 124, 136, 153–55, 166, 172, 178–79, 203–4, 208–10, 215–18, 267

Sachs, J. S. 6
Sacks, H. 29
Sala, L. S. 61
Samuels, S. J. 36–37, 53, 61
Sanders, E. 60
Sanford, A. 215–17
Sawyer, J. C. 55–56, 70–79, 105–6, 114
Scarborough, H. S. 52–53
Schachter, P. 6, 9–11
Schaier, A. H. 6
Schallert, D. L. 215
Schank, R. C. 20, 25, 29–34, 71, 111–16, 124, 136, 156, 166, 176, 194, 202–4, 264–67
Schegloff, E. 29
Scheidt, B. J. 169
Schlosberg, H. 71
Schmidt, C. F. 25, 124
Schmidt, R. A. 34
Schneider, W. 36–37, 53
Schnur, P. 107
Scholtz, K. W. 113
Schulman, H. G. 60
Schvaneveldt, R. 61
Schwartz, S. P. 27
Schweller, K. G. 13, 114–15
Scribner, S. 17, 203
Searle, J. R. 10–12, 114, 167, 208
Seidenberg, M. S. 60
Sengul, C. J. 53
Shaffer, W. O. 37
Shankweiller, D. 52
Shiffrin, R. M. 36–37, 53
Shoben, E. J. 29
Simmons, R. F. 11
Simon, H. A. 24, 124, 175, 218
Simpson, J. C. 55, 108
Simpson, R. 215
Singer, M. 114–15, 193, 201
Smets, G. 108
Smith, D. A. 20, 56, 70–79, 83, 87, 93–104, 200–201
Smith, E. E. 29, 61
Smith, W. R. 64–67
Snyder, C. R. 36, 54
Spilich, G. J. 53, 69, 79, 115, 203, 213–16
Spiro, R. J. 72, 95
Spoehr, K. T. 61
Sridharan, N. S. 25, 124
Stanovich, K. E. 60
Steedman, M. J. 167
Stein, N. L. 14–15, 18, 24, 111, 154–55, 177–79
Sternbergs 178
Stevens, A. L. 20–21, 27, 33, 42–43, 175
Stillings, N. A. 113–15
Stockwell, R. P. 6, 9–11
Streby, W. J. 44
Swets, J. A. 94
Swinehart, D. 23, 79, 128–31, 178–79, 203–11
Swinney, D. A. 60

Tanehaus, M. K. 60
Tannen, D. 34, 267
Taylor, S. 28, 52
Taylor, S. E. 69, 81
Tesser, A. 29
Thorndyke, P. W. 14–19, 24, 72, 111, 154–55, 203
Tinker, M. A. 42
Todres, A. K. 169
Toppino, T. 201
Townsend, D. J. 53
Townsend, J. T. 178
Trabasso, T. 20, 24–25, 115, 132, 168, 194
Treisman, A. 36
Tulving, E. 30, 61
Turner, A. 49
Turner, T. J. 27, 70–75, 114–15, 200, 208, 213–15
Tversky, A. 108
Tyler, L. K. 61

Vallacher, R. R. 28
Vendler, Z. 6, 167
Verbrugge, R. R. 10
Vesonder, G. T. 53, 69, 79, 115, 203, 213–16
Vipond, D. 53, 69, 115, 216–17
Voss, J. F. 53, 69, 79, 115, 203, 213–16

Walker, C. 115, 201, 215, 261
Wallace, W. P. 71
Wanner, E. 6, 49
Warren, R. E. 36–37, 53
Warren, R. P. 14, 151
Warren, W. H. 20, 24–25, 115, 132, 168, 194
Waterman, D. A. 175
Waugh, N. C. 36
Wegner, D. M. 28
Wehausen, E. 54
Weiner, S. L. 29
Weinreich, U. 10
Welsh, A. 60–61
West, R. F. 60
Westbrook, R. D. 54
Wheeler, D. 61
Wickelgren, W. A. 178
Wilensky, R. 15–16, 23–25, 29, 115, 124, 153–56, 168, 264
Wilks, Y. 20–23
Wilson, T. D. 218
Winograd, T. 172, 178
Woll, S. B. 56, 70–79, 83–7, 93–201
Wolverton, G. S. 215
Woods, W. 43
Woodworth, R. S. 71
von Wright, G. H. 23
Wulff, F. 95
Wyer, R. S. 28

Yales, J. 53
Yekovich, F. R. 44, 215, 261
Yonas, A. 52
Yngve, V. H. 49

Zadeh, V. H. 32, 152
Zangwill, O. 79, 208
Zeigler, R. 54
Zola, D. 215

Subject Index

Abstraction-summarization editor 79, 171, 176–78, 208–13
Amount of information 231–33, 247–48, 261–65
Arc categories 22, 124–30, 137, 150–51, 158–59, 169, 186, 190, 192, 257–58, 268–71
  Consequence 125, 127–29, 147
  distributions 137, 151, 158–59, 186, 190, 192
  Initiate 125–27, 146
  Manner 125, 129–30, 146
  Property 125, 130, 149
  Reason 125–26, 144
Attention 34, 105
Augmented transition network 43, 48–50
Automatization 36–37, 52–53

Binding 259, 271

Causal conceptualization 19–22, 122, 127–28, 137, 147–48, 165–66, 207, 268–71
Causal connectivity 22
Clausal juncture 53
Clusters 169–70, 260–61
Cognitive resources 36–67
  allocation of 37–59, 105–6
  limitations of 36, 49, 53–54
Cognitive science 2–4
Coherence graph 153–54
Complex protocol analysis 218–19, 273
Comprehension difficulty 18–21, 29–30, 67, 262–71
Comprehension score 18–21, 55–59, 65–67
Conceptual graph structure 103, 134, 136–44, 158–72, 183–84, 189, 214, 220, 262–63
Connective 9, 144, 147, 157
Construction chart 237–39
Context 38, 43, 63, 88–91, 120, 220–62, 265
Converging evidence 194–98
Critical node 176–78, 194–98, 201–2

Ecological validity 2
Expectation 34, 43, 220–23, 236–62, 264–71
Eye fixation 49, 52, 215–17

Familiarity of passage 18–19, 44–48, 50–52, 54, 57–58, 64–67, 107–8
Feedback 35
Filtering hypothesis 69–70
Foregrounding 44, 261
Free generation 75–76, 86–88, 157, 164–65

Genre 14–19, 44–58, 136–57, 229, 232
  descriptive 14, 16
  expository 14, 16, 18–19, 44, 64–67, 149–57, 232

narrative 14–19, 44–48, 50–54, 57–58, 64–67, 136–49, 152–57, 232
persuasive 14, 16, 232
Given-new distinction 154
Goal-oriented conceptualization 23–26, 35, 122–24, 137, 144–47, 156, 204–11, 243, 268–71
Guessing 62, 66, 69–70, 75, 81, 84–88, 91–95, 102–3

Hierarchical state transition theory 24–25, 204

Inference 21, 33–34, 72, 75, 93–95, 112–16, 130–33, 136–37, 149, 192–202, 216–17, 227–33, 235–71
bridging 115, 217, 259–60, 271
disconfirmation 222–23, 232–33, 236, 244–48, 253–55, 264–68
pragmatic 112–14
propositional 112–13
Instantiation 31–32
Intentional conceptualization (*see* Goal-oriented conceptualization)
Interest 15, 65, 156

Lamination effect 251–53, 267–68
Letters 42, 45–47, 50–53, 57–63
Linguistic knowledge 5–13
lexicon 5–6, 52
phoneme 5–6, 52, 59–61
pragmatics 5–6, 12–13, 26, 113–14, 213
semantics 5–12
syntax 5–6, 13, 42–43, 45–50, 53–54, 57–61

Macrostructure 6, 45–46, 51–53, 57–59
Means-end analysis 24, 124
Memory 11, 17–19, 25, 30, 49, 53, 67–108, 202–13
conceptually driven retrieval 88–92, 97–104
data-driven retrieval 88–92, 98–104
false-alarm rate 70, 75, 78–79, 84–88, 92–93, 96, 102
intrusions 70, 75, 81–82, 86–88, 96, 102
limitation 49, 53
recall 11, 17–19, 25, 30, 67–71, 81–83, 88–91, 95–107, 202–13
recognition 70, 78–80, 84–86, 88–107
retention interval 70, 95–108, 201–3
Mental model 21–22
Message center 61–62
Microstructure 6, 45–46, 51–53, 57–59, 203

Node categories 17–18, 116–23, 137, 149–51, 166–69, 203, 206–12, 257–58, 266–71
distributions 118, 137, 151, 241, 244, 246, 248
Goal 122–26, 166–67, 210–11, 242
Internal Event 121–22, 127, 168–69, 211–12, 243
Internal State 120–1, 127, 168–69, 212–13, 243
Physical Event 119–20, 169, 212, 243
Physical State 117–19, 169, 212–13, 243
Style 123, 129, 146

Objects 29
On-line comprehension 215–20, 226–71
Output order of statements 13–14, 18, 171, 178
Overlap score 186, 224–25, 230–31, 256–57

Personality 28, 69–70, 81–86
Problem reduction analysis 24–25
Production system 175–78, 183, 197–202
Proposition 6–12, 42, 45–48, 50–53, 57–58
argument 7–11, 43–48, 50–52, 57–59
embedding 8, 11, 116–17
index 10
predicate 7–11
truth 10, 12

Question-answering 130–36, 158, 164–65, 179–92, 205, 220–7, 233–35
method of exposing inferences 130–33, 158, 164–65, 220–27, 233–35
symbolic procedures of 179–192, 205

Reading 17, 39–67
goals 51–53, 63–67
models 59–63
reading time 17, 39–59, 62–64, 215–17, 261
Reference 7–9, 11, 153
spatial 8, 153
temporal 8, 153
von Restorff effect 70–71, 106
Rhetorical knowledge 13–19, 155–57, 171
Role 28, 81–86 (*see also* Stereotype)

Schema 29–35, 68–108, 157–65, 198–99, 213, 219–20, 263–65, 272
Script 71–72, 75–81, 84–107
Secondary task technique 53–54, 215–17

Serial position 44–47, 57, 247–48, 261–62
Spatial knowledge 26–28
Speech acts 12–13, 26, 207–8
Stereotype 28, 69–70, 81–86
Story grammar 14–18
Structure 162–63, 263, 268–71
  hierarchical 11, 17, 23–25, 124, 126, 144–47, 161–66, 203–11, 213, 243, 263, 268–71
  network 128–29, 148, 161–64, 263, 268–71
  transformation of 249–55, 259, 266, 267–71
Structural centrality 194–98, 201–2, 205–8
Surface structure 6, 9
Suspension of disbelief 152–53
Syllables 42, 45, 50–53, 57–59

Think aloud protocols 218–19
Typicality 32, 68–108, 203, 213

Verification processes 192–202

Words 42, 45–47, 50–53, 57–63

MIX
Papier aus verantwortungsvollen Quellen
Paper from responsible sources
FSC® C105338

If you have any concerns about our products,
you can contact us on
ProductSafety@springernature.com

In case Publisher is established outside the EU,
the EU authorized representative is:
Springer Nature Customer Service Center GmbH
Europaplatz 3, 69115 Heidelberg, Germany

Printed by Libri Plureos GmbH
in Hamburg, Germany